Praise for *Chicken Soup for the Soul in the Classroom*

"One of the best motivational tools I have found in education is a good Chicken Soup for the Soul story. This curriculum guide combines the best stories from this phenomenal series with tested classroom activities and discussion guides. If you want to motivate your students while teaching valuable lessons about life, this is the perfect resource for you."

—**Hanoch McCarty, Ed.D.**, retired associate professor of education
and author of *Motivating Your Students: Before You Can Teach Them, You Have to Reach Them*

"Teachers have long been using Chicken Soup for the Soul stories to turn nonreaders into readers, motivate the unmotivated, and inspire students to reach out and make a difference in the lives of others. Now we have this powerful curriculum guide chock full of the best stories from the series accompanied by lesson plans with discussion starters, writing prompts, and interactive exercises. If you want to build self-esteem, increase motivation, and teach emotional literacy, ethics, and values, or just have a resource of filler activities for those times you need a change of pace, then this curriculum guide is a must have."

—**Robert Reasoner**, former superintendent, author, trainer,
and president of the International Council for Self-Esteem

"Many teachers who come to our training seminars have used Chicken Soup for the Soul stories to help to create classroom bonding and a supportive atmosphere that eventually permeates the whole school. This exciting *new* approach . . . expands classroom possibilities. These plans often focus on self-awareness, personal empowerment, and on feeling connected to each other and to the world at large. Many of the activities offer a variety of directions and options that allow teachers to move wherever they need to go with a concept. If a teacher is short on time, students can be sent out the door with a 30-second inspirational story to ponder. Or they may become so involved that a year-long classroom project to help the homeless might be in order. This curriculum offers options for critical thinking and personal involvement at every turn."

—**Gaye Barker**, senior policy analyst, NEA Human & Civil Rights

"In classrooms where there is never enough time and much required preparation for mandated testing, I have found Chicken Soup for the Soul stories to provide a wealth of resources in a short and sweet format. These stories expose students to new ideas, and with classroom discussion, they act as a catalyst for this required writing. Finally, as one of the classroom test groups for this curriculum, I found a wonderful range of stories, questions, and activities to enhance the learning in my classroom and to inspire my students to care about each other and the world."

—**Mary Rose Davis**, third-grade cluster classroom

"One of the greatest challenges for educators is helping students connect academia with the 'real' world. Sometimes we need a hook to snag their non-collected thoughts. Chicken Soup stories are short nonfiction, and just the lure needed. Think of Chicken Soup stories as the perfect over-the-counter medicine that restores and revitalizes tired lessons. And having a wide variety of lesson plans ready-to-go for teachers is truly a gift."

—**Christine N. Heerlein, M.** od School District

"From the beginning, *Chicken Soup for the Soul* made our lives. As I read for myself one story after another, through smiles and ith my family. As a teacher, I am excited to see the lesson plans and activit amazing stories."

—**Linda Carter**, mother of two, grandmother of three, teacher of hundreds

"Quality and meaningful 'prompts' help all students to identify feelings and values in the decision-making process. Academically gifted students need this challenge to use their critical thinking skills as they analyze, interpret, and question both themselves and society. In general, the compact nature of Chicken Soup for the Soul stories lends itself to this process. More specifically, these lesson plans and activities address multiple intelligences and the higher level thinking skills that are required to motivate gifted students."

—**Eunice Wollin Crockett**, teacher of language arts and social studies for gifted students

"This book, with its combination of wonderful stories, leading questions, and thought-provoking activities, helped to pave the way for many important discussions and heart-to-heart conversations with my two daughters. I felt empowered using this resource to help my children to survive the many minefields, daunting decisions, and temptations they are facing daily."

—**Lori Slonim**, mother of Becky (age 12) and Tori (age 11)

"These are straightforward and easy-to-use lessons that spurred on into dinner conversations. Later, when we were in the car my son said, 'Mom, remember the bully story we talked about? Today I told a boy to leave this other kid alone. And he did! It really made me feel good to do something like we talked about.' My sons are able to apply many of these informal discussions into real situations in their lives. Many of the activities found in this book are providing children an arsenal of coping methods, social skills, and awareness for growing up today."

—**Christine Brillhart**, mother of Brett (age 9) and Garrett (age 6)

"As a substitute teacher for years and now a full time teacher, I am thrilled that this book is available. Because it is so versatile, it is a fantastic resource for teachers to leave for their substitutes and an easy document for them to follow. Having tried some sample plans in a variety of classrooms, I know it will add a much greater measure of quality to 'Emergency Lesson Plans!'"

—**Jennifer DeRego**, teacher

"I have had the pleasure of teaching a high school service learning class, where Chicken Soup stories have been a big part of our inspiration and motivation, especially during the 'down time' between community projects. I am excited that Chicken Soup for the Soul has expanded what they are doing to include lesson plans and projects for students of all ages. Many of the activities found in *Chicken Soup for the Soul in the Classroom* focus on community involvement and giving back to the world—a perfect asset to any classroom, but especially to a service learning class."

—**Carol Gardner-Neurath**, teacher

"My high school Spanish students LOVE being read to! The students don't allow me to skip this part of the day. I've noticed that the students truly are taking these lessons they have learned and are applying them in their lives, and are *mostly* treating each other with so much more respect. Simply taking less than five minutes a day to read a story has completely changed the environment in our classroom. The stories inspire, uplift, motivate, relate, and engage the students. I attribute these stories to helping create a safe environment for learning and also helping to grow a community within our classroom. My students have told me time and time again at the end of the semester that they feel like they are leaving summer camp and that they'll miss the stories and the feeling of the class."

—**Laura Krogh**, Spanish teacher, San Dieguito Academy

"I used a number of the Chicken Soup stories when I was coaching, and I continue to use some of these stories when I go into classrooms to give a talk. Some of my favorites stories for all ages come from *Chicken Soup for the Teenage Soul.* I remember telling the 'Champ' story before a county cross-country championship meet a few years ago. Neither our girls' nor boys' teams were particularly good that year. In fact, our cross-town rivals were picked to win both the boys' and girls' races that day. My teams were so fired up after hearing that story that they went out to run their best time of the year and ended up winning both championships. Having ready-made lesson plans attached to some of these stories is a real boon for anyone who deals with our youth in any capacity."

—**Ernest Carter**, recently retired elementary teacher and high-school coach

"Chicken Soup for the Soul stories have long been used in home schooling situations for their character-building messages and their doorway to opening communication. Now, having lesson plans attached to these stories is a real asset for these parent-teachers. Oftentimes, home schooling families have multiple children and therefore multiple grade levels at the same time. The lesson plans and activities in this book are clearly identified and cover a wide range of ages and abilities, with much versatility for these families to use. This offers a measure of reassurance for the non-certified teacher. And the comprehensive version is a particular asset in these situations."

—**Chris Kelley**, K–7 home study coordinator, Lucia Mar School District

"*Chicken Soup for the Soul in the Classroom* offers activities and lesson plans that provide students of all ages the opportunity to reflect upon their lives and the lives of others—while at the same time developing their reading, listening, and writing skills. Every educator should have a copy."

—**Catherine E. Hull, MSEd.**, Sylvan Learning Center Franchisee

"As a school board member, I try to spend a fair amount of time visiting classrooms. I've observed what works and what makes certain classrooms more successful than others. I have noticed Chicken Soup for the Soul books on many classroom shelves and am aware of the powerful messages that these stories impart. Lesson plans are extremely important as a support system to these stories and add value to the outcome. As I reviewed several sections of *Chicken Soup for the Soul in the Classroom*, I found the content to be clear and concise. I look forward to the availability of this curriculum for educators to use."

—**Suzii LaCross**, Board of Education, Midland, Michigan

"As 'Leaders for Life' participants, my friends and I decided that we wanted to do a project to empower younger girls to believe in themselves, to discover solutions, and to 'dream big.' After much discussion and many *wouldn't it be cool if's* . . . we were still at a loss as to *how* to do this. Trusting there was a solution, one appeared. In this case, I was asked to look at a new curriculum project: *Chicken Soup for the Soul in the Classroom*, to see if we would be interested in using it somehow with other teens. The rest is history. We now had the answer to *how* to complete our project idea. The Chicken Soup stories selected are wonderful stories of inspiration, hope, and personal empowerment. We see high school students working with middle school girls in classrooms. We see college women working with high school girls in camps. We see girls of all ages hearing these Chicken Soup stories and then writing in journals to express their feelings. We see many of the lesson plans, activities, and projects in this curriculum acting as springboards for other projects and plans. *Chicken Soup for the Soul in the Classroom* planted the seeds for us as teenagers. We are ready to go . . .and to grow."

—**Tara Huggins**, Age 15

Chicken Soup for the Soul®

in the CLASSROOM

Lesson Plans and Students' Favorite Stories for:

- Reading Comprehension
- Writing Skills
- Critical Thinking
- Character Building

**High School Edition
Grades 9-12**

**Health Communications, Inc.
Deerfield Beach, Florida**

www.hcibooks.com
www.chickensoup.com

Library of Congress Cataloging-in-Publication Data

Canfield, Jack, 1944-
     Chicken soup for the soul in the classroom / Jack Canfield, Mark Victor Hansen, and
Anna Unkovich. — High school ed.
          p. cm.
     Includes index.
     ISBN-13: 978-0-7573-0696-9 (trade paper)
     ISBN-10: 0-7573-0696-9 (trade paper)
     1. Education, Secondary—Curricula—United States. 2. Storytelling—Social aspects—
United States. 3. Social skills—Study and teaching (Secondary)—United States.
     I. Hansen, Mark Victor. II. Unkovich, Anna. III. Title.
     LB1628.C36 2007
     373.19—dc22

                                                                                                        2007025864

HCI, its logos and marks are trademarks of Health Communications, Inc.

Publisher: Health Communications, Inc.
              3201 S.W. 15th Street
              Deerfield Beach, FL 33442-8190

Cover design by Andrea Perrine Brower
Interior graphics by Taffy French-Gray, Jonny Hawkins, and Robb Waters
Inside design by Lawna Patterson Oldfield
Inside formatting by Dawn Von Strolley Grove

This book is dedicated to all the children of the world
and to the teachers and parents who guide them.

Our future is in your hands.

Contents

Part One: How to Use This Book

Part Two: The Stories and Lesson Plans

Part Three: Additional Stories That Inspire and Motivate

A Note to Parents and Teachers

This curriculum was originally designed and written as a K–12 comprehensive document for classrooms and home schools. With that in mind, all stories were selected to meet a variety of ages, interests, and abilities.

In our never-ending quest to make this the best book possible, it was reviewed and tested by a wide range of potential user groups—public-school teachers, private-school teachers, alternative education, special education, parents, grandparents, substitute teachers, teen mentors, and so on. Some of their specific comments are reflected in the testimonials at the beginning of this book, and many of their suggestions have been incorporated into this book.

Three main issues repeatedly arose in their feedback, and as a result:

1. We added new sections to the book that were grade-specific in content and ability. The main document still has its wide-range concept, but sections of each edition are now specifically geared toward elementary, middle school, or high school.

2. While keeping the comprehensive version for certain audiences, it was later decided to break this document into grade-level books. The result of this four-year journey is the book that you now hold in your hands.

3. Finally, many of our test groups produced repeated requests from *parents* for a book that could be used at home and for family discussions.

So, we have kept those K–12 concepts and the original stories whenever possible. And you can expect to see a wide variety of topics, abilities, activities, and plans in all editions of *Chicken Soup for the Soul in the Classroom.*

While some of these stories and plans may not have the *look* or *feel* of a typical high school curriculum, our test groups found that the students "*got it.*" And, perhaps because the stories are true, they took the messages to heart with greater measure than normal.

We had thousands of stories from which to choose, and almost as many decisions to be made in publishing a project of this size. For a variety of reasons it became impossible to include everything that we would have wished. So in an attempt to provide you with some on-going support, with the purchase of this book, we are offering you **10 FREE lesson plans** to start you on your journey, with additional new plans added from time to time. Simply go to www.chickensoup.com. **Under Free Soup Stories**, go to **Lesson Plans** and enter code: **CSBONUS**.

We hope you enjoy working with this document and that you find much success in this journey. We welcome your feedback at comments@chickensoupforthesoul.com.

—Jack Canfield, Mark Victor Hansen, and Anna Unkovich

How the Stories Were Chosen

Our intention with this curriculum was to put together a variety of stories that would suit multiple age groups in communities across the land.

Many of those selected here are favorites of Anna Unkovich's middle school and high school students since the very first *Chicken Soup for the Soul* in 1993. Others have been sent to test groups in Michigan, Missouri, South Carolina, and California for elementary input, as well.

While there are thousands of Chicken Soup for the Soul stories that would make great classroom readings, these were chosen to reflect the variety of topics within several Chicken Soup titles. In some cases, a story was chosen to reflect an important concept. In other cases, it was simply a student favorite over the past fourteen years.

After two years of this selection and testing process, plans were written and further test groups were sought in order to make this book worthy of the Chicken Soup for the Soul name.

Acknowledgments

We wish to express our heartfelt gratitude to the following people who helped make this book possible.

Our families, who have been chicken soup for our souls . . . especially to Anna's husband, Don Dirkse, who is new to this Chicken Soup level of commitment!

Our Publisher, Peter Vegso, for his continuous support and allegiance to all of us and to the Chicken Soup brand.

Patty Aubery and Russ Kalmaski, for being there on every step of the journey, with love, laughter, and endless creativity.

Patty Hansen, for her thorough and competent handling of the legal and licensing aspects of the Chicken Soup for the Soul books. You are magnificent at the challenge!

D'ette Corona, Veronica Romero, Teresa Collett, Robin Yerian, Jesse Ianniello, Lauren Edelstein, Barbara LoMonaco, Laurie Hartman, Patti Clement, Debbie Lefever, Basia Christ, Jenny Jones, Karyn Philippsen, and Marty Robinson who support Jack's and Mark's businesses with skill and love.

Michele Matrisciani, Carol Rosenberg, Andrea Gold, Allison Janse, Katheline St. Fort, Larissa Hise Henoch, Lawna Patterson Oldfield, Dawn Von Strolley Grove, and Andrea Perrine Brower at Health Communications, Inc., for their devotion to excellence.

Terry Burke, Lori Golden, Kelly Maragni, Sean Geary, Patricia McConnell, Kim Weiss, Paola Fernandez-Rana, Christine Zambrano, and Jaron Hunter for doing such an incredible job supporting our books.

This project would not have been possible without the many teachers and hundreds of students who helped us with this lengthy process, and we extend our heartfelt gratitude to every one of them. But, Denise Bujalski, teacher at Northeast Middle School, and the following fourteen students from Michigan to California deserve extra recognition for spending weeks and months poring over their favorite Chicken Soup books to help us select these stories for you:

Demitria Castañon	T.J. Armbruster	Cydney Millhisler
Taylor Castañon	Matt Magirl	Alan Ham
Laura Baker	Jenna Stevens	Catherine Shull
Sarah Baker	Ben Kozuch	Steven Elmer
Brandon MacKay	Warren Elmer	

They have our special thanks for making *Chicken Soup for the Soul in the Classroom* the best possible for students everywhere.

Introduction by Jack Canfield

The genesis of the Chicken Soup for the Soul series took place in my classroom when I was a high school history teacher in Chicago, in the late 1960s. While I had many bright students and some of lesser abilities, most of my students were not motivated. They did not have high aspirations, and they were plagued with low self-esteem and even lower visions of what was possible for them in their futures. It was because of this that I began to collect stories of real people who had escaped conditions worse than theirs and who became successful in life.

Some of the stories came from magazines aimed at the African American community such as *Ebony* and *Jet*. Others came from the mainstream media: *Reader's Digest, Life, Look,* and the *Parade Magazine* from the Sunday paper. There were also news stories clipped from the local Chicago newspapers, as well as stories I saw on television or heard on the radio. I would read these stories to my classes: stories of overcoming obstacles, triumphing in the face of adversity, and fulfilling one's dreams in the face of prejudice. Some stories, I would simply post on the bulletin board for them to read. Little by little, a transformation began to occur. Students began to believe that they, too, could overcome their conditions of poverty, race discrimination, and lack of educational resources. They began to believe in their abilities to create a future they chose for themselves. They began to dream bigger dreams and to believe they could achieve them.

I was witnessing first-hand the transformative power of real-life stories in the lives of my students. Based on the success I was having, I began to collect other kinds of stories as well—stories of people making a difference in the world rather than only chasing selfish goals, stories of people finding alternatives to violence as a way to solve their differences, stories of people expressing more love and kindness than was the norm in my classroom. Students loved these stories because it called forth what was best and highest in them. Hope and optimism felt better than hopelessness and pessimism. Possibility felt better than resignation.

As time passed I began to find stories and poems about and often written by students their own age—students who were sharing their feelings about dealing with abusive parents, uncaring teachers, institutional racism, drug dealers, gang wars, and inner city violence. Now they realized they weren't alone in their struggles to cope with life. And when the stories had endings that showed it was possible to transcend all of these horrors, the effect was even more powerful.

Over the course of two years, I had gathered hundreds of stories, poems, and fables that held powerful lessons for my students.

A few years later, I left the classroom to become a teacher-trainer in the area of raising student self-esteem. Once again, I found that stories were the most *powerful tools* I had to reach teachers and to get them to open their hearts to each other and to their students. I gathered more stories about transformations that teachers had witnessed, or that they had created in their classrooms. When I shared these anecdotes with other teachers, they could easily relate to the wisdom in the stories and instantly apply them in their classrooms. For years, I continued to collect stories that would awaken the heart, inspire, motivate, and give direction to teachers.

When I started offering trainings and seminars on Self-Esteem and Peak Performance for the general public, I continued to use stories to touch people at the soul level. By then, I had learned that all great teachers—Jesus, Buddha, the great rabbis, and the greatest spiritual teachers from every tradition—used stories, fables, and parables to make their points more memorable and more easily understood. It was during this period that the inspiration came to collect these stories into the first *Chicken Soup for the Soul*. While chicken soup was long thought to nourish the physically ill, this title was chosen to feed the soul—to nourish the spiritually sick in the world.

Following a talk I had given in Boston, a man asked me if the story I had told about the little boy and the puppy could be found somewhere in a book. I had to tell him "no," because it was a story I had heard from another speaker. A week later, someone asked me if the story I had told about the Girl Scout winning the *Guinness Book of Records* was anywhere in a book. Again, I had to answer "no." Magically, I kept getting these questions every day for months. It was as if God were tapping me on the shoulder and saying, "Put these stories into a book."

On a plane ride back from the east coast to Los Angeles, I made a list of all of the stories that I had been sharing in my talks over the past few years. There were sixty-eight of them. I decided it was time to compile them into a book. So I made a commitment to myself to write up two of these stories every week in order to finish the book within a year. When I was approximately half way through the writing, I happened to have breakfast with my long-time friend, Mark Victor Hansen. By the end of the meal, we had decided to team up to finish the book together, and it turned out to be a match made in heaven. Mark brought more great stories to the book, as well as his marketing genius, which proved invaluable once the book was finally published.

Over the course of the next several years, that book went on to sell over eight million copies in the United States. It continued to spread throughout the world, selling millions of books in more than thirty languages, and spawning a series that now has more than 145 titles. Teachers everywhere began using Chicken Soup stories in their classrooms to get kids to read, to introduce lessons on values, morals, and character, and to motivate them to think and to dream bigger dreams. We began to get thousands of letters from teachers and students alike, telling us how much the stories were changing their lives.

As a result, we began our line of Chicken Soup books for teenagers, preteens, kids, and little souls (two- to eight-year-olds). There are now more than fifteen books in that series, many of them having been adopted as ancillary reading texts. Tens of thousands of dedicated and caring teachers have spent hundreds of their own dollars to stock their classrooms with Chicken Soup for the Soul books—from the teens, preteens, and kids books to the perennial favorites like the original *Chicken Soup for the Soul,* and *Chicken Soup for the Pet Lover's Soul, Chicken Soup for the Sports Fan's Soul, Chicken Soup for the African-American Soul,* and *Chicken Soup for the College Soul.* Hundreds of school libraries have stocked all of these titles, and many more, including *Chicken Soup for the Teacher's Soul.* And, because of the universal appeal of the stories, thousands of teachers in China, Japan, and Korea have been using the books to teach English to their Asian students.

Over the years, many teachers developed complete lesson plans around the stories in these books. We were excited to hear that. And we loved that our books were making such a difference, and that they were being used in such a structured way to teach everything from reading comprehension and writing skills to values, education, and building self-esteem.

Several years ago, Anna Unkovich, a middle school and high school teacher who was living in nearby Arroyo Grande, California, approached me and told me about her extraordinary experiences using Chicken Soup stories with her students. Later she proposed that we create a teacher's manual for the use of Chicken Soup for the Soul stories in the classroom. After checking out her experience, credentials, and writing abilities, I enthusiastically jumped at the chance to work with her to create this guide you now have in your hands.

I am thrilled that this wonderful resource now exists. I believe it will help you to achieve many exciting things in your classroom, and it will provide many deep, meaningful, and magical moments for you and your students. I want you to know, as a former teacher, that I honor you for having the courage and commitment to be in the classroom day after day, making a difference in the lives of our children. In some small way, I feel as if Mark, Anna, and I, are there with you—cheering you on as you engage your students in exploring the lessons and messages contained in the Chicken Soup stories. Whether you are using these stories to teach reading, subject matter, self-awareness, emotional literacy, character education, or English as a second language, we wish you all the best.

As always, I would love to hear from you about your successes when using the stories and lesson plans contained in this guide. Feel free to write to me at Jack Canfield, Chicken Soup for the Soul, PO Box 30880, Santa Barbara, CA 93130, or e-mail me at comments@chickensoup forthesoul.com. I look forward to hearing from you. Until then, have great fun with these stories, activities, and lesson plans.

Introduction by Anna Unkovich

Three roads converged to make me a good teacher. The first occurred as early as age five. I knew that I would love school long before I ever attended. We had no money, but there were always books around the house. We were avid users of our public library. And, as a second-generation American born of Serbian descent, I learned the value of obtaining a good education from my parents. So on my first day of school, I knew without a doubt that I would become a teacher, and forevermore, I was passionate about it.

The second event happened in the middle of my third grade year. Our one-room schoolhouse merged with another to become a two-room school with a gym. It was here that I met Mrs. Ferguson. And it was here that I fell in love with the "story" as a big part of learning.

Mrs. Ferguson started each day with a chapter from a storybook, mostly the *Little House On The Prairie* series. But it was sometimes *Nancy Drew* or the *Hardy Boys* having a daily adventure for us. I could hardly wait to get to school each day! From that moment on, I was never without a book, and I sometimes had five or six that I was reading at the same time. Even at this young age, I realized the power of stories to take me to another time, another land. But it wasn't until my teenage years that I recognized the power of stories to help me to learn.

With the exception of the hated story problems that I had to do in math, I found that I would remember things far better every time a teacher attached a story, or example to the concept. Teachers who taught using stories were always my favorite teachers, and I was always more successful in their classes.

The third important leg of this journey occurred about ten years before the official end to my thirty-one-year, award-winning teaching career. It was the first day back to school following a Christmas vacation. Apparently, I wasn't totally "with it" that day, for I had five minutes remaining at the end of a class period and nothing planned.

As a veteran teacher, I always over prepared for each class by twenty to thirty minutes. It was simply unthinkable to have extra time with a group of seventh graders! But, as an old-timer, I also knew how to pull out a spontaneous plan, much as a magician pulls a rabbit from a hat.

I had just received my first Chicken Soup for the Soul book as a Christmas present. The friend who gave it to me had just returned from a Jack Canfield seminar, where she had obtained the book. She knew that the highly motivational stories were right up my alley.

The rest is history. To fill those five minutes, I read them a story. They loved it. The next day, they asked for more. Each day thereafter included a Chicken Soup for the Soul story. Sometimes it would start the class as the lesson plan for the day, while other times it would conclude with some final words of wisdom before sending them out the door.

After teaching middle school for more than twenty years, I was moved back into a high school classroom. I now had juniors and seniors, and I suggested to these older students that we try these readings for a week. I particularly feared that the seniors would consider it as childish or too elementary for me to read to them. It turned out they loved it no matter what the age. If we missed a story one day, they wanted two the next.

I started developing longer lesson plans or activities related to the stories. And I began using stories at every opportunity and with every age group, even at parent meetings. I repeatedly noticed that people felt encouraged to make a difference in the world after hearing these stories. Students were treating classmates more kindly. Parents were looking at their teens with different eyes. Nonreaders were asking their parents to buy them Chicken Soup for the Soul books.

One day, I had a parent almost run me down in a parking lot. This made me a bit nervous when the opening question was, "What did you do to my daughter?" The fact that I also taught sex education in this small community made this query especially disconcerting. As I was looking for a place of safety, she continued, "My daughter has never read a book in her life! Now she's asking for this Chicken Soup thing. What is it?"

That was just the beginning of many wonderful examples of stories changing lives, including my own. Chicken Soup for the Soul became a huge aspect of my personal and professional life. Students started calling me "the Chicken Soup lady." In fact, it was so much of my identity as a teacher that at retirement I was presented with a gift book entitled *Chicken Soup for Anna Unkovich's Soul.* This book contained motivational stories and testimonials about me, compiled by my colleagues and students. To this day it is one of my most cherished possessions.

Following my retirement from teaching in Michigan, I moved on to teach at a small college in California. I continued to inspire students with a daily dose of messages from the many Chicken Soup for the Soul books. Age was never a factor in my students' enjoyment of these stories.

The roads converged, and the idea for this book was born. It seemed to be a perfect merging of mission statements: Jack and Mark's is "to change the world, one story at a time;" mine is "to change the world one student at a time."

It is with a lifetime of passion that I share my favorite stories and lesson plans with you. Read them to your students. Do the follow-up activities. Use them often. They do change lives! And they will motivate your students to change the world.

PART
ONE

How to Use
This Book

Before You Begin

We can only hope that you fully understand the importance of being prepared *before* you start this Chicken Soup for the Soul journey.

Research indicates that when we learn something new, we will remember:

10 percent of what we read
20 percent of what we hear
30 percent of what we see
50 percent of what we see and hear
55 percent of what we see and take notes on
70 percent of what we discuss with others
80 percent of what we personally experience
85 percent of what we see, take notes on, and review within five hours
95 percent of what we teach others.

While Chicken Soup for the Soul stories are not exactly note-taking experiences, they are true stories that teach to our hearts, rather than solely to our heads. As we hear them, we relate to them, and they become personal experiences for us. We laugh with them, we cry with them, and most of the activities encourage us to discuss these new experiences with others.

These stories lead us through many life experiences vicariously, while under the guidance and supervision of a teacher. They provide character education at its best.

Because every story provides for some discussion, we refer you to many suggestions and guidelines entitled **Circle Talks**, found on page 311 in the Appendix.

Here are a few guidelines and reminders to set the tone for success:

★ preview the story and plans
★ whenever possible, read the story aloud to yourself first
★ know the intended direction of questions and activities
★ allow for spontaneity and shifting of direction for "teachable moments" (*because when the mind is open, the heart will hear*)
★ have materials ready for any activities, and whenever possible have samples to show
★ be sure that students are clear on any directions before they start an activity
★ if possible, do a "walk-through" to assure understanding
★ encourage students to participate with an open attitude
★ allow time for students to process and reflect
★ unless you are deliberately sending students out the door with their own thoughts following a story, provide some sense of closure for the group
★ remember that it is your energy that sets the tone for the entire experience

Suggestions for Using
Chicken Soup for the Soul in the Classroom

We have three main goals for teachers using this program:
- ★ to get students to enjoy *reading*
- ★ to get students to express themselves in *writing*
- ★ to *empower* students to make a difference in the world

For optimal success, we recommend the following:

1. **Choose your story to match your lesson.**

    Although each Chicken Soup for the Soul story is motivating in some way, for maximum value it is best for it to be an integral part of your lesson plan.

2. **Choose your story to match your audience.**

    Mild swear words may be acceptable for high school students or adults, but not so for elementary students. Can you "soften" them without changing the power of the story? Strong references to God or religion may be an important part of your life, but forbidden in most public schools. Do you leave out those references, modify them, or switch to another story? It is important to know your story before reading it aloud.

3. **Select the placement of your story.**

    Will you start class with it? Do you plan to fit it into the middle of the lesson? Do you intend to use the follow-up activities? Have you allowed enough time? Is it your "out-the-door," thought-provoking message at the end of class for students to ponder, and perhaps journal about?

4. **How long does it take to read it aloud?**

    Have you planned your time accordingly? It is not wise to be in the middle of your story when a bell is ringing signifying the end of class.

5. **What type of follow-up will you do?**

    Will you use the questions provided or develop some of your own? If the questions will be used for classroom discussion, have you allowed enough time? Can you adjust plans easily to allow for a longer (or shorter) discussion than you anticipated? If the questions will be answered in writing or journal format, will this be done during class time? For homework? For credit? Will the writing become a part of your classroom routine? If student reading is your goal, do you have classroom quantities of Chicken Soup for the Soul books available? Will students be allowed to choose their own stories with corresponding follow-up activities?

6. **What is your PURPOSE in using the story?**

   Is it for motivation? Inspiration? Is it part of a specific lesson (*e.g., friendship, history of an era, attitude, civil rights, etc.*)? Will it be used to establish classroom routine (*e.g., the value of daily reading or writing*)? Is it a time-filler at the end of the hour (*oops, three minutes to spare*)? Or, is it your desire to "change the world one story at a time?"

7. **Every student needs to be "heard."**

   For this reason, discussion questions are best shared in dyads and/or **Circle Talks** before examining in a full-class interaction. There are numerous ways to randomly pair students in a nonthreatening way to form dyads or small groups. We have included set-up directions for **Circle Talks**, (Appendix, page 311) and **Creative Ways to Get into Groups** (Appendix, page 336).

8. **Practice reading stories aloud, at least once.**

   A poorly read story is like a joke with the wrong punch line—it will lose its potentially huge impact. A practice run will let you know which phrases to emphasize so you won't be surprised by any words or concepts, and the story will flow more smoothly.

   > These stories are not recommended for students to read aloud, unless practiced in advance. The power of *Chicken Soup for the Soul* stories lies in the message. There is an art to reading aloud, which most students have not yet mastered. However, they could be successfully used with drama or speech classes where the art of speaking aloud is rehearsed.

9. **Are other teachers in your building using Chicken Soup for the Soul stories as a regular part of their teaching?**

   In elementary school, there is probably no problem with this. But whenever students rotate from teacher to teacher, they may be hearing the same stories frequently, and you may lose the impact of a powerful or surprising ending. If this is the case, you may wish to do some minor coordinating between staff for the maximum effect with your students.

10. **The questions and activities are geared for students at a midrange level.**

    In most cases, they can easily be adjusted to higher or lower abilities and competencies. Always remember that you are the expert regarding your students and their capabilities. A plan that is labeled for the sixth grade may be perfect for your fifth graders and the issues they are facing. Or, it might work best for a particularly challenging group of ninth graders. The age levels indicated are merely guidelines to help you to select the stories and activities.

11. **Not all stories are suitable for all students.**

Some of the stories selected deal with very tough issues (*e.g., divorce, discrimination, abuse, death, etc*). A rural school in Michigan will have very different needs than an inner-city school in New York. We have included a variety of these sensitive topics in case you have the need to address them as a class. Teachers have a responsibility to use their good judgment in selecting appropriate stories for their students.

12. **Activities have been designed that will touch several aspects of students' lives: physical, emotional, social, spiritual, mental, artistic.**

We have found this "whole life" learning to stay with students longer and to empower them to make a difference in their homes, their schools, their communities, and the world. We refer to it as "teaching to the heart, rather than the head." And we encourage you to use this method regardless of the subjects that you teach. For more information on teaching to multiple intelligences, we suggest that you go on-line to any popular search engine and simply type in "multiple intelligences." We consider Thomas Armstrong and Howard Gardner to be the leading experts in this field.

13. **Use these stories to trigger personal stories of your own.**

Recall the childhood memories or turning points in your own life. Remember a friend who had a tough decision to make. Tell of a former student who made a difference in your school. Students need to know that you, as a teacher, are human, that you have had obstacles to overcome, painful experiences to endure, and joys to share. Learning to tell your own stories may be the most powerful aspect of using this program. We think you will be pleased with the strong student-teacher bonding that will occur with the use of stories in your classroom. We do suggest, however, that you use discretion in sharing too many personal details of your life with your students.

14. **Finally, have fun!**

Your attitude about reading and the use of stories is contagious. If you love a good story, so will your students. Your passion for stories will become their passion.

Do not underestimate the power of having a consistent reading diet of Chicken Soup for the Soul stories, without always doing the lesson plans. Refer to the Short Shorts and the Just for Fun chapters for stories with a powerful impact, but no plans. We think you will find that the frequent use of story in the classroom can literally change the world, one student at a time, and one story at a time.

Designing the Plans, Using the Plans, and Adapting the Plans

As we sought to select the best stories from the thousands that were available to us, our main criterion was to find anecdotes that contained inspiring content and those that would potentially have a high impact on students of all ages. We wanted these stories to make a difference in students' lives, while dealing with a variety of topics. And, we wanted stories that would connect with anyone, regardless of age, sex, race, religion, or socioeconomic background.

The plans are available for you to select and use to meet individual and classroom needs. One class may have a student dealing with the death of a parent. Another may have several students dealing with divorce and remarriage issues. One community may have gang or drug problems. Still another may have no concept of the needs of the homeless, and you might wish to bring this awareness to the classroom. For this reason, we have included a wide variety of stories from thirty of the Chicken Soup for the Soul books.

Although there are plans included for most of the stories in this curriculum guide, we strongly recommend that you not make every story into a lesson plan. Sometimes, the most powerful lesson is to simply read the story and send students out the door with their own thoughts on the matter. The plans that are included here have been designed to enhance the message of the story. If, however, they become overused, students will begin to dread Chicken Soup time, rather than to experience the joyfulness of story and the make-a-difference aspect of the Chicken Soup for the Soul stories.

Finally, it is our intention that the stories in this document be **read to the students** by the teacher. We further recommend that you obtain a variety of Chicken Soup for the Soul books for your classroom, and set aside some time each day or each week for Silent Sustained Reading (SSR). Much research recommends that students silently read for twenty minutes immediately following lunch, to help to settle them back into "classroom mode." The reading level for most of these stories is at grades five or six, with content that captures the hearts of all ages and backgrounds.

Understanding the Format

Part One of this book has the introductory information regarding the background and suggested use of this book, its lesson plans, and its activities.

Part Two contains three main chapters of stories, lesson plans, and activities. The first of these has stories that are general in content and were selected for all age levels. While originally designed with three levels of plans, the volume that you hold contains only the high school plans and activities.

Each story throughout the book is preceded by an information page listing:

- ★ Title of the story
- ★ Original book that printed the story
- ★ Page number from the original book
- ★ Amount of time necessary to read the story aloud
- ★ Major theme of the story presented in **bold** print
- ★ Related story topics indicated in standard print
- ★ Appropriate age level for the story content and plans
- ★ Short synopsis of the story
- ★ Additional notes for the teacher

The second chapter in this section has stories that are suitable for all age levels, but contains a single, K-12 plan that can easily be adapted for any group or ability. This chapter may not look like typical high school stories or lesson plans, but our test groups found them to be highly successful with students in these classrooms. Furthermore, those teachers found the wide range of activities to be especially valuable with the academically gifted or challenged, or with those students who seem to "march to a different drummer."

The third chapter is age-specific in its content and scope. These stories, plans, and activities have a special appeal to high school students.

Part Three contains stories that have no lesson plans, but are included because of their powerful impact, humor, or inspiration. These chapters include Short Shorts, Just for Fun, Consider This, Teacher Motivation, Parent Inspiration, and Final Thoughts. Lesson plans could easily be attached to any of these stories, but we strongly recommend reading them for fun or inspiration.

Within each chapter, the stories are grouped by similar content or theme whenever possible. Suggested worksheets are located within the story sections, following the plans, and preceding the stories. Occasionally, teachers will be referred to the Appendix at the back of the book for additional information or more detailed plans.

NOTE: *All worksheets and activities in this document that are borrowed from other sources are used with permission.*

This compilation includes selections from many of the more than one hundred Chicken Soup for the Soul books that are available. For a complete listing of Chicken Soup for the Soul books, go to www.chickensoupforthesoul.com.

It is just the beginning. . . .

Some Research on Reading

With a plethora of research available, there are as many possible solutions as there are problems that center on reading in America. We could write an entire book on these findings, but have chosen to refer you to a few recommended experts for a limited review of research and opinions that specifically relate to this document (see Resources, page 377, for full citations). These sources were chosen for their highly respected reputations concerning education and the developing child, and for their ongoing contact with other brilliant minds in this field.

What is fairly common knowledge is that our children are not testing well on reading, and like many adults, they are not reading or are alliterate. Unlike the illiterate person who is unable to read, the alliterate person chooses not to read.

Let us present some key concepts and some possibilities for how this curriculum guide can offer a new kind of solution to this growing problem.

1. **The invasion of technology.**

   Starting in infancy, we now have products and television shows designed to capture the attention of even our youngest learners. In a special report in *Time* magazine that appeared on January 16, 2006, it is suggested that these products do capture the eyes and ears of infants. But far more crucial to the child's development is a life filled with rich sensory experiences of human interactions. In fact, according to the article in *Time*, "The American Academy of Pediatrics recommends no TV viewing of any kind before age two."

   In a 1998 interview, author Joseph Chilton Pearce reported a "20–25 percent reduction in sensory awareness of the technological child as opposed to the preliterate, or 'primitive' child in the grass shacks of the jungles . . . and that kids' minds go catatonic in front of the 'tube.'"

   In a study of fourth-grade comprehension and retention of textbook material reported by Pearce, information studied from a TV monitor had a severely reduced retention and comprehension level of 3 to 5 percent, compared to 85 percent retention from the paper copy (http://pediatrics.aappublications.org/cgi/content/full/118/4/e1061). Pearce, a former faculty member on child development at the Jung Institute in Switzerland, has had educational conferences throughout Canada, Japan, and the United States that have featured his work.

   And while this data may appear to be old by researchers' standards, the trend is still evidenced today. A study reported in *Pediatrics,* April 2004, found early television exposure to be associated with attention problems at age seven. Another study found "excessive television viewing in childhood may have long-lasting adverse consequences for educational achievement and subsequent socioeconomic status and well-being." (*Archives of Pediatrics and Adolescent Medicine,* July, 2005).

   On the other hand, a 2006 study by Gentzkow and Shapiro found some positive effects of educational television, particularly in households where English is not the primary language.

   We recommend that you search the internet for the latest research on this issue.

So, while technology has its place, it appears that overexposure to entertainment technology clearly may be detrimental to the young, developing mind. And reading is still a necessary element for success in school in *every* discipline. For a detailed list of reading strategies across multiple curricula, see *Reading Reminders* by Jim Burke (see Resources, page 377).

Since reading is critical to every aspect of education, the best of technology cannot replace the written word, nor the brain activity generated from reading. This guide, and the regular use of stories to teach, offers students new perceptions of life. Throughout history, young people have resisted "convention." Chicken Soup for the Soul offers guidance of an "unconventional" sort, where students are often unaware they are learning something important.

2. The political pressure for high standardized test scores.

With the No Child Left Behind law, attaching tax dollars to test scores and threatening loss of jobs for teachers whose classes do not perform well, it is a tough time to be a teacher, especially in the public schools. Top-notch, innovative educators are being pushed to "teach to tests" and to create a student-product, while students are being "scripted" into test scores. By their very nature, these kinds of tests expect a single, correct answer, and they stifle the very essence of creative thinking.

Furthermore, according to author and education-system critic Jonathan Kozol, teachers are being accused of harboring "low expectations," as though "genetically predisposed to mediocrity."

It's fairly safe to say that most teachers have not chosen this career for the income that it generates. Rather, it is a "calling" for most . . . a passion driven by a love of our own early school days and a joyfulness in a classroom somewhere.

Today's classrooms are still filled with future poets, doctors, artists, musicians, leaders, parents, and rebels. However, Kozol says these future achievers are now viewed as human capital, a potential worker somewhere in the distance. We can't help but wonder how many youngsters coming through this test-driven, anxiety-ridden environment will grow up *wanting* to be teachers someday.

There is no scripted curriculum that will put joy into a classroom. There is no single score on a single test that can ever measure the joyfulness of reading a good story. This Chicken Soup curricula is not meant to replace state-mandated curricula, but to act as a supporting player—perhaps a more joyful means of improving standardized test scores. Children who *want* to read will read more frequently, and ultimately their test scores are more likely to improve. Feedback from across America has shown that frequent exposure to Chicken Soup for the Soul stories has led to students of all ages *wanting* more of these uplifting narratives.

3. Much required reading today consists of "problem novels."

In an article written in *American Educator*, 2005, Barbara Feinberg gives us something else to ponder. She feels that much literature presented to students often centers on a problem, not on the character's whole life. And while it may be "realistic," it is often catastrophic, painful, sad, dark, and downright depressing, sometimes leaving children feeling that they are the cause of all of the terrible things that occurred. She contends that these stories are rarely filled with humor, play, or childhood fantasy, which are comforting elements for youngsters of any age. Feinberg sums up these feelings by saying, "I don't remember feeling anxiety upon opening a book."

The Chicken Soup for the Soul stories found in this curriculum are not designed to replace the great literature of the world. Rather, the stories selected seek to provide a balance of reading materials by consistently providing humor, hope, and a sense of connection. It is a connection to the story, to others in the room, and to the world at large. Even the heaviest of topics end with hope and a sense that "I can do that, too," or, "I can make a difference to others in this world."

If Feinberg's premise has any measure of truth, we are still not suggesting that all "problem novels" or painful stories be pulled from classroom shelves. We are simply recommending a balance to provide young people with a sense of well-being that creates a desire to pick up a good book and find friendship in a good story.

4. **There are too many things that have to be done, with no time available for stories.**

    With such pressure for student performance on standardized tests, most teachers will tell you that they simply don't have time to take away from curriculum and test preparation in order to read stories to their students. Most of the Chicken Soup for the Soul stories take less than three minutes to read. Anna found this investment in time greatly enhanced the overall behavior and atmosphere within her classroom, excluding the use of any lesson plans at that time.

    For those of you who need to justify this time spent, either to yourself or to an administrator, these attached plans were specifically designed to foster joyfulness in reading, and thereby improve reading and writing scores. Questions and activities are based on *Bloom's Taxonomy*, as well as Armstrong's and Gardner's work with multiple intelligences. So there is adequate depth to the follow-up work to justify a three-minute story.

    One of the most fascinating and comprehensive examinations of the research on reading is found in Jim Trelease's *The Read Aloud Handbook*. It is here that we report on our final research issue:

5. **There are very few role models who read often for children to witness.**

    Essentially, Trelease's research shows that reading aloud to students of all ages improves their reading, writing, listening, speaking, and attitudes toward reading. In fact, in a 1985 Commission on Reading Report, it was found that ". . . the single most important activity for eventual success in reading is reading aloud to children . . . in the home and classroom . . . and throughout the grades."

    International studies in the 1990s and reported in Trelease's book found two main factors influencing higher reading achievement:

    ★ frequency of teachers reading to students

★ frequency of SSR (Silent Sustained Reading), or pleasure-reading *within schools*

Further studies reported by Trelease indicate the importance of male role models for reading. We live in a society where males are not shown the value of reading. Fathers who value sports produce sons who value sports. For school success to occur, it is critical that males (particularly fathers and male teachers) be intellectually involved in children's lives, not just athletically.

Anna has a dear friend and colleague who is a highly respected coach in the community where they both taught. Ernie is known to recite lengthy pieces of poetry to his athletes on a regular basis. He models for them the beauty of poetry, and shows how it relates to sport and to life. More than one of his athletes has gone on to read books of poetry; it is likely the athletes would never have considered doing so without Ernie's influence.

When selecting the stories for this curriculum guide, much consideration was put into choosing stories that would appeal to males, and test groups were chosen with the idea of igniting males' interest in reading. Females are easier to please when it comes to literature, so less concerted effort was made on their behalf.

So, remember that it is critical to create a passion and a pleasure associated with reading. Don't always make it a lesson or a test-question. Rather, make it a joyful experience, and make it a repeated experience. The more you do it, the better you get . . . just like riding a bike.

Also remember that every time you read aloud to a class, you offer yourself as a role model. So it is best to start early when children want to imitate you, and it is best to choose material full of interest and excitement to capture their attention. It is an easy, and somewhat expected, task to read to elementary students. We do not underestimate the value of creating joyfulness and a habit of reading at this early age.

However, we challenge you to consider that for the most part, it will be your secondary students who will take the content of these stories out into the world, in order to change the world. This curriculum is designed to transcend age levels and subject matter. It is designed to empower your students at all ages and stages. We strongly suggest that you regularly read to your high school students and give them the opportunity to make a difference in your classroom and in life.

We firmly believe that a regular diet of Chicken Soup for the Soul in your classroom will lead to greater reading achievement, improved vocabulary, and higher test scores. These are not the reasons for reading, but merely a byproduct of a good story or a good book. Our primary intention is that you will use these stories to inspire your students to change the world.

The Importance of Reading

It will be suggested over and over and over again that . . .

you recognize, and value, the concept of helping students to develop images in their minds. This cannot be accomplished solely in front of a television, nor with a computer screen or a picture book. When children are presented with *words,* their minds must learn to fill in the gaps with all of the sensory details. Teachers who read to their students offer them this opportunity to exercise their brains in this manner, at every age level.

In a 1999 interview, Joseph Chilton Pearce stated that "the simple act of watching television has profoundly negative effects on the physiology of human beings." The uncomplicated version of what happens is that the brain closes down due to the effects of the radiant light that is emitted from television and computer monitors. In a sense, it hypnotizes the brain, actually preventing neural growth in developing brains and suppressing imagination. For a plethora of information on this subject, we suggest that you search the internet for the "hypnotic effect of television on developing brains."

By reading to young people, crucial skill areas of the brain are accessed, particularly those relating to creativity and problem-solving. This may be one of the most important skills that students can acquire to help provide balance to their technical world of high-speed visual images that flash before their eyes.

Initially, you might suggest to students that they close their eyes during story time, in order to see the events unfolding in their minds. For those students who have had extensive time in front of television or computer monitors, this practice of listening to a story gives them an opportunity to redesign their internal world. We contend that even if they happen to fall asleep, they will still be hearing, and getting, the message from the story.

It will be suggested over and over and over again that . . .

you model the joyfulness of reading for your students. If you are passionate about anything, it is contagious. Show your passion for the written word. Fill your classroom with books. Allow your students to "catch you" reading before school or at the end of a lunch period. One of the single most important factors for igniting their passion is your passion. Let it show. You don't have to be an English teacher to enjoy reading.

It will be suggested over and over and over again that . . .

you designate a regular story time for students, regardless of their age or the subject matter that you teach. Over the years, Anna read to her students, grades seven through college, on a daily basis. The minute or two that she devoted at the end of class did not cut into course content in any way, but it did significantly change classroom behavior and atmosphere with these high-impact stories. Initially, she did not have any lesson plans attached. But, as she recognized the power of these stories, she later developed plans to go with the key concepts in her curriculum. Ultimately, it became the seed for this book.

It will be suggested over and over and over again that . . .

you have planned some time each day, or week, in which students read silently on their own. Light their fire for reading and then turn them loose. SSR (Silent Sustained Reading) programs are being implemented across the nation in an effort to help improve reading comprehension test scores. We encourage you to fill the room with Chicken Soup for the Soul books so their souls get filled, as well as their minds.

It will be suggested over and over and over again that . . .

you remind students that stories can take them anywhere in time and space, and give them experiences they might not ever have in their lives. According to Pearce, "Children's emotional experience, how they feel about themselves and the world around them, has a tremendous impact on their growth and development. It's the foundation on which all learning, memory, health and well-being are based. When that emotional structure is not stable and positive for a child, no other developmental process within them will function fully. Further development will only be compensatory to any deficiencies." The Chicken Soup for the Soul stories selected here help to provide pathways to greater self-esteem, access emotional experiences, and empower students to change their lives and their world.

It will be suggested over and over and over again that . . .

everything you do in your classroom can help to create a safe and secure emotional environment that is crucial to students' ultimate success in learning. Many of our students come from negative households that are lacking in unconditional love, and they are starving for touch. These young people turn to socially unacceptable substitutes that don't satisfy those needs. Stories, particularly the warm, caring, compassionate stories found in the Chicken Soup for the Soul books, take them to a safe place. It is only when children of all ages feel safe that they will learn.

It will be suggested over and over and over again that . . .

our secondary students be given this story-time experience on a regular basis. It is not uncommon for this to occur with elementary students. However, it is extremely rare for a high school student to have a daily diet of stories read to them in any classroom. Perhaps one of the most important messages we would like to extend to you is the importance of frequently reading to children of *all ages*.

The gift of a story is truly magical! And, while it is habit-forming, it is not life-threatening, nor does it have any harmful side effects!

The Importance of Writing

Writing with competence is a crucial skill to possess in this modern world. Indeed, with all that has been added into curricula, schools across the nation are struggling to find a way to incorporate this essential practice. To add to the problem, getting students to write, and eventually to enjoy writing, can be a monumental task. It has been our experience that attaching a writing assignment to a story that students enjoy makes this undertaking more palatable.

There are a couple of important things to keep in mind for the writing assignments found in this book. First of all, every assignment can be a writing assignment, if you so choose. We don't recommend this kind of overkill, but merely mention it so you will recognize that virtually any plan in this book can be made or adapted into a writing practice.

Some compositions may be assigned mainly for the purpose of improving one's writing skill. Style, form, sentence structure, grammar, and punctuation—the mechanics of writing—would necessarily have teacher access and comment.

However, other writing may be done to connect both sides of the brain, or to get students to access and identify their deepest feelings on a subject. This type of written expression should be private in nature and not available to anyone but the writer.

The teacher needs to be very clear about his or her intent before posing the questions to the students. In every case where the content is to be read by the teacher, or shared with the class, students should be told in advance. In addition, when pre- or post-questions deal with highly sensitive or personal issues, it is initially recommended that students write their responses in continuing journals, rather than to discuss them aloud. However, we believe it is important to teach students how to safely talk about their feelings as a part of developing emotional literacy. A good technique for doing this is the use of *Circle Talks*, described in detail in the Appendix, page 311. Student responses will vary depending upon the topic, or on the quality of the bonding within the group. Always, as the teacher, you set the tone and the boundaries for this type of exchange.

Assess your individual and classroom needs, then determine the writing assignments accordingly. Don't forget to share your excitement about writing. It is your energy and enthusiasm that will set the tone for writing success.

Chicken Soup Classroom Activities

Sometimes, we need a word or a thought to jolt us into creating the perfect lesson plan. The following is a compilation of dozens of activities that could be used with any of the stories in this book, or with any other reading or writing assignments. There is no order to this list, other than when the ideas popped into our minds.

Create cartoons to recapture the story in a new way.
Draw images that reflect the storylines.
Paint to give insights to various concepts of the story.
Make masks that reflect feelings portrayed in a story.
Share first impressions of someone or something.
Make timelines that show the progression in the story.
Make personal timelines to show past and future goals.
Invite speakers to share personal experiences that relate to the story.
Create a personal journal or writing folder, then write in it regularly.
Rewrite the story as seen through the eyes of a lesser character.
Write a sequel to the story.
Maintain regular classroom bulletin boards that relate to the stories.
Stop the story before the ending to let students devise their own ending.
Write a diary of one of the characters.
Write a shopping list of one of the characters.
Use the story to generate a debate.
Volunteer somewhere in the community that relates to the story.
Use music—classical or old, popular or new—that has a related message.
Write, sing, or play a song of your own.
Develop a school-wide campaign to deal with a relevant issue.
Write and perform puppet shows or plays.
Use dance as an expression of the main theme of the story.
Use movement to show your opinion on something:
> *Move to the left side of the room if you are left-handed.*
> *Clap your hands once if you liked the main character.*
> *Hop on your left foot if you watch more than three hours of TV each day.*
> *Wink if you liked this story.*
> *(Create several choices and movements to get students energized.)*
Prepare foods that relate to a story.
Use related videos, movies, or other books.
Make gifts to give to the needy.
Make coupon books (*e.g., hugs, clean my room, take out garbage, etc.*).
Create games (*e.g., name-games, truth and lies, "telephone," TV quiz shows, etc.*).
Establish graffiti boards, or a reserved graffiti wall (*allow only positive messages*).
Create an advice column, movie review, or restaurant review.

Make bumper stickers, rally signs, or posters.

Research holidays in other countries.

Create a new holiday . . . what is it called? What does it celebrate?

Throw a "come-as-you-will-be-party" (*e.g., in five years, ten years, twenty years*).

Use mind-maps, thought-wheels, or other quick ways to generate ideas.

Create a crossword puzzle, word search, or other word game with vocabulary words.

Produce want ads, advertisements, or TV commercials.

Make school announcements to share the stories and related activities.

Create tongue twisters or riddles.

Formulate a recipe for _____ (*e.g., life, success, happiness, etc.*).

Write directions for _____ (*e.g., making peanut butter sandwiches, washing hands, etc.*).

Write a bedtime story for a small child.

Read to a child.

Have a child read to you.

Brainstorm to generate ideas quickly.

Have brainstorming contests between groups within the class.

Role-play, or act out a skill that needs practice (*e.g., saying "no," meeting someone, making a decision, dealing with a conflict, etc.*).

Send happy-grams to parents.

Leave notes or quotes daily for loved ones or special friends.

Make a series of lists that reflect who you are:

> *Favorite foods*
> *Favorite television programs*
> *Famous people you would like to talk to or meet*
> *Dreams you've had*
> *Top ten jobs or professions you would like to pursue*
> *Ten ways to find inner peace*
> *Things you think about when you can't sleep*
> *Places you want to see and things you want to do before you die*
> *Things you want to say to the President*
> *(Lists can be made about anything when you use your imagination.)*

Use puzzles, optical illusions, or brain-teasers to generate thoughts.

Use interviews to gather information about a certain topic or time in history.

Use photographs or magazine pictures to create a related story board or goal board.

Plan a treasure hunt to look for objects that relate to the story.

Have a "people hunt," searching for classmates or teachers that connect to the story.

Compile a collection of classroom favorite music.

Play music when working on classroom projects.

Generate a comic strip that reflects classroom activities.

Create fun and friendly nicknames for everyone in the class (*tie it to a specific story*).

Develop a classroom newspaper (*e.g., main news of the class, comics, editorials, sports, and a life section featuring articles on students' lives*).

Start a "gratitude journal" and write in it daily at bedtime.

Write letters of gratitude to important people in your life, past, or present.

Post goals and affirmations in prominent places, in the classroom, and at home.

Predict the outcome of the story, or a character within the story.

Read the story and have students create the title.

Have options for homework or extra credit. (*Young people appreciate having the power to choose!*)

Using the Worksheets and the Appendix

Throughout this plan book you will find many student worksheets and activities, in addition to the discussion and journaling questions.

The basic format for your ease of use is this:

★ If the worksheets and activities are story-specific, they will be included immediately following the lesson plan sheets and prior to the story.

★ Occasionally, the directions will have several components and may require several pages of explanation. In that case, they will be located in and referenced to the Appendix (*e.g., the* **Good Boy/Bad Boy Kinesiology** *Demonstration*).

★ Any materials that are more general in nature, and may be related to several stories, will also be located in the Appendix (*e.g., listening skills, decision-making skills, how to say "no," etc.*).

★ **With the purchase of this book, you have our permission to copy any of these worksheets for use in your classroom.**

★ In the event that your budget is too limited for copying costs, you will be able to use these worksheet concepts on any available paper (*recycled paper, or old, unused worksheets will do*).

★ Our goal is to provide you with an ample selection of materials for your use. Choose the ones that best fit your needs.

★ Our ultimate desire is to spark students' enthusiasm for reading, and to empower them to make changes in their lives and in the world. For this reason, it is strongly recommended that you choose the worksheets and activities in this curriculum with care. Overuse can create boredom and may sabotage the more primary goal.

★ This Chicken Soup for the Soul lesson plan book is not designed to be the main course of your curriculum. Rather, it should be the appetizer to tease students' taste buds and create passion for stories in their day. Or, it can whet their appetites to want more, and to do more, in their lives and in their world. Or, it could be the dessert that creates a sense of contentment and completion, leaving them with an attitude of gratitude.

Regardless of how you use this book, the act of using it regularly over time will create positive changes in your students' attitudes and behavior, as well as in your overall classroom atmosphere. It will also spark a desire for the written word and might correspondingly raise reading test scores.

Home-Schooling Suggestions

There are a number of reasons parents choose to educate their children at home. Suffice to say, they are looking for a better way for their kids to learn. For them, the "system" is not a good match for their child or children.

Home-schools have two huge advantages over the structured public classroom. They have time flexibility, and they have the ability to integrate subjects together surrounding a common theme. In addition, time can justifiably be spent on actively educating for character-building and social responsibility—essentially, teaching family values.

Chicken Soup for the Soul stories are a natural fit for dealing with these issues. Most, if not all, of these stories offer motivation and inspiration, and send messages of:

respect	responsibility	character
hope	honesty	fairness
tolerance	self-discipline	empathy
hard work	cooperation	positive attitude
compassion	overcoming obstacles	safe and healthy habits
moral courage	thoughtful decision-making	appreciation
making a difference	good citizenship	conflict-solving
humility	sportsmanship	choosing positive role models
family relationships	inner strength	friendships
problem-solving	resilience	personal goals

and the list goes on. . . .

Lesson plans in this document tap into these issues and allow for students to experience physical, emotional, mental, social, and spiritual growth.

Every story can be a lesson in reading:
★ Silent Sustained Reading (SSR)
★ Partner reading
★ Small group reading
★ Comprehension
★ Analysis of story
  * identification of plot
  * identification of character
  * identification of setting
  * identification of problem
  * identification of solution
  * sequencing of events
  * point of view
  * cause and effect

* ★ Where writers get ideas
* ★ Connecting feelings with stories
* ★ Determining why the author chose that time, place, topic
* ★ Types of stories
    * * fables
    * * fiction
    * * nonfiction
    * * poetry
* ★ Most important, the pure enjoyment of the story!

Every story can be a lesson in writing:
* ★ Daily journal prompts relating to the story
* ★ Triggers for creative writing
* ★ Rewrites from the perspective of another character
* ★ Rewrites with a different ending
* ★ Style and form
* ★ Writing for communication
* ★ The process of writing
* ★ Writing spontaneously
* ★ Poetry: types, forms, techniques, rhyming, repetition, verse
* ★ Learning to edit and rewrite
* ★ Keeping a notebook of writing ideas

Every story can be an English or grammar lesson:
* ★ Vocabulary—understanding and choosing the right words
* ★ Identifying and/or diagramming sentence structure
* ★ Punctuation, mechanics, structural analysis
* ★ Parts of speech (*e.g., nouns, verbs, compound words, prepositions, etc.*)
* ★ Active and passive voice
* ★ Spelling
* ★ Sentence structure

Every story can be used to develop listening skills and comprehension (see Appendix, page 363).

Every story can be used to practice note-taking skills.

Every story can be used to develop critical thinking skills:
* classify
* compare
* contrast
* describe
* discuss
* evaluate
* illustrate
* list
* prove
* review
* summarize
* use Venn diagrams or graphic organizers to show similarities and differences

In addition, some stories can provide:
* personal **history** lessons (*e.g., Vietnam War, slavery, Holocaust, Civil Rights, 9/11*)
* **geography** lessons related to study in other parts of the country or world (*e.g., deep South, Pakistan, Vietnam, etc.*)
* lessons related to **science** (*e.g., animal behavior, environmental or natural issues, etc.*)
* **health** lessons (*e.g., smoking, drugs, drinking, eating disorders, depression, grief, etc.*)
* lessons of **social or societal** issues (*e.g., bullies, family relations, love, homeless, racial, war, etc.*)
* **art, music, culture** (*many student activities tie in these aspects to the stories*)

We think you get the idea . . .

Essentially, children learn what they love. It has been our experience that they love being read to, and they particularly love the heart-warming inspiration and hope found in Chicken Soup for the Soul stories. A daily diet of Chicken Soup stories considerably changes the attitude and behavior of many students.

Dealing with Feelings

When doing the research for this book, in almost every case we found that our male test groups of all ages did not enjoy the sad stories as much, even if they ended happily.

We suspect this to be a reflection of our society and the need for males to suppress their feelings, particularly when they are in a group setting. Since many of the Chicken Soup for the Soul stories elicit strong emotions, a class discussion of dealing with feelings is suggested.

Our ability to feel is a gift of being human. Talking about one's feelings and learning the various ways of expressing them is a healthy tool for life. By establishing classroom guidelines and your expectations for students' behavior regarding emotional situations, you are creating an atmosphere of safety. The more often that you read them stories that elicit feelings, the more opportunity you give them to practice appropriate ways of dealing with their feelings in a safe, but public place (see Appendix, page 363, for practice worksheets).

On a related note, it is desirable that you, as the teacher, examine your own comfort levels regarding the showing of your emotions to your classes. What you model for young people is the highest form of teaching. Is this particular life lesson one that you are willing to impart to your students?

Anna was raised with three brothers and a no-crying policy in her house. When she burst into tears in her classroom following the death of a five-year-old friend, she found out how important it was to be human in front of her students. They told her that they were "never given a chance to care," or that, "adults always tell them it's okay to cry, but never do it themselves." They also told her she was "always there for them . . . now they would be there for her." It was a huge eye-opener for Anna, and a gift to her students to share tears when they were feeling sad.

After that, she no longer avoided the sad Chicken Soup for the Soul stories, nor did she hide her tears when she read them. As many times as she read "Bopsy," she would still cry when she got to the ending. When her seventh graders started requesting a "cry story," she realized that she was modeling for them what adults have often said, but have rarely shown—that it really is okay to cry. In the end, it acted as a strong bonding agent with her class, and it became a wonderful lesson that she learned from her students.

Not all of you will be comfortable with showing your feelings to students. At times, it may seem appropriate to do so, while at other times, it may not. That, in itself, is okay.

Anna had a male colleague who found himself very emotional whenever a story would trigger the thought of a possible loss of his little daughter. With certain groups of students, he felt comfortable sharing these intense feelings. There were other classes, however, where he held back the tears forming in his eyes and attempted to hide the crackling in his voice. The difference may have been the students, or it may have been him coping with his own personal issues on that particular day. The point is that you should be prepared for either possibility, and you should avoid any self-judgment that may occur.

Remember that you are the one to select the best stories to fit the emotional climate and goals of your class. We do challenge you to risk showing a bit more of yourself to your students, and we think that you will find it to be rewarding in the end.

Changing the World

Most of the stories in this book have a common thread, a feeling of making the world better. For this reason, plans can easily be adapted from story to story so you can teach the particular concept you desire to reinforce.

Many students want to change the world after hearing these true accounts. They feel empowered to do so because the stories are about real people, just like themselves.

In the stories of famous people, students learn of their obstacles, their failures, and their *human*-ness. From this, students are inspired to follow their own dreams and to make it happen in the world, whatever "it" may be for them.

Following each and every story, students can be challenged to ask themselves:

"What did I say or do today to make the world better?"
"What life lesson did I learn from this story . . . this experience?"
"What have I shared of myself that gives back to the world?"
"What has this story inspired me to do . . . more of . . . less of . . . differently?"

Every story could have sentence completions:

"I learned_____."
"I learned that I _____."
"I relearned that I _____."
"I felt_____."
"I felt that I _____."

We are committed to increasing students' awareness of their power to make a difference in the lives of others. This might be single one-on-one behavior, such as listening more deeply or smiling at someone. Or, it may be the larger social behaviors that impact the world, such as eliminating racism, sexism, poverty, violence, and abuse.

After hearing these stories, the ultimate question we're looking to have students answer is: "How do I intend to use my life to change the world?"

Remember that stories create experiences for us. Our heart races when the main character is scared. Tears form when a child dies. We feel courage and determination when a youngster overcomes obstacles to become a famous surgeon, an Olympian, or the owner of a large horse ranch. As the teacher, you are the catalyst. You are the one to connect your students to the story and to the world. You can provide them with a variety of life experiences every day. You can challenge them with every story. You can inspire them to ask these questions of themselves. You can create for them a desire to make a difference. *You* can motivate them to change the world!

PART TWO

The Stories
and
Lesson Plans

Stories Selected for Three Levels of Lesson Plans

Stories in this chapter are the top student favorites of all ages and were specifically chosen to be general in content to cover a wide variety of topics and to be suitable for grades one through twelve. This versatility is reflected in selections from several different Chicken Soup for the Soul books. While the stories here cover a broad range of ages and interests, the plans and activities are specific to the high school grades.

Each story is preceded by an information page listing:

- ★ Title
- ★ Book
- ★ Page number
- ★ Amount of time necessary to read the story aloud
- ★ Major topics in **bold** print
- ★ Lesser referencing topics in standard print
- ★ Appropriate age level for the story content and plans
- ★ Short synopsis of the story
- ★ Additional notes to the teacher.

Additional worksheets are located within the story section whenever possible. Occasionally, teachers will be referred to the Appendix for further information.

TITLE: **KINDNESS IS CONTAGIOUS**

BOOK: **Chicken Soup for the Kid's Soul**

PAGE: **328**

TIME TO READ: **4 minutes**

TOPICS: **Acting with Kindness**
World issue—elderly
Giving and receiving

AGE LEVEL: **Grades 9–12**

SYNOPSIS: **A young girl leaves a backpack and a library book in a waiting room while helping elderly strangers to get to their doctors' appointments. Upon returning, there is a $50 bill tucked in her wallet.**

NOTES TO TEACHER:

You can easily leave out the reference to God for public school use.

The plans and activities in this section focus on the elderly and on growing old. You could just as easily focus on the issue of exhibiting acts of kindness.

Look in Appendix, page 349, for further ideas on spreading kindness.

Chicken Soup for the Kid's Soul,
Kindness is Contagious

HIGH SCHOOL:

PRE-QUESTIONS:

What are your feelings about the elderly?

Picture yourself as "old." . . . how old are you?
- What is your life like?
- What do you look like?
- What are you doing?
- Where do you live?

Read Story

POST-QUESTIONS:

Discuss various ways that teens can help the elderly in your community.

"What goes around, comes around. . ." (*What you give out to people eventually comes back around as gifts to you . . . in spirit, not as "exact" possessions.*).
- In circle groups, discuss personal examples of this quote.

STUDENT ACTIVITIES:

Compare the United States with other countries and cultures in its treatment of the elderly. Where would you like to grow old?
- Why did you choose this place?

Explore the topic of "elder abuse."
- How prevalent is it?
- Why does it occur?
- How can it be prevented?
- Write a three to five page paper on the subject.

What are the volunteer "requirements" and corresponding "responsibilities" at your local hospital?
- Consider volunteering.

Are there any nursing homes, or assisted living facilities in your community?
- Volunteer at a facility that helps the elderly.

Conduct a debate on an issue involving the elderly (*socialized medicine, Social Security, buying prescription drugs from Canada, etc.*)

Kindness Is Contagious

*The place to improve the world is first
in one's own heart and head and hands . . .*

Robert M. Pirsig

When I was through with my doctor's appointment, I made my way down to the lobby. My mom was going to pick me up, but knowing how she was always late, I realized I had some time to spare. I took a seat in the lobby and smiled politely at the three elderly people sitting near me. There were two women and one old man. Then I dug into my backpack for my library book.

Just as I started to read, one of the women struck up a loud conversation with anyone who would listen. She relayed her adventures purchasing her new eyeglasses. I smiled and listened to her tale; she had a lot to say. When her husband pulled up in front of the big glass doors, her story ended abruptly. She was gone.

The old man's ride arrived just as quickly. His daughter pulled up in a station wagon filled with kids. She burst through the doors, saying, "Pop, are you ready?" That left just me and a beautiful gray-haired woman in the lobby.

I looked directly at her. She appeared dignified, serious, and stern. I thought she might be a former English teacher because she impressed me as a person with knowledge and confidence. She intentionally avoided my direct glance, but as I lifted my book to read, I could feel her eyes carefully gazing in my direction.

Concentrating on reading was impossible. My thoughts kept shifting from the beautiful gray-haired woman to thoughts of school.

Everyone was talking about graduation. The other kids had been discussing what presents to buy for each other. My face turned red at the thought. It had never occurred to me that kids bought presents for graduation. In our home, relatives bought the graduate presents, not friends. I had no money. And I couldn't ask my parents; they hadn't any money either. Yet I longed to be able to share with my best friends something that would help them remember our friendships, even if it was just something little.

I prayed, Oh God, help. What am I going to do?

My mind was still deep in thought when suddenly I heard a commotion at the entrance doors. There was an elderly woman in a wheelchair and another older woman trying to push her along. They were struggling with the heavy glass door. A bustling crowd too busy to help sidestepped them to get by, leaving them to struggle alone.

I jumped up to help them. It was only then that I realized the woman pushing the wheelchair could barely walk. I eased them through both sets of doors and helped them to the elevator. They thanked me, but I could see that they still had a monumental struggle ahead. They still needed to get on and off of the elevator, and into their doctor's office safely.

I decided to ride with them on the elevator. I asked them which floor they needed, and then I made sure they found the correct office. They thanked me again. I told them it was my pleasure, and I really meant it. I was truly happy to help them.

30

I was on my way down in the elevator when I realized that I had left my backpack on the lobby chair. My backpack had nothing of value in it, just a wallet with fifty-nine cents in change, a small mirror, a comb, and some tissues. But then I remembered that my precious library book was also on the chair.

The elevator could not go fast enough. As the doors opened, I held my breath, hoping against all hope that my backpack and library book were still there. I rushed into the lobby.

They were both safely on the chair, just as I had left them.

As I sat down, I could feel the beautiful gray-haired woman's smiling eyes on me. She seemed proud for some reason. Then her taxi arrived, and, without a word, she was gone.

I decided to pick through my pennies to see if I had enough money to buy a package of peanuts at the little pharmacy. I opened my backpack. To my surprise, tucked neatly inside my wallet was a fifty dollar bill!

My mind flashed to the beautiful woman with the proud look in her eye. I had been kind to a stranger, and in turn, a stranger had been kind to me. I knew that God had answered my prayer.

Kristin Seuntjens

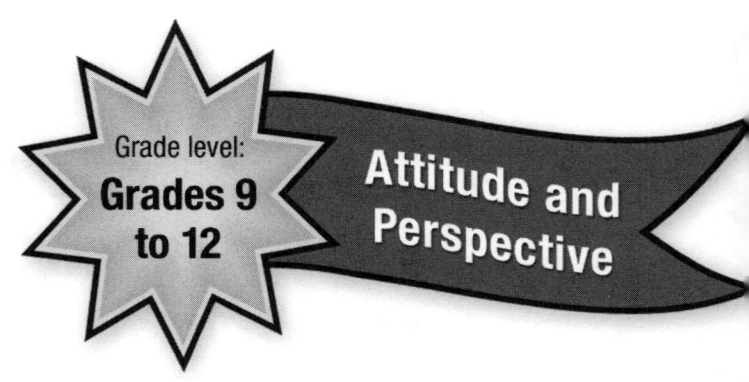

TITLE: **GLENNA'S GOAL BOOK**

BOOK: **Chicken Soup for the Soul**

PAGE: **188**

TIME TO READ: **5 minutes**

TOPICS: **Attitude and Perspective**
Following your dream
Visual imagery

AGE LEVEL: **Grades 9–12**

SYNOPSIS: **A woman creates picture books to capture her dreams and to make them happen.**

NOTES TO TEACHER:

We deleted specific references to God or the Bible when reading this story in the public schools.

We suggest that you identify the difference between dreams and goals for students. (*A dream is a wish or desire for something. A goal is a wish that is specific, measurable, and has a deadline.*) See information on Smart Goals (Appendix, page 353).

It is highly recommended that you encourage students to write goals that have to do with personal achievements and are more attainable (*e.g., becoming an artist, doctor, Olympian, astronomer, writer, etc.*), instead of fairytale dreams like becoming the greatest basketball player in history or marrying a crown prince.

Anna has read the story to students, ages twelve to sixty. And she has given the goal book assignment with amazing results over the years. She has included her own true story (*Following Glenna*), which portrays the main reason for the inclusion of the original story.

Chicken Soup for the Soul,
Glenna's Goal Book

HIGH SCHOOL:

PRE-QUESTIONS:

Which is more powerful, pictures or words? Explain your answer.

How do dreams and goals differ? *(Dreams are wishes or desires. Goals are wishes that are specific, measurable, action-oriented, and have time-lines.)*

Do you think it's important to see your dreams? Why, or why not?

Do you think it's important to write your goals? Why, or why not?

Why is it important to be very specific when writing goals? *(There is a saying that goes "Be careful what you wish for." The more specific you are, the more clearly your mind can identify, and then help you to manifest your goals.)*

Read Story

POST-QUESTIONS:

Do you think this picture process can work for anyone? Explain.

How does the **I x V = R Principle** work? *(**I**magination mixed with **V**ividness becomes **R**eality.)*

What is the theory behind making goal books? *(That the mind sees things in pictures, not in words. By cutting out pictures that represent your wishes, you are creating a space in your brain that sees these dreams as real possibilities. The act of repeatedly viewing the pictures helps to add the emotional, feeling-desire component, as well as to regularly reinforce your dream. It is also a reminder to put some action behind it.)*

STUDENT ACTIVITIES:

Do **Goal Book/Goal Poster Activity** (see Appendix, page 354 for directions).
 • Have a cut-and-paste day in class, where classmates can help each other to find pictures.

Look at these visual goals every day. Report your progress to the class every two or three weeks until the end of the school year.

NOTES TO TEACHER:

Show students the **Good Boy/Bad Boy Kinesiology Demonstration** (Appendix, page 317).

Follow up with **Fingers Come Together** exercise (Appendix, page 322).

Following Glenna

When I first read *Glenna's Goal Book* many years ago, I found it to be too much of a fairytale for my liking. At the time, I was reading *Chicken Soup for the Soul* stories to my classes on a daily basis. It was our ritual ending to each class period. Without discussion or homework, it was just food for thought as I sent them out the door.

While I did believe in the power of visualization, this particular story just seemed too good to be true. Hence, I skipped reading it to students in favor of other stories that were more believable.

Several weeks went by, and I shared with a friend my Chicken Soup journey through my classroom. She immediately mentioned Glenna's story and how she had made a picture book of her own, and she found that it was all coming true! I was quite surprised and highly skeptical. Nevertheless, we made plans to spend New Year's Eve making a picture-goal book instead of writing New Year's resolutions. Regardless of the outcome, I thought it would be an entertaining way to spend a dateless evening.

New Year's Eve rolled around. Kay and I sat in the middle of her living room floor in our most comfortable flannel pajamas, talking, laughing, and finding the pictures that represented our deepest dreams. We had such a great time that I decided to give it a try in my classroom. At the very least, this cut-and-paste project would be a short break from the serious, "real" work of my classes.

My students loved it! I obtained a box of old magazines from the library, and I had students bring in some of their own for cutting. There was a lot of noise and laughter as students helped each other find the more difficult pictures. "Hey! If anyone sees a motorcycle picture, I need one." "I'm looking for a picture of a doctor." "Anyone have any horse pictures?"

All in all, I felt good about getting my students to think about their dreams, convert them to goals, and to have a fun day cutting out pictures of them all. Not wanting to judge their goals, I assigned points to the project merely for following directions in the labeling process.

The assignment was done and I thought nothing more of it, until students started coming back to me and reporting that one of their goals had come true after doing this class project. Months and years later, I was hearing how several, or all, of their goals had come true.

As for my own goal book, I had shoved it in a closet and didn't find it until years later when I was moving from Michigan to California. Even though they were pictures of my dreams and not written as goals, almost everything in the book had manifested in my life!

Needless to say, this is now a regular assignment in all of my classes, whether I'm teaching seventh graders or college students.

I challenge you to try it. It may make a believer out of you, too.

Anna Unkovich

Glenna's Goal Book

In 1977 I was a single mother with three young daughters, a house payment, a car payment, and a need to rekindle some dreams.

One evening I attended a seminar and heard a man speak on the I x V = R principle. (Imagination multiplied by Vividness becomes Reality.) The speaker pointed out that the mind thinks in pictures, not in words. And as we vividly picture in our mind what we desire, it will become a reality.

This concept struck a chord of creativity in my heart. I knew the Biblical truth that the Lord gives us "the desires of our heart" (Psalms 37:4) and that "as a man thinketh in his heart, so is he" (Proverbs 23:7). I was determined to take my written prayer list and turn it into pictures. I began cutting up old magazines and gathering pictures that depicted the "desires of my heart." I arranged them in an expensive photo album and waited expectantly.

I was very specific with my pictures. They included:

1. A good-looking man
2. A woman in a wedding gown and a man in a tuxedo
3. Bouquets of flowers (I'm a romantic)
4. Beautiful diamond jewelry (I rationalized that God loved David and Solomon and they were two of the richest men who ever lived)
5. An island in the sparkling blue Caribbean
6. A lovely home
7. New furniture
8. A woman who had recently become vice president of a large corporation. (I was working for a company that had no female officers. I wanted to be the first woman vice president in that company.)

About eight weeks later, I was driving down a California freeway, minding my own business at 10:30 in the morning. Suddenly a gorgeous red and white Cadillac passed me. I looked at the car because it was a beautiful car. And the driver looked at me and smiled, and I smiled back because I always smile. Now I was in deep trouble. Have you ever done that? I tried to pretend that I hadn't looked. "Who me? I didn't look at you!" He followed me for the next fifteen miles. Scared me to death! I drove a few miles, he drove a few miles. I parked, he parked . . . and eventually I married him!

On the first day after our first date, Jim sent me a dozen roses. Then I found out that he had a hobby. His hobby was collecting diamonds. Big ones! And he was looking for somebody to decorate. I volunteered! We dated for about two years, and every Monday morning I received a long-stemmed red rose and a love note from him.

About three months before we were getting married, Jim said to me, "I have found the perfect place to go on our honeymoon. We will go to St. John Island down in the Caribbean." I laughingly said, "I never would have thought of that!"

I did not confess the truth about my picture book until Jim and I had been married for almost a year. It was then that we were moving into our gorgeous new home and furnishing it with the elegant furniture that I had pictured. (Jim turned out to be the West Coast wholesale distributor for one of the finest Eastern furniture manufacturers.)

By the way, the wedding was in Laguna Beach, California, and included the gown and tuxedo as realities. Eight months after I created my dream book, I became the vice president of human resources in the company where I worked.

In some sense this sounds like a fairy tale, but it is absolutely true. Jim and I have made many "picture books" since we have been married. God has filled our lives with the demonstration of these powerful principles of faith at work.

Decide what it is that you want in every area of your life. Imagine it vividly. Then act on your desires by actually constructing your personal goal book. Convert your ideas into concrete realities through this simple exercise. There are no impossible dreams. And, remember, God has promised to give his children the desires of their hearts.

Glenna Salsbury

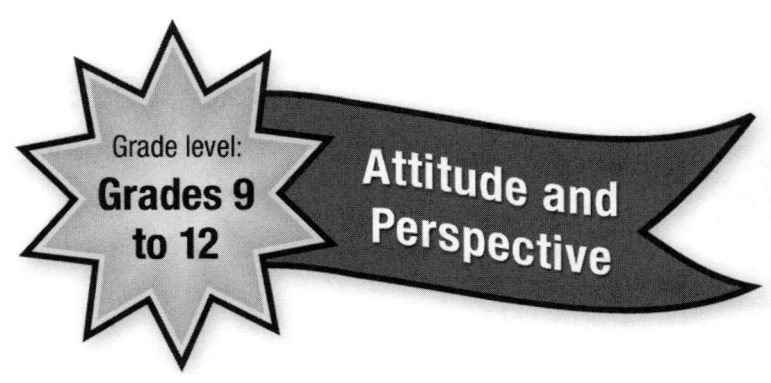

TITLE: **A SILENT VOICE**

BOOK: **Chicken Soup for the Preteen Soul**

PAGE: **254**

TIME TO READ: **2 minutes**

TOPICS: **Attitude and Perspective**
World issues—poverty
Nonmaterial wealth
Giving and receiving
Acting with kindness

AGE LEVEL: **Grades 9–12**

SYNOPSIS: **An isolated young boy reaches out to "give" to the annual Christmas collection. It turns out that he is at the top of the "most needy" list.**

NOTES TO TEACHER:

When this plan was tested on some third grade students in Michigan, their initial responses on the worksheets were very self-centered and materialistic in nature. They wanted things for themselves, such as an iPod, a Game Boy, a new bike, etc. After making and delivering no-sew blankets to a homeless shelter, one of the students raised her hand and asked, "Can we do those worksheets again?" The responses this time were "other-centered" and altruistic, such as feeding the poor, helping victims of disaster, etc. The underlying message from the story, followed by the experience of making and delivering the blankets, became a life-altering event for this classroom of eight-year-olds.

Two related stories that your students might enjoy are "The Man Who Had Plenty," found on page 162 of *Chicken Soup for the Kid's Soul,* and *"My Homeless Man,"* found in *Chicken Soup for the Soul: Stories for a Better World,* page 97.

Chicken Soup for the Preteen Soul,
A Silent Voice

HIGH SCHOOL:

PRE-QUESTIONS:

In writing, answer the following questions:

If you were granted any three wishes, what would they be?

What is your most important possession? *(This could be an item like a car, or a quality or state of being like inner peace or health.)*

If you had unlimited money, what would you do with it?

Have you ever given money to a homeless person? Why, or why not?

Have you ever been, or know someone closely, that is or was very poor?

Describe the lifestyle of the very poor *(clothing, housing, food, responsibilities, daily life, etc.)*.

Read Story

POST-QUESTIONS:

Would you consider Willard to be rich, or poor? Why?

What made him "give" when he was one of the most needy in the class?

List "riches" that are not related to money? *(Health, loving relationships, fame, wisdom, inner peace, etc.)*

You have $5 million that you must give away.

- List the places or people who would receive your gift. Explain your selections.

STUDENT ACTIVITIES:

Keep a gratitude journal, listing the things for which you are grateful.

Make **No-Sew Blankets** for the homeless (see directions, page 39).

Start a service club in your school. Identify local needs.

- Determine ways the club can donate time and/or money.

NOTES TO TEACHER:

Carole Gardner-Neurath teaches a "Service Class" at Cadillac High School in Michigan. Students research local agencies that need help. Students then design and execute projects to raise money for these charities. They also participate in volunteering their time. Project plans, as well as hours donated, help to determine their grade for the class. "Down-time" between projects is spent reading from a variety of Chicken Soup for the Soul books to inspire and motivate them.

MAKING NO-SEW BLANKETS

1. Start with two pieces of fleece fabric. (Blankets can be made to any length, but one to two yards works best.)

2. Lay both pieces together, right sides facing outward.

3. Make cuts around the entire perimeter that are approximately one inch wide and three inches deep. (Adults will need to do the cutting when younger children are involved. We recommend using parent volunteers to help cut and supervise this task.)

4. Tie two strips of fabric in a tight double knot, top to bottom, around the edge of the blanket.

5. Cut off and remove strips at the corners. (It will become evident where this is necessary once you've tied one entire edge.)

Tying-teams of four eight-year-old students can complete a blanket in less than an hour. Teens can do it in a fraction of that time.

You can make it reversible by putting a solid color on one side, and a print on the other. Blankets wash and dry easily.

This makes a nice gift to give to the elderly or to the homeless.

Some stores may donate fabric or offer discounts for a classroom venture such as this one. If you choose to do this as a continuing project from year to year, you may ask stores to alert you of sales on fleece fabric.

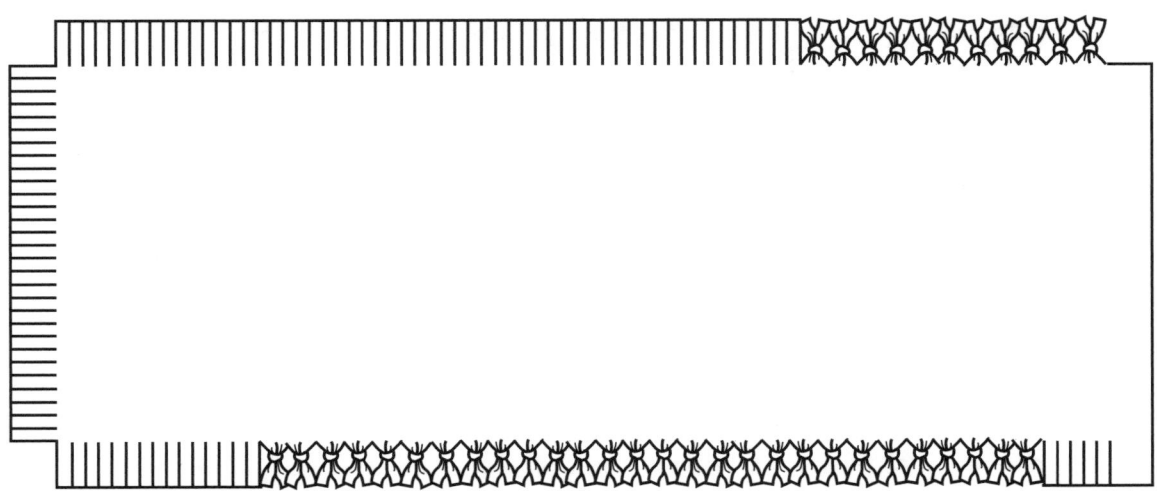

A Silent Voice

If there are people at once rich and content, be assured they are content because they know how to be so, not because they are rich.

Charles Wagner

The situation seemed hopeless.

From the first day he entered my junior high classroom, Willard P. Franklin existed in his own world, shutting out his classmates and me, his teacher. My attempts at establishing a friendly relationship with him were met with complete indifference. Even a "Good morning, Willard" received only a barely audible grunt. I could see that his classmates fared no better. Willard was strictly a loner who seemed to have no desire or need to break his barrier of silence.

Shortly after the Thanksgiving holiday, we received word of the annual Christmas collection of money for the less fortunate people in our school district.

"Christmas is a season of giving," I told my students. "There are a few students in the school who might not have a happy holiday season. By contributing to our Christmas collection, you will help buy food, clothing, and toys for these needy people. We start the collection tomorrow."

When I called for the contributions the next day, I discovered that almost everyone had forgotten. Except for Willard P. Franklin. The boy dug deep into his pants pockets as he strolled up to my desk. Carefully, he dropped two quarters into the small container.

"I don't need no milk for lunch," he mumbled. For a moment, just a moment, he smiled. Then he turned and walked back to his desk.

That night, after school, I took our meager contribution to the school principal. I couldn't help sharing the incident that had taken place.

"I may be wrong, but I believe Willard might be getting ready to become a part of the world around him," I told the principal.

"Yes, I believe it sounds hopeful," he nodded. "And I have a hunch we might do well to have him share a bit of his world with us. I just received a list of the poor families in our school who most need help through the Christmas collection. Here, take a look at it."

As I gazed down to read, I discovered Willard P. Franklin and his family were the top names on the list.

David R. Collins

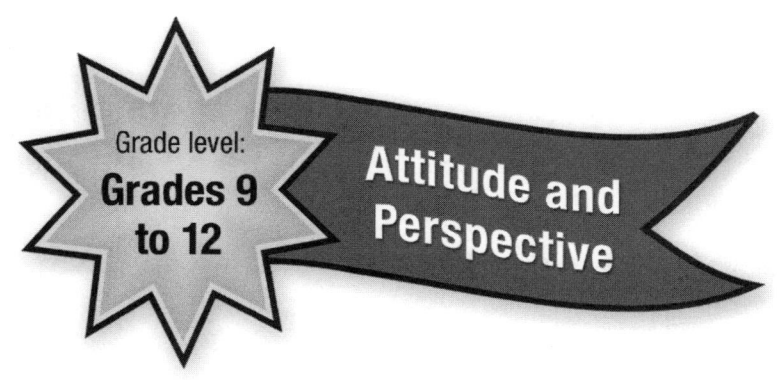

TITLE: **TO BE ENORMOUSLY GORGEOUS**

BOOK: **Chicken Soup for the Kid's Soul**

PAGE: **167**

TIME TO READ: **2 minutes**

TOPICS: **Attitude and Perspective**
Self-esteem
Making choices
Family

AGE LEVEL: **Grades 9–12**

SYNOPSIS: **A young girl chooses her father's idea of "gorgeous" rather than accepting her friends' opinions on the subject.**

NOTES TO TEACHER:

l   While this story has a childlike feeling to it, the concepts and activities are important for all ages.

Chicken Soup for the Kid's Soul,
To Be Enormously Gorgeous

PRE-QUESTIONS:

List five things you like or appreciate about yourself.

List five things that others appreciate about you.

Define "gorgeous."

What attributes are found in someone who you consider to be gorgeous? *(Discuss whether or not any inner qualities were listed, such as a beautiful spirit, a kind heart, a calm and peaceful manner, etc.)*

What do you think is more important, having good looks or having ability?

- Which would you rather have? Explain.

Read Story

POST-QUESTIONS:

Why does the author choose to believe her father?

Who decides what gorgeous means? *(Parents? Friends? Television? Teachers? Magazines? The President? etc.)*

In dyads, or **Circle Talk** groups (Appendix, page 311), discuss the issues of "inner" vs. "outer" beauty. Follow with a discussion of "beauty" vs. "talent."

NOTES TO TEACHER:

Introduce students to the Mirror Exercise (Appendix, page 307).

- Have them complete this task for forty nights. Report back at the end of that time to discuss the results. Does anyone feel more powerful, more at peace, or more successful?

STUDENT ACTIVITIES:

Complete some of the *self-awareness worksheets* (Appendix, page 366).

Interview three people of different age categories (someone younger than age 12, age 13–20, age 21–40, age 41–60, age 61–80, or someone older than 80).

- Ask them what "gorgeous" means to them.
- Is there a difference with age? If so, what did you find?

Using popular magazines, make a collage of currently held or personal views of gorgeous.

Your parents have nominated you as "Teen of the Year." What qualities have they listed about you for the judges' consideration?

After making your own list, ask your parents what they would list.

- Compare the lists. Were there any surprises?

To Be Enormously Gorgeous

My dad says I am ENORMOUSLY GORGEOUS. I wonder if I really am.

To be ENORMOUSLY GORGEOUS . . . Sarah says you need to have beautiful long, curly hair like she has. I don't.

To be ENORMOUSLY GORGEOUS . . . Justin says you must have perfectly straight, white teeth like he has. I don't.

To be ENORMOUSLY GORGEOUS . . . Jessica says you can't have any of those little brown dots on your face called freckles. I do.

To be ENORMOUSLY GORGEOUS . . . Mark says you have to be the smartest kid in the seventh-grade class. I'm not.

To be ENORMOUSLY GORGEOUS . . . Stephen says you have to be able to tell the funniest jokes in the school. I don't.

To be ENORMOUSLY GORGEOUS . . . Lauren says you need to live in the nicest neighborhood in town and in the prettiest house. I don't.

To be ENORMOUSLY GORGEOUS . . . Matthew says you can only wear the coolest clothes and the most popular shoes. I don't.

To be ENORMOUSLY GORGEOUS . . . Samantha says you need to come from a perfect family. I don't.

But every night at bedtime my dad gives me a big hug and says, "You are ENORMOUSLY GORGEOUS, and I love you."

My dad must know something my friends don't.

Carla O'Brien

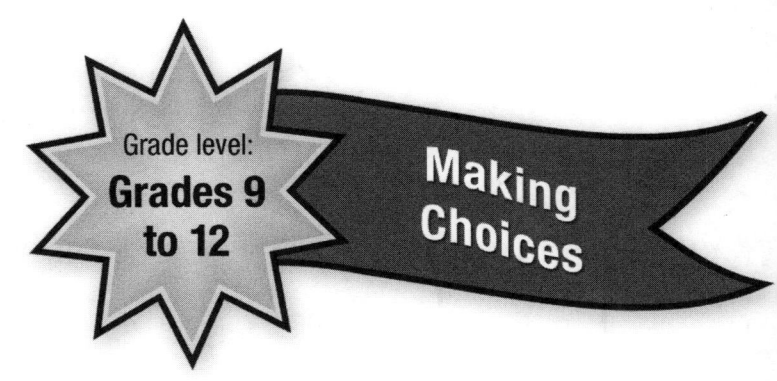

TITLE: **LOST AND FOUND**

BOOK: **Chicken Soup for the Preteen Soul 2**

PAGE: **279**

TIME TO READ: **6 minutes**

TOPICS: **Making Choices**
Living and learning
Acting with kindness

AGE LEVEL: **Grades 9–12**

SYNOPSIS: **A twelve-year-old finds $1,000 in a secondhand nightstand. He decides to return it to the store to find the owners.**

NOTES TO TEACHER:

As educators, we instill societal values in our students mostly by the examples we set on a daily basis. This is a good reinforcement for "doing the right thing" at any age!

You might choose to focus on the decision-making aspect of this story. For worksheets and practice skills on making decisions, go to the Appendix, pages 342–347.

Chicken Soup for the Preteen Soul 2,
Lost and Found

PRE-QUESTIONS:

If no one knew that you found $1,000, what would you do with the money?
- Explain your answer.

Read Story

POST-QUESTIONS:

Most of us would agree that returning the money is the *right* thing to do.
What circumstances might justify keeping the money:
- Your family is hungry?
- Your mother needs life-saving surgery?
- A homeless shelter will close its doors if it doesn't get immediate funding?
- The owners cannot be found?
- A major flood in a nearby community caused many to be homeless?

Make a list of as many reasons as you can that would justify keeping the money.
Assess and discuss the issue of "life as shades of gray."

STUDENT ACTIVITIES:

Rewrite the story with a different ending.
Rewrite the story from the viewpoint of the person who once owned the nightstand.
- Capture the feelings of the situation.

Lost and Found

*The measure of a man's real character is what he would
do if he knew he would never be found out.*

Thomas B. Macaulay

It was my twelfth birthday, and what I really wanted most was a new bicycle. A blue low-rider with fat tires. But I knew that my family couldn't afford one. My parents said that I should be happy that I had a bicycle at all—if you can call that rickety old thing that I owned a bike.

A new bike was just a dream, so I settled for a nightstand. I figured that at least I would have a safe place to keep my private stuff, away from the reach of my pesky younger brothers. So I asked my parents for a nightstand with lockable drawers. And that's what I got.

We went to the secondhand furniture store and found an old, dark brown nightstand. It didn't look too cool, but at least it had drawers that I could keep locked. I decided that I would paint it and glue some stickers on it to make it look better.

After we took it home, I was getting ready to paint it. When I pulled the drawers out, I felt something stuck to the back of the lowest drawer. I reached in all the way to the back, and guess what I found? A Ziploc bag with some papers in it.

Cool! *Maybe I've found somebody's secret stuff,* I thought. When I opened the bag, I realized that the papers were some kind of official-looking documents. And wrapped in the papers were a bunch of ten and twenty dollar bills! Talk about finding a treasure! And on my birthday!

"Is this some kind of joke?" I said aloud. Maybe my family was playing a trick on me. Maybe this was fake money. But it looked pretty real. Somebody had been stashing money in this bag and hiding it in the back of the locked drawer. I went ahead and read the papers, and it turned out to be a will. Some old lady was leaving her savings for her son and grandchildren.

All this was too weird. My mind was going crazy. Was I the luckiest twelve-year-old ever? With this money I could buy the coolest bicycle. I could even buy bicycles for my brothers. Who knows? Maybe I even had enough here to get a car for my parents, so they could trash that embarrassing old junker that we had for a car.

"Finders keepers, losers weepers," I started singing as I began counting the money. When I reached a thousand dollars, I had to stop. My mother was knocking on my bedroom door. I quickly closed the drawer with the money in it.

"How is your painting job coming along? Do you want some help?"

"No . . . thanks, Mom, I haven't even started. I . . . I'll call you when it's ready."

"Is everything all right?" she asked.

No, everything was not right. Actually, my stomach was growling.

"I'm okay," I fibbed. "I'll let you know when it's ready."

When my mother left my room, I lay on my bed, and, staring at the ceiling, I started thinking about this past week. First, I didn't make the basketball team. Then I flunked the math test. Finally, my little brother destroyed my science project. (That's why I needed a nightstand with locked drawers.) And now, I found this money on my birthday—the only good news in a long time. A solution to my problems. Yet I didn't feel good about it. How come?

I would have to make up lies to tell my family and friends. "Finders keepers . . ." the saying goes. But that money wasn't really meant for me, was it? The lady had been saving it for her family. She must have died and nobody knew about the money hidden in the nightstand. Her family donated it to the secondhand store, and now it was in my hands.

What a dilemma! I could keep it and get all kinds of stuff for me and my family. It wouldn't be too bad for me to keep it, if I shared it . . . right? I bargained with myself. What about keeping some and returning the rest? After all, nobody knew how much money was there . . . and it was my birthday! Or I could give it all back. Tell the truth. No new bicycles. No car.

"Somebody help me with this!" I pleaded. But I really didn't need someone else to give me the answer. I already knew right from wrong. That's why I flunked the math test even though I could have cheated. I decided not to flunk this test. It was a test of honor. My honor.

I called my parents and my brothers into my bedroom and showed them what I had found. They were wide-eyed—speechless! When they asked, "What should we do about this?" I already had the answer.

"Let's take it back to the store and find her family." As I said this, my stomach quieted down.

The store owners could not believe it when we told them the story.

"You mean to say you found over a thousand dollars in cash and you are here to return it?" they asked, almost at the same time.

Looking through their donation records, they found the family's telephone number. They phoned them right there and then, and within a few minutes, they all came over to the store: her son, his wife, and their three children—a family pretty much like ours. The parents had tears in their eyes. The old lady's twelve-year-old grandson just kept looking at me as people were telling the story over and over.

You see, they were all still sad about her death. And the father had just lost his job. They had been praying for help, and it turned out that I brought in the answer to their prayers. My act of honesty not only helped them pay the rent, but strengthened their faith and gave them hope.

I had never felt better. No new bicycle could have made me feel as good about myself as I felt that day. I may have flunked the math test, but I passed a more important one—a lost and found test of my own character.

Antonio Angulo Jr., twelve
As told by Marisol Muñoz-Kiehne

Grade level:
Grades 9 to 12

Following Your Dream

TITLE: **BOPSY**

BOOK: **Chicken Soup for the Soul**

PAGE: **61**

TIME TO READ: **4 minutes**

TOPICS: **Following Your Dream**
Tough stuff—dying child
Friendship and community
Family

AGE LEVEL: **Grades 9–12**

SYNOPSIS: **With the help of his mother, and the Phoenix Fire Department, a terminally ill child fulfills his dream of becoming a fireman.**

NOTES TO TEACHER:

A dream is simply a wish or a desire to have something, to do something, or to be something. A goal becomes much more specific. It should be measurable, have some action involved to complete it, and have a time-line by when it will be accomplished (see **SMART Goals,** Appendix, page 353).

This would be a good opportunity to bring in a speaker from Hospice, or for use following a grief situation in the classroom.

Chicken Soup for the Soul,
Bopsy

PRE-QUESTIONS:

Do you remember your dreams for the future that you had as a small child?
  • What were they?

Read Story

POST-QUESTIONS:

What did you think of Fireman Bob and what he did?

Do you know anyone in your school or community who has acted in such a manner?
  • Who was it? What have they done?

Can you think of others who would contribute in this kind of way?

Are there generous ways that you could contribute in your community?
  • If so, what would you do? Why?

What would you like to accomplish or contribute to the world before you die?

STUDENT ACTIVITIES:

List 25 goals in **SMART** format (Appendix, page 353): **S**pecific, **M**easurable, **A**ction-oriented, **R**ealistic, **T**ime-lined.
  • Possible categories include: adventure, recreation, artistic, creative, school, future career, relationship, health, appearance, financial, personal, and spiritual growth.

Put all goals on 3x5 cards. Review each card twice a day. Then visualize it, or see it in your mind as if it's already completed. Feel the feelings you would have if it were already accomplished. Avoid letting your limiting beliefs stand in the way of these dreams.

Help someone else to accomplish a life-time dream. How does that feel?

Determine some specific need within your community.
  • Do a classroom or small group volunteer project to meet this need.
  • Report on the results.

Make a list of things that you would be willing to do to help someone who was dying.

Bopsy

The twenty-six-year-old mother stared down at her son who was dying of terminal leukemia. Although her heart was filled with sadness, she also had a strong feeling of determination. Like any parent, she wanted her son to grow up and fulfill all his dreams. Now that was no longer possible. The leukemia would see to that. But she still wanted her son's dreams to come true.

She took her son's hand and asked, "Bopsy, did you ever think about what you wanted to be when you grew up? Did you ever dream and wish about what you would do with your life?"

"Mommy, I always wanted to be a fireman when I grew up."

Mom smiled back and said, "Let's see if we can make your wish come true." Later that day she went to her local fire department in Phoenix, Arizona, where she met Fireman Bob, who had a heart as big as Phoenix. She explained her son's final wish and asked if it might be possible to give her six-year-old son a ride around the block on a fire engine.

Fireman Bob said, "Look, we can do better than that. If you'll have your son ready at seven o'clock Wednesday morning, we'll make him an honorary fireman for the whole day. He can come down to the fire station, eat with us, go out on all the fire calls, the whole nine yards! And, if you'll give us his sizes, we'll get a real fire uniform made for him, with a real fire hat—not a toy one—with the emblem of the Phoenix Fire Department on it, a yellow slicker like we wear, and rubber boots. They're all manufactured right here in Phoenix, so we can get them fast."

Three days later Fireman Bob picked up Bopsy, dressed him in his fire uniform and escorted him from his hospital bed to the waiting hook and ladder truck. Bopsy got to sit up on the back of the truck and help steer it back to the fire station. He was in heaven.

There were three fire calls in Phoenix that day, and Bopsy got to go out on all three calls. He rode in the different fire engines, the paramedics' van, and even the fire chief's car. He was also videotaped for the local news program.

Having his dream come true, with all the love and attention that was lavished upon him, so deeply touched Bopsy that he lived three months longer than any doctor thought possible.

One night all of his vital signs began to drop dramatically and the head nurse, who believed in the Hospice concept that no one should die alone, began to call the family members to the hospital. Then she remembered the day Bopsy had spent as a fireman, so she called the fire chief and asked if it would be possible to send a fireman in uniform to the hospital to be with Bopsy as he made his transition. The chief replied, "We can do better than that. We'll be there in five minutes. Will you please do me a favor? When you hear the sirens screaming and see the lights flashing, will you announce over the PA system that there is not a fire? It's just the fire department coming to see one of its finest members one more time. And will you open the window to his room? Thanks."

About five minutes later a hook and ladder truck arrived at the hospital, extended its ladder up to Bopsy's third floor open window and fourteen firemen and two firewomen climbed up the ladder into Bopsy's room. With his mother's permission, they hugged him and held him and told him how much they loved him.

With his dying breath, Bopsy looked up at the fire chief and said, "Chief, am I really a fireman now?"

"Bopsy, you are," the chief said.

With those words, Bopsy smiled and closed his eyes for the last time.

Jack Canfield and Mark V. Hansen

Grade level:
Grades 9 to 12

Following Your Dream

TITLE:	FOLLOW YOUR DREAM
BOOK:	Chicken Soup for the Soul
PAGE:	207
TIME TO READ:	3 minutes
TOPICS:	**Following Your Dream** Overcoming obstacles Attitude and perspective Making choices
AGE LEVEL:	Grades 9–12
SYNOPSIS:	Young Monty Roberts chooses to take an **F** on his paper, but to keep his dream.

NOTES TO TEACHER:

l You might begin the reading in the second paragraph " . . . a story about a young man . . ."

Chicken Soup for the Soul,
Follow Your Dream

PRE-QUESTIONS:

Make a ***Timeline*** (Appendix, page 374) of your life, including things you have already accomplished, as well as things you still wish to do.

Read Story

POST-QUESTIONS:

Had you been given the same choice as Monty Roberts, would you have taken the F?
  • Why, or why not?
How important are grades to you?
What kinds of things will people do in order to get a good grade?
Do you know anyone who cheats?
  • What percentage of students in this class do you think cheat?
  • What percentage of students in your grade do you think cheat?
  • What percentage of students in this school do you think cheat?
Why do you think they do this?
How do you think they feel when they do this?
What would you do, or how far would you go, to keep your dreams?
  • Discuss positive and negative possibilities (*e.g., sell your car, move to Tasmania, use steroids, lie, cheat, steal? etc.*).

STUDENT ACTIVITIES:

Write an essay, such as Monty did, describing a dream of yours in great detail.
  • Save it to show your children someday.
Choose the most important dream or goal that you currently have.
  • Establish a time frame for its completion.
  • Set up a step-by-step plan to accomplish it.
  • Establish mini-rewards for steps taken.
  • Keep a journal of your feelings about your progress.
  • Write a one-page essay at the end of the year, reporting on this process.

Follow Your Dream

I have a friend named Monty Roberts who owns a horse ranch in San Ysidro. He has let me use his house to put on fund-raising events to raise money for youth-at-risk programs.

The last time I was there he introduced me by saying, "I want to tell you why I let Jack use my house. It all goes back to a story about a young man who was the son of an itinerant horse trainer who would go from stable to stable, race track to race track, farm to farm and ranch to ranch, training horses. As a result, the boy's high school career was continually interrupted. When he was a senior, he was asked to write a paper about what he wanted to be and do when he grew up.

"That night he wrote a seven-page paper describing his goal of someday owning a horse ranch. He wrote about his dream in great detail, and he even drew a diagram of a 200-acre ranch, showing the location of all the buildings, the stables, and the track. Then he drew a detailed floor plan for a four-thousand-square-foot house that would sit on the 200-acre dream ranch.

"He put a great deal of his heart into the project and the next day he handed it in to his teacher. Two days later he received his paper back. On the front page was a large red F with a note that read, 'See me after class.'

"The boy with the dream went to see the teacher after class and asked, 'Why did I receive an F?'

"The teacher said, 'This is an unrealistic dream for a young boy like you. You have no money. You come from an itinerant family. You have no resources. Owning a horse ranch requires a lot of money. You have to buy the land. You have to pay for the original breeding stock, and later you'll have to pay large stud fees. There's no way you could ever do it.' Then the teacher added, 'If you will rewrite this paper with a more realistic goal, I will reconsider your grade.'

"The boy went home and thought about it long and hard. He asked his father what he should do. His father said, 'Look, son, you have to make up your own mind on this. However, I think it is a very important decision for you.'

"Finally, after sitting with it for a week, the boy turned in the same paper, making no changes at all. He stated, 'You can keep the F and I'll keep my dream.'"

Monty then turned to the assembled group and said, "I tell you this story because you are sitting in my four-thousand-square-foot house in the middle of my 200-acre horse ranch. I still have that school paper framed over the fireplace." He added, "The best part of the story is that two summers ago that same schoolteacher brought thirty kids to camp out on my ranch for a week. When the teacher was leaving, he said, 'Look, Monty, I can tell you this now. When I was your teacher, I was something of a dream stealer. During those years I stole a lot of kids' dreams. Fortunately, you had enough gumption not to give up on yours.'"

Don't let anyone steal your dreams. Follow your heart, no matter what.

Jack Canfield

TITLE: **THE POWER TO SHINE**

BOOK: **Chicken Soup for the Latino Soul**

PAGE: **189**

TIME TO READ: **8 minutes**

TOPICS: **Following Your Dream**
Bias issues—stereotypes
Bias issues—gender
Bias issues—cultural

AGE LEVEL: **Grades 9–12**

SYNOPSIS: **A Latina overcomes gender and cultural bias in the business world.**

NOTES TO TEACHER:

If your classroom or school population is highly Latino, you may wish to spend more time on the cultural implications of this story.

If you choose to do any of the interview activities listed, you may want to use the ***Repeating Question Technique*** (Appendix, page 331) to keep the activity structured and moving.

Chicken Soup for the Latino Soul,
The Power to Shine

HIGH SCHOOL:

PRE-QUESTIONS:

In journals, write about the following:
- Have you ever experienced any kind of discrimination *(race, religion, gender, ability, body size, etc.)*? If so, what? Was it obvious, or subtle? How did you feel at the time? What, if anything, did you do when it happened?

Read Story

POST-QUESTIONS:

Discuss the journey from ghetto-poor, little, Latina girl, to founder and owner of a multi-million-dollar business.
- What things helped, or hindered her journey?
- Have you faced any similar obstacles? If so, what?

Who is Mama Juanita? How does she fit into this story?

Discuss various roles, places, and cultures, where being female is clearly more difficult *(Middle Eastern cultures, Hispanic cultures, Asian cultures, Slavic cultures, etc.)*.

STUDENT ACTIVITIES:

Make a list of all cultures represented in this classroom.
> Choose one that is not your ethnic background. Report on the pros and cons of growing up in this culture or subculture *(It is best to pair with a student of a dissimilar ethnic background and to interview* each other)*.

Interview* someone outside of class with an ethnic background that is not familiar to you. Question this person about their cultural experiences.

Research other cultures and the responsibilities held by teens in these cultures.
- Write a two-page essay on which teen you would rather be and why.
- Be sure to include gender issues as a part of your discourse.

Within the class, pair up with someone of the opposite sex. Then interview* each other to discuss expectations and advantages and disadvantages of females and males.

Conduct a debate on gender merits and responsibilities in this society—Is it easier to be a male, or a female, in our society? Defend your position.

*Using the ***Repeating Question Technique*** (Appendix, page 331) will help to keep this process structured and moving.

The Power to Shine

Anyone who saw me standing at the podium during the awards ceremony that June day would have called me a success. At thirty-five, I was the founder and sole owner of a multimillion-dollar business. I traveled the country speaking to businesspeople. I had three beautiful sons and was prosperous enough not to need to work another day in my life. But I had spent so much of my early life feeling lost and powerless that I wasn't able to savor my own good fortune.

As a girl, growing up poor in the South Bronx, I wasn't sure what success looked like, but I was pretty sure it didn't look like me. There was no chubby, freckled, bespectacled Puerto Rican girl in any movie I'd ever seen or book I'd ever read—nor had I ever heard of a Latina CEO or scholar. And there weren't too many successes on view outside my window either. The women I saw were worn-out domestics and shop clerks, carrying groceries to their walk-ups, trying to scrape together enough energy to make it through another day.

Without realizing what I was doing, I began putting together a model for myself from bits and pieces of those around me—that one's straight back, this one's spirit—a kind of rag doll I kept by my side.

As I grew up and moved out into the world, I worked hard to overcome the impoverishment of my childhood years. But early versions of myself were stacked inside me like Russian dolls: the four-year-old who was beaten up the first day of school because she was mistaken for white; the frightened teenager at a South Bronx high school where police stood in riot gear; the college freshman at Wellesley whose roommate requested to be moved because she didn't want to room with a kid from the ghetto. I couldn't get rid of them entirely, nor did I want to. They were part of me, reminders of where I was from, although I made sure to keep them hidden.

Then completely by chance, at seventeen, I found a niche for myself in New York after dropping out of Wellesley. I landed a job as a customer-service clerk at a company that made umbrellas and tote bags. Business fascinated me—all the gyrations of people and product, the ups and downs, the whole cycle of making something out of nothing. Eventually, I decided I wanted to move into sales, but the company turned down my request. Not to be deterred, I called in sick one day so that I could call on the American Museum of Natural History, a potential customer. I left there with a huge order and a new customer. After I brought the order to the office, I met with the company president and asked, "Are you guys gonna let me sell now or what?"

They did. A few years later, when I was twenty-one, I was promoted to account executive and put in charge of my own category of business. Two years after that, I went to work for a rival firm in California to expand their umbrella business. I was making a lot of money for someone my age, and with a goal in mind, I consciously lived well below my means.

After working for that company for a few years, I had enough money to step out on my own. Suddenly, I was an entrepreneur without a salary. Flying by the seat of my pants, I was losing money, but I didn't let my early mistakes discourage me. I continued to move forward, doing what I felt I had to do, even when I wasn't sure whether I was right.

By this time, I was married with two young children, and my world was split down the middle. I kept the professional strictly separate from the personal, and never spoke about my background in business circles. It was lonely being a woman CEO, but I was used to that. I was vaguely aware that

I was hiding, but I didn't feel ready to take the risk of revealing myself.

My company, Umbrellas Plus, continued to grow and expand, landing several major retail accounts. Eventually, I relocated to New Jersey to be closer to the industry action. One day as I was flipping through a magazine, I came across an announcement for the Women of Enterprise Awards sponsored by Avon and the Small Business Association (SBA). The award was given to women business owners who had overcome significant odds to build a successful enterprise. It sounded right up my alley.

As I filled out the essay questions, it occurred to me that this kind of award might bring me smack up against my carefully constructed identity, but I completed the application anyhow. Who said I was going to win? A month later I opened a notice from Avon, read the first word—"Congratulations!"— and whooped out loud. This Puerto Rican, a one-time public-housing resident, was going to be honored in front of fifteen hundred luminaries during a reception at the Waldorf-Astoria! I'd been awarded a stay in New York, with theater, dinner, media appearances, a cash gift, and a makeover. I was on cloud nine.

The day of the awards luncheon, I felt like Cinderella as I walked into the legendary Waldorf-Astoria, surrounded by well-wishers. But once I was seated in the hotel's grand ballroom, looking around at the crystal chandeliers, the linen tablecloths, and the impeccably dressed crowd, I grew increasingly anxious.

When it was my turn to speak, my ears roared and my legs shook as I made my way to the podium. Looking out over the glittering crowd, the old voices I had battled all my life came thundering back at me: Who do you think you are? What's a ghetto girl like you doing here? By this point in my life, I "had it all"—the well-tailored suits, the fine jewelry, the business, the family, the house. What was still missing? I stared out beyond the crowd to an illuminated patch of floor at the back of the ballroom . . .

And then an amazing thing happened. A vision of an old woman with a bucket and rag flashed before me: a widow who spoke no English, whose only option had been to leave her children and homeland to work as a domestic in the United States. That woman was my great-grandmother, Juanita. You see, my great-grandmother had left Puerto Rico and found a job at a large, fancy hotel in New York—this hotel, the Waldorf-Astoria. She had worked on her knees, in this very building where her great-granddaughter was now standing in a place of honor.

As I looked out over the audience, I felt such a connection to Mama Juanita, her spirit of fortitude and resolve, and all the other women who came before me, women who worked hard without knowing how it would affect future generations. If they could push through their fears and achieve so much, then so could I. I would let my real life shine, not only for my great-grandmother, but also so that other women could see it for themselves. With my sons, parents, and business associates looking on, I spoke. For the first time publicly, I shared, with pride, my true story, not a sanitized version. As I gave that speech, I came to terms with where I came from and where I was going. In embracing my own history, I was connecting to a story larger than myself.

To this day, whenever I feel discouraged, I stand at the kitchen sink and wash dishes. When I make that circular motion with a brush or cloth, I feel the power of so many women before me, whether they washed dishes at a river or cleaned the floors of a hotel. I think about my children, their children, and their children's children. I think of my great-grandmother Juanita and how she scrubbed floors on her knees, so that one day, I might shine.

Deborah Rosado Shaw

TITLE: **A GOOD REASON TO LOOK UP**

BOOK: **Chicken Soup for the Kid's Soul**

PAGE: **154**

TIME TO READ: **4 minutes**

TOPICS: **Living and Learning**
Class clown
Family
Making choices

AGE LEVEL: **Grades 9–12**

SYNOPSIS: Shaquille O'Neal, famous former L.A. Laker's basketball player, was a prankster in junior high school. In this story, he tells of his growing up process and his desire to be a positive role model.

NOTES TO TEACHER:

Many people do not realize that Shaquille O'Neal does way beyond average in his efforts to improve the world. He is trained as a sheriff. He puts on programs to teach children how to protect themselves from Internet predators, and has even asked Congress for tougher laws against child predators. This additional information about Shaq creates interesting discussion following the story.

Chicken Soup for the Kid's Soul,
A Good Reason to Look Up

HIGH SCHOOL:

PRE-QUESTIONS:

Do you think that great athletes are "born" or "made"? Explain.

Name some of your heroes, past or present.

Do you feel that heroes have a greater responsibility to society? Explain.

Do you think good sportsmanship is more important than winning?

- Or is it the other way around . . . "winning at all costs"? Explain.

Read Story

POST-QUESTIONS:

What is the "Golden Rule"? (*Treat others as you want them to treat you.*)

- Did Shaq live by it? Cite examples.

Do you think it's important for athletes to set a good example?

- All athletes? Just the good ones? Just the famous ones? Explain.

Do we "look up" to athletes, even if they're not as big as Shaq?

Do athletes act as "leaders" for us? In what ways?

- Is this mostly positive or negative? Cite examples.

Which athletes do you look up to?

What other heroes do you have? Why do you admire these people?

Brainstorm qualities we want our heroes to have.

- Are these qualities only found in heroes, or do we all possess these traits?

STUDENT ACTIVITIES:

Do further research on Shaq and his efforts to protect children.

Choose a hero or leader you admire. Research his or her childhood. Write a 2-page report on how the past affected his or her success.

Start a hero or leader of the week campaign within your school. Establish criteria for the award, a selection committee, and involve the community (*local businesses to give pizza or movie coupons, etc.*).

- Establish a "Hero Board" or "Hero Announcement" of the week.
- See if you can get the entire school involved in recognizing and honoring hero or leadership qualities among your classmates.

A Good Reason to Look Up

Much is required from those to whom much is given,
for their responsibility is greater.

Luke 12:48

When I was in junior high school, what my friends thought of me was real important to me. During those years I grew much taller than most of my peers. Being so tall made me feel uncomfortable. In order to keep the focus off of me and my unusual height, I went along with the crowd who would play practical jokes on other kids at school. Being one of the class clowns gave me a way to make sure that the jokes were directed at others, and not at me.

I would pull all kinds of pranks that were hurtful, and sometimes even harmful, to others. Once before gym class, my friends and I put Icy Hot in the gym shorts of one of the kids on the basketball team. Not only was he terribly embarrassed, but he also had to go to the school nurse's office. I thought it was going to be funny, but it ended up that no one thought it was—least of all my father.

My parents didn't always think that my behavior was funny. They reminded me about the Golden Rule: Treat others as I would like to be treated. Many times, I was disciplined for the hurtful way I was treating others. What I was doing was hurting other kids, and in turn hurting my reputation as someone to be looked up to. My friends were looking up to me because I was tall, but what did they see?

My parents wanted me to be a leader who was a good example to others—to be a decent human being. They taught me to set my own goals and to do the best at everything that I set out to do. During the lectures I got from my father, he told me over and over again to be the leader that I was meant to be—to be a big man in my heart and actions, as well as in my body. I had to question myself whether or not it was important to be the kind of leader and person my father believed I was inside. I knew in my heart that he was right. So I tried my best to follow my father's advice.

Once I focused on being the best that I could be at basketball and became a leader in the game, I took my responsibility to set a good example more seriously. I sometimes have to stop and think before I act, and I make mistakes occasionally—everyone is human. But I continue to look for opportunities where I can make a difference and to set a good example because of my father's advice. I now pass it on to you:

"Be a leader, Shaq, not a follower. Since people already have to look up to you, give them a good reason to do so."

Shaquille O'Neal

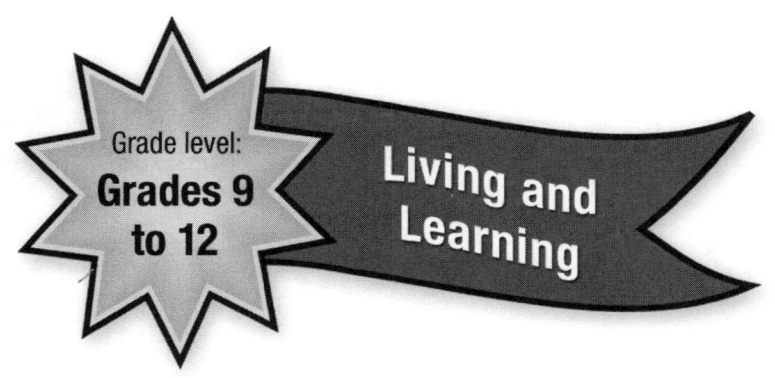

Grade level:
Grades 9 to 12

Living and Learning

TITLE: **SCHOOL—MOVING UP**

BOOK: **Chicken Soup for the Kid's Soul**

PAGE: **240**

TIME TO READ: **9 minutes**

TOPICS: **Living and Learning**
Attitude and perspective
Bias issues—racial
Motivation
Self-esteem
Family

AGE LEVEL: **Grades 9–12**

SYNOPSIS: A struggling student goes on to become a famous surgeon, with a little help and encouragement from his mother.

NOTES TO TEACHER:

This would be a good story to read at the beginning of the school year to set the tone for the year and to discuss expectations, goals, and students doing their best. By having students make a list of goals, and keeping track of them throughout the school year as a part of your classroom procedure, you could help to establish, and guide them through, this potential lifelong habit.

If you choose to assign the **Treasure Map** activity (worksheet **D**, Appendix, page 376), it is suggested that you, the teacher, do one first. This is a good exercise for you to focus on your own goals, for students to see a sample *Treasure Map* before beginning one of their own, and for them to see teachers modeling this important habit. If you have done several over the years, you may want to show slides or other visuals of them.

HIGH SCHOOL:

PRE-QUESTIONS:

Is success in school an important value held by your family? By you? Explain.

List your important life goals. Are any of these goals related to, or dependent upon, success in school? Explain.

Choose a male and a female classmate who you would name as "most likely to succeed."
   • What reasons would you give for your choices?

Do you think that television has an effect on school success? If so, what?

How many hours per week do *you* watch TV?

Read Story

POST-QUESTIONS:

How did getting glasses affect Ben's success? Why didn't he get them sooner?

Do you think Ben's self-esteem had anything to do with his early "lack of success"?

What happened for Ben to *begin* to *like* school?

What were the subtle racial issues that evolved around Curtis?

What goals did Mrs. Carson have for her children? Why were they important?

What goals do your parents have for you? *Ask them!*

Give some examples of how Mrs. Carson "motivated" Ben or Curtis.

What are some important "motivators" that help you to find success?

What are other ways you can find inspiration when you need a "boost?" *(movies, books, counselors, other role models)*

STUDENT ACTIVITIES:

Research the effects of watching TV on school success. Discuss recent findings.

Ben Carson became a very famous surgeon. Read *Gifted Hands, Think Big or The Big Picture*, all by, and about, Ben Carson (Resources, page 379).

Go online and research Dr. Carson's professional success with the separation of Siamese twins.

Research statistics on high school dropouts *(expected lifetime wage? types of jobs? etc.)*.

Write a poem or short story indicating the importance of getting a high school diploma.

School—Moving Up

"You look tired," I said one evening when Mother trudged into our narrow apartment. It was already dark, and she had put in a long day working two jobs.

"Guess I am," she said as she collapsed into the overstuffed chair and kicked off her shoes. With a smile she asked, "What did you learn in school today?"

No matter how tired she was, if we were still up when she got home, Mother asked about school. I got the idea pretty early in life that school was important to her.

She was satisfied with my schoolwork in Boston. I got good grades at the small, private church school Curtis and I attended. Mother thought that place would give us a better education than the public schools.

But when we moved back to Detroit in 1961, I found out that we had been mistaken. The fifth-graders at Higgins Elementary School knew so much more than I that they left me in the dust in every subject. There was no doubt in anyone's mind that I was the dumbest kid in the whole class. I felt stupid from the top of my head to the bottom of my sneakers.

I thought I was too stupid to even read the letters in an eye test that we took halfway through the year. The boy in front of me rattled off every single letter on the examination chart. I squinted, tried to focus, and just barely made out the first line.

But there the problem was not with my brain; it was my eyes. I had no idea that my eyesight was so bad. The school provided me with free glasses, and when I wore them to school, I was amazed. I could actually see the writing on the chalkboard from the back of the classroom! Getting glasses started me on my climb upward from the bottom of the class.

When my next report card came out, I was thrilled to see that I had gained a D in math. "Benjamin, on the whole you're doing so much better," Mrs. Williamson said to me. *I'm improving,* I thought. *There's hope for me. I'm not the dumbest kid in the school.*

Despite my excitement and sense of hope, though, my mother was not happy. "Oh, it's an improvement all right," she said. "And I'm proud of you for getting a better grade. But you can't settle for just barely passing. You're too smart to do that. You can make the top math grade in the class."

"But Mother, I didn't fail," I moaned. "I'm doing the best I can."

"But you can still do better, and I'm going to help you." Her eyes sparkled. I should have known from that look that she had already started hatching a plan.

Mother was a goal-setter by nature. That was why we had moved back to Detroit in the first place. Mother had her heart set on getting back into our old house, which she was still renting out. For the time being, we lived in a top-floor apartment in a smoggy industrial area while she worked two and three jobs at a time. But as the weeks and months passed, she said, "Boys, just wait. We're going back to our house on Deacon Street. We may not be able to afford living in it now, but we'll make it."

Mother set the same kind of high goals for Curtis and me, and she wouldn't take no for an answer. I remember when Curtis came home with a note from his junior high counselor. Curtis had to read some of the words to her, but she understood exactly what the counselor had done. He had placed Curtis in the less challenging classes for those kids who would not be going to college.

Curtis was one of the few black kids in the school. Mother had no doubt that the counselor thought blacks were not capable of doing college work.

"They're not going to treat my boy that way," she declared, staring at the paper Curtis had given her.

"What are you going to do?" I asked in surprise. I never imagined that anyone could argue with a decision made by school authorities.

"I'm going right over there in the morning and get this straightened out," she said. The tone of her voice showed she meant business. That evening, Mother told us what had happened. "I said to that counselor, 'My son Curtis is going to college. I don't want him in any vocational courses.'" Then she put her hand on my brother's head. "Curtis, you are now in college prep courses."

Mother refused to lower her sights for her boys. At the same time, she would not settle for anything less than the best we could give. She certainly was not going to let me be content with a D. "I've got two smart boys," she insisted. "Two mighty smart boys. Now, since you've started getting better in math, Bennie, you're going to go on. And here's how you'll do it. First thing you're going to do is memorize your times tables."

"My times tables?" I cried. "Do you know how many there are? Why, that could take a year!"

She stood up a little taller. "I only went through third grade, and I know them all the way through my twelves."

"But Mother, I can't . . ."

"You can do it, Bennie. You just have to set your mind to it. You work on them. Tomorrow when I get home from work, we'll review them."

I argued a little more, but I should have known better.

"Besides"—here came her final shot— "you're not to go outside and play after school until you've learned those tables."

I was almost in tears. "Look at all these things!" I cried, pointing to the columns in my math book. "How can anyone learn all of them?" But talking to Mother was like talking to a stone.

I learned the times tables. I just kept repeating them until they fixed themselves in my brain. Mother kept prodding me and went over them with me at night. Within days after learning my times tables, math became so much easier. I'll never forget how I practically shouted my score to Mrs. Williamson after another math quiz. "Twenty-four! I got twenty-four right!" School became much more enjoyable. Nobody laughed or called me dummy anymore.

I thought I was on top of the world, but Mother was far from satisfied. She had proved to me that I could succeed in one thing. The next part of her plan was to keep setting higher goals. I can't say I cared much for this plan.

"I've decided you boys are watching too much television," she said one evening, snapping off the set in the middle of a program.

"We don't watch that much," I protested. I tried to argue that some of the programs were educational and that the smartest kids in the class watched television.

As if she did not hear a word, she said, "From now on, you boys can watch no more than three programs a week." She had also decided what we were going to do with all those hours we had spent on television. "You boys are going to go to the library and check out books. You're going to read at least two books every week. At the end of each week, you'll give me a report on what you've read."

I couldn't believe it. Two books? I had never read a book in my life except those they made us read at school. But a day or two later, Curtis and I dragged our feet the seven blocks from home to the public library. We obeyed Mother because we loved her and because we could tell when she meant business. But that did not stop us from grumbling the whole way.

Several of Mother's friends criticized her strictness. I heard one woman ask, "What are you doing to those boys, making them study all the time? They're going to hate you."

"They can hate me," she answered, "but they're going to get a good education just the same."

Of course, I never hated her. I did not like the constant pressure, but she made me realize the hard work was for my own good. Almost every day, she would say, "Bennie, you can do anything you set yourself to do."

Since I have always loved animals, nature, and science, I chose library books on those subjects. My fifth-grade science teacher, Mr. Jaeck, discovered my interest and gave me special projects to do, such as identifying fish or rocks. By the end of the year, I could pick up just about any rock along the railroad tracks and tell what it was. After reading fish and water-life books, I started checking streams for insects. Mr. Jaeck let me look at water samples under his microscope.

Slowly, I began looking forward to my trips to the library. The staff there got to know Curtis and me. They began offering suggestions on what we might like to read. Soon my interests widened to include books on adventure and scientific discoveries.

As I continued reading, my vocabulary and spelling improved. Up until the last few weeks of fifth grade, our weekly spelling bees were one of the worst parts of school for me. I usually dropped out on the first word. Mrs. Williamson gave us one final spelling bee that covered every word we were supposed to have learned that year. As everyone expected, Bobby Farmer won the spelling bee. He was clearly the smartest boy in the fifth grade. But to my surprise, the final word he spelled correctly to win the contest was agriculture.

I can spell that word, I thought with excitement. I had learned it just the day before from my library book. As Bobby sat down, a thrill swept through me. I thought, *I'll bet I can spell any other word in the world. I'll bet I could learn to spell better than Bobby.*

Learning to spell better than Bobby Farmer challenged me. I kept reading all through the summer. By the time I began sixth grade, I had learned to spell a lot of words. In the sixth grade, Bobby was still the smartest boy in the class, but I was gaining ground on him. I kept improving until, by the time I entered seventh grade at Wilson Junior High, I was at the top of the class.

The very kids who once teased me about being dumb started coming up to me and asking, "Bennie, how do you solve this problem?" I beamed when I gave them the answer. It was fun to get good grades, to earn people's respect. But by then, making it to the top of the class was not good enough for me. Mother's influence had started to sink in. I did not work hard just to be better than the other kids. I did it because I wanted to be the very best I could be—for me.

Ben Carson, M.D.

[EDITORS' NOTE: *Ben Carson, M.D., is a graduate of Yale University and the University of Michigan Medical School. He is currently the director of pediatric neurosurgery at Johns Hopkins Medical Institutions in Baltimore, Maryland. In 1987, Dr. Carson gained worldwide recognition for his part in the first successful separation of Siamese twins joined at the back of the head, which took five months of planning and twenty-two hours of surgery.*]

TITLE: **THE GREATEST BASEBALL STORY EVER**

BOOK: **Chicken Soup for the Sports Fan's Soul**

PAGE: **199**

TIME TO READ: **1 minute**

TOPICS: **Making a Difference**
Overcoming obstacles
Sport—baseball
Heroes
Acting with kindness

AGE LEVEL: **Grades 9–12**

SYNOPSIS: **A ten-year-old polio victim makes a deal with Lou Gehrig . . . "If you hit a home run today, I'll go to therapy and learn to walk again."**

NOTES TO TEACHER:

You may need to introduce students to Lou Gehrig. He was an outstanding first baseman for the New York Yankees in the 1930s. He held the lifetime home run record of 493 until recently, and was the first athlete with the Yankees to have his number retired—jersey #4. Lou Gehrig is also famous for bringing ALS (*amyotrophic lateral sclerosis*) to the public eye. This debilitating disease is now commonly referred to as "Lou Gehrig's disease." For more information go to www.lougehrig.com.

Most students will also be unaware of polio. It was a widely known crippling disease in the early 1900s. President Franklin Delano Roosevelt contracted it in 1921 at the age of thirty-nine. It wasn't until 1954 that the Salk vaccine was tested and approved for use in 1955. It is almost totally eradicated at this point in time.

Chicken Soup for the Sports Fan's Soul,
The Greatest Baseball Story Ever

PRE-QUESTIONS:

When you don't want to do something that *has* to be done, what do you do to motivate yourself?

Make a list of your "self-motivators," or ways that you motivate yourself (*a promised reward of 30 minutes of TV after completing your homework, a new pair of jeans after cleaning out your closet, or a "pep talk" with yourself in front of the mirror focusing on the image of what you want, etc.*).

NOTE TO TEACHER:

Having an *image* of what you want, plus the *reality* of what you don't have, equals *tension*, which creates the *desire to change*.

Read Story

POST-QUESTIONS:

Who is the one person who could motivate you the most?
   • Why did you choose this person?
Why did Lou Gehrig consider himself to be "*. . . the luckiest man on the face of the earth*"? (*Because he was able to motivate Tim to walk again.*)

STUDENT ACTIVITIES:

You are being honored by having something very important named after you (*e.g., street, library, stadium, school, award, etc.*).
   • What would you want it to be?
   • Why did you choose that?
   • What significance does it hold for you?
   • What would the dignitaries say about you at the ceremony?
   • Write the keynote speech.
   • If time permits, give this 5–10 minute speech to the class.
(This assignment focuses on the *legacy* that you want to leave for the world.)

The Greatest Baseball Story Ever

*A hero is someone who has given his or her life
to something bigger than oneself.*

Joseph Campbell

In 1937, Lou Gehrig, the outstanding first baseman of the New York Yankees, was asked to go to the Children's Hospital in Chicago, while there to play the White Sox, and visit a boy with polio. Tim, ten years old, had refused to try therapy to get well. Lou was his hero, and Tim's parents hoped that Lou would visit Tim and urge him to try the therapy.

Tim was amazed to meet his hero. Lou told Tim, "I want you to get well. Go to therapy and learn to walk again."

Tim said, "Lou, if you will knock a home run for me today, I will learn to walk again." Lou promised.

All the way to the ballpark, Lou felt a deep sense of obligation and even apprehension that he would not be able to deliver his promise that day. Lou didn't knock one home run that day. He knocked two.

Two years later, when Lou Gehrig was dying with the dreaded muscular disease that to this day bears his name, on July 4, 1939, they celebrated Lou Gehrig Day at Yankee Stadium.

Eighty thousand fans, the governor, the mayor, and many other celebrities paid their respects. Lou was one of America's great heroes.

Just before the mike was turned over to Lou to respond, Tim, by this time twelve years old, walked out of the dugout, dropped his crutches, and with leg braces walked to home plate to hug Lou around the waist.

That's what Lou Gehrig meant when he exclaimed those immortal words: "Today I consider myself the luckiest man on the face of the earth."

Mack R. Douglas

TITLE: **INNOCENT HOMELESS**

BOOK: **Chicken Soup for the Pet Lover's Soul**

PAGE: **54**

TIME TO READ: **8 minutes**

TOPICS: **Making a Difference**
World issues—homelessness
Bias issues—stereotypes

AGE LEVEL: **Grades 9–12**

SYNOPSIS: A woman feeds a homeless man and his dogs to keep him from having to sell one dog in order to feed the other.

NOTES TO TEACHER:

This is a great story to break the stereotype of the homeless as being lazy, crazy, or uncaring.

Questions and activities can focus on either the plight of homeless people or homeless animals.

For additional stories of understanding the homeless, read "My Homeless Man," found in *Chicken Soup for the Soul: Stories for a Better World,* page 97. Or read "Suzannah's Story," previously unpublished, and found on page 171 of this book.

Chicken Soup for the Pet Lover's Soul,
Innocent Homeless

PRE-QUESTIONS:

What thoughts go through your mind when you see a homeless person?
Brainstorm some stereotypes about homeless people.

Read Story

POST-QUESTIONS:

Have your thoughts about the homeless changed at all since hearing this story?
 • Why, or why not?

STUDENT ACTIVITIES:

Contact a manager or supervisor from a local homeless shelter.
 • Ask this person to speak to the class about homeless people and their plight.
Read the Pulitzer-prize winning novel *Ironweed* by William Kennedy, (see Resources, page 378 for full citation), to put some "heart" into the concept of the "homeless."
Instead of getting your next pet from a store, consider adopting from one of the many animal shelters. You may be saving an animal from euthanasia.
Debate the issue of how communities should deal with the indigent or homeless.
Form small groups to discuss the world-wide implications of poverty.
 • Brainstorm some possible solutions locally and worldwide.

Innocent Homeless

*No matter how little money and how few possessions
you own, having a dog makes you rich.*

Louis Sabin

The hastily scrawled sign on the crumpled cardboard read: "BROKE—NEED DOG FOOD." The desperate young man held the sign in one hand and a leash in the other as he paced back and forth on the busy corner in downtown Las Vegas.

Attached to the leash was a husky pup no more than a year old. Not far from them was an older dog of the same breed, chained to a lamppost. He was howling into the brisk chill of the approaching winter evening; his wail could be heard for blocks. It was as though he knew his own fate, for the sign that was propped next to him read: "FOR SALE."

Forgetting about my own destination, I quickly turned the car around and made a beeline back toward the homeless trio. For years, I've kept dog and cat food in the trunk of my car for the stray or hungry animals I often find. It's been a way of helping those I couldn't take in. It's also what I've used to coax many a scared dog off the road to safety. Helping needy animals has always been an automatic decision for me.

I pulled into the nearest parking lot and grabbed a five-pound bag of dog food, a container of water, and a twenty-dollar bill from my purse. I approached the ragged-looking man and his unhappy dogs warily. If this man had somehow hurt these creatures or was using them as come-ons, I knew my anger would quickly take over. The older dog was staring up at the sky, whining pitifully. Just before I reached them, a truck pulled up alongside of them and asked how much the man wanted for the older dog.

"Fifty bucks," the man on the corner replied, then added quickly, "but I really don't want to sell him."

"Is he papered?"

"No."

"Is he fixed?"

"No."

"How old is he?"

"Five. But I really don't want to sell him. I just need some money to feed him."

"If I had fifty bucks, I'd buy him." The light turned green, and the truck sped off.

The man shook his head and continued dejectedly pacing the sidewalk. When he noticed me coming in his direction, he stopped walking and watched me approach. The pup began wagging his tail.

"Hi," I offered as I drew nearer. The young man's face was gentle and friendly, and I could sense just by looking in his eyes that he was someone in real crisis.

"I have some food here for your dogs," I said. Dumbfounded, he took the bag as I set down the water in front of them.

"You brought water, too?" he asked incredulously. We both knelt down next to the older dog, and the puppy greeted me enthusiastically.

"That one there is T. C., and this one's Dog. I'm Wayne." The sad, older dog stopped crying long enough to see what was in the container.

"What happened, Wayne?" I asked. I felt a bit intrusive, but he answered me directly and simply. "Well, I just moved out here from Arizona and haven't been able to find work. I'm at the point where I can't even feed the dogs."

"Where are you living?"

"In that truck right there." He pointed to a dilapidated old vehicle that was parked close by. It had an extra long bed with a shell, so at least they had shelter from the elements.

The pup had climbed onto my lap and settled in. I asked Wayne what type of work he did.

"I'm a mechanic and a welder," he said. "But there's nothing out here for either. I've looked and looked. These dogs are my family; I hate to have to sell them, but I just can't afford to feed them."

He kept saying it over and over. He didn't want to sell them, but he couldn't feed them. An awful look came over his face every time he repeated it. It was as if he might have to give up a child.

The time seemed right to casually pass over the twenty-dollar bill, hoping I wouldn't further damage his already shaky pride. "Here. Use this to buy yourself something to eat."

"Well, thanks," he slowly replied, unable to look me in the face. "This could get us a room for the night, too."

"How long have you been out here?"

"All day."

"Hasn't anyone else stopped?"

"No, you're the first." It was late afternoon and quickly getting dark. Here in the desert, when the sun dropped, the temperature would dip into the thirties.

My mind went into fast-forward as I pictured the three of them going without even a single meal today, perhaps for several days, and spending many long, cold hours cooped up in their inadequate, makeshift shelter.

Seeing people beg for food isn't anything new in this city. But this man stood out because he wasn't asking for food for himself. He was more concerned with keeping his dogs fed than with his own welfare. As a pet-parent of nine well-fed and passionately loved dogs of my own, it hit a deep chord in me.

I don't think I'll ever really know what came over me at that moment, inspiring me to do what I did next, but I just knew it was something I had to do. I asked him if he'd wait there for a few minutes until I returned. He nodded his head and smiled.

My car flew to the nearest grocery store. Bursting with urgency, I raced in and took hold of a cart. I started on the first aisle and didn't quit until I reached the other side of the store. The items couldn't be pulled off the shelves fast enough. Just the essentials, I thought. Just food that will last a couple of weeks and sustain their meager existence. Peanut butter and jelly. Bread. Canned food. Juice. Fruit. Vegetables. Dog food. More dog food (forty pounds, to be exact). And chew toys. They should have some treats, too. A few other necessities, and the job was done.

"The total comes to $102.91," said the checker. I didn't bat an eye. The pen ran over that blank check faster than I could legibly write. It didn't matter that the mortgage was due soon or that I really didn't have the extra hundred dollars to spend. Nothing mattered besides seeing that this family had some food. I was amazed at my own intensity and the overwhelming motivation that compelled me to spend a hundred dollars on a total stranger. Yet, at the same time, I felt like the luckiest person in the world. To be able to give this man and his beloved companions a tiny bit of something of which I had so much opened the floodgates of gratitude in my own heart.

The icing on the cake was the look on Wayne's face when I returned with all the groceries. "Here are just a few things . . . " I said as the dogs looked on with great anticipation. I wanted to avoid any awkwardness, so I hastily petted the dogs.

"Good luck to you," I said and held out my hand.

"Thank you and God bless you. Now I won't have to sell my dogs." His smile shone brightly in the deepening darkness.

It's true that people are more complicated than animals, but sometimes they can be as easy to read. Wayne was a good person—someone who looked at a dog and saw family. In my book, a man like that deserves to be happy.

Later, on my way home, I purposely drove past that same corner. Wayne and the dogs were gone.

But they have stayed for a long time in my heart and mind. Perhaps I will run into them again someday. I like to think that it all turned out well for them.

Lori S. Mohr

TITLE: **ONE AT A TIME**

BOOK: **Chicken Soup for the Soul**

PAGE: **22**

TIME TO READ: **1 minute**

TOPICS: **Making a Difference**
Acting with kindness
Living and learning
Changing the world

AGE LEVEL: **Grades 9–12**

SYNOPSIS: **When an old man was questioned about throwing starfish into the sea, his response was, "It made a difference to that one."**

NOTES TO TEACHER:

The focus of this plan is on the intrinsic value, or inner feeling, associated with doing acts of kindness for others. Some of the extended activities do shift the focus to extrinsic rewards, such as being recognized or rewarded for doing nice things. Should you choose to do these externally motivated tasks, it is strongly recommended that you remind students of the power of their intrinsic worth.

A good ancillary story is "Practice Random Kindness and Senseless Acts of Beauty," page 34 in *A 2nd Helping of Chicken Soup for the Soul.*

Chicken Soup for the Soul,
One at a Time

HIGH SCHOOL:

PRE-QUESTIONS:

What, if anything, have you done during the past week to make the world a better place?

Brainstorm possibilities or realities *(e.g., helped to tutor a classmate who was having difficulty with math, read a story to a younger sibling, bought a sandwich for a homeless person, etc.).*

Read Story

POST-QUESTIONS:

What is the message of this story?

What are some simple things that you could do to make a difference for just one person in the world?

What would be the impact on the world if everyone in your class did one small positive thing every day?

What if everyone in your school did something? Your town? Your state? Your country? The world?

Discuss the merits of intrinsic rewards *(inner joy of doing)* vs. extrinsic rewards *(recognition)*.

STUDENT ACTIVITIES:

Read the book, or watch the movie *Pay It Forward* for similar concepts (see Resources, page 379 for full citation).

Do one small, positive thing every day for two weeks. Keep a journal of your feelings when doing this.

Start a school-wide *Acts of Kindness* for one week or a year (Appendix, page 349).

Get local businesses to give a cash award that would be donated to a local charity selected by the "winning" class.

Read *Random Acts of Kindness* (see Resources, page 379 for full citation).

Do something nice that is *totally anonymous (you do not tell a single soul about it!).*
• Write in your journal about how that feels.

At Christmastime, instead of being a "Secret Santa" who leaves "gifts," become a "Secret Elf" who does nice things for others.

Hold a debate to determine which carries greater value in this society, intrinsic or extrinsic rewards.

One at a Time

A friend of ours was walking down a deserted Mexican beach at sunset. As he walked along, he saw another man in the distance. As he grew nearer, he noticed that the local native kept leaning down, picking something up, and throwing it out into the water. Time and again he kept hurling things out into the ocean.

As our friend approached even closer, he noticed that the man was picking up starfish that had been washed up on the beach, and one at a time, he was throwing them back into the water.

Our friend was puzzled. He approached the man and said, "Good evening, friend. I was wondering what you are doing."

"I'm throwing these starfish back into the ocean. You see, it's low tide right now and all of these starfish have been washed up onto the shore. If I don't throw them back into the sea, they'll die up here from lack of oxygen."

"I understand," my friend replied, "but there must be thousands of starfish on this beach. You can't possibly get to all of them. There are simply too many. And don't you realize this is probably happening on hundreds of beaches all up and down this coast. Can't you see that you can't possibly make a difference?"

The local native smiled, bent down, and picked up yet another starfish, and as he threw it back into the sea, he replied, "Made a difference to that one!"

Jack Canfield & Mark V. Hansen

Grade level:
Grades 9 to 12

On Love

TITLE: **ON COURAGE**

BOOK: **Chicken Soup for the Soul**

PAGE: **27**

TIME TO READ: **1 minute**

TOPICS: **On Love**
Making a difference
Tough stuff—dying child
Family

AGE LEVEL: **Grades 9–12**

SYNOPSIS: **A small boy believes that giving a blood transfusion to his sister means giving *all* of his blood and that he will die.**

NOTES TO TEACHER:

This is a wonderful story to discuss the concept of sacrifice with various age levels.

Chicken Soup for the Soul,
On Courage

PRE-QUESTIONS:

What is your definition of "sacrifice?"

What kinds of sacrifices, if any, have you made in your life? *(Gave up playing soccer in order to get a job to help with family expenses, gave up time with friends in order to take your little brother to the playground, gave your favorite jacket to a homeless person, etc.)*

Read Story

POST-QUESTIONS:

Most people take our *free* life for granted. Yet, throughout history there are many people who have willingly gone to jail defending a cause. *(Nelson Mandela, Freedom Riders, etc.)*

What, if anything, would you face prison for, in order to defend it?
  • Explain your answer.

What, if anything, would your risk your *life* for?
  • Explain your response.

STUDENT ACTIVITIES:

Brainstorm a time in history when people gave up their freedom, or their life, in order to defend or protect others.

Research someone who did this. Write a two-page report on this person *(this could be someone famous, lesser known, or perhaps a relative).*

Spend two hours a month for three months, with someone in a nursing home.
  • Get their memory of turbulent times in history when sacrifice was common.
  • Write a two-page report on this person and/or their thoughts on this topic.

On Courage

"So you think I'm courageous?" she asked.

"Yes, I do."

"Perhaps I am. But that's because I've had some inspiring teachers. I'll tell you about one of them. Many years ago, when I worked as a volunteer at Stanford Hospital, I got to know a little girl named Liza who was suffering from a rare and serious disease. Her only chance of recovery appeared to be a blood transfusion from her five-year-old brother, who had miraculously survived the same disease and had developed the antibodies needed to combat the illness. The doctor explained the situation to her little brother, and asked the boy if he would be willing to give his blood to his sister. I saw him hesitate for only a moment before taking a deep breath and saying, 'Yes, I'll do it if it will save Liza.'

"As the transfusion progressed, he lay in a bed next to his sister and smiled, as we all did, seeing the color returning to her cheeks. Then his face grew pale and his smile faded. He looked up at the doctor and asked with a trembling voice, 'Will I start to die right away?'

"Being young, the boy had misunderstood the doctor; he thought he was going to have to give her all his blood.

"Yes, I've learned courage," she added, "because I've had inspiring teachers."

Dan Millman

Reprinted by permission of Dan Millman. 1991. As appeared in Source Book: Sacred Journey of the Peaceful Warrior *(HJ Kramer/New World Library).*

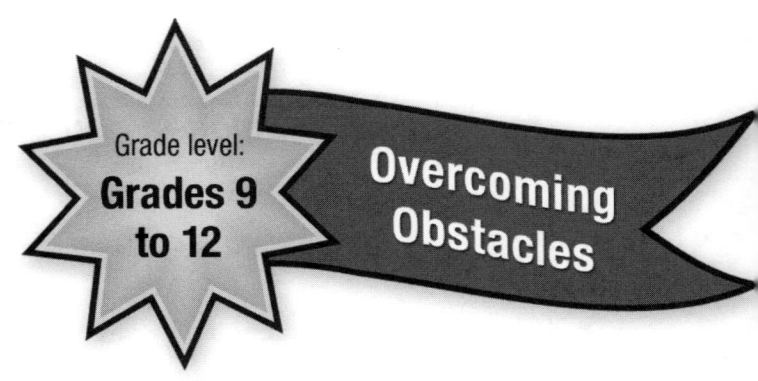

TITLE: **JUST BEN**

BOOK: **Chicken Soup for the Kid's Soul**

PAGE: **139**

TIME TO READ: **4 minutes**

TOPICS: **Overcoming Obstacles**
Acceptance and belonging
Communication
Sport—soccer

AGE LEVEL: **Grades 9–12**

SYNOPSIS: **Six-year-old Ben hides his missing hand in order to be treated the same as everyone else on the soccer team. Teammates eagerly question what happened, and within minutes, he becomes just another guy on the team.**

NOTES TO TEACHER:

This is a good introductory story to use when students are new to one another. Or, once students have bonded, this story can be used to bring up the subject of handicaps or to introduce physical or mental challenges.

It would be particularly useful if you have a handicapped student in your classroom. However, use with caution unless you know that your physically challenged student feels okay about his or her handicap. Not everyone is as confident as Ben.

Chicken Soup for the Kid's Soul,
Just Ben

PRE-QUESTIONS:

Think back to a time when you were totally new at something *(the first day of school, joining a new team, etc.)*. What were you feeling as the new person?

Have you ever felt like "the only one who . . ."?

Have you ever hidden something just because you wanted to be accepted by others? If so, write about it in your journal. If not, are you a totally open person, or extremely confident in who you are, or are you simply blessed that you have nothing worth hiding? Write in your journal about this.

Write about what you think and feel when you see someone with a handicap.

• If you have some form of handicap, write about what that is like for you.

Brainstorm a list of things that may "handicap," or "hinder" a person in some way *(look beyond the obvious ones for things like beauty, wealth, brilliance, superior athletic ability, etc.)*.

Discuss how these less-obvious attributes might hinder someone's growth. *(When always treated as special, one never has to pull their own load, nor are they certain of why people seek their friendship.)*

Read Story

POST-QUESTIONS:

What do you think of Ben?

How much of Ben's behavior was confidence and how much was simply wanting to be accepted? Explain your answer.

STUDENT ACTIVITIES:

Write a story or poem about someone with one of the less-obvious handicaps as brainstormed above.

Re-write the story as seen through Ben's eyes.

Play **Truth and Lies** (Appendix, page 351).

Discuss how much of a "handicap" is in one's "attitude."

Watch and discuss "Armed with Hope," the story of John Foppe, who was born without arms (see Resources, page 378 for citation).

Just Ben

It was late August and quite chilly outside. I was coaching a soccer team for kindergarteners and first-graders, and it was the day of our first practice.

It was cold enough for the kids to be bundled up in extra sweatshirts, jackets, gloves, and mittens.

I sat the kids down on the dugout bench—soccer in Austin is played on the outfield grass at the softball complex. As was normally the case any time I was coaching a new team, we took the first few minutes to get to know one another. We went up and down the row a few times, each kid saying his or her name and the names of all the kids sitting to the left.

After a few minutes of this, I decided to put the kids to the ultimate test. I asked for a volunteer who thought he or she knew the names of all eleven kids on the team and could prove it to all of us right then. There was one brave six-year-old who felt up to the challenge. He was to start at the far left end of the bench, go up to each kid, say that kid's name, and then shake his or her right hand.

Alex started off and was doing very well. While I stood behind him, he went down the row—Dylan, Micah, Sara, Beau, and Danny—until he reached Ben, by far the smallest kid on the team. He stammered out Ben's name without much trouble and extended his right hand, but Ben would not extend his. I looked at Ben for a second, as did Alex and the rest of the kids on the bench, but he just sat there, his right hand hidden under the cuff of his jacket.

"Ben, why don't you let Alex shake your hand?" I asked. But Ben just sat there, looking first at Alex and then at me, and then at Alex once again.

"Ben, what's the matter?" I asked.

Finally Ben stood up, looked up at me and said, "But coach, I don't have a hand." He unzipped his jacket, pulling it away from his right shoulder.

Sure enough, Ben's arm ran from his right shoulder just like every other kid on the team, but unlike the rest of his teammates, his arm stopped at the elbow. No fingers, no hand, no forearm.

I'll have to admit, I was taken aback a bit and couldn't think of anything to say or how to react, but thank God for little kids—and their unwillingness to be tactful.

"Look at that," said Alex.

"Hey, what happened to your arm?" another asked.

"Does it hurt?"

Before I knew it, a crowd of ten players and a bewildered coach encircled a small child, who was now taking off his jacket to show all those around him what they all wanted to see.

In the next few minutes, a calm and collected six-year-old explained to all of those present that he had always been that way and that there was nothing special about him because of it. What he meant was that he wanted to be treated like everybody else.

And he was from that day on.

From that day on, he was never the kid with one arm. He was just Ben, one of the players on the team.

Adrian Wagner

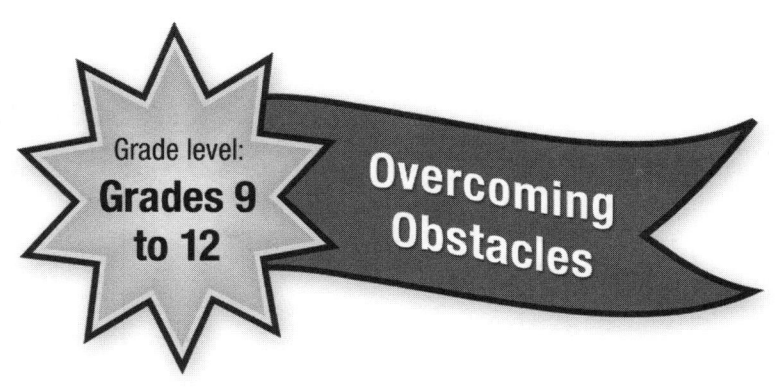

TITLE: **THE POWER OF DETERMINATION**

BOOK: **Chicken Soup for the Soul**

PAGE: **259**

TIME TO READ: **3 minutes**

TOPICS: **Overcoming Obstacles**
Attitude and perspective
Making choices

AGE LEVEL: **Grades 9–12**

SYNOPSIS: **Badly burned as a child, determination takes Glenn Cunningham to the world's fastest mile.**

NOTES TO TEACHER:

This story would work well with an early American history unit in the era of one-room school-houses and potbellied stoves.

This is a good place to introduce the concept of $E + R = 0$ (see Appendix, page 327).

Chicken Soup for the Soul, The Power of Determination

PRE-QUESTIONS:

What is more important in life, ability or determination? Defend your response.

Which would you rather have? Explain your answer.

Discuss the concept of being a "victim" (*a person who suffers for some reason*).

- Cite examples (*e.g., a quadriplegic, a person who is deaf, someone who has been robbed, a person who has been slandered, a child who has been abused, etc.*).

Discuss "disability" (*having a physical or mental incapacity*).

- Cite examples (*having Down's syndrome, having no legs, having no sight, etc.*).

Can something usually seen as positive, such as beauty or wealth, ever be considered a handicap or a disadvantage?

- Explain why or why not (*e.g., people may consider you less intelligent, they may respond to your beauty or your money rather than your "person," etc.*).

If you have a disability or a handicap, are you also a "victim"?

- Explain your answer (*generally, being a "victim" is an attitude*).

Who determines any of this (*Society? The media? Your peers? You?*)?

Read Story

POST-QUESTIONS:

Discuss the role that attitude plays in any hardship.

NOTES TO TEACHER:

| This is a good place to introduce the concept of $E + R = O$ (see Appendx, page 327).

STUDENT ACTIVITIES:

Select someone who has overcome major obstacle(s) to become successful.

- This may be someone you personally know, or it may be someone famous. Write a two-page essay about their journey and its impact on you.

Form debate teams to deliberate the issues of "nature" vs. "nurture," "heredity" vs. "environment," "ability" vs. "determination."

Write a one-page essay describing any obstacle that you have had to overcome, and what, if anything, that you are currently doing to deal with this challenge.

Bring in any popular music, past or present, that portrays the power of determination.

The Power of Determination

The little country schoolhouse was heated by an old-fashioned, potbellied coal stove. A little boy had the job of coming to school early each day to start the fire and warm the room before his teacher and his classmates arrived.

One morning they arrived to find the schoolhouse engulfed in flames. They dragged the unconscious little boy out of the flaming building more dead than alive. He had major burns over the lower half of his body and was taken to the nearby county hospital.

From his bed the dreadfully burned, semiconscious little boy faintly heard the doctor talking to his mother. The doctor told his mother that her son would surely die—which was for the best, really—for the terrible fire had devastated the lower half of his body.

But the brave boy didn't want to die. He made up his mind that he would survive. Somehow, to the amazement of the physician, he did survive. When the mortal danger was past, he again heard the doctor and his mother speaking quietly. The mother was told that since the fire had destroyed so much flesh in the lower part of his body, it would almost be better if he had died, since he was doomed to be a lifetime cripple with no use at all of his lower limbs.

Once more the brave boy made up his mind. He would not be a cripple. He would walk. But unfortunately from the waist down, he had no motor ability. His thin legs just dangled there, all but lifeless.

Ultimately, he was released from the hospital. Every day his mother would massage his little legs, but there was no feeling, no control, nothing. Yet his determination that he would walk was as strong as ever.

When he wasn't in bed, he was confined to a wheelchair. One sunny day his mother wheeled him out into the yard to get some fresh air. This day, instead of sitting there, he threw himself from the chair. He pulled himself across the grass, dragging his legs behind him.

He worked his way to the white picket fence bordering their lot. With great effort, he raised himself up on the fence. Then, stake by stake, he began dragging himself along the fence, resolved that he would walk. He started to do this every day until he wore a smooth path all around the yard beside the fence. There was nothing he wanted more than to develop life in those legs.

Ultimately through his daily massages, his iron persistence, and his resolute determination, he did develop the ability to stand up, then to walk haltingly, then to walk by himself—and then—to run.

He began to walk to school, then to run to school, to run for the sheer joy of running. Later, in college, he made the track team.

Still later in Madison Square Garden this young man who was not expected to survive, who would surely never walk, who could never hope to run—this determined young man, Dr. Glenn Cunningham, ran the world's fastest mile!

Burt Dubin

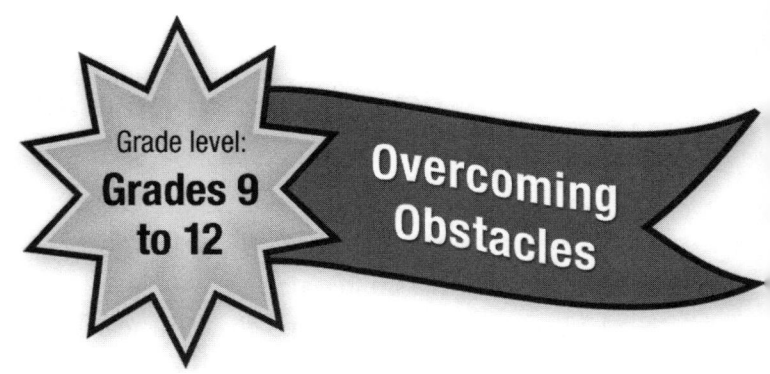

Grade level:
Grades 9 to 12

Overcoming Obstacles

TITLE:	**THEIR BULLET, MY LIFE**
BOOK:	**Chicken Soup for the Soul Stories for a Better World**
PAGE:	**244**
TIME TO READ:	**7 minutes**
TOPICS:	**Overcoming Obstacles** World issues—gangs Making choices Making a difference
AGE LEVEL:	**Grades 9–12**
SYNOPSIS:	A seventeen-year-old sneaks out to join friends in a rough part of town and ends up becoming a quadriplegic in a gang shooting. Later, he goes into schools to tell his story.

NOTES TO TEACHER:

We rarely suggest the use of other media and materials in this document. However, we are going to recommend that you check out three amazing pieces of material in conjunction with this story (see Resources, pages 378–379 for full citations).

#1. *Armed With Hope* is a highly motivational story of John Foppe, a young man who was born without arms and has learned to do everything with his feet.

#2. Have students go online to check out the Association of Mouth and Foot Painting Artists (AMFPA or MFPA) to see some amazing artwork painted with either mouth or foot. Their website is www.amfpa.com.

#3. *No Excuses: The True Story of a Congenital Amputee Who Became a Champion in Wrestling and in Life,* by Kyle Maynard. The title tells it all.

Chicken Soup for the Soul: Stories for a Better World, Their Bullet, My Life

PRE-QUESTIONS:

Respond in writing to the following questions:

Do you know anyone in a gang?

What kinds of things cause people to join gangs? *(Rebellion, acceptance, excitement, sense of "family," etc.).*

Do you think that it is safe to simply be friends with a gang member without ever joining a gang?

• Why, or why not?

Read Story

POST-QUESTIONS:

What were Cruz's dreams before he was shot?

What was his reality after being shot?

"Birds of a feather, flock together" and *"Guilt by association"* are two famous quotes.

• How do they relate to this story?

How do people get out of gangs?

STUDENT ACTIVITIES:

Read the book or watch the DVD, *Armed With Hope,* the story of John Foppe.
For full citation, see Resources, page 378.

Read *No Excuses: The True Story of a Congenital Amputee Who Became A Champion in Wrestling and in Life* by Kyle Maynard (see Resources, page 379 for full citation.)

Compare John or Kyle *(born without limbs)*, with Cruz *(who lost the use of his arms and his legs at age seventeen).*

• Discuss the obstacles that each had to face.

Invite a police officer to discuss gang issues in your community.

Simulate a handicap for a day *(do everything with your non-dominant hand, do everything in a wheelchair, etc.).* Discuss how this feels after a few hours.

Their Bullet, My Life

The strongest principle of growth lies in the human choice.

George Eliot

Entering the large assembly room, the motor of my powered wheelchair humming in my ears, I could feel the eyes of every boy, all local gang members, staring at me. I wondered how they would react to my computer-activated voice. Would they listen to what I had to say? Would they understand the violence and pain they were causing? Could I really make a difference?

"Hello, I'm Cruz Carrasco," I began. "As you can see and now hear, I am unable to walk or talk by myself. I wasn't always in this wheelchair, and once I could speak as well as any of you. In fact, up until I was seventeen years old, I lived a life probably very similar to yours. My dream then was to play pro football. I loved it! I started as a sophomore for East L.A.'s Roosevelt High School Rough Riders and was soon their star running back.

"By the time I was in the twelfth grade, UCLA had offered me a full scholarship, and I was ready to take it. I was going to be the first college graduate in my family. I promised my mom I would buy her a big house with a pool when I was a star. And then, without warning, my plans and dreams were literally blown away. I don't remember that day now, so what I am going to tell you is what my family and friends have told me.

"November 4, 1986, was a normal school day. After football practice, I headed home, had dinner with my mom, and then went up to my room to do my homework. I heard one of my football buddies calling to me outside my window. My friends knew Mom couldn't hear them back there. I sneaked out the window to go for a ride with him on his new moped. If I had asked my mom, she wouldn't have let me go.

"We rode around and stopped to hang out with another football buddy at his house, even though we knew his neighborhood was heavily infested with gangs and drugs. Unfortunately, before we arrived at my friend's house, a bad drug deal had gone down in the neighborhood. Little did I know that this would be the last time I would walk by myself, talk by myself, have normal vision or live the life of my dreams.

"Once the gang realized the cocaine they had bought was really soap, they came back, armed with a .44-caliber Magnum, driving down the street and spraying bullets into the neighborhood. In sheer panic, we started to run for cover. My two friends fell as bullets ripped through their legs. My terror was ended abruptly when a bullet exploded in my head.

"For the next four and a half months, I lay in a coma, machines feeding me and making me breathe. There was not much hope that I would recover. Can you imagine what it was like for me to awaken to the helpless horror of what had become of me?

"The two years after the shooting are a blur to me now. I do know that, throughout the seemingly endless year and a half that followed, I was in rehab; my mother refused to give up on me and vowed to eventually bring me home. Her determination was contagious, and in spite of my suffocating despair, I clung to hope.

"I was nineteen when I finally returned home. I had not become the college football hero I had dreamed I would be. Instead, I was having to start over from infancy, physically. I was filled with grief over the life I had lost. It was agonizing to realize that my friends had all gone to our prom and graduated from high school. Some had gone on to college; some were working; some were living in their own apartments; some were even married with kids.

"Once home, my mother did what she knew how to do best: she loved me. She enrolled me in a program for disabled adults, and I finished high school. But I still couldn't communicate or move my own wheelchair; I was trapped in my own body. I was filled with anger and frustration. I realized that Mom's love wasn't enough. It was then that Zoe came to work with me.

"Zoe began as my occupational therapist and became first my friend, and then my partner in life. With Zoe, I finally had someone listening to my dreams rather than focusing on my disabilities. Zoe made sure I received the voice-output computer to speak with and the power wheelchair so I could get around independently. Once I realized I could again interact with people, I wanted to find a way to keep what happened to me from happening to anyone else.

"That is why I am here today, eight years after I was shot, to let you know about the effects of the choices you make. Before you make those choices, I hope you will take the time to think about how they will affect your life and the lives of the people around you. They never caught the guys who shot me, although I did learn a most painful truth: one of the men in the car was my best friend from elementary school! I never dreamed that the boy I loved like a brother would take away my life as I knew it. I'm sure he didn't, either. What a cruel result his choices and mine made on my life. While I had been pursuing football, he had joined a gang. I never thought it was cool belonging to a gang, but I did think it was okay to be friends with gang members. I never realized that simply associating with gang members would change my life forever."

I spoke for about fifteen minutes and showed them a video of myself before and after the shooting. When I was finished, they shared with me that they had never met someone who had been affected by gun violence like I had. They knew they had affected a lot of lives through their violence, but they had never seen the true impact of their actions. When we were finished talking, they all came up to shake my hand. I was filled with hope.

A few weeks later, I received letters from some of the boys thanking me for coming and vowing to get out of the gang. Some even said they wanted to look for a more peaceful way of life. I was ecstatic. What had happened to me finally had some meaning. I would never play football, but I could make a difference in young people's lives.

In May 2000, Zoe and I adopted a child. As I see the wonder and hope in my son's eyes, I dream of a future when the only gun violence he will know about is the cause of my disability. I'll never be the same as before, but we all have to be the best we can be. When I look out into the audience during a presentation, I hope that this won't happen to any of them. I beg them, "Please stay away from guns, drugs, and gangs. Stop the violence! It is the only way we can all live together in peace."

Cruz Carrasco and Zoe McGrath

Stories with One Multilevel Plan

As with the previous section, these stories were student and teacher-selected to encompass a wide variety of issues for all age groupings, and includes selections of topics from several Chicken Soup for the Soul books.

It differs from the previous section in that it contains a *single* plan, easily adaptable to all ages and abilities, rather than plans that are specifically grouped by grade level.

Each story is preceded by an information page listing:
* ★ Title
* ★ Book
* ★ Page number
* ★ Amount of time necessary to read the story aloud
* ★ Major topics in **bold** print
* ★ Lesser referencing topics in standard print
* ★ Appropriate age level for the story content and plans
* ★ Short synopsis of the story
* ★ Additional notes to the teacher

Additional worksheets are located within the story section whenever possible. Occasionally, teachers will be referred to the Appendix for further information.

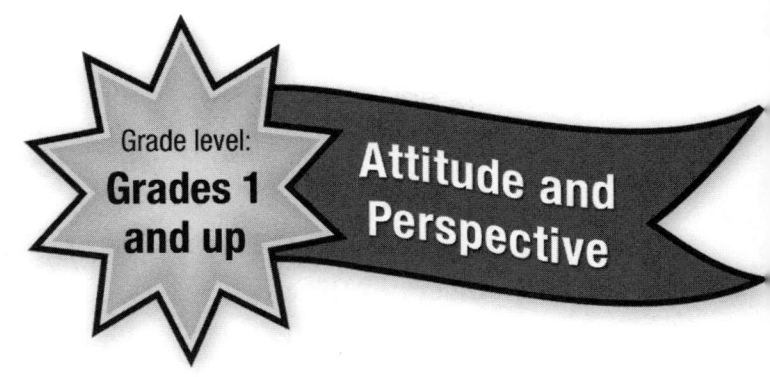

Grade level:
Grades 1 and up

Attitude and Perspective

TITLE: DID THE EARTH MOVE FOR YOU?

BOOK: Chicken Soup for the Soul

PAGE: 171

TIME TO READ: **2 minutes**

TOPICS: **Attitude and Perspective**
Overcoming obstacles
Following your dream

AGE LEVEL: Grades 1 and up

SYNOPSIS: Despite medical opinion, eleven-year old Angela was determined to walk again. While visualizing herself moving with incredible concentration, she felt the bed move! Unbeknownst to her, it was the middle of the San Francisco earthquake . . . a few years later, she was walking!

NOTES TO TEACHER:

Henry Ford once said, "He who thinks he can, and he who thinks he can't, are both correct." This very short story is a good beginning lesson relating to that thought.

The **Inner Smile Visualization** (Appendix, page 323) is a safe way to introduce this concept.

A related story parents might also enjoy is "If You Think You Can, You Can," found on page 242 of *Chicken Soup to Inspire the Body and Soul.*

Chicken Soup for the Soul, Did the Earth Move for You?

PRE-QUESTIONS:

Has anyone ever told you that you couldn't accomplish something that was important to you? If so, what was it? Why did they tell you that? How did you feel?

Have you ever accomplished something that only you believed you could do?

- If so, what was it, and how did it feel?

Read Story

POST-QUESTIONS:

Why did the doctors feel that Angela wouldn't be able to walk again?

What is visualization?

- How does it work? (see Appendix, page 375, for simple directions or use ***Inner Smile Visualization***, Appendix page 323 , as an introduction.)

How did Angela get the bed to move (*what happened to move the bed*)?

What is the main message in this story?

STUDENT ACTIVITIES:

Draw or paint a picture that represents your belief in yourself (*either who you are now, or who you want to be in the future*).

- Laminate this picture and place it in a prominent spot where you will look at it daily.
- Use this activity along with the ***Mirror Exercise*** (Appendix, page 307).
- Report back to your ***Circle Groups*** (Appendix, page 311) each week to discuss any differences in your feelings or abilities after doing this.

Make up a song or dance that shows the power of belief (*music adds power to the idea*).

Research and report on people who have overcome extreme obstacles to succeed at something.

Research medical facilities that focus on using visualization to help heal.

- Report on one or more of these, citing their success rates.

Take a challenge you are currently facing (*e.g., your math grade, extreme shyness, your speed in the one hundred meter dash, test anxiety, stuttering, etc.*) and practice visualizing for thirty days. Report back on your success.

Did the Earth Move for You?

Eleven-year-old Angela was stricken with a debilitating disease involving her nervous system. She was unable to walk, and her movement was restricted in other ways as well. The doctors did not hold out much hope of her ever recovering from this illness. They predicted she'd spend the rest of her life in a wheelchair. They said that few, if any, were able to come back to normal after contracting this disease. The little girl was undaunted. There, lying in her hospital bed, she would vow to anyone who'd listen that she was definitely going to be walking again someday.

She was transferred to a specialized rehabilitation hospital in the San Francisco Bay area. Whatever therapies could be applied to her case were used. The therapists were charmed by her undefeatable spirit. They taught her about imaging—about seeing herself walking. If it would do nothing else, it would at least give her hope and something positive to do during the long waking hours in her bed. Angela worked as hard as possible in physical therapy, in whirlpools and in exercise sessions. But she worked just as hard lying there, faithfully doing her imaging, visualizing herself moving, moving, moving!

One day, as she was straining with all her might to imagine her legs moving again, it seemed as though a miracle happened: the bed moved! It began to move around the room! She screamed out, "Look what I'm doing! Look! Look! I can do it! I moved, I moved!"

Of course, at this very moment everyone else in the hospital was screaming, too, and running for cover. People were screaming, equipment was falling, and glass was breaking. You see, it was a San Francisco earthquake. But don't tell that to Angela. She's convinced that she did it. And now only a few years later, she's back in school. On her own two legs. No crutches, no wheelchair. You see, anyone who can shake the earth between San Francisco and Oakland can conquer a piddling little disease, can't they?

Hanoch McCarty

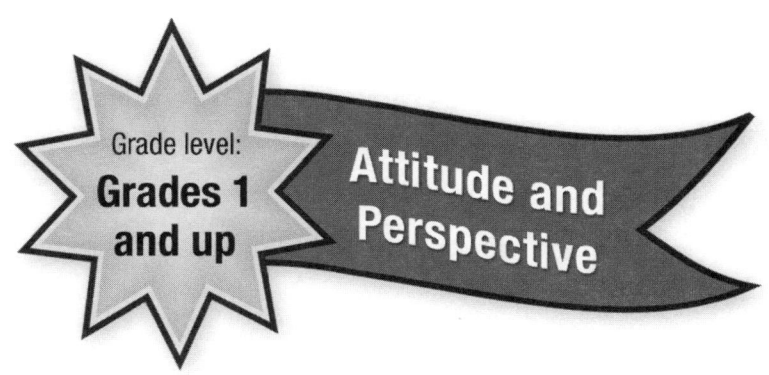

TITLE: **JUST ME**

BOOK: **Chicken Soup for the Teenage Soul**

PAGE: **287**

TIME TO READ: **1 minute**

TOPICS: **Attitude and Perspective**
Living and learning
Overcoming obstacles
Sport—basketball

AGE LEVEL: Grades 1 and up

SYNOPSIS: This rhyming verse is about a basketball player who goes from blaming everyone else to taking responsibility for his mistakes, and ultimately improving as a result.

NOTES TO TEACHER:

After reading this poetry to younger students, you may need to break it down stanza by stanza, for their understanding.

It is important to help students recognize that *everyone* has winner moments and loser moments. However, it is critical to focus on those winner moments in order to draw more energy to them.

If you have your students read "*99 Percent Is Tough; 100 Percent Is Easy*" (Appendix, page 305), you will initially need to spend time helping them to grasp the concept and to choose an area for practice and growth. Like any other practice, it will pay off in the end. Because of the nature of the assignment, you cannot "order" commitment to be done as homework. You can, however, encourage it, and perhaps offer extra credit for those who choose to try it. Spend time helping students choose simple tasks to work on with this activity.

ALL LEVELS:

PRE-QUESTIONS:

When unpleasant things happen to you, how often do you blame others (*parents, teachers, coaches, teammates, friends, the President, your dog, the weather, etc.*)?

Complete the **Winners and Losers** worksheet.

Discuss the *feelings* involved in each scenario.

Can possessing extreme amounts of talent ever be an obstacle? Explain.

Do you ever claim 100 percent responsibility for your actions and their resulting consequences?

Read Story

POST-QUESTIONS:

Who was blamed for all that went wrong in this poem?

Why did this basketball player always blame others?

• What happened to change that?

Do you think that parents, coaches, or society in general help to create athletes who do not take responsibility for their actions?

Does fame or success make you a "good" human being? Explain.

STUDENT ACTIVITIES:

Choose four or five famous athletes and research their lives on and off the playing fields (*e.g., O.J. Simpson, Kristin Yamaguchi, Mark McGwire, Kobe Bryant, Shaquille O'Neal, Tiger Woods, Lance Armstrong, Michael Jordan, Marion Jones, Billie Jean King, etc.*).

• Do you think that being athletically talented, and the resulting fame, contributed to their attitudes, successes, or failures in their sport, or in life?

• Write a one-page report on your findings and feelings.

Choose one small area of your life where you can practice taking 100 percent responsibility for your thoughts and actions and their consequences. Choose something small and build on that success (*e.g., making your bed daily, drinking eight glasses of water each day, doing all of your math homework daily, etc.*). Report on your success weekly throughout the year.

Watch or read *The Secret* (see Resources, page 378 for full citation). Discuss its key concepts of "law of attraction" and "power of intention" (*what you think about, you create*).

WINNERS AND LOSERS

1. The last time I felt like a winner was . . .

2. I feel like a real winner when . . .

3. When I think of winners, I think of people like . . .

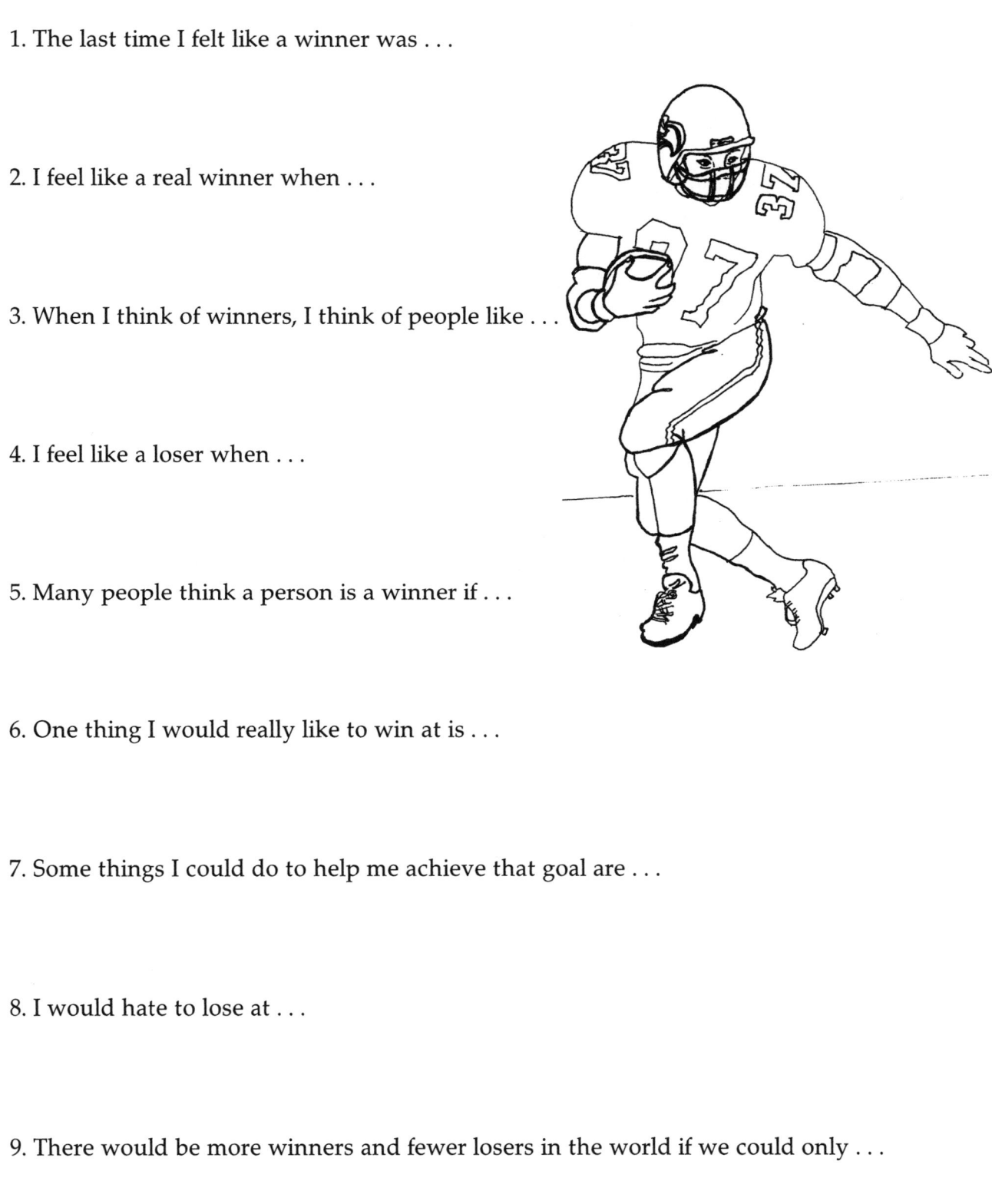

4. I feel like a loser when . . .

5. Many people think a person is a winner if . . .

6. One thing I would really like to win at is . . .

7. Some things I could do to help me achieve that goal are . . .

8. I would hate to lose at . . .

9. There would be more winners and fewer losers in the world if we could only . . .

Just Me

From the time I was little, I knew I was great
'cause the people would tell me, "You'll make it—just wait."
But they never did tell me how great I would be
if I ever played someone who was greater than me.

When I'm in the back yard, I'm king with the ball.
To swish all those baskets is no sweat at all.
But all of a sudden there's a man in my face
who doesn't seem to realize that I'm king of this place.

So the pressure gets to me; I rush with the ball.
My passes to teammates could go through the wall.
My jumpers not falling, my dribbles not sure.
My hand is not steady, my eye is not pure.

The fault is my teammates—they don't understand.
The fault is my coaches—what a terrible plan.
The fault is the call by that blind referee.
But the fault is not mine; I'm the greatest, you see.

Then finally it hit me when I started to see
that the face in the mirror looked exactly like me.
It wasn't my teammates who were dropping the ball,
and it wasn't my coach shooting bricks at the wall.

That face in the mirror that was always so great
had some room for improvement instead of just hate.
So I stopped blaming others and I started to grow.
My play got much better and it started to show.

And all of my teammates didn't seem quite so bad.
I learned to depend on the good friends I had.
Now I like myself better since I started to see
that I was lousy being great—I'm much better being me.

Tom Krause

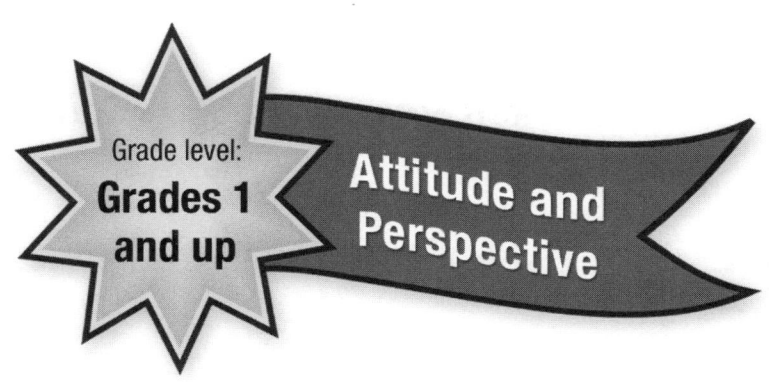

TITLE: **NOBODY KNOWS THE DIFFERENCE**

BOOK: **Chicken Soup for the Kid's Soul**

PAGE: **285**

TIME TO READ: **4 minutes**

TOPICS: **Attitude and Perspective**
Making choices
Living and learning
Christmas spirit

AGE LEVEL: **Grades 1 and up**

SYNOPSIS: A small child returns to pay for a performance seen the night before. As he insists on paying, he teaches an important lesson to a nearby grumpy parent.

NOTES TO TEACHER:

In a society where many people try to get away with things, this is a wonderful story about integrity from a small child who knows the difference. It is critical that this message be presented to students of all ages.

ALL LEVELS:

PRE-QUESTIONS:

If you had the opportunity to sneak into some kind of show or event without paying, do you think that you would do so?

How do you think you would feel?

- Explain your answers.

Read Story

POST-QUESTIONS:

Why did the small boy choose to pay when he could have gotten in for free?

What did the grumpy parent learn from the small boy in this story?

Integrity is doing the right thing when no one is watching.

- Where, or how, does someone learn this?

Compare and contrast the young child in this story with Willard in "A Silent Voice," page 40 of this curriculum.

- What part did wealth play in each of their decisions?
- What part did attitude play in each of their decisions?

STUDENT ACTIVITIES:

Use puppet diagrams (on pages 101 and 102) to make hand puppets from paper bags or fabric.

- Perform this story for elementary classes or shows can be done for elders in an assisted living facility.

Write a song that reflects this story.

PUPPET DIAGRAMS

FINGER HOLES

PAPER-BAG PUPPETS

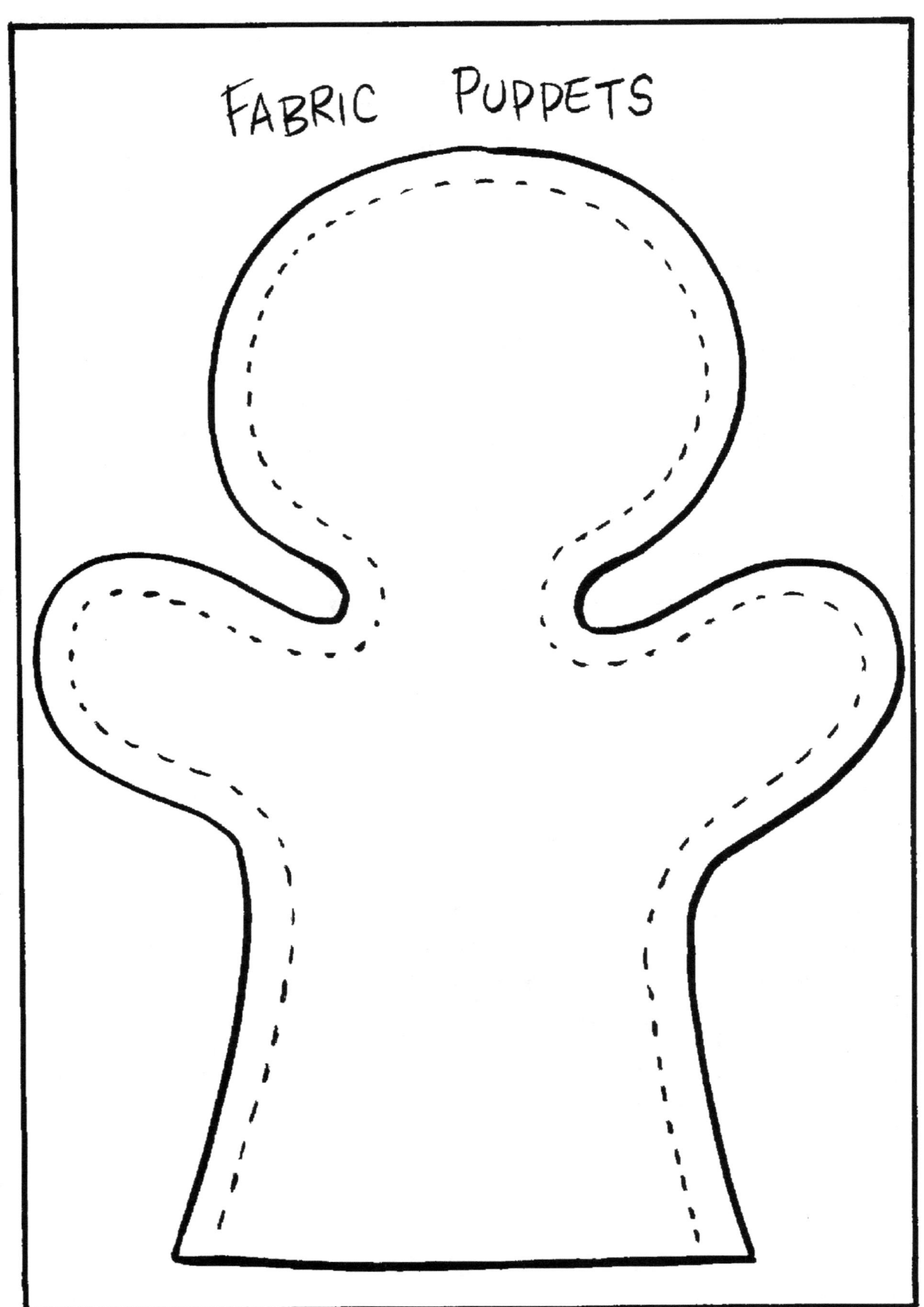

FABRIC PUPPETS

Nobody Knows the Difference

School volunteers don't get paid money, but sometimes we receive special gifts. One morning, just before Christmas vacation, I was selling tickets to our grade school's last evening performance of *The Nutcracker*. The evening before had been a sellout. People had lined the walls of the auditorium. Some had even peeked in from outside to watch the show.

One of my customers that day was a parent. "I think it's awful that I have to pay to see my own child perform," she announced, yanking a wallet from her purse.

"The school asks for a voluntary donation to help pay for scenery and costumes," I explained, "but no one has to pay. You're welcome to all the tickets you need."

"Oh, I'll pay," she grumbled. "Two adults and a child."

She plunked down a ten-dollar bill. I gave her the change and her tickets. She stepped aside, fumbling with her purse. That's when the boy waiting behind her emptied a pocketful of change onto the table.

"How many tickets?" I asked.

"I don't need tickets," he said. "I'm paying." He pushed the coins across the table.

"But you'll need tickets to see the show tonight."

He shook his head. "I've already seen the show."

I pushed the pile of nickels, dimes, and quarters back. "You don't have to pay to see the show with your class," I told him. "That's free."

"No," the boy insisted. "I saw it last night. My brother and I arrived late. We couldn't find anyone to buy tickets from, so we just walked in."

Lots of people in that crowd had probably "just walked in." The few volunteers present couldn't check everyone for a ticket. Who would argue, anyway? As I'd told the parent ahead of this boy, the donation was voluntary.

He pushed his money back to me. "I'm paying now, for last night," he said.

I knew this boy and his brother must have squeezed into the back of that crowd. And being late to boot, they couldn't possibly have seen the whole show. I hated to take his money. A pile of coins in a kid's hand is usually carefully saved allowance money.

"If the ticket table was closed when you got there, you couldn't pay," I reasoned.

"That's what my brother said."

"Nobody knows the difference," I assured him. "Don't worry about it."

Thinking the matter was settled, I started to push the coins back. He put his hand on mine.

"I know the difference."

For a moment our hands bridged the money. Then I spoke. "Two tickets cost two dollars."

The pile of coins added up to the correct amount. "Thank you," I said.

The boy smiled, turned away and was gone.

"Excuse me." I looked up, surprised to see the woman who had bought her own tickets moments earlier. She was still there, purse open, change and tickets in hand.

"Why don't you keep this change," she said quietly. "The scenery is beautiful, and those costumes couldn't have been cheap." She handed me a few dollar bills, and left.

Little did that boy know that he had given us both our first gift of the Christmas season.

Deborah J. Rasmussen

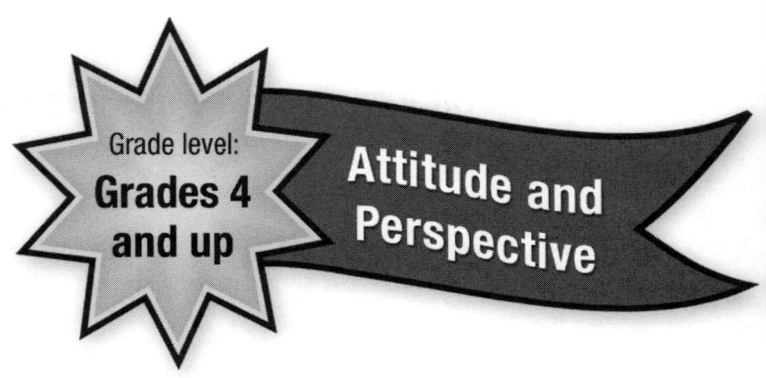

Grade level:
Grades 4 and up

Attitude and Perspective

TITLE: **THE POWER OF ATTITUDE**

BOOK: **Chicken Soup for the Kid's Soul 2**

PAGE: **168**

TIME TO READ: **2 minutes**

TOPICS: **Attitude and Perspective**
Living and learning
Making choices

AGE LEVEL: **Grades 1 and up**

SYNOPSIS: **A youngster finds that a change in *attitude* makes any task easier.**

NOTES TO TEACHER:

The concepts of self-fulfilling prophecy (*the outcome that we expect from something is generally the outcome that we experience*), E + R = O (*event plus our response equals outcome*), and the law of attraction (*like a magnet, we draw to us what we think about and focus on—positive or negative*) are all extremely powerful ideas that successful people seem to simply know.

The sooner we present these ideas to our students, the greater are their chances for success, in school, and in life.

For further details on these concepts, refer to the Appendix, page 327 and page 330 or watch *The Secret* (cited in Resources, page 378).

For a wonderful related story, read to your students "The Optimist," found on page 180 of *A 2nd Helping of Chicken Soup for the Soul.*

Adjust any of the time amounts or writing requirements to suit appropriate ages.

Chicken Soup for the Kid's Soul 2, The Power of Attitude

PRE-QUESTIONS:

What does the word "attitude" mean to you? How do you think it affects your life?
- Give some examples (*e.g., simple things like hating lima beans or loving math class, or more profound things like whether you quit when things get tough or see them through to the end*).

Do you think that your successes or failures in life were caused by your own thoughts?
- Explain your answer.

Read Story

POST-QUESTIONS:

How did attitude affect the outcome in this story?

What was some of the self-talk the author experienced?
- Do you ever find yourself talking to yourself like that?
- Which side wins, the positive or the negative?

Has your idea about attitude changed since hearing this story?

STUDENT ACTIVITIES:

Draw faces or characters, or make masks that represent various aspects of your self-talk.
- Give these characters names such as Likeable Lucy, Positive Paul, Negative Nellie, Positive Penny, Do-Good Dan, Negative Nate, Trouble-Making Terry, etc.
- Make a conscious effort to have more inner conversations with the positive ones.

Make a list of all of the things that you remember saying in the past hour.
- Put (+) signs next to the positive comments and (–) signs next to the negative statements. What percentage of your communication is positive?

In **Circle Talks** (Appendix, page 311), share ways to increase your positive list.

Now that you have more awareness, keep track of your self-talk for the next twenty-four hours. Tabulate how much is positive and how much is negative.

For the next two weeks, practice some of the concepts presented by your teacher ($E + R = O$, *the law of attraction, etc.*) and write a report on its effect.

Start two new journals—one that starts your day with positive intention, and the other that ends your day by focusing on gratitude for things, people, or happenings in your day. In three or four weeks, write a half-page paper, or share in **Circle Groups**, if either of these journals had an effect on your daily attitude.

The Power of Attitude

*People forget how fast you did a job—but
they remember how well you did it.*

Howard Newton

I strongly believe that your outlook on life has a lot to do with whether or not you will succeed. A very wise man once told me, "Life is an attitude." During the summer that I turned nine, I learned that lesson firsthand.

Early one morning, my mom asked me to do some yard work for her.

"Do I have to?" I grumbled.

"Yes, you do," came the answer I had dreaded. Then my mom followed that up with, "If you have a good attitude about it, it will be easier!"

"That's what you think," I mumbled under my breath. I waited and stalled as long as possible, but eventually my mother wouldn't wait any longer. So I shuffled slowly outside. My feet felt very heavy—almost as though there were magnets attached to them and the ground was metal, or like my socks were filled with wet sand. Or maybe my feet were just glued to the ground. I felt miserable.

As I started to work, I could feel my conscience knocking away at the door of my heart. The words "It will be easier if you have a good attitude," popped back and forth in my head. I knew that my mom was right, but at that moment I would never admit it.

The work was really frustrating. It took me forever to dig through the ground and find the flower bulbs so we could put them away for planting the following year. The muddy dirt seeped through my hands almost as though it was trying to get away from me and my lousy attitude. The whole time, the little voice inside of me kept repeating, *If you change your attitude, it will be easier!*

"Shut up," I yelled, "just shut up!" I couldn't believe it! I was arguing out loud with myself!

After awhile, my better self won the argument. I decided that I had to change my attitude. I have to admit, the minute my attitude changed, the happier I became and the easier my work was. I finished my work humming every dumb song that popped into my head.

As I walked into the house later that day, I turned to Mom, who was peeling potatoes, and said, "You were right, my work was easier once I changed my attitude." My mom just smiled and said, "I told you. Now go take a bath and help me make dinner."

WHAT??!!

Melea Wendell, fourteen

TITLE: REST IN PEACE: THE "I CAN'T" FUNERAL

BOOK: Chicken Soup for the Soul

PAGE: 156

TIME TO READ: 7 minutes

TOPICS: **Attitude and Perspective**
Overcoming obstacles
Teacher impact

AGE LEVEL: Grades 4 and up

SYNOPSIS: Fourth graders bury their "I can't" statements in a classroom funeral service.

NOTES TO TEACHER:

| This "funeral" process can be used with any age.

Chicken Soup for the Soul, Rest in Peace: The "I Can't" Funeral

PRE-QUESTIONS:

Discuss "May I . . .?" versus "Can I . . .?"

Discuss "can't" versus "won't" (*e.g., I can't do math, or I won't do math; I can't read, or I won't read; I can't run fast, or I won't run fast, etc.*).

Discuss the concept of trying to do something.

Read Story

POST-QUESTIONS:

Discuss in **Circle Groups** (Appendix, page 311), then as a full class, the typical "I can't" comments of kids your age.

Make your own personal list of "I Can't" statements. Add the word "try" to your list of things to eliminate.

STUDENT ACTIVITIES:

Perform an "I Can't" ceremonial funeral or cremation. Organize the funeral, eulogy, and wake. (*Note to teacher: You should supervise these plans for appropriateness.*)

• Reflect back on this activity at one week, one month, and the end of the school year.

• Add the word "try" to the casket.

Banish "try" from your vocabulary and from the classroom.

• Create a "Banish the Word 'Try' Campaign."

• Make elaborate posters banishing the word "try."

• At the bottom of each poster, end with the question, "Want to know more? Ask _____" (followed by the student's name).

• If asked, demonstrate "trying" to take a pencil.

• Make announcements to get other teachers and classrooms involved.

• Have contests between classrooms.

• See if you can banish the word "try" from the entire school.

NOTES TO TEACHER:

Demonstration of "try." (*Have a student try to take a pencil out of your hand. They will either take it out of your hand, or not take it out of your hand. Ask them again to TRY to take the pencil. Again, they will take it, or not take it. Point out that the word "try" is a useless word. You either DO something, or you DON'T DO something. You can't try. . . .*)

Rest in Peace: The "I Can't" Funeral

Donna's fourth-grade classroom looked like many others I had seen in the past. Students sat in five rows of six desks. The teacher's desk was in the front and faced the students. The bulletin board featured student work. In most respects it appeared to be a traditional elementary classroom. Yet something seemed different that day I entered it for the first time. There seemed to be an undercurrent of excitement.

Donna was a veteran small-town Michigan schoolteacher only two years away from retirement. In addition, she was a volunteer participant in a county-wide staff development project I had organized and facilitated. The training focused on language arts ideas that would empower students to feel good about themselves and take charge of their lives. Donna's job was to attend training sessions and implement the concepts being presented. My job was to make classroom visitations and encourage implementation.

I took an empty seat in the back of the room and watched. All the students were working on a task, filling a sheet of notebook paper with thoughts and ideas. The ten-year-old student closest to me was filling her page with "I Cant's."

"I can't kick the soccer ball past second base."

"I can't do long division with more than three numerals."

"I can't get Debbie to like me."

Her page was half full and she showed no signs of letting up. She worked on with determination and persistence.

I walked down the row glancing at students' papers. Everyone was writing sentences, describing things they couldn't do.

"I can't do ten push-ups."

"I can't hit one over the left-field fence."

"I can't eat only one cookie."

By this time, the activity engaged my curiosity, so I decided to check with the teacher to see what was going on. As I approached her, I noticed that she too was busy writing. I felt it best not to interrupt.

"I can't get John's mother to come in for a teacher conference."

"I can't get my daughter to put gas in the car."

"I can't get Alan to use words instead of fists."

Thwarted in my efforts to determine why students and teacher were dwelling on the negative instead of writing the more positive "I Can" statements, I returned to my seat and continued my observations. Students wrote for another ten minutes. Most filled their page. Some started another.

"Finish the one you're on and don't start a new one," were the instructions Donna used to signal the end of the activity. Students were then instructed to fold their papers in half and bring them to the front. When students reached the teacher's desk, they placed their "I Can't" statements into an empty shoe box.

When all of the student papers were collected, Donna added hers. She put the lid on the box, tucked it under her arm and headed out the door and down the hall. Students followed the teacher. I followed the students.

Halfway down the hall the procession stopped. Donna entered the custodian's room, rummaged around, and came out with a shovel. Shovel in one hand, shoe box in the other, Donna marched the students out of the school to the farthest corner of the playground. There they began to dig.

They were going to bury their "I Can'ts"! The digging took more than ten minutes because most of the fourth-graders wanted a turn. When the hole approached three-feet deep, the digging ended. The box of "I Can'ts" was placed in position at the bottom of the hole and quickly covered with dirt.

Thirty-one ten- and eleven-year-olds stood around the freshly dug grave site. Each had at least one page full of "I Can'ts" in the shoe box, four-feet under. So did their teacher.

At this point Donna announced, "Boys and girls, please join hands and bow your heads." The students complied. They quickly formed a circle around the grave, creating a bond with their hands. They lowered their heads and waited. Donna delivered the eulogy.

"Friends, we gather today to honor the memory of 'I Can't.' While he was with us on earth, he touched the lives of everyone, some more than others. His name, unfortunately, has been spoken in every public building—schools, city halls, state capitols and, yes, even the White House.

"We have provided 'I Can't' with a final resting place and a headstone that contains his epitaph. He is survived by his brothers and sister, 'I Can,' 'I Will,' and 'I'm Going to Right Away.' They are not as well known as their famous relative and are certainly not as strong and powerful yet. Perhaps some day, with your help, they will make an even bigger mark on the world.

"May 'I Can't' rest in peace and may everyone present pick up their lives and move forward in his absence. Amen."

As I listened to the eulogy I realized that these students would never forget this day. The activity was symbolic, a metaphor for life. It was a right-brain experience that would stick in the unconscious and conscious mind forever.

Writing "I Cant's," burying them, and hearing the eulogy. That was a major effort on the part of this teacher. And she wasn't done yet. At the conclusion of the eulogy she turned the students around, marched them back into the classroom, and held a wake.

They celebrated the passing of "I Can't" with cookies, popcorn, and fruit juices. As part of the celebration, Donna cut out a large tombstone from butcher paper. She wrote the words "I Can't" at the top and put "RIP" in the middle. The date was added at the bottom.

The paper tombstone hung in Donna's classroom for the remainder of the year. On those rare occasions when a student forgot and said, "I Can't," Donna simply pointed to the RIP sign. The student then remembered that "I Can't" was dead and chose to rephrase the statement.

I wasn't one of Donna's students. She was one of mine. Yet that day I learned an enduring lesson from her.

Now, years later, whenever I hear the phrase "I Can't," I see images of that fourth-grade funeral. Like the students, I remember that "I Can't" is dead.

Chick Moorman

TITLE: **RIVER RECIPE**

BOOK: **Chicken Soup for the Nature Lover's Soul**

PAGE: **336**

TIME TO READ: **1 minute**

TOPICS: **Attitude and Perspective**
Making a difference
World issues—environment
World issues—nature

AGE LEVEL: **Grades 3 and up**

SYNOPSIS: **An eleven-year-old has written a "recipe" for his favorite river.**

NOTES TO TEACHER:

While this particular story lends itself to the same lesson plan for all levels, certain aspects may be more suitable for young ages (*recycling*), while others might work better for older students (*writing letters to Congressional leaders*). However, all age groups can do some version of the activities listed.

ALL LEVELS:

PRE-QUESTIONS:

What do you value most about nature or the beauty of our world?

Where is your favorite place in the world (*this could be somewhere you've been, or somewhere you wish to go*)?

- Tell why this place is so special to you.

Read Story

POST-QUESTIONS:

Did this "recipe" help you to appreciate the details of your favorite place?

Do you feel that it is important to conserve and protect the Earth?

- Explain your reasoning.

What are some things that anyone can do to protect the beauty of Mother Earth (*recycle, pick up litter, conserve water when brushing teeth by not allowing the water to run continuously, shut off lights when not in use, turn off the TV and read a good book, etc.*)?

STUDENT ACTIVITIES:

Write your own "recipe" for a special place of yours.

Start a school-wide campaign to protect our natural treasures.

- Choose a specific goal (*e.g., recycling, eliminating litter, etc.*), or an informational blitz on many environmental topics (*e.g., wetlands, endangered species, the ozone, letters to Congressional leaders regarding laws of protection, less packaging of products, water conservation, global warming, etc.*).
- See how many ways you can list where we can all work to protect the Earth.

Watch Al Gore's movie *An Inconvenient Truth* about global warming. Or go to one of the following websites on the topic: www.climatecrisis.net or www.stopglobalwarming.org.

- Discuss your agreement or disagreement with these assessments.

River Recipe

Ingredients
- Freshly melted snow from the spires of the Cascades
- Navy-blue blackberries as dark as the summer night's sky
- The stars and the planets mixed together in a puree
- Marshmallow clouds
- Wild mushrooms (can be found in any nearby heart of a forest; make sure they are finely pounded by the sleek hooves of neighboring elk)
- About one hundred thousand acres of lush, green farmland

Directions
1. Mix all ingredients together except for the clouds and the farmland.
2. After many moons, stop stirring and let it sit for five days. Then soak in the finest silks from India and sprinkle across a dry landscape in Washington.
3. Surround your river with the farmland and then wait until they connect.
4. Float the clouds up to the sky; wait until they have made themselves comfortable in heaven.
5. Take yourself on a walk in the misty morning and find a comfortable spot on the bank of the river. Gaze into the river until you've found your reflection. Learn something special about yourself.

Robin Andrews, age eleven

TITLE: **TROUBLED**

BOOK: **Chicken Soup for the Soul, The Book of Christmas Virtues**

PAGE: **167**

TIME TO READ: **4 minutes**

TOPICS: **Bias Issues—Stereotypes**
Giving and receiving
Christmas spirit
World issues—homelessness

AGE LEVEL: **Grades 5 and up**

SYNOPSIS: A man totally misjudges four teenagers and a homeless person. The story unfolds to show a contagious Christmas spirit.

NOTE TO TEACHER:

| This is a Christmas story that is appropriate for all religions and all seasons.

Chicken Soup for the Soul: The Book of Christmas Virtues, Troubled

PRE-QUESTIONS:

What are your first thoughts when you see . . .
- A teen who is heavily tattooed?
- An old person who is driving slowly?
- A screaming toddler who won't stop crying?
- A person with multiple body piercings?
- A homeless person pushing a shopping cart?
- A large man wearing heavy gold chains, many big diamonds, and driving a big, expensive, black car with darkened windows?

Where do stereotypes originate?
- Are they accurate?
- Explain your answers.

Read Story

POST-QUESTIONS:

What were the judgments made in this story?
- Were they accurate?

Do you think you will view others differently after hearing this story?
- Why, or why not?

Complete worksheet **B** (Appendix page 372).

STUDENT ACTIVITIES:

Start a ***Kindness Is Contagious—Pass It On*** campaign. Essentially, the teacher begins by doing something extra special for three people—one in the classroom and two outside of the class.
- Within twenty-four hours, the student selected in class passes on three acts of kindness—one to a class member and two others outside of the classroom. That "in-class" student, in turn, passes it on to three others, etc.

For a more comprehensive version of this activity, see Appendix, page 349.

At the end of a month, report on how it felt giving and receiving an act of kindness.

Troubled

A song sung by Faith Hill in the blockbuster movie *The Grinch* asks: "Where are you, Christmas? Why can't I find you?" Well, sometimes the Christmas spirit is like a misplaced sock—you find it when you aren't looking and where you'd least expect it to show up.

I found it at a quarter past one in the morning.

On my way home from work, I stopped at the neighborhood doughnut shop. After parking in its ghost town of a parking lot, I was headed toward the door when I spotted trouble.

What lit a warning light on my intuition radar was a group of teenagers—three boys and a girl. Understand, I wasn't alarmed by their tattoos (the girl included) or their earrings (boys included—eyebrows as well as each of their ears). Rather, it was the extremely late hour and the fact they loitered on the sidewalk in a semicircle around an elderly man sitting in a chair. Wearing a tattered flannel shirt and barefoot, the man looked positively cold and probably homeless.

And in trouble with a capital T.

Against my better judgment, I went inside the store and ordered three doughnuts—while keeping a worried eye on the group outside. Nothing seemed to be happening.

Until I headed toward my car.

Something was indeed "going down." As ominously as a pirate ordering a prisoner to the plank, the teens told the old man to stand up and walk.

Oh, no, I thought. *Capital tee-are-oh-you-bee-el-ee.*

But wait. I had misjudged the situation. And I had misjudged the teens.

"How do those feel?" one of the boys asked. "Do they fit?"

The cold man took a few steps—maybe a dozen. He stopped, looked at his feet, turned around and walked back. "Yeah, they'z about my size," he answered, flashing a smile that, despite needing a dentist's attention, was friendly and warm on this cold night.

The teens, all four, grinned back.

"Keep them. They're yours," one of the boys replied. "I want you to have them."

I looked down. The teen was barefoot. The kid had just given the cold-and-probably-homeless man his expensive skateboarding sneakers—and, apparently his socks, as well.

The other two boys sat on their skateboards by the curb, retying their shoelaces. Apparently, they, too, had let the man try on their sneakers to find which pair fit the best. The girl, meanwhile, gave the cold man her oversized sweatshirt.

With my heart warmed by the unfolding drama, I went back into the shop.

"Could I trouble you for another dozen doughnuts?" I asked, then told the clerk what I had witnessed.

Christmas spirit, it seemed, was more contagious than flu or chicken pox. Indeed, the cold night got even warmer when the woman not only wouldn't let me pay for the doughnuts, but added a large coffee, too.

"These are from the lady inside. Have a nice night," I said as I delivered the warm doughnuts and piping-hot cup. The old man smiled appreciatively.

"You have a nice night, too," the teens said.

I already had.

Woody Woodburn

Grade level: **Grades 1 and up**

Following Your Dream

TITLE: **ASK, ASK, ASK**

BOOK: **Chicken Soup for the Soul**

PAGE: **168**

TIME TO READ: **5 minutes**

TOPICS: **Following Your Dream**
Asking
Attitude and perspective
Living and learning

AGE LEVEL: **Grades 1 and up**

SYNOPSIS: **Markita Andrews started selling Girl Scout cookies at age seven. Asking, asking, asking was her means of accomplishing her goal to take her mother around the world. This story shows the importance of asking and "selling ourselves" in all that we do.**

NOTES TO TEACHER:

This story is introduced at a young age because learning how to ask is an important skill to develop. The story is appropriate for all ages, however, and the questions and activities can easily be adapted for any group.

For a related story on asking that is appropriate for any age, read, "Just Ask," found in *Chicken Soup for the Kid's Soul,* page 228.

Refer to the Appendix, page 302, for detailed information on the importance of asking, taken with permission from *The Success Principles: How to Get from Where You Are to Where You Want to Be* (see Resources, page 377, for full citation).

Chicken Soup for the Soul, Ask, Ask, Ask

PRE-QUESTIONS:

If you had a magic wand that would grant you any wish just by asking for it, what would you ask for?

Do you ever have a problem asking for things?

• Give some examples.

Read Story

POST-QUESTIONS:

What is the main message of this story?

What was Markita's real goal in this story?

Name some specific examples of Markita asking for things in order to achieve her goal.

NOTE TO TEACHER:

Information on *assertive communication* can be found in the Appendix, page 338.

STUDENT ACTIVITIES:

Make a classroom list of typical things that kids your age will ask for.

• Using this list, or the examples below, role-play asking for things.
• Remember to use assertive communication to do so.

Examples:

• asking a question in class when you don't know something
• asking for help with homework
• asking someone to buy something from you
• asking your parents for a bigger allowance
• asking someone to dance
• asking for a later curfew
• asking someone to sponsor you for a charity walk
• asking to borrow your father's corvette for prom night.

Ask, Ask, Ask

The greatest saleswoman in the world today doesn't mind if you call her a girl. That's because Markita Andrews has generated more than eighty thousand dollars selling Girl Scout cookies since she was seven years old.

Going door-to-door after school, the painfully shy Markita transformed herself into a cookie-selling dynamo when she discovered, at age thirteen, the secret of selling.

It starts with desire. Burning, white-hot desire.

For Markita and her mother, who worked as a waitress in New York after her husband left them when Markita was eight years old, their dream was to travel the globe. "I'll work hard to make enough money to send you to college," her mother said one day. "You'll go to college, and when you graduate, you'll make enough money to take you and me around the world. Okay?"

So at age thirteen when Markita read in her Girl Scout magazine that the Scout who sold the most cookies would win an all-expenses-paid trip for two around the world, she decided to sell all the Girl Scout cookies she could—more Girl Scout cookies than anyone in the world, ever.

But desire alone is not enough. To make her dream come true, Markita knew she needed a plan.

"Always wear your right outfit, your professional garb," her aunt advised. "When you are doing business, dress like you are doing business. Wear your Girl Scout uniform. When you go up to people in their tenement buildings at 4:30 or 6:30 and especially on Friday night, ask for a big order. Always smile, whether they buy or not, always be nice. And don't ask them to buy your cookies; ask them to invest."

Lots of other Scouts may have wanted that trip around the world. Lots of other Scouts may have had a plan. But only Markita went off in her uniform each day after school, ready to ask—and keep asking —folks to invest in her dream. "Hi. I have a dream. I'm earning a trip around the world for me and my mom by merchandising Girl Scout cookies," she'd say at the door. "Would you like to invest in one dozen or two dozen boxes of cookies?"

Markita sold 3,526 boxes of Girl Scout cookies that year and won her trip around the world. Since then, she has sold more than forty-two thousand boxes of Girl Scout cookies, spoken at sales conventions across the country, starred in a Disney movie about her adventure, and has coauthored the best-seller, *How to Sell More Cookies, Condos, Cadillacs, Computers . . . and Everything Else.*

Markita is no smarter and no more extroverted than thousands of other people, young and old, with dreams of their own. The difference is Markita has discovered the secret of selling: ask, ask, ask! Many people fail before they even begin because they fail to ask for what they want. The fear of rejection leads many of us to reject ourselves and our dreams long before anyone else ever has the chance—no matter what we're selling.

And everyone is selling something. "You're selling yourself everyday—in school, to your boss, to new people you meet," said Markita at fourteen. "My mother is a waitress: she sells the daily special. Mayors and presidents trying to get votes are selling. . . . One of my favorite teachers was Mrs. Chapin. She made geography interesting, and that's really selling. . . . I see selling everywhere I look. Selling is part of the whole world."

It takes courage to ask for what you want. Courage is not the absence of fear. It's doing what it takes despite one's fear. And, as Markita has discovered, the more you ask, the easier (and more fun) it gets.

Once, on live TV, the producer decided to give Markita her toughest selling challenge. Markita was asked to sell Girl Scout cookies to another guest on the show. "Would you like to invest in one dozen or two dozen boxes of Girl Scout cookies?" she asked.

"Girl Scout cookies?! I don't buy any Girl Scout cookies!" he replied. "I'm a federal penitentiary warden. I put two thousand rapists, robbers, criminals, muggers, and child abusers to bed every night."

Unruffled, Markita quickly countered, "Mister, if you take some of these cookies, maybe you won't be so mean and angry and evil. And, mister, I think it would be a good idea for you to take some of these cookies back for every one of your two thousand prisoners, too."

Markita asked.

The warden wrote a check.

Jack Canfield & Mark V. Hansen

Grade level:
Grades 3 and up

Giving and Receiving

TITLE: **THE ANONYMOUS DONOR**

BOOK: **Chicken Soup for the NASCAR Soul**

TIME TO READ: **1 minute**

TOPICS: **Giving and Receiving**
Making a difference
Acting with kindness

AGE LEVEL: **Grades 3 and up**

SYNOPSIS: **An anonymous child donates $10 to the Speedway Children's Charities every year. There's never a name or address, just a child's drawing and unconditional giving.**

NOTES TO TEACHER:

Even very young children can get excited about donations in lieu of some gifts. Anna has her youngest friends sit down with their parents to discuss and select a significant charity for donations. She then makes the donations in their names, instead of buying them presents, and instructs the receiving charity to send acknowledgment and gratitude to these young kids. As small children, Taylor chose the Pacific Whale Foundation because of his passion for marine life, while Demitria selected the American Diabetes Association because of her grandmother's diabetes and her love and concern for her "Noni."

Chicken Soup for the NASCAR Soul, The Anonymous Donor

PRE-QUESTIONS:

Have you ever anonymously given something to someone (*"Secret Santa,"* an anonymous card, etc.)?

Have you ever done something for someone without identifying yourself? (*put money in someone else's expired parking meter or brushed off six inches of new snow from your teacher's car in the school parking lot—this actually happened to Anna twenty years ago, and she still has no idea who did it!*)?

Have you ever done anything special for someone without telling another living soul?

• How does it feel to do these things?

Read Story

POST-QUESTIONS:

What is the reason this particular donation stood out among millions?

What would prompt a small child to make an anonymous donation such as this?

What are the pros and cons (*advantages and disadvantages*) of doing something anonymously? Be sure to discuss the feelings involved in this.

STUDENT ACTIVITIES:

Choose a jar, can, or box to decorate and make into a charity jar.

Research many possible charities to select one that has special meaning for you. Set aside a charity jar to personally collect money all year. Once a year, make a donation to this charity, either anonymously, or including your name.

As a class, select a charity that is meaningful to the group. Have a car wash, bake sale, or simply a collection box to work toward this cause together.

Start, or join, an existing service club within your school to give back to the community and the world.

Consider requesting from family and friends that they make a charitable donation in lieu of any gifts for you. Do the same for them.

Design and make personal cards, telling others of your donation choices made in their honor.

For further ideas, read "Practice Random Kindness and Senseless Acts of Beauty" found in *A 2nd Helping of Chicken Soup for the Soul,* page 34. Or read *Random Acts of Kindness* by Conari Press (see Resources, page 379, for full citation).

The Anonymous Donor

It has been my pleasure to help facilitate and coordinate donations and sponsorships on behalf of Speedway Children's Charities over the last six years as national marketing director. All of the funds are deeply appreciated and always come from the heart from both donors and sponsors alike, no matter the amount of the contribution.

One donation that sticks in my mind, however, is a donation that comes in to us every six to eight weeks. It has no return address, usually has a small drawing on the envelope (obviously a child's drawing), and a cashier's check for ten dollars mailed from Harrisburg, North Carolina. It definitely is not the largest donation we receive throughout the month, but it's one that touches all the employees here at the Speedway Children's Charities every time it's received.

The reason it means so much to us is twofold. One, somewhere out there is an adult(s) who has taken the time to drive the child to the convenience store that the cashier's check is drawn on, making the act of giving a special activity. Second, the child never leaves a name or return address; he or she just gives unconditionally to other children in need. Speedway Children's Charities is fortunate to have such supporters as this child and his or her parents; I only hope that I can raise my own children to know what the true meaning of giving is, as our anonymous donor does.

Deb Wilson

TITLE: SHE DIDN'T PRAY FOR A MIRACLE

BOOK: Chicken Soup for the Jewish Soul

PAGE: 2

TIME TO READ: 6 minutes

TOPICS: **Giving and Receiving**
Overcoming obstacles
Acting with kindness
Tough stuff—Holocaust survivor

AGE LEVEL: Grades 5 and up

SYNOPSIS: Sonya, a Holocaust survivor, finds solace from her nightmares by helping two children who are also survivors. The surprising ending shows the reality of "in giving, we receive."

NOTES TO TEACHER:

This is a wonderful story of hope and survival—and of giving and receiving. However, it is a post-Holocaust story, and it does contain references to God and prayer. It should be previewed carefully and used with caution in some classrooms.

It is recommended that you discuss the Holocaust prior to reading this story in order to set the stage for Sonya's dilemma.

Another powerful story that takes place in this era is "Stranger on the Bus." found on page 134 of *Chicken Soup for the Jewish Soul.*

Chicken Soup for the Jewish Soul, She Didn't Pray for a Miracle

ALL LEVELS:

PRE-QUESTIONS:

Share what you already know about the Holocaust.
- In **Circle Talk** groups (Appendix, page 311), discuss the feelings that Holocaust survivors might have.

Have you ever been to a Holocaust museum? If so, what were your impressions?

Read Story

POST-QUESTIONS:

Explain Sonya's nightmares.

Initially, why didn't Sonya want to help these two children?
- Why did she change her mind?

Who were the two children who came to live with her?

The ending is what we refer to as a miracle (*an extraordinary event, often attached to divine intervention*), or a moment of serendipity (*the experience of finding things not sought for*) or synchronicity (*unexpected coincidences, not explainable by conventional means*).
- Have you ever experienced a "magical moment" such as this? What was it?

STUDENT ACTIVITIES:

Using puppets, or performing this story as a skit, retell it to other classes.

Invite a guest speaker to share a personal experience of this era (*an older relative who may be a survivor or whose family may have helped Jews to safety*).

Create and perform a dance to represent this story.

Draw or paint your feelings regarding this story or this era in time.

Explore the mathematical probability of Liese and Karl's being Sonya's lost relatives.

Research more recent periods of ethnic cleansing (*Rwanda, Yugoslavia, etc.*).

Discuss what brings people to this kind of thinking—and action.

What can individuals do to prevent this? Politicians? Governments?

Discuss and plan ways to bring peace to the planet—one person at a time (*starting in your classroom, your school, your community, state, nation, and the world*).

Begin a journal to capture the daily gifts in your life (*it can be called Miracle Journal, Magical Moments, Serendipity in my Day, Bits of Synchronicity, etc.*). Focus on these positive moments to help attract and create more of them for yourself.

She Didn't Pray for a Miracle

One who has compassion for others
will receive compassion from Heaven.

Talmud, Tractate Shabbat

That morning, as every morning, Sonya awoke from a nightmare, her heart thudding. She had heard it all again so clearly—the shouts of the soldiers, the pounding on the door. Quickly, she got out of bed, pressing her hands to her head. She could not, would not, let the past intrude on her. After a moment, she willed herself back to calmness, and then, methodically, she began dressing for work.

Sonya had escaped from Hitler's Germany the year before. She and her family had been active in the resistance movement in their small city—and they had paid for it. Her husband had been taken away in the night. For questioning, the SS men had said. But as they led him out, he and Sonya had managed a brief embrace. They knew it was farewell. Her brother-in-law had disappeared in the same way; her sister, niece, and nephew had been taken off to work as slave laborers in a weapons factory.

Last of all, the soldiers had come for Sonya's son. They had arrested him at school. That time there wasn't even the chance for a good-bye. Shortly afterwards, Sonya had been smuggled out of Germany through American intervention, and she resettled in New York City. An apartment had been found for her, and a job as well, doing alterations and fine needlework in a large department store. She had a life—but not really. To survive, Sonya had not only sealed up her past, she had closed herself off. During the day, she was as removed from the rest of the world as if she was a stone. In fact, that's how she thought of herself. As made of stone. Only at night, as she slept, would the unwanted past come creeping back.

At the store, Sonya did her work efficiently and well—and silently. She never spoke to any of the people who sat near her, and they knew better than to try and speak to her. At lunch, too, she sat alone.

Only on this day, as she sat in the store cafeteria, a voice interrupted her.

Sonya looked up, startled. "Mrs. Stein!" She gestured to the heavyset woman in the elaborate hat. "Yes, please, please sit."

Mrs. Stein was on the refugee assistance committee that had found Sonya her apartment and her job. "We have two children, from Germany," Mrs. Stein began. "They've been through so much. The girl is ten; the boy is seven. They need a home. Not just a place to live, a home. I thought maybe you needed someone, too."

Ten and seven. The exact ages her niece and nephew would have been now. Of course, she couldn't take these children. They'd be living reminders of the past. Sonya shook her head. "I cannot."

"Will you at least think about it, Sonya? I'll come back tomorrow and you can give me your answer then."

"There's no need," Sonya said stiffly. "I cannot take them."

For a few moments more, she felt Mrs. Stein's eyes on her. Kindly eyes, but eyes that saw too much. Sonya kept her head down until the woman moved away.

Sonya worked faster than usual that afternoon and left work early. She hurried home, turned off the lights, and crawled into bed. That's what she did on the bad days, struggling alone in the darkness to keep the door shut on the past. But tonight it wasn't working and she knew why. The mention of those children had started up memories she couldn't stop. The ache within became an actual physical pain. The only way she could ease it was with tears. For the first time since she'd left Germany, Sonya began crying.

Sobbing, stumbling, she went to the closet and pulled out the small satchel she'd carried with her from Germany. Wrapped in heavy cloth were three photographs: her husband, her son, and her sister. Tenderly, she unwrapped the pictures and then she set them on the bureau. It hurt to look at them . . . but they also brought comfort. She began to remember the good times again, the happy times as well as the bad. And she knew that she had to start reaching out again, not only for herself, but for the people in the pictures. She had to carry on for all of them.

Sonya knelt by her bed. It had been a long time since she'd prayed, and the words came hard. "I want to come alive again," she whispered. "I don't know how, but I'm hoping you can help me. Amen."

It had been a very disjointed kind of prayer, but maybe God would understand.

For the first time since her husband had been taken, Sonya slept through the night. And when she awoke, it was naturally, peacefully. She knew what she had to do. She would take the children! That would be the first step in reaching out.

At noon, Sonya stood nervously at the door to the cafeteria, watching for Mrs. Stein. As soon as she saw her, she started to speak, "The children—they still need a home?"

"Yes, but . . ."

"Then I will take them! It will be crowded, my apartment is so tiny, but we'll manage. I want to take them!"

Mrs. Stein's face broke into a big smile. She took Sonya's hand. "Good! I'll bring them over tonight."

Right after work, Sonya began baking the traditional German pastries she hadn't made in so long. She would reach out to those children with good food—and love. They would be shy, of course. Maybe they would even be like she had been—closed off, closed in. But it didn't matter. She would keep trying.

"Sonya!" It was Mrs. Stein. Quickly, Sonya opened the door. The girl stood on one side of Mrs. Stein, the boy on the other. Sonya's heart lurched. They looked so sad. And why shouldn't they? They'd lost everything—and everyone. And there was something else, too, something strangely familiar about them that tugged at her.

"Please come in," she said. Each child carried a small satchel and wore clean clothes that didn't quite fit. The look of a refugee, Sonya thought. The look she herself had worn not so long ago. Was that why they seemed so familiar? Because they reminded her of the other refugee children she'd seen on the ship coming to America?

"Sonya," Mrs. Stein said, "this is Liese and Karl."

Her niece's and nephew's names. Sonya's stomach dropped away; her heart began beating hard. It couldn't be. Things like that didn't happen. It would be a miracle, and she hadn't prayed for a miracle.

She'd only prayed to be able to reach out again. But still she took a step closer, searching the children's faces. It had been so long, and they would have changed in so many ways. As she had changed.

Puzzled, Mrs. Stein said, "Is something wrong, Sonya?"

Sonya shook her head, still staring. The girl lifted her eyes, wide and dark—wrenchingly familiar. It was as if she was searching Sonya's face, too. And then the boy cried out.

"Karl?" Mrs. Stein asked. "Are you all right?"

The boy pointed a trembling hand toward the three pictures Sonya had set out the night before. He ran toward the bureau, grabbed up the picture of Sonya's sister and held it to his heart.

"Mama," he whispered.

Cynthia Mercati

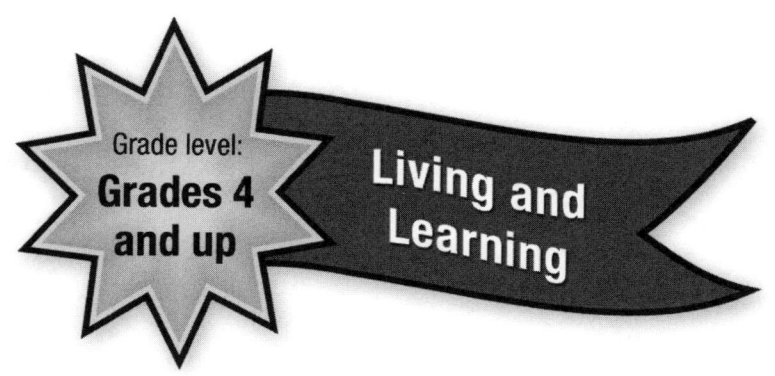

TITLE: **A FRIEND . . .**

BOOK: **Chicken Soup for the Kid's Soul**

PAGE: **57**

TIME TO READ: **1 minute for the story, 6 minutes for the follow-up examples**

TOPICS: **Living and Learning**
Friendship and community
Communication

AGE LEVEL: **Grades 4 and up**

SYNOPSIS: **This story is about confronting a close childhood friend who moved, changed, and began doing harmful things. It follows with viewpoints on friendship from students, ages nine to fourteen.**

NOTES TO TEACHER:

While it takes place in the author's middle school years, the story, the plans, and the discussion of changing friendships are appropriate for all ages.

You may wish to post the follow-up examples, or share them over a period of time, rather than to read them all at once.

Other recommended stories on friendship are:
"Tom(my) Boy," page 89, *Chicken Soup for the Teenage Soul IV.*
"Forever Beyond a Goodbye," page 143, *Chicken Soup for the Teenage Soul on Love and Friendship.*

Chicken Soup for the Kid's Soul, A Friend . . .

PRE-QUESTIONS:

List qualities you expect in a close friendship.

Do attached worksheet listing what you want in a friend.

List your three closest friends. Tell what it is that you most admire about them.

Read Story

POST-QUESTIONS:

How honest are you with your closest friends?

Would you tell them if . . .
- they had bad breath?
- their boyfriend or girlfriend was cheating on them?
- your vehemently disagreed with their political or religious views?
- you had a deep, dark secret that no one else knows?
- you were worried about their health?
- you were worried about their behavior?

Would you tell a trusted adult if you were worried about a close friend's behavior being illegal, immoral, or dangerous?

Where do we learn about how to be a good friend?

Have you lost any close friends because one or both of you changed your values or behaviors?

Discuss the concept of having different friends for different reasons (*help with homework, go to a movie, need advice, go for a bike ride, have a need to "vent," want a good laugh, need to cry, play a sport, want a totally honest answer about something, get some ice cream, etc.*).

STUDENT ACTIVITIES:

Write your best friend a letter of appreciation. Thank this person for the qualities they possess and the things they have done to enhance your friendship.

Write and/or illustrate a children's book on friendship. You might partner with a classmate, with one person writing the story and the other doing the illustrations.

Make a large, artistic poster of friendship qualities. Laminate it and hang in the classroom or your bedroom.

Make a book or poster of quotes and favorite "friendship" pictures.

Write some poetry about friendship.

Make a collage of your favorite friendship snapshots.

Complete the friendship recipe worksheets that follow.

WHAT I WANT IN A FRIEND

In the space below, list the qualities that you seek in your closest friends.

_____

_____

_____

_____

_____

_____

_____

_____

_____

_____

_____

_____

_____

_____

_____

_____

_____

_____

_____

_____

_____

_____

Now, go back over your list and put an asterisk (*) next to any of the qualities that you possess. In general, we seek people who are much like ourselves. If you have very few *s above, you may find that you are not being the kind of friend that you seek. Or that the people you "hang out with" are not really friends.

FRIENDSHIP RECIPE

Cook up a friendship recipe by deciding which ingredients are necessary to create a healthy relationship. Use the words on the side of the page and the example to help you. Be sure to add some of your own words to the lists.

Power
Prestige
Kindness
Humor
Love
Strength
Honesty
Appreciation
Caring
Sensitivity
Loyalty
Wealth
Intelligence
Affection
Sincerity

Enthusiasm
Faith
Respect
Trust
Morals
Understanding
Joy
Abundance
Optimism
Generosity
Responsibility
Strength
Patience
Devotion
Dedication

> *Example:*
> **Love Recipe**
> MIX:
> 3 tablespoons of kindness
> 2 cups respect
> ADD:
> 1 cup of sensitivity
> 2 teaspoons understanding
> a dash of humor
> a sprinkle of honesty
>
> Stir thoroughly and enjoy!

Recipe Terms

Blend
Cut in
Whisk
Dash
Garnish
Mash
Bake
Mix
Stir
Boil
Broil
Chop
Dice
Marinate
Poach
Simmer

Blanch
Dip
Sprinkle
Combine
Squeeze
Pour
Toss
Beat
Fry
Baste
Chill
Cool
Grate
Mince
Saute
Steam

Title: _____

Ingredients:

_____

_____

_____

_____

_____

_____

_____

Directions: _____

_____

_____

RELATIONSHIP RECIPE QUESTIONS

1. Which ingredients do you most value in your relationships?

2. Which ingredients are the easiest/hardest for you to offer others? Why?

3. Which ingredients are the easiest/hardest for you to receive from others? Why?

4. Which ingredients are currently missing from your relationships?

5. What steps will you take to develop them? List these steps.

A Friend . . .

Friendships multiply joys and divide grief.

Thomas Fuller

Recently, one of my best friends, whom I've shared just about everything with since the first day of kindergarten, spent the weekend with me. Since I moved to a new town several years ago, we've both always looked forward to the few times a year when we can see each other.

Over the weekend we spent hours and hours, staying up late into the night, talking about the people she was hanging around with. She started telling me stories about her new boyfriend, about how he experimented with drugs and was into other self-destructive behavior. I was blown away! She told me how she had been lying to her parents about where she was going and even sneaking out to see this guy because they didn't want her around him. No matter how hard I tried to tell her that she deserved better, she didn't believe me. Her self-respect seemed to have disappeared.

I tried to convince her that she was ruining her future and heading for big trouble. I felt like I was getting nowhere. I just couldn't believe that she really thought that it was acceptable to hang with a bunch of losers, especially her boyfriend.

By the time she left, I was really worried about her and exhausted by the experience. It had been so frustrating, I had come close to telling her several times during the weekend that maybe we had just grown too far apart to continue our friendship—but I didn't. I put the power of friendship to the ultimate test. We'd been friends for far too long. I had to hope that she valued me enough to know that I was trying to save her from hurting herself. I wanted to believe that our friendship could conquer anything.

A few days later, she called to say that she had thought long and hard about our conversation, and then she told me that she had broken up with her boyfriend. I just listened on the other end of the phone with tears of joy running down my face. It was one of the truly rewarding moments in my life. Never had I been so proud of a friend.

A Friend . . .
Won't allow you to self-destruct.
Will take all the time that's needed, no matter what time of day, to listen to your problems and give you her best advice.
Is someone who can open up and be herself around you.
Will swallow her pride to take your advice.
Will never write you off.

—Danielle Fishel

Is someone who keeps promises, tells the truth, makes time for you, and is someone to laugh with.

—Leah Hatcher, age fourteen

Is a person who knows what you are saying, even if you're not talking.
Understands what you're feeling, even if you don't understand your own feelings.
Will always forgive you, usually before you forgive yourself.

—Sarah Bennett, age thirteen

Will do something for you and not ask for a favor in return.
Comes and cheers for you at your games.

—Roman Zaccuri, age twelve

Will always say that you look great—even if you don't.
Will tell you if you have something in your teeth.

—Katie Adnoff, age thirteen

Doesn't talk bad about you.

—Martina Miller, age twelve

Has a special place in your heart and is always there when you need them.

—Meghan Gilstrap, age fourteen

Is someone who will hold in a laugh when you make a fool out of yourself.
Stays after school when you get in trouble to help you write 250 sentences.

—Danielle Uselton, age twelve

Is someone that you respect, who respects you, and shares their feelings.

—Jorge Prieto, age eleven

Makes you feel good about yourself.
Encourages you to reach for your goals.
Never gets jealous of you.

—Megan Preizer, age twelve

Shares the good times and helps out by listening during the bad times.

—Molly Oliver, age nine

Never tells a secret they promise not to tell.
Doesn't talk about you to other friends.
Is forever and for life.

—Angie Porter, age twelve

Is there for you even when you feel like the world is against you.

—MeShelle Locke, age thirteen

Will open the door for you no matter how late it is.
Would never betray you.
Helps you make new friends.

—Eun Joo Shin, age thirteen

Might get in fights with you but will always forgive you.

—Gina Pozielli, age twelve

Is someone who will share lunch with you if you forgot yours.

—Hayley Valvano, age twelve

Doesn't laugh when someone makes a mean joke about you.

—Brittany Miller, age twelve

Likes you for who you are and not what you look like, because that is
    what really matters.

—Marleigh Dunlap, age eleven

Never makes fun of anything you have or do.

—Jessica Ann Farley, age ten

Helps you get up when you fall at the roller-skating rink.

—Elisabeth Hansen, age twelve

Is not about beauty or popularity, but it is someone who likes your personality.
Is with you to the end.

—Renny Usbay, age twelve

Doesn't always think the way that you do.
Is a person who will tell on you when you are doing drugs or smoking.
Is someone that tells you when you are wrong, but not in a bad way.

—Stephanie Lane, age twelve

Is someone that your own mom trusts too.

—Mike Curtis, age thirteen

Is not afraid to be seen with you.
Will laugh at your jokes, even if they're bad.

—Geoff Rill, age twelve

Never blames everything on you.

—Tania Garcia, age thirteen

Will give you the last bite of their candy bar.
Is a present that you can open again and again.

—Natalie Citro, age twelve

Is someone who believes you when nobody else will.

—Ashley Parole, age twelve

Danielle Fishel

TITLE: **WHAT A DIFFERENCE A WALK MAKES**

BOOK: Chicken Soup for the Nature Lover's Soul

PAGE: **334**

TIME TO READ: **1 minute**

TOPICS: **Living and Learning**
Attitude and perspective

AGE LEVEL: Grades 3 and up

SYNOPSIS: While walking, an encounter with a ninety-year-old provides important insights on having happiness in life.

NOTES TO TEACHER:

Having your students list 30–200 things that make them happy is a great family activity. However, we suggest that you assign it as extra credit for family involvement. The task is made easier for the student, yet the student is not penalized if his or her family is uncooperative. A shorter list is more appropriate for younger students.

We also suggest that you select one or two "happy package" activities for your students to share, or allow the students to choose their favorite "package" (used with permission from *100 Ways to Enhance Self-Concept in the Classroom.* See Resources, page 378, for full citation).

We feel it is critical for young people of all ages to learn how to express feelings appropriately. This is most successful under the structure and guidance of an emotionally safe classroom environment.

For a related story, read "Happiness," found in *Chicken Soup for the Teenage Soul IV,* page 139.

Chicken Soup for the Nature Lover's Soul,
What a Difference a Walk Makes

PRE-QUESTIONS:

Define happiness (*a state of pleasure, joy, contentment, good fortune*).

What makes you happy?

Do you ever take a simple walk and think about life?

Read Story

POST-QUESTIONS:

What important life lesson was learned on this walk?

What was the old lady's secret to happiness?

In this moment, what things create a sense of happiness or gratitude for you? See how many simple things you can list (*toilets that flush, electricity, warm clothing, bicycles, friends, books to read, pencils, family, shoes and socks, pets, being able to hear your favorite music, etc.*).

STUDENT ACTIVITIES:

Do the **Happy Package** activity as described by your teacher on page 140, (*100 Ways to Enhance Self-Concept in the Classroom.* See Resources, page 378, for full citation).

Make a list of 20, 50, 100, or 200 "Things That Make Me Happy."

- Extra credit will be given if you get your family involved in compiling the list. You must obtain their signatures for the extra credit points.

Bring in your favorite happy music, and create a happy dance to accompany it.

Create a deck of cards showing and listing happy things in your life.

Create a "Happiness" bulletin board for the classroom.

Make a series of happy posters to display throughout the building.

Create a series of happy story problems for your math class.

See if you can create a happy assignment for each of your classes.

Start a Gratitude Journal. Every day, write five things for which you are grateful. Read your list every night at bedtime and each day upon awakening. Notice if your daily attitude improves with this habit.

HAPPY PACKAGE

The first duty to children is to make them happy.

Sir Thomas Fowell Buxton

Have the class sit in a circle.

Ask the students to pretend that they can have a package of any size or shape they want. Inside this imaginary box they are to place whatever it is in the whole wide world that would make them happy.

Ask the students to share with the rest of the group what would be in the box and why it would make them happy.

Ask the students to share with the class things they have brought from home that make them happy.

Ask the students to leave the group, go find an object in the class that makes them happy, and return to the group and share the object.

Ask the students to share with the group a happy incident that happened in the past week.

Ask the students to tell the class about a person who makes them happy.

Ask the students to describe how it feels to be happy. Where do they feel it? How do they know?

Ask the students to complete the sentence: "Happiness is . . ."*

Used with permission, 100 Ways to Enhance Self-Concept in the Classroom, Jack Canfield and Harold C. Wells (Needham Heights, MA: Allyn & Bacon, 1976).

What a Difference a Walk Makes

Be part of the miraculous moment.

Thich Nhat Hanh

My father and I had walked together a lot, but after he underwent both heart bypass and back surgery, we faced the possibility that his long-distance hiking days were over at seventy. But miraculously, only one year after his setbacks, he was able to join me on a 180-mile coast-to-coast trek across Wales.

One late afternoon, while traversing a long, curving ridge, we came upon an elderly woman and her beagle hiking toward us. Teetering along on a walking stick, she wore a motoring cap and clutched a bunch of wildflowers.

I said hello, and after some discussion she told us that she was almost ninety. I studied her carefully and couldn't believe what great shape she was in. She seemed so fit and content.

"What's the secret to a long and happy life?" I asked.

She smiled and spoke softly, "Moments." There was a quiet pause before she carried on. "Moments are all we get. A true walker understands this."

She bid us good-bye and continued on her way, her dog trotting a few steps in front. Just before she disappeared into the horizon, I looked back at her, plodding ahead with timeless poise and bearing, and sent a smile to my father.

She was right; that is all we get.

Bruce Northam

TITLE: **A TRUE HERO**

BOOK: Chicken Soup for the Baseball Fan's Soul

PAGE: 157

TIME TO READ: 4 minutes

TOPICS: **Making a Difference**
Overcoming obstacles
Attitude and perspective
Sport—baseball

AGE LEVEL: Grades 1 and up

SYNOPSIS: Jim Abbott is special, not just because he is a professional baseball player with only one hand, but because of how he helps a young boy who has a missing arm.

NOTES TO TEACHER:

For two other hero-baseball stories, read "True Heroes Earn the Title," in *Chicken Soup for the Baseball Fan's Soul*, page 147, and "Roberto's Last At-Bat," in *Chicken Soup for the Volunteer's Soul*, on page 53. Both stories are about the legendary Roberto Clemente.

Chicken Soup for the Baseball Fan's Soul, A True Hero

PRE-QUESTIONS:

Who are the people you admire, or who you might consider to be heroes?
- What qualities do they possess that makes them so special to you?

Read Story

POST-QUESTIONS:

What made Jim Abbott so special?

What did he do in this story to make a difference in someone else's life?

Do you think that all athletes are heroes in some way?
- Explain your answer.

STUDENT ACTIVITIES:

Create a bulletin board of heroes.

Research some current heroes.
- Write a one-page report on what they have done, and what makes them a hero to you.

Give a one or two minute speech on your favorite hero.

Read or watch *Armed With Hope,* or read *No Excuses* (see Resources, pages 378 and 379, for full citations).
- Compare Jim Abbott with John Foppe or Kyle Maynard.
- What do these men have in common?
- Create a Venn diagram to show their commonalities and differences.

Debate the pros and cons of being a hero-athlete.

A True Hero

The life of a Major League baseball player involves more than playing baseball. Especially for those who are popular.

Jim Abbott was one of the most popular players from the moment he first donned a Major League uniform for the California Angels in 1989. Abbott, just twenty-one at the time, was one of the rare few who skips the minor leagues completely and begins his professional career in the big leagues.

But that's not what made Abbott so special to so many.

Abbott was born without a right hand. In fact, Abbott's right arm extended from his shoulder to just past the elbow joint.

Abbott, though, didn't make the big leagues because people felt sorry for him. Abbott could pitch.

The Angels took a chance on him by drafting him out of the University of Michigan, and he proved in spring training that year that he was ready for the big leagues.

Using a skill he developed as a kid, Abbott could pitch with his left hand, then quickly transfer a right-hander's glove from the stub of his right arm onto his left hand, in case he had to field the ball.

If a ball was hit back to him, Abbott would catch it, stick the glove under his right armpit, then pull the ball out with his left hand so he could throw it again. And he did all of this in a second or two.

Abbott became a media magnet. Wherever he went, reporters wanted to hear his story. Abbott was overwhelmed, but never lost his pleasant disposition.

Abbott had a smile for everyone, writers and fans alike.

Many times the media relations department of a Major League team gets requests for fans to meet their favorite baseball players. Abbott was no different.

What was different about one particular fan was what made him similar to Abbott.

The Angels had set up a meeting between Abbott and a young boy from the Midwest. The boy, about nine or ten years old, had lost an arm in a farming accident.

Before one game during a long and arduous baseball season, the boy was brought onto the field to meet Abbott. The boy was obviously nervous, his body language telling the story. Head down, shoulders slumped forward, he had no idea what he was in for.

Abbott and the boy met on the field during batting practice before a game. But they weren't getting much privacy. The media are allowed to remain on the field up to forty-five minutes before game time, and there were plenty of curious onlookers.

So Abbott had an idea. He took the boy down the left-field line and away from anyone who wanted to get close. The two stood in the outfield, talking, watching batting practice, and laughing for about an hour.

When the two returned to the dugout after batting practice, the boy's eyes sparkled. His head was up and his chest was thrust forward. Abbott was asked what he said to the boy, but he wouldn't reveal what was said.

That was about ten years ago, and the boy is now an adult. I often wonder whatever became of him, but after his meeting with Abbott, I have no doubt he is leading a happy and productive life. Abbott, after all, was living proof for the boy that he could do anything he wanted. Even pitch in the big leagues.

Joe Haakenson

Grade level:
Grades 5 and up

Making a Difference

TITLE: **DO IT NOW!**

BOOK: **A 2nd Helping of Chicken Soup for the Soul**

PAGE: **46**

TIME TO READ: **5 minutes**

TOPICS: **Making a Difference**
            On love
            Communication

AGE LEVEL: **Grades 5 and up**

SYNOPSIS: A teacher gives an "I love you" assignment to a class of adult students. A middle-aged man in the class completes the assignment with his father just two days before his dad has a heart attack.

NOTES TO TEACHER:

It is important to stress the key concept of this story—Do it now!—since none of us knows what tomorrow will bring.

The ***Unfinished Business*** assignment is a powerful tool to accompany this story. Many students in the past have reported that it was the most important assignment they have ever done (after it was over!). They strongly resisted doing it at the onset, so a firm deadline is important. We suggest two weeks.

We also highly recommend that you do this assignment at the same time. Anna waited until she had only fifteen minutes left on her deadline to tell her mother that she loved her. The best that her mother could say was, "We feel the same way." It was not the outcome Anna wanted, but she had said what she needed to say. This became a perfect example to share with her classes in the coming years.

We suggest you use this opportunity to share your own personal stories where seizing the moment, or not procrastinating, was important.

A recommended related story is "My One Regret," found on page 284 of *Chicken Soup for the Preteen Soul.*

ALL LEVELS:

PRE-QUESTIONS:

In your journal, write about the following:
- Have you ever had a time when you wished you had, or hadn't, said or done something?
- If so, what was it?

Read Story

POST-QUESTIONS:

Write about what might have happened if the man hadn't told his father "I love you," and his dad had died two days later.

Discuss the feelings this story brings about.

Is there a difference in how males and females deal with these feelings?
- If so, what?

Is it important for both sexes to learn how to share feelings?
- Why, or why not?

STUDENT ACTIVITIES:

Do the ***Unfinished Business*** assignment found in the Appendix, page 357.

Do the ***Warm Fuzzy*** assignment found in the Appendix, page 352.

Write letters to special teachers, friends, or relatives, telling them how they are important to you.

Do It Now!

If we discovered that we had only five minutes left to say all that we wanted to say, every telephone booth would be occupied by people calling other people to stammer that they loved them.

Christopher Morley

In a class I teach for adults, I recently did the "unpardonable." I gave the class homework! The assignment was to "go to someone you love within the next week and tell them you love them. It has to be someone you have never said those words to before, or at least haven't shared those words with for a long time."

Now that doesn't sound like a very tough assignment, until you stop to realize that most of the men in that group were over thirty-five and were raised in the generation of men that were taught that expressing emotions is not "macho." Showing feelings or crying (heaven forbid!) was just not done. So this was a very threatening assignment for some.

At the beginning of our next class, I asked if someone wanted to share what happened when they told someone they loved them. I fully expected one of the women to volunteer, as was usually the case, but on this evening one of the men raised his hand. He appeared quite moved and a bit shaken.

As he unfolded out of his chair (all six feet, two inches of him), he began by saying, "Dennis, I was quite angry with you last week when you gave us this assignment. I didn't feel that I had anyone to say those words to, and besides, who were you to tell me to do something that personal? But as I began driving home my conscience started talking to me. It was telling me that I knew exactly who I needed to say 'I love you' to. You see, five years ago, my father and I had a vicious disagreement and really never resolved it since that time. We avoided seeing each other unless we absolutely had to at Christmas or other family gatherings. But even then, we hardly spoke to each other. So, last Tuesday, by the time I got home I had convinced myself I was going to tell my father I loved him.

"It's weird, but just making that decision seemed to lift a heavy load off my chest.

"When I got home, I rushed into the house to tell my wife what I was going to do. She was already in bed, but I woke her up anyway. When I told her, she didn't just get out of bed, she catapulted out and hugged me, and for the first time in our married life she saw me cry. We stayed up half the night drinking coffee and talking. It was great!

"The next morning I was up bright and early. I was so excited I could hardly sleep. I got to the office early and accomplished more in two hours than I had the whole day before.

"At 9:00 I called my dad to see if I could come over after work. When he answered the phone, I just said, 'Dad, can I come over after work tonight? I have something to tell you.' My dad responded with a grumpy, 'Now what?' I assured him it wouldn't take long, so he finally agreed.

"At 5:30, I was at my parents' house ringing the doorbell, praying that Dad would answer the door. I was afraid if Mom answered that I would chicken out and tell her instead. But as luck would have it, Dad did answer the door.

"I didn't waste any time—I took one step in the door and said, 'Dad, I just came over to tell you that I love you.'

"It was as if a transformation came over my dad. Before my eyes his face softened, the wrinkles seemed to disappear, and he began to cry. He reached out and hugged me and said, 'I love you too, son, but I've never been able to say it.'

"It was such a precious moment I didn't want to move. Mom walked by with tears in her eyes. I just waved and blew her a kiss. Dad and I hugged for a moment longer and then I left. I hadn't felt that great in a long time.

"But that's not even my point. Two days after that visit, my dad, who had heart problems but didn't tell me, had an attack and ended up in the hospital, unconscious. I don't know if he'll make it.

"So my message to all of you in this class is this: don't wait to do the things you know need to be done. What if I had waited to tell my dad—maybe I will never get the chance again! Take the time to do what you need to do, and do it now!"

Dennis E. Mannering

Grade level:
Grades 3 and up

Making a Difference

TITLE: IF I COULD CHANGE THE WORLD FOR THE BETTER, I WOULD . . .

BOOK: **Chicken Soup for the Preteen Soul**

PAGE: **25**

TIME TO READ: **8 minutes total (we recommend reading one example a day, rather than all of them at one sitting).**

TOPICS: **Making a Difference**
Giving and receiving
World issues

AGE LEVEL: **Grades 3 and up**

SYNOPSIS: **Several students, ages nine to eighteen, tell what they would do to change the world for the better.**

NOTES TO TEACHER:

It is suggested that you have students write their own statements to share in dyads or **Circle Talks** (Appendix, page 311), and then share as a full class discussion. After classroom sharing, read them the examples from the *Chicken Soup for the Soul* story list.

Chicken Soup for the Preteen Soul,
If I Could Change the World for the Better, I Would . . .

PRE-QUESTIONS:

Complete the following statement in writing: "If I Could Change the World for the Better, I Would_____"

Share in dyads, **Circle Groups** (Appendix, page 311), and then as a class.

Read Story

POST-QUESTIONS:

Is there anything you would like to add to your list after hearing everything so far?

How would you like to be remembered when you die?

Do worksheet **C** (Appendix, page 373).

STUDENT ACTIVITIES:

Select one or two concepts from your list on "changing the world" to work on as a year-long class project.

Design a bumper sticker with an important message that you wish to share with the world.
  • Present your design to the class in a one-minute speech, explaining why this message is so important to you.
  • Laminate and post these signs throughout the building.

You are marching for a *positive* cause.
  • Design a sign to carry.
  • Present your sign in a one-minute speech, explaining why this message is important to you.

If I Could Change the World for the Better, I Would . . .

Melt every cold heart and mold them into new warm ones.

—Scarlett Kotlarczyk, age eleven

Help people realize that people like me who learn and do things differently than them are still really the same underneath it all. We want to be liked and smiled at.

—Wilson Cook, age nine

Find another way to test drugs instead of using them on animals.

—Brandon Barger, age thirteen

Make it so every kid would have a warm meal, and no one would go starving.

—Timothy Blevans, age eleven

Open a house for all of the orphans of the world. I would get lots of people to help me take care of them.

—Stacey Bergman, age fifteen

Stop kids from making fun of other kids. Prejudice is just what we don't need. Kids hate being ridiculed.

—Rachel Force, age eleven

Make people realize that it's not what other people think of you, but what you think of yourself. You shouldn't put yourself down when people say cruel things about you or do things to you, because they're the ones that need a little chicken soup for their soul.

—Sarah Hampton, age fourteen

Travel back in time, and make sure the people who invented drugs and smoking never discovered or invented them.

—Lisa Cline, age eleven

Find a cure for diabetes. My little brother's friend has juvenile diabetes. Every year my family "Walks for the Cure." I wish there wasn't such a disease because he has to take shots and stuff.

—Kristin Boden, age thirteen

Want everyone to keep an open mind about everything, because with an open mind, you can accomplish anything.

—Annemarie Staley, age fourteen

Make everything solar powered including factories, vehicles, and all types of machinery. By doing this, there wouldn't be as much air pollution and people could breathe easier.

—Tracye Paye, age thirteen

Give every child a grandmother like mine. She may not be rich and famous, but she has enough love in her heart for her twenty-one grandchildren and great-grandchildren, and plenty more to spare. How many millionaires can say that?

—Casey Singleton, age eighteen

Make it so that kids don't have to go through child abuse.

—Kristen Hamilton, age eleven

Make every capable person do one hour of community service per month. This would include cleaning up rubbish, bathing and feeding homeless people, and planting trees.

—Trevor Burton, age nineteen

Make sure that no one in the world is harmed because of their religion.

—Pratima Neti, age eleven

Stop child labor, which is unfortunately still going on in this world. Children deserve the right to live, and working at a very young age will not give you that freedom.

—Jessilyn Yoo, age twelve

Pay teachers more, because teachers are the foundation of all learning. Without teachers, the world would just be a useless space full of useless people.

—Angela Rotchstein, age fourteen

Make sure that everybody in the world is able to read. Reading is the world's greatest gift for the mind and imagination.

—Jessica Behles, age fourteen

Have everybody just agree to disagree instead of fighting. After all, we are all different, and have our own ways; this is the spice of life.

—Jill Ananda, age fourteen

Plant the rainforests back all over the world, so that the trees will grow and the rivers will flow. I would bring back the animals that have died out, but without the dinosaurs!

—Kyla Cangemi, age ten

Make the world a happier place with no bombings or school shootings.

—Chap Arst, age thirteen

Show everyone the love that my adoptive mother showed me. I was angry at the world because I thought no one loved me or could ever love me. No one wanted a thirteen-year-old girl, but she came along and showed me that people could and do care about me. I would definitely give that to any person in this world. Love is all the world needs.

—Mia Sifford, age seventeen

Give every child a blanket, not only to keep them warm, but to snuggle with. We each need something to hold onto, and a fuzzy blanket would help keep away the problems of the world, if only for a moment or two.

—Steve Hayden, age thirteen

Let all the kids in the whole world know that they can succeed in anything that they put their hearts into. There is always a solution for problems; you just have to look in your heart to find them.

—Alysia Escalante, age thirteen

Fix that hole in the ozone layer so the heat of the sun won't kill us.

—Nikole Pegues, age eleven

[EDITORS' NOTE: *Since the printing of this story, education, awareness, and a concerted effort have largely corrected this problem.*]

Ask everyone in school to say one nice thing to another person every day. Have every family tell each other they love one another.

—William Baun, age twelve

Have people talk to each other and listen more, and make sure that everybody would have enough play time.

—Neil Gogno, age nine

Stop all the violence that is on TV, which is where people get the idea that it is okay to hurt or kill someone. When we were channel surfing, my stepmom and I saw seven guns and three acts of violence all in one minute; even my dog got scared!

—Bethany Hicks, age twelve

Want everyone to have at least one best friend that they could count on.

—Andrea Hawsey, age eleven

Create vehicles that would run on natural resource waste material to stop the pollution.

—Rosie Huf, age eleven

Get more clubs and activities going so that people would stay away from gangs, drugs, and crimes.

—Stacy Luebbe, age fourteen

Bring back all our lost loved ones for a day.

—Rita Koch, age ten

Make sure that all children in the world can go to school, and have Chicken Soup for the Soul books so they know that they aren't alone.

—Allison Opsitnick, age twelve

TITLE: **IT ONLY TAKES A FEW**

BOOK: **Chicken Soup for the Volunteer's Soul**

PAGE: **247**

TIME TO READ: **2 minutes**

TOPICS: **Making a Difference**
Changing the world
Friends and community
Making choices
Overcoming obstacles

AGE LEVEL: **Grades 4 and up**

SYNOPSIS: This rhyming poem shows how easily people give up on a task, and how you can get "replacements" on board to get important work done, if you are willing to work as a community.

NOTES TO TEACHER:

After reading this poetry to younger students, you may need to break it down, one stanza at a time, for their understanding.

ALL LEVELS:

PRE-QUESTIONS:

How many people does it take to make a change in the world?
Is there any kind of age requirement for making a difference?
  Explain or defend your answers.

Read Story

POST-QUESTIONS:

What is the main message of this poem?
What were the excuses given as each person left the group?
  • Do you believe they were valid or important reasons?
What were the reasons that caused the group to grow again?

STUDENT ACTIVITIES:

Discuss how many people it takes to make changes in the world.
  • What do these people have in common?
  • Are these qualities that you possess, or wish to possess?
Write this piece of poetry in the form of a short story where you are the main character.
Write some poetry about any topic that is near and dear to you (*older students can experiment with different forms such as limericks or Haiku, or rewrite this same story-line as a different poetry form*).
As a class, select a school or community project where it only takes a few to make a difference. Be the one to get it started.

It Only Takes a Few

A group of ten cared about kids,
And had an idea that was very fine.
But one was asked to donate money,
And now there are only nine.

Nine caring people,
Thought helping kids would "be great!"
But one was asked to commit some spare time,
And now there are only eight.

Eight thought that a new youth center,
Would be a special gift from heaven.
But one was asked to join a committee,
And now there are only seven.

Seven concerned about juvenile crime,
Wished it was something that they could fix.
But one was asked to spend time with a teen,
And now there are only six.

Six were thankful for the gifts,
They had acquired in their lives.
But when asked about planned giving,
The six soon became five.

Five were frustrated,
Wishing for just a few more.
But one became tired of people leaving,
And suddenly there are four.

Four people asking themselves,
Will the next one be me?
One asked the question too many times,
Now they are down to three.

With only three remaining,
And so much work to do,
One decides to just give up on kids,
And now there are only two.

But the two that remain are leaders,
And to help kids they will find some more.
They each call up their own best friend,
And suddenly there are four!

Four friends who share a common thought,
Helping kids is great!
They each recruit their own personal banker,
And now their team is eight.

Soon these eight recruit eight more,
And I think you will begin to see,
That the number of people helping kids,
Can start with you and me.

Now you can be like the eight who left,
Or be more like the final two.
But when you make your decision,
Just please remember . . . It only takes a few.

Dave Krause

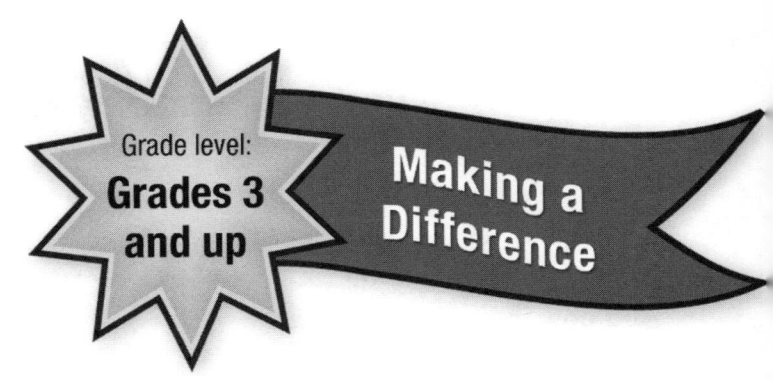

TITLE: **LOVE: THE ONE CREATIVE FORCE**

BOOK: **Chicken Soup for the Soul**

PAGE: **3**

TIME TO READ: **1 minute**

TOPICS: **Making a Difference**
Teacher impact
Overcoming obstacles
Changing the world

AGE LEVEL: **Grades 3 and up**

SYNOPSIS: A sociology class evaluates kids in the Baltimore slums, and "condemns" them to a life of "failure." Twenty years later, another study finds that the surprising success of these young men was due to a teacher.

NOTES TO TEACHER:

This makes a great classroom farewell story. We recommend using it on the last day of class to say goodbye, as well as to provide an opportunity to obtain a final teacher evaluation from your students.

The vocabulary may need to be addressed or modified with younger students.

Chicken Soup for the Soul, Love: The One Creative Force

PRE-QUESTIONS:

What qualities does a good teacher have?

Do you think that teachers can make a difference in students' lives?

- Why, or why not?
- Cite any personal examples you may have.

Read Story

POST-QUESTIONS:

Why do you think that these kids were expected to be failures?

(*Because they lived in the slums.*)

Doesn't that usually result in the self-fulfilling prophecy?

(*What you expect is what you get.*)

Why do you think they turned out to be successful?

(*Because the teacher expected them to be successful.*)

What did the teacher do that made a difference?

(*She showed her love for them.*)

STUDENT ACTIVITIES:

After hearing this story, complete a short, anonymous evaluation that includes the question: "Do you think I care about you?"

- Cite specific examples that show that I either care or do not care about you.

ACTIVITY FOR THE TEACHER—THE LAST FAREWELL:

As students leave the classroom for the final day, have them indicate if they want a handshake, a high-five, or a hug as they leave.

You, the teacher, stand at the door to honor their farewell request.

Love: The One Creative Force

Spread love everywhere you go: first of all in your own house.
Give love to your children, to your wife or husband, to a next
door neighbor. . . . Let no one ever come to you without leaving
better and happier. Be the living expression of God's kindness:
kindness in your face, kindness in your eyes, kindness in your
smile, kindness in your warm greeting.

Mother Teresa

A college professor had his sociology class go into the Baltimore slums to get case histories of two hundred young boys. They were asked to write an evaluation of each boy's future. In every case the students wrote, "He hasn't got a chance." Twenty-five years later another sociology professor came across the earlier study. He had his students follow up on the project to see what had happened to these boys. With the exception of twenty boys who had moved away or died, the students learned that 176 of the remaining 180 had achieved more than ordinary success as lawyers, doctors, and businessmen.

The professor was astounded and decided to pursue the matter further. Fortunately, all the men were in the area and he was able to ask each one, "How do you account for your success?" In each case the reply came with feeling, "There was a teacher."

The teacher was still alive, so he sought her out and asked the old but still alert lady what magic formula she had used to pull these boys out of the slums into successful achievement.

The teacher's eyes sparkled and her lips broke into a gentle smile. "It's really very simple," she said. "I loved those boys."

Eric Butterworth

TITLE:	MRS. VIRGINIA DeVIEW, WHERE ARE YOU?
BOOK:	Chicken Soup for the Teenage Soul
PAGE:	170
TIME TO READ:	6 minutes
TOPICS:	**Making a Difference** Teacher impact Following your dream
AGE LEVEL:	Grades 5 and up
SYNOPSIS:	Students at age thirteen are forced to choose a career, and later look back to thank the teacher who made them think about it.

NOTES TO TEACHER:

| Writing a letter of appreciation to a teacher works well as an extra-credit assignment.

Chicken Soup for the Teenage Soul, Mrs. Virginia DeView, Where Are You?

PRE-QUESTIONS:

Think about every teacher that you can remember having had.
- What qualities did they possess that made them a good teacher?
- What, if anything, made each of them a good person?
- What characteristics made them memorable?

When you think of "bad" teachers, what characteristics do you attribute to them?

Can someone be a good person and a horrible teacher, or vice versa?
- Cite examples.

List qualities of your favorite teachers.

Read Story

POST-QUESTIONS:

Does being hard or easy make a teacher good or bad?
- Which one was Mrs. DeView?
- Explain your answers.

Was Mrs. DeView appreciated at the time that she taught her students?
- When, and why, was she appreciated?

Did she ever find out how her students felt about her?
- Why, or why not?

STUDENT ACTIVITIES:

Write your favorite teacher or teachers a letter of appreciation. Otherwise, they may never know of their value to you.

Mrs. Virginia DeView, Where Are You?

There are high spots in all of our lives, and most of them come about through encouragement from someone else.

George Adams

We were sitting in her classroom, giggling, jabbing each other and talking about the latest information of the day, like the peculiar purple-colored mascara Cindy was wearing. Mrs. Virginia DeView cleared her throat and asked us to hush.

"Now," she said smiling, "we are going to discover our professions." The class seemed to gasp in unison. Our professions? We stared at each other. We were only thirteen and fourteen years old. This teacher was nuts.

That was pretty much how the kids looked at Virginia DeView, her hair swirled back in a bun and her large, buck teeth gaping out of her mouth. Because of her physical appearance, she was always an easy target for snickers and cruel jokes among students.

She also made her students angry because she was demanding. Most of us just overlooked her brilliance.

"Yes, you will all be searching for your future professions," she said with a glow on her face—as though this was the best thing she did in her classroom every year. "You will have to do a research paper on your upcoming career. Each of you will have to interview someone in your field, plus give an oral report."

All of us went home confused. Who knows what they want to do at thirteen? I had narrowed it down, however. I liked art, singing, and writing. But I was terrible in art, and when I sang my sisters screamed: "Oh, please shut up." The only thing left was writing.

Every day in her class, Virginia DeView monitored us. Where were we? Who had picked their careers? Finally, most of us had selected something; I picked print journalism. This meant I had to go interview a true-blue newspaper reporter in the flesh, and I was terrified.

I sat down in front of him barely able to speak. He looked at me and said: "Did you bring a pencil or pen?"

I shook my head.

"How about some paper?"

I shook my head again.

Finally, I think he realized I was terrified, and I got my first big tip as a journalist. "Never, never go anywhere without a pen and paper. You never know what you'll run into."

For the next ninety minutes, he filled me with stories of robberies, crime sprees, and fires. He would never forget the tragic fire where four family members were killed in the blaze. He could still smell their burning flesh, he said, and he would never forget that horrid story.

A few days later, I gave my oral report totally from memory, I had been so mesmerized. I got an A on the entire project.

As we neared the end of the school year, some very resentful students decided to get Virginia

DeView back for the hard work she put us through. As she rounded a corner, they shoved a pie into her face as hard as they could. She was slightly injured physically, but it was emotionally that she was really hurt. She didn't return to school for days. When I heard the story, I felt a deep, ugly pit fill my stomach. I felt shame for myself and my fellow students who had nothing better to do than pick on a woman because of how she looked, rather than appreciate her amazing teaching skills.

Years later, I forgot all about Virginia DeView and the careers we selected. I was in college scouting around for a new career. My father wanted me in business, which seemed to be sound advice at the time, except that I had no sense of business skills whatsoever. Then I remembered Virginia DeView and my desire at thirteen to be a journalist. I called my parents.

"I'm changing my major," I announced.

There was a stunned silence on the end of the phone.

"What to?" my father finally asked.

"Journalism."

I could tell in their voices that my parents were very unhappy, but they didn't stop me. They just reminded me how competitive the field was and how all my life I had shied away from competition.

This was true. But journalism did something to me; it was in my blood. It gave me the freedom to go up to total strangers and ask what was going on. It trained me to ask questions and get answers in both my professional and personal lives. It gave me confidence.

For the past twelve years, I've had the most incredible and satisfying reporting career, covering stories from murders to airplane crashes and finally settling in on my forté. I loved to write about the tender and tragic moments of people's lives because somehow I felt it helped them in some way.

When I went to pick up my phone one day, an incredible wave of memories hit me, and I realized that had it not been for Virginia DeView, I would not be sitting at that desk.

She'll probably never know that without her help, I would not have become a journalist and a writer. I suspect I would have been floundering in the business world somewhere, with great unhappiness shadowing me each day. I wonder now how many other students in her class benefited from that career project.

I get asked all the time: "How did you pick journalism?"

"Well, you see, there was this teacher . . ." I always start out. I just wish I could thank her.

I believe that when people reflect back over their school days, there will be this faded image of a single teacher—their very own Virginia DeView. Perhaps you can thank her before it's too late.

Diana L. Chapman

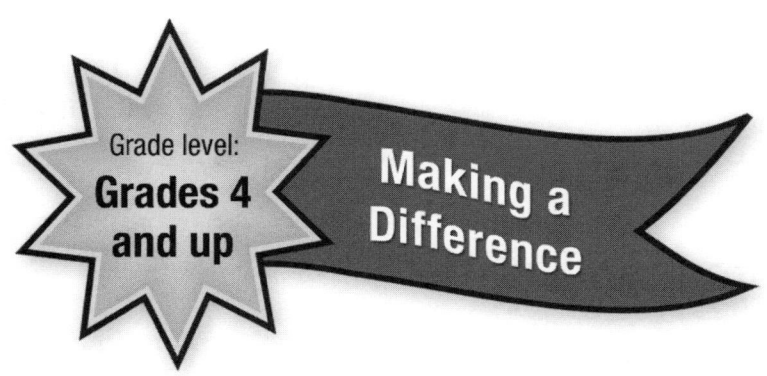

Grade level:
Grades 4 and up

Making a Difference

TITLE: **WEARING 9/11**

BOOK: **Previously unpublished**

TIME TO READ: **6 minutes**

TOPICS: **Making a Difference**
Giving and receiving
Acting with kindness

AGE LEVEL: **Grades 4 and up**

SYNOPSIS: **Wearing a bracelet with the name of a fallen firefighter from 9/11, the author decides to find his family in New York City. Her journey becomes one of many moments and miracles of synchronicity.**

NOTES TO TEACHER:

Use caution when reading to younger students.

We suggest having a tissue box handy for this wonderful story of several magical moments that followed one fallen firefighter from the tragedy of September 11, 2001.

Because this is an event in recent history, check to see if any students have been personally affected, and be prepared for emotions that may surface.

Refer to Appendix, pages 362–364, for handouts on dealing with feelings.

Invite your students to contact the author, Mary Jane West-Delgado at mmjdelgado@comcast.net. She would love to hear their responses about her true story.

Wearing 9/11

PRE-QUESTIONS:

What do you remember about September 11, 2001?

Has anyone here personally lost a family member or friend in the 9/11 tragedy?

What were you doing when you heard the news of this event?

Is there any other event in history that you remember vividly?

    If so, what was it, and why do you remember it so well?

Read Story

POST-QUESTIONS:

What is the main idea behind wearing "name bracelets" of any sort?

What name bracelets did the author wear?

    What did they represent?

Why do you think that she wanted to find the firefighter's family?

Explain why this is a story of hope, not hatred.

STUDENT ACTIVITIES:

Write an imaginary letter to the family of the firefighter.

Interview parents or grandparents to find out what they were doing when:

    • they heard about President Kennedy's assassination;

    • they heard about the landing on the moon;

    • they heard about the ending of the Vietnam War;

    • they heard about the Challenger explosion.

Interview classmates regarding their thoughts about 9/11.

Make this story into a high-level math problem to determine the probability of the author connecting with three people directly related to the name on her bracelet.

Brainstorm things that you could do to bring about peace among people, religions, and nations who differ.

What is stopping you from doing them?

Write a story about what the world would be like if we were all the *same.*

Send an e-mail to the author of this story, telling her what it meant to you. She can be reached at mmjdelgado@comcast.net.

Wearing 9/11

Living in California, I didn't know anyone who was personally affected by the 9/11 tragedy. However, I did want to support the Fire Department of New York (FDNY) families, so I purchased one of the copper name bracelets.

It was similar to the one I had worn during the Vietnam War, holding the name of a POW/MIA. This one was engraved with the name of a heroic New York firefighter with whom I had no connection, except that my own husband is a firefighter.

Looking at the name on the bracelet, I felt compelled to speak with this firefighter's family. I thought they might like to know that the bracelet was being worn by someone who really cared about him. I didn't know where to begin, so I started at the most public place, New York City Hall.

I called directory assistance, got a number and dialed. I had no idea what I would say, but I hoped that something intelligent would spew forth. The lady who answered the phone was polite but seemed preoccupied, so I stated my business as simply and quickly as possible. She began crying uncontrollably and then transferred me to another clerk. When I stated my request to the second lady, she too, burst into tears and transferred me to a third clerk who happened to be a man. I felt badly that I was rekindling emotions that obviously still ran high, so I apologized to the man before I repeated my request.

"I live in California and I purchased one of the copper name bracelets of a fallen firefighter. I want to contact his family."

He asked what the firefighter's name was. I read him the name that was carved on the bracelet I was wearing.

There was a pause.

I was beginning to feel that my request was just too much to ask of the people who had lived through this tragedy. I was ready to give up when he said in a shaky voice, "The women whom you spoke to before me are the mother and the sister of that fallen firefighter."

He said he would give them a hug for me, then he thanked me and hung up. I thought that was the end of my quest.

Several months later, it was time for the annual Fallen Firefighters Memorial in Washington, D.C. It is a ceremony that honors all firefighters from throughout the United States who died in the line of duty over the previous twelve months. This year, the FDNY would have a much larger presence than in the past. My husband was chosen by lottery to represent the Ventura County Firefighters at that ceremony. I accompanied him.

On October 10, 2002, approximately one mile of Pennsylvania and Constitution Avenues were closed down for this memorial occasion. This historic route was lined with thousands of people standing silently and tearfully saluting as thirty-seven buses passed carrying the grieving families of the entire nation's fallen firefighters. The solemn parade was lead by an honor guard of proud comrades from every state, and the bagpipe brigade repeatedly playing their familiar refrain of tragedy and sorrow.

Later, we all arrived at the huge MCI Center for the official ceremony. Over the next four hours, each name of a fallen comrade was read aloud, his/her photo was displayed, and that person's family and friends were asked to stand and be acknowledged. From our seats on the upper levels, I watched carefully for the name on my bracelet. I wanted to see what he looked like, and I anxiously waited to see where his family was seated. I thought that after the ceremony I could run down and meet them.

Finally, the last speech was given, and we all took a deep breath. We were exhausted from hours of crying and grieving. I kept my eye on the family as we filed out, but it was in vain. The stadium became total chaos. There was no way I was ever going to find his family among this moving crowd. But I didn't give up. I didn't know what I was looking for, but I had to keep trying. I was so close.

The firefighters from FDNY are easy to spot because they wear a very traditional style uniform. As I was being herded out of the stadium, I looked up to find a proud member of the FDNY right in front of me. I tapped him on the shoulder, and he looked down at me and smiled.

"Excuse me. I have this memorial bracelet and I want to find his family to show them that I am honoring him. I don't know where to begin to find them in this crowd. Could you help me?"

The man stared momentarily at the bracelet that I showed him. He turned to me with tears in his eyes and said, "He was my best friend. Thank you. I will definitely tell his family about this. Thank you."

We hugged and the crowd pushed me away toward the door.

I had made my connection.

Mary Jane West-Delgado

Mary Jane would love to hear from you at mmjdelgado@comcast.net if this story meant something special to you.

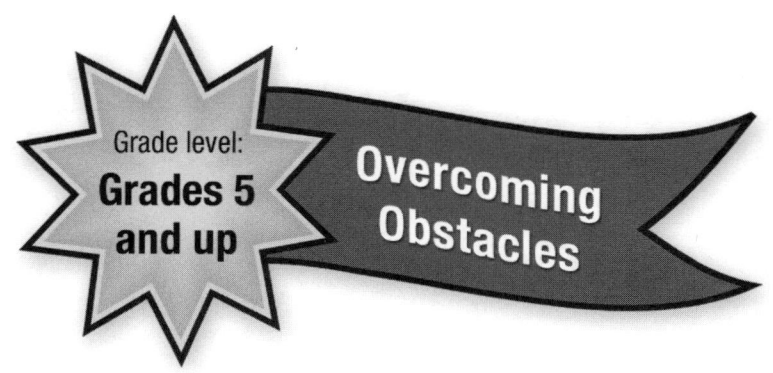

Grade level:
Grades 5 and up

Overcoming Obstacles

TITLE: **SUZANNAH'S STORY**

BOOK: **Previously unpublished**

TIME TO READ: **8 minutes**

TOPICS: **Overcoming Obstacles**
Making choices
Making a difference
World issues—homelessness
Tough stuff—potential suicide

AGE LEVEL: **Grades 5 and up**

SYNOPSIS: **Homeless, pregnant, and considering suicide, Suzannah tells this true episode of reading a *Chicken Soup for the Soul* story that saved her life.**

NOTES TO TEACHER:

We have repeatedly heard stories of how *Chicken Soup for the Soul* has changed lives or improved lives. But there is probably no story more dramatic than that of Suzannah Crowder. We recommend reading "Puppies for Sale" to your students (*Chicken Soup for the Soul,* page 65) prior to reading this story to them.

For a more recent account of Suzannah, read "Magic Happens," page 174.

Preview carefully for use with younger students.

References to God within the story can be omitted for use in public schools.

Suzannah's Story

PRE-QUESTIONS:

In your journals, answer the following questions:

Do you know of anyone who has ever considered suicide?

What kind of things might push a person to consider such drastic measures (*e.g., physical abuse, emotional abuse, sexual abuse, homelessness, extremely painful illness or disability, etc.*)?

Have you heard of someone being "saved" from a near-suicide?

> What happened to save this person (*e.g., a phone call, an unexpected visitor, something that caused them to reconsider life or think of it in a new way*)?

Read Story

POST-QUESTIONS:

What caused Suzannah to consider suicide? What caused her to change her mind?

Suzannah obviously valued life because she intended to release Matt for adoption prior to taking her own life in front of a train. Why didn't she value her own life?

How did a simple story about a puppy change Suzannah's life?

What changed to cause people to say "Yes" to Suzannah who had previously said "No"?

What has Suzannah done since reading "Puppies for Sale" that has turned her life around? Why didn't Suzannah pursue these possibilities sooner?

Has there even been a person, story, or life episode that became a defining moment in your life? Write about it in your journal, or share it in dyads or **Circle Talks** (Appendix, page 311).

STUDENT ACTIVITIES:

Read "Ask, Ask, Ask" found on page 119.

Compare and contrast the issue of asking for Markita and Suzannah.

Using the guidelines on how to ask (Appendix, pages 302–304), ask for something today, that you normally wouldn't consider requesting.

Rewrite Suzannah's story with a different beginning—a different childhood.
  • How would that have affected her as a teen?

Write Matt's story (Suzannah's son) as if his mother had gone through with her planned suicide. What would his life have been like without her? What kinds of questions may have plagued him throughout his life?

As a class, generate a Teen Help-Line Resource List of local, state, and national agencies and phone contacts to help with a variety of teen issues and problems. Laminate this list and post it in the classroom, throughout the school building, and in public facilities where teens might hang out.

Write a skit or short play that captures Suzannah's story. Perform it for other classes.

Suzannah's Story

The morning cold wakes me. Glancing around the alley, I realize again that I am homeless, as the baby in my belly kicks announcing its hunger. The sound of traffic on Broad Street tells me that it is just after seven in the morning, the rush hour. I know the priests will soon be parking less than twenty feet from where I've slept. I quickly brush my stringy blonde hair with my fingers, trying to put it back into a neat ponytail. If I'm caught, I may look homeless and be told to stay away. I'm not sure if church people would do that, but I can't take that risk.

If you live on the streets of downtown Columbus, it's best to wait until eight in the morning to go Dumpster diving for food. That's when the best stuff is there. If I'm lucky, half-wrapped breakfast sandwiches and leftover pancakes are sometimes still warm. I've gotten so big with my pregnancy that it's tough to get over the side of the dumpster, but going without food makes my baby kick so hard that I become sick. So I have no choice.

I feel sorry for the baby inside of me because he's stuck with me as his mother. I've been thinking about finding a family to raise him so he's not homeless with me. The thought of doing that is terribly painful. But I'm his mother, so it's up to me to figure out what is best for him, and then to do it. While the thought of giving him away hurts, the thought of my own suicide sounds comforting to me.

If I kill myself, I'll jump onto the train tracks right after I deliver him and he goes to his new family. I've already climbed the hill to the tracks to inspect the area, and I have a plan. For now though, I need to get this kid fed, so I head to the Dumpsters behind McDonald's.

After eating, I decide to sneak inside the restaurant to get cleaned up in their bathroom. I hope to go to the air-conditioned library to read, and I want to get cleaned up enough so that the librarians don't kick me out for stinking.

Standing in front of the Columbus Public Library, I'm overcome with the feeling that the answers to all my problems must be inside those walls. That's what my grade-school teachers used to tell us when we would visit the library on field trips. The answer to every question is inside there. But my problems have never been so desperate as they are today. Could this huge white building, with its thousands of books, contain my answer? If the answers aren't in there, I tell myself, there are no answers.

Just like I once did as a little girl, I make my way to the second floor. I'm in search of an inspirational book, a Bible, a psychology journal, or anything that may explain what's haunting me. I feel desperate to shake the worthlessness I've felt since I was a child. I wish to banish those ghosts inside of me that keep telling me I'm nobody. Terror and pain are normal feelings for me. I've got to do something about this. I must figure out what I did to become the "crazy, homeless, pregnant lady of Broad Street." I hate being called that. How can I be crazy if I'm smart? But wait, I've heard that very smart people are often crazy. Mom always told me I was nuts. But she was neurotic, so was she wrong? Damn, I wish these thoughts would stop going through my brain!

I see a librarian setting up a table of books. There's a sign on the table that reads "Inspiration." BINGO! I grab the book that is closest to me. As I sit down, I say a little prayer that a Divine Guidance will give me a helping hand and tell me how to get myself out of this mess.

The book I've chosen is called *Chicken Soup for the Soul.* It must be new. I open the book to a story entitled "Puppies for Sale."** I feel like a dog anyway, so I may as well try this one. It turns out that God was listening when I asked for that guidance.

The story is about a little boy who sees a sign that says "Puppies for Sale," and he goes into a pet store with his life savings of $2.37. From the full litter of puppies, he notices that one of the pups is lame. He quickly tells the shopkeeper that he wants the lame pup. The shopkeeper tries to dissuade him and offers to give him the runt for free, as the puppy is worthless because of a missing hip socket. The little boy becomes angry and tells the storeowner that the puppy is worth every bit as much as the others.

I'm transformed as I read, savoring each word as if it's a gift. How wonderful that the little boy sees the lame pup as valuable! As I continue the story, the boy then pulls up his pants leg, exposing a mangled leg surrounded by a metal brace. He exclaims that the puppy will need someone who understands. Wow! The wheels are turning inside my head. The brace on the boy's leg means that he'd gotten help for his problem. And with that help, he became able to show understanding to others in need. Perhaps, someday, someone might come to understand me as well.

My chest feels heavy and I'm breathing quickly now. "Maybe I'm valuable too" is the thought that circles my head and heart, enveloping me in comfort. One person saw the lame pup as worthless, but another saw him as a perfect fit. I'm suddenly at peace with myself. I'm no longer alone. I'm not sure who is with me, but I am surrounded by compassion. I'm valuable. I no longer feel that I'm damaged goods.

Like a movie, much of my life's pain appears, then vanishes before me. Pain from the past comes and goes, and is gradually replaced by comfort. The awfulness of my drunken mother horrifically abusing me as a child becomes less intense and then fades. The sexual abuse I endured begins to slowly vanish. Being told a thousand times that I am worthless now feels like a lie. My traumatic past slowly becomes strength. It's as apparent as if someone is standing in front of me and saying, "Suzannah is no longer damaged goods." I was born special. I have value. With help, I can have a life. This spiritual message is presented to me in such a simple, clear way that I can't ignore it. I must get some help to improve my life. I'm desperate to begin immediately.

And, that's exactly what I did.

I went to every homeless shelter that had already turned me down for lodging. Apparently, if you are pregnant and homeless in Columbus, you are not considered a "family," so you can't get into a family shelter. At the same time, they won't take you in a single women's shelter because of the liability risk of the pregnancy.

I finally convinced the Homeless Families Foundation to ignore that rule, to take pity on me, and to listen to my story. I told them of the boy and the lame puppy for sale. I told them of my transformation and asked if they would be the ones to see me as valuable. It worked. They gave me a tiny apartment in their building, complete with a crib for baby when he arrived. It cost them approximately three thousand dollars a month in lost funding from the shelter board, but they did it anyway just because I asked a second time.

That baby inside of me was delivered in November 1997 and named Matt. He is now a gorgeous eight-year-old who plays goalie on his soccer team.

It took me five years of intensive psychotherapy to rid myself of the demons that stole my self-esteem. I had no insurance, so I sought out a program to pay for it. I studied visualization and learned to see myself as a significant being, highly capable of great success. I went back to college and studied psychology so I might understand what happened to me as a child and master the principles behind overcoming adversity.

I now teach women basic welfare-to-work skills, and I do my best to convince them that they are not damaged goods, but rather "divas in training." I live in a beautiful home in suburban Columbus with a wonderful, loving family and a once-lame pup named Ashley. I'm an author and a speaker. I've become a successful, single mom.

In addition to saving my life, "Puppies for Sale" initiated a major change inside of me. If Jack Canfield and Mark Victor Hansen, the cocreators of the *Chicken Soup for the Soul* series, had kept the story inside, I may never have realized that I'm important. Their love of sharing, and their own journey of persistence, introduced me to an idea that improved my life forever.

This morning I almost bumped into a burly man outside of our neighborhood coffee shop. As he cheerfully greeted me, I realized I am now surrounded by friendly people who truly care about me.

I stopped, smiled, and whispered, "Thank you, God. " And I remembered that we are here to care for one another and to provide for a need when one is presented. *Chicken Soup for the Soul* and "Puppies for Sale" did that for me when I desperately needed help and hope.

Suzannah L. Crowder
Author, Damaged Goods: Adults Can Heal From Childhood Trauma

** *"Puppies for Sale," Chicken Soup for the Soul, page 65.*

Magic Happens

When you come from a place of gratitude and abundance, magic happens. Such was the case at Jack Canfield's Breakthrough to Success, Level II Training, in February 2007. As with all of Jack's trainings, the focus was on finding your inner joy and your inner power in order to manifest your personal destiny. Gratitude and abundance are always critical keys to that success.

Suzannah Crowder, one of the participants in the seminar, had come a long way from her days on the streets as a homeless woman in Ohio. As the result of being profoundly impacted by reading the story "Puppies for Sale" in the first *Chicken Soup for the Soul* book, she had turned her life around and gone on to found Chicken Soup Kitchens to feed and educate the homeless. In addition to being its CEO and visionary, she also runs programs to provide job training and empowerment skills for women.

In a spontaneous moment during one of the breaks, Rick Mars, the drummer featured in the classic 1960s song "Wipe Out" did a "drum-sync" re-enactment of this famous drum solo on the bottom of a black plastic trashcan.

When you put 100 positive, free-thinking people together in one room, ideas begin to fly. Nigel Risner, another participant from Great Britain, suggested that the drum-trashcan should be auctioned off and that the money generated would go to Suzannah's Chicken Soup Kitchens. It was to be a quick, five-minute affair, with lunch eagerly awaiting everyone.

The auction began. Everyone dug deep into their hearts and pockets, and the "drum" quickly sold for $1,000.

That, in itself, would have been a pretty amazing ending to this story, except that Judy, the winner of the drum, "released" it to be auctioned again.

Again, the drum sold for $1,000. And that person released it.

Again, it sold for $1,000. Again, it was released. Again and again and again, it was sold and released.

In the thrill of the auction, someone silently and anonymously approached Jack to offer matching funds up to $17,500.

The excitement rose, and the bidding continued.

Somewhere around $1,000, Suzannah was in tears. Fifteen minutes and $35,000 later, everyone was in tears.

It takes only sixty-seven cents to feed one homeless person for a day. That day, one hundred people were late for lunch so that more than fifty thousand homeless people would be fed.

An interesting side-note is that Judy, the first person who won and then released the drum, did not have the $1,000 to spare. In an act of pure faith, she knew without a doubt that she would have the money when the time came to write the check. This act of faith and courage spurred over a dozen others to win and release a simple trashcan.

Yes, when you come from a place of generosity based on the heartfelt gratitude for all the abundance you already have, magic does indeed happen.

Jack Canfield & Anna Unkovich

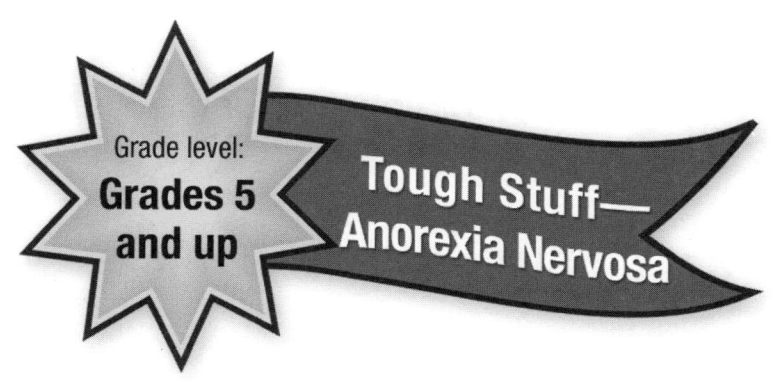

Grade level:
Grades 5 and up

Tough Stuff— Anorexia Nervosa

TITLE: **The Perfect Figure**

BOOK: **Chicken Soup for the Preteen Soul**

PAGE: **287**

TIME TO READ: **4 minutes**

TOPICS: **Tough Stuff—Anorexia Nervosa**
Living and learning
Acceptance and belonging
Making choices

AGE LEVEL: **Grades 5 and up**

SYNOPSIS: A shopping trip for a bathing suit leads to a discussion of losing a little "baby fat." This innocent beginning gets out of control and becomes a life-threatening illness called anorexia.

NOTES TO TEACHER:

This story is included for all age levels because according to an April '06 television news report, there are seven million females, and one million males, with eating disorders, and they are occurring as early as ages eight and nine. Recent research indicates that a probable genetic factor may be involved, as well. It is a very serious and deadly problem!

Use with CAUTION with younger students! And, with every age, be careful not to glorify this killer disease.

You will need to adjust questions and activities slightly to accommodate various age levels.

Other recommended stories on anorexia nervosa:

"Gabby, You're Sooooo Skinny," page 232, *Chicken Soup for the Teenage Soul*

"Already Perfect," page 135, *Chicken Soup for the Teenage Soul II*

"I Just Wanted to Be Skinny," page 253, *Chicken Soup for the Teenage Soul III*

Chicken Soup for the Preteen Soul, The Perfect Figure

ALL LEVELS:

PRE-QUESTIONS:

What is society's attitude toward skinny people? Toward overweight people?
If there were one thing that you could magically change about your body, what would it be? Why?

Read Story

POST-QUESTIONS:

Did Nikki, the author, plan to get that skinny? What happened?
Do body image worksheets *Here I Am #1* and *Here I Am #2* that follow this plan.
What percentage of young people do you think are satisfied with their body image?
   • Take an anonymous poll in your class or school on this issue.
Do you think that the media helps to cause eating disorders? Explain.
Discuss the differences between anorexia and bulimia (*e.g., "Anorexia is starvation, perfection, control, pride. Bulimia is binge and purge, shame, hiding."*).
Focus on warning signs and the importance of students of any age getting help from a trusted adult.

STUDENT ACTIVITIES:

Research Twiggy and the beginning of the "thin-is-in" movement.
Go on-line to search for successful programs for people with eating disorders.
Go to www.edap.org or call hotline 800-931-2237 for information or referral on prevention.

In Anna's experience, she found that using local speakers or former students who were recovering** allowed students to identify more closely with the problem, and not to see it as an issue that exists only in Hollywood.

> *One recovering bulimic started her talk by placing on the table two large bags of potato chips, a large bag of Oreo cookies, two liters of Diet Coke, and an empty half gallon ice cream container. She proceeded to tell students that this was a typical binge for her. She went on to explain various ways she purged, and the resulting pain, shame, and long-term damage to her body. At the end of her speech, she served the food to the students. There was more than enough food to feed the entire class!*

**Just as with alcoholism or drug addiction, the disease never fully goes away.*

HERE I AM #1

Imagine that the body outline shown is you as you are right now. Color or write on it or around it—commenting on each part of you, head to toe (*e.g., short, curly hair—okay; stomach— flabby; feet too big—shoes hurt*). Remember to comment on your insides *(heart, lungs, brain, etc.)* as well.

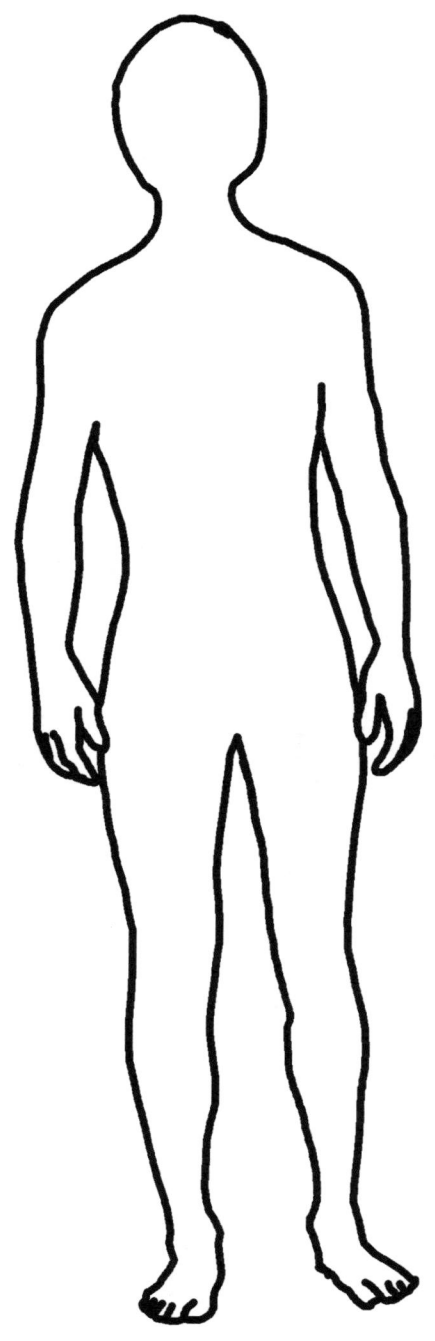

HERE I AM #2

Now imagine that this is your ideal self. Write all over or around the outline, commenting on yourself as you would like to be (*e.g., 20/20 vision—no more glasses; 120 pounds—looking good; lungs clear—asthma gone*).

Compare your two selves. You may find you are unduly critical of yourself. Some things simply cannot be changed—accept them. Focus on your positive points instead, or on those aspects that can be changed.

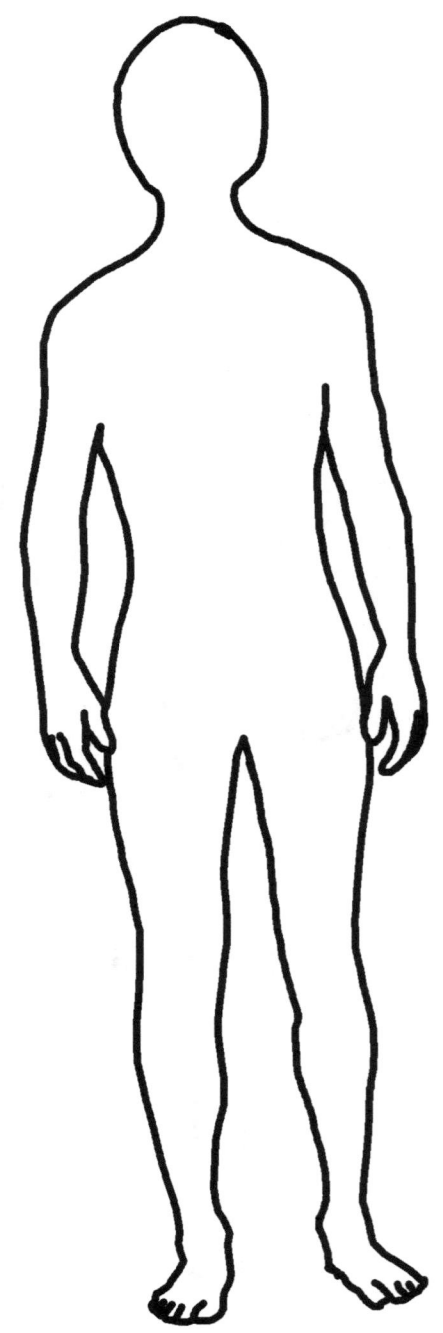

Chicken Soup for the Soul in the Classroom

The Perfect Figure

I am as my Creator made me, and since he is satisfied, so am I.

Minnie Smith

"Oh my gosh, it looks sooo good on you," exclaimed my best friend. "That color flatters you, and I'm getting it for you for your birthday. After all, it's in two weeks!"

I had gone bathing-suit shopping with my best friend. Since we were going into the seventh grade we needed to look cooler. We tried two-piece suits in hopes that we would get more attention from the guys. We wound up purchasing them, and the topic of conversation came up about going on a diet. The only reason for going on one would be to lose a little bit of our "baby fat." I thought all the guys would like me if I was pretty and thin.

So I decided to stick to the diet, even though it would be hard because I am a chocoholic. I had always been a big girl. Not necessarily fat, but tall with a solid build. All the courses in school I took were advanced placement and I played many sports. I thought, *A thin, pretty, smart, athletic girl—everyone will love me.* When I would come home I wouldn't snack, and I cut down on my dinner portions. I had cravings for ice cream, but I just looked at beauty magazines and my bathing suit. The craving disintegrated quickly.

My mom noticed when I dropped five pounds. She told me to stop because I could hurt myself. I promised her I'd stop, but I couldn't. My best friend lost about ten pounds and stopped because she knew she looked good. I started getting complimented by my peers at school. I wore my same clothes, which kept getting baggier and baggier. Some people would ask me where my lunch was. I lied to them and made up excuses.

Since I lost weight by dropping lunch, I did the same with breakfast. I tricked my dad into thinking that I ate my bagels, but I fed them to the deer. My weight dropped drastically, and my best friend threatened to tell my parents if I didn't eat. I fooled her so she thought I was eating, but I wasn't. When I looked at myself in the mirror every day, I saw bulgy thighs that had to go.

My gym teacher confronted me about my immense weight loss. I told her I was losing weight, but that it was all through exercise.

Finally, dark circles formed under my eyes, and I stopped physically developing. It was a struggle for me to even walk up my driveway. I couldn't sleep at night, and I wore layers of clothing in eighty-degree weather but I was still cold. That didn't matter. I still needed to be thinner, and I started wondering how many calories were in toothpaste and communion wafers.

About a month and a half after I had bought the bathing suit, I tried it on again and it fell right off me. My mom told me to look in the mirror. I could see my eye sockets, my transparent skin, the dark circles under my eyes, and my cheekbones popping out of my skin. That was the day I realized how skinny I was.

I went to our family doctor and a psychiatrist. My total weight loss was about twenty-five pounds in one month and a week. It took one year for my body to start working normally again.

Sometimes I want to go back to being thin, but I would never do what I did again. It's not worth it. Please don't go on diets when you're young. You will regret them. I know I do. Get help right away because you'll slowly kill yourself and suffer greatly. Don't judge and compare yourself to others. Try to love yourself for who you are, not for how you look. Besides, you probably look fine just the way you are.

Nikki Yargar, age fourteen

[EDITORS' NOTE: *For information regarding eating disorders, log on to the Eating Disorders Awareness and Prevention website at www.edap.org or for information and referrals call the hotline at 800-931-2237.*]

Favorite High School Stories

High school students selected these favorite stories to cover a variety of the more serious issues facing them and their peers. Unlike the previous sections that could be used with any age group, these stories are recommended for older and more mature students.

The lesson plans and activities that accompany this section range from short and simple to those involving higher level thinking skills. Our teacher test groups appreciated having a wide range of choices to meet a multitude of abilities within their classrooms.

As with all stories in this book, we caution you to use your discretion and judgment to select stories that meet with the needs of your students within the community that you teach.

As with the other sections, the stories are preceded by an information page, and the accompanying worksheets are located with the story, whenever possible.

TITLE: **DROWNING IN SOMEBODY I'M NOT**

BOOK: **Chicken Soup for the Teenage Soul IV**

PAGE: **85**

TIME TO READ: **3 minutes**

TOPICS: **Acceptance and Belonging**
Living and learning
On love

AGE LEVEL: **Grades 9 to12**

SYNOPSIS: **A teen finds that being himself gets him a date, and that learning to love himself allows another to love him.**

NOTES TO TEACHER:

This is a wonderful story that prompts each of us to question and to think about who we *really are.*

For further exploration of "self," we have included several pages of handouts in the Appendix, on page 366.

Chicken Soup for the Teenage Soul IV,
Drowning in Somebody I'm Not

HIGH SCHOOL:

PRE-QUESTIONS:

Have you ever tried to act like someone you weren't in order to impress another person?

• If so, what happened?

List ten words to describe yourself.

• You may use the Personal Strengths list to help you (taken from *101 Ways to Develop Student Self-Esteem and Responsibility* by Jack Canfield and Frank Siccone).

How much time, if any, do you spend thinking about who you really are?

• If so, what is the result of that thought process?

• If not, why don't you spend time on this important issue?

Read Story

POST-QUESTIONS:

What things did Mark do in order to try to get Mary's attention?

Have you ever done anything like that?

If so, what?

What finally worked for Mark?

What did Mark learn from this experience?

STUDENT ACTIVITIES:

Do the sentence completion sheets that follow this plan.

Write a personal ad describing the qualities you have to offer in a relationship.

Make a collage of pictures reflecting who you are.

• It could be a double-sided poster, double-sided mask, or a shoebox.

• On the outside, place pictures that represent who you are publicly, or how others might see you. On the inside or backside, the pictures should reflect your inner self, or hidden self.

My Personal Strengths

able to give orders
able to take care of self
able to take orders
accept advice
admire others
affectionate
alive
appreciative
articulate
artistic
assertive
athletic
attractive
brave
bright
businesslike
calm
can be firm if necessary
caring
clean
committed
common sense
communicates well
compassionate
considerate
cooperative
courteous
creative
daring
dedicated
dependable
diligent
disciplined
do what needs to be done
don't give up
eager to please
effective
efficient
elegant
encourage others
enjoy taking care of others
fair
feeling forceful
frank and honest
friendly

generous
get along with others
get things done
give a lot
goal setter
good cook
good dancer
good friend
good leader
good listener
good looking
good manners
good neighbor
good parent
good singer
good with details
good with words
good with my hands
graceful
grateful
happy
hard worker
healthy
helpful
honest
humorous
independent
inspiring
intelligent
joyful
keep agreements
kind and reassuring
leadership
like responsibility
lots of friends
lovable
loving
loyal
make a difference
make a good impression
mathematical
mechanical
motivate others
musical

never give up
observant
often admired
on time
orderly
organized
open
patient
peaceful
physically fit
pleasant
positive in attitude
quick learner
religious
resilient
respected by others
respectful of authority
responsible
risk taker
self-confident
self-reliant
self-respecting
sense of humor
sensitive
speak many languages
spiritual
spontaneous
stand up for myself
straightforward/direct
strong
team player
tolerant
trusting
truthful
understanding
unselfish
visionary
warm
well-dressed

Used with permission, 101 Ways to Develop Student Self-Esteem and Responsibility *by Jack Canfield and Frank Siccone (Needham Heights, MA: Allyn & Bacon, 1993).*

Complete the following sentences
(usually your *first* thought is your best response):

1. I have fun when I . . .
2. I want to . . .
3. I get my way by . . .
4. The world would be a better place if . . .
5. One thing I like about my friends is . . .
6. I worry about . . .
7. More than anything else, I would like to . . .
8. If I were older, I would . . .
9. The best thing about me is . . .
10. I hate . . .
11. Someone I'd like to get to know better is . . .
12. Something that I do for my mother is . . .
13. Something that I do for my father is . . .
14. If I were President, the first thing I would do is . . .
15. The one thing that I want people to admire me for is . . .
16. I love to . . .
17. I feel brave when . . .
18. My face is . . .
19. Something that I want, but I'm afraid to ask for is . . .
20. I like it when somebody tells me that I am . . .
21. I'd like my friends to . . .
22. I'm happiest when I . . .
23. I like to hear stories about . . .
24. If I were the teacher, I would . . .
25. I feel sad when . . .
26. Something that I like to do now, that I didn't like last year is . . .
27. When I want something from my parents, I . . .
28. I can help others by . . .
29. What I especially like about my best friend is . . .
30. I like my mother when . . .
31. I like my father when . . .
32. I get angry when . . .
33. Older people are . . .
34. Little children are . . .
35. I wish people would . . .
36. I wish my family would . . .
37. I admire people who . . .
38. I have no respect for people who . . .
39. I think . . .

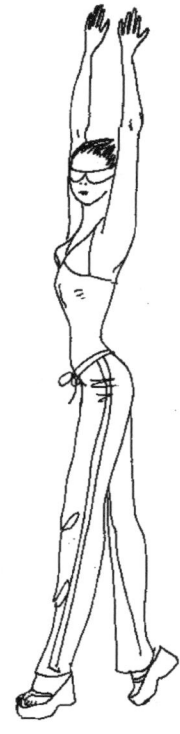

40. I need help to . . .
41. Something I've never told anyone about before is . . .
42. My favorite teacher is awesome because . . .
43. My closest friends would say that I am . . .
44. My favorite music is . . .
45. My favorite color is . . .
46. My favorite subject is . . .
47. My biggest hero is . . .
48. If I could have one wish, it would be . . .
49. I'm happiest when I . . .
50. I feel the most important when I . . .
51. One question I have about life is . . .

52. The one thing that I most want to do in life is . . .
53. The one thing I most want to be in life is . . .
54. The one thing I most want to have in life is . . .
55. I used to . . .
56. When I feel sad, I . . .
57. When I feel scared, I . . .
58. The thing that scares me most is . . .
59. I do my best work when . . .
60. My body is . . .
61. When people try to boss me around, I . . .
62. When somebody is nice to me, I . . .
63. The thing that makes me a good friend is . . .
64. The things I look for in a friend are . . .
65. My parents . . .
66. My siblings . . .
67. Something that I do well is . . .
68. I am proud that I . . .
69. I'd like my parents to . . .
70. I once got in trouble when I . . .
71. The nicest thing anyone every said about me was . . .
72. The best thing about my body is . . .
73. The best thing about my mind is . . .
74. People like me because . . .
75. The most important thing in the world to me is . . .

Drowning in Somebody I'm Not

*I know for me the subject of how to be in a relationship
is precious and complicated and challenging.
It wouldn't be right to make it look too easy.*

Helen Hunt

There is nothing like being young and in love. Your body trembles all over, and you long for that special person. I was sixteen when it first happened. Her name was Mary; she was one grade ahead and the most beautiful girl in the entire school. I was smaller than the rest of the guys my age but had many friends. I would walk by her locker, act cool, and do just about anything to gain her attention.

Nothing worked.

I often pondered to myself, *How would such a beautiful and amazing girl ever fall for a guy like me?* I constantly thought that if I were a "hip guy," she would eventually have to notice. Once, I "accidentally" dropped my letter jacket by her feet, just so she would note my varsity pins—and me.

She only laughed.

Then, at a weekend gathering one evening, she was there with all of her frightening friends. I decided that this had to be it; I couldn't live with myself one second more without at least trying to talk to her. I checked my ego at the door—and decided to be myself. She was alone outside for one moment, and all I can remember is that she was so incredibly beautiful it made me dizzy. I walked up to her and said, "Hi, I'm Mark. You seem really nice; can we talk?" My belly rolled with butterflies while my head rushed with anxiety.

Time stood still for a moment.

She replied, "I know who you are; you're different when your friends aren't around." And then she smiled and said, "I'm walking up the street to meet a friend. Would you like to go?" I could hardly breathe: how could this beautiful girl ever talk to a guy like me? Needless to say, we walked and talked, and she was everything I thought she would ever be. We giggled about the world and how stupid our friends were.

Then, to my amazement, she gave me her phone number. That night, Mary revealed that dropping my letter jacket in front of her was a stupid thing to do. She didn't care about what sports guys lettered in, she only cherished wonderful people with substance. After I began being myself, we quickly fell for one another and became "high school loves."

We later went on to separate colleges and grew apart, but one thing that I learned from the experience has stuck with me my entire life. If you try to act like somebody you're not, any love or approval you gain won't mean anything.

It's best to just be yourself.

Mark Whistler

TITLE:	**MORE ALIKE THAN DIFFERENT**
BOOK:	Chicken Soup for the African American Soul
PAGE:	225
TIME TO READ:	7 minutes
TOPICS:	**Bias Issues** Bias issues—racial stereotypes World issues—culture
AGE LEVEL:	Grades 10 to 12
SYNOPSIS:	Multiethnic, multiracial students at a camp share stories of racial injustice and find a common bond in truly looking in each other's eyes.

NOTES TO TEACHER:

The eye-to-eye activity is a powerful bonding agent, but requires trust among classmates, and maturity in dealing with the emotions that surface. It is suggested that you do several team-building exercises over time before attempting this circle activity.

Chicken Soup for the African American Soul,
More Alike Than Different

HIGH SCHOOL:

PRE-QUESTIONS:

When is the last time that you truly looked into the eyes of a friend or a classmate?

- How did it feel to do this?

Discuss stereotypes of all varieties (*e.g., age, race, sex, culture, religion, body size, handicaps, hair color, financial status, etc.*)

Read Story

POST-QUESTIONS:

What part did Calvin play in the changes within the group?

What qualities created the impact?

STUDENT ACTIVITIES:

Form small groups. Discuss heritage, ethnicity, stereotypes, racial and biracial issues, sexual bias, and, essentially, any form of discrimination.

Spend time in small groups before moving to large group discussions.

- It is best to spend several class sessions sharing and bonding.

NOTES TO TEACHER:

When you feel the students are ready, do the ***Circle Exercise***, eye-to-eye, as described in the story.

Write in your journal about your feelings during this exercise.

- Eventually, share aloud about this experience.

While initially it is uncomfortable to share feelings with others, we feel it is an important developmental growth experience. We encourage you to provide a safe environment for your students to share in this way.

More Alike Than Different

I never considered my race as a barrier to me. In fact, it's become an asset because it allows me to have broader perspective.

James Kaiser

I met Calvin at Camp Unitown. He was our leader. At Unitown teenagers come together to participate in activities that focus on how we are all more alike than different.

Calvin was five feet, seven inches tall with medium brown skin and "locks" to his shoulders—and the teens loved him. Calvin possessed a calmness that made you want to be near him. Where you felt okay to be yourself. Calvin spoke straight from the heart. His voice thundered when he told the group stories about acts of racism.

It was a cold and snowy February in the northern Arizona mountains. About sixty kids attended that weekend. Half came from an inner-city school in Phoenix. The other half were from a low socioeconomic community near the camp. Probably about 40 percent of all the teens there were white, 20 percent black, 20 percent Hispanic, 10 percent Native American, and the other 10 percent of the kids were of varied ethnic backgrounds.

They were typical teenagers: loud, unruly, having fun. At first the students didn't mix with each other. The Phoenix teenagers stayed with their group; the rural kids hung with their friends. Everyone was in their own cliques.

We participated in large groups led by Calvin and broke into small groups of six to eight to share individually. The first evening Calvin led us through a scenario of racial injustice and violence. Calvin's story appeared so real in our minds that most of the teens were in tears. Tenderly, Calvin assisted the group in personalizing the inhumanness of any kind of prejudice.

One white girl sitting next to me pushed her head into my chest. She was sobbing. When she lifted her head to look at me, her sky-blue eyes were clear and wide and full of compassion. I kissed her forehead.

In the morning we discussed our different heritages. Calvin told us about individual cultures and described admirable qualities about each one. As he expanded on the honorable attributes of varying ethnic groups he would ask students of that ethnicity to stand as he described their heritage. The last group he asked to stand included kids of mixed ethnic groups. Calvin's voice was passionate. "Here we have brothers and sisters who come from more than one racial background. These individuals came from two parents or parental lines that had different races. Look each one of them in the eyes. See their beauty. Here, my brothers and sisters, is the future of our world."

By the afternoon we had heard and watched each other reveal our best-kept secrets. We all shared. No one was left out.

That night we went through a litany of exercises to demonstrate how we discriminate against each other based on sex. Calvin showed us how the belief systems we had been taught verbally or nonverbally affect us. Surprisingly we saw that the girls were just as guilty as the boys in stereotyping others because they were male or female.

Calvin told the boys to stand in rows so they were facing each other. The girls made a circle around the perimeter of the room. Then Calvin played soft music on his CD player. The music was from cultures around the world: drums, flutes, chants. The directions Calvin gave to the boys were: "Look into your brother's eyes. Do not say a word to him. But with your eyes tell your brother, 'I am there for you. I care for you, and I understand. You don't have to be tough anymore. You can come to me if you need someone to help you remember your commitment.'"

To the girls he said, "Please silently witness the boys making this commitment to each other."

Calvin gave each pair of boys time to connect their eyes and silently make their vow. Then he announced, "Change," and the boys moved up one space to encounter a new person in the row. A few of the "tougher" boys laughed. It didn't take long, though, for them to honor the seriousness of this event. Outside, snow fell swiftly as if to solidify their vows to each other. The girls watched in awe as boys became men that day.

Afterwards, Calvin told these young men to hug every person in the room. With each hug I said a silent blessing. Earlier that day most of these guys had been strangers to me. It felt to me like they each received my blessing with honor.

Now it was the girls' turn. Calvin instructed us to take the men's place in the middle of the room. The men encircled us. As Calvin played music created by great women from all around the world, he told us, "Look into your sister's eyes. See her beauty. Tell her how beautiful she is. Tell her with your eyes, not words. Promise her you will be there for her when she needs you. Remind her to respect herself."

Powerful emotions built up inside of me as I gave each girl a silent message using only my eyes. I felt such compassion.

Calvin called, "Change," and I met a new pair of eyes. I looked into brown, black, blue and green eyes that evening; each time I saw beauty and grace. I felt proud to be among these girls, like I was taking part in a sacred ceremony. The snow kept falling.

As the weekend came to an end, I felt like I had grown two inches taller. Before we boarded our buses to go home, we made a large circle and stood in the snow hand in hand. There was no separation by skin color, schools, or cliques. Calvin, with his openness and tell-it-like-it-is manner, had somehow transformed a group of immature teenagers into men and women of integrity.

I thank Calvin for the gift he shared with us that weekend. In my mind he is a real twenty-first-century hero.

Mary Cornelia Van Sant

TITLE: **THE BIRTH OF AN ADULT**

BOOK: **Chicken Soup for the Teenage Soul on Tough Stuff**

PAGE: **170**

TIME TO READ: **10 minutes**

TOPICS: **Friendship and Community**
Tough stuff—teen pregnancy
Tough stuff—adoption
Living and learning

AGE LEVEL: **Grades 9 to 12**

SYNOPSIS: **A teenage boy becomes a man as he supports his friend through her unplanned pregnancy and her abandonment by the father of the child.**

NOTES TO TEACHER:

While the foundation of this story is teen pregnancy, the true message lies in friendship and growing up.

More appropriate terminology is now "releasing for adoption," rather than "giving up for adoption."

While this is a wonderful story about friendship and maturity, it is also a story about teenage pregnancy. This is a reality for many teens, despite their knowledge of contraception. Be very aware of your students and your community before using this story in your classroom. And, make sure it is appropriate for the class that you teach (*e.g., health, personal development, life-skills, child development, etc.*).

Students may want to extend their discussions to contraception and abortion issues. Establish firm boundaries for your student discussion on these highly controversial topics. Know your state laws and local policies on these issues and adhere to them firmly!

This is a terrific story. Just consider caution in how you use it in a classroom.

For a related story and activity of understanding adoption, read "My Toughest Decision" found on page 213 of this book, and do the *Valued Treasure Activity* on page 212.

Chicken Soup for the Teenage Soul on Tough Stuff,
The Birth of an Adult

HIGH SCHOOL:

PRE-QUESTIONS:

In your journal, write about the following questions:

Has there ever been a time when you have totally put aside your needs and wants, and faced the criticism or judgment of classmates, in order to really be there for a friend?

> • If so, write about the experience and how it felt.

Has anyone ever shown you this level of friendship?

> • Write about it, if it occurred.

> • If not, write about what you think it takes to reach that level of friendship.

Read Story

POST-QUESTIONS:

Discuss the things Jonathan did to support Jamie throughout the story.

In the end, how was Jonathan affected by all of this?

STUDENT ACTIVITIES:

Rewrite the story as seen through the eyes of Jamie, the pregnant teen.

Invite a speaker from a local adoption agency to explain the adoption process, laws, paternity rights, and the open adoptions that are now available.

Debate the issue of Jamie keeping her child versus releasing for adoption.

> • Discuss the pros and cons of either option. (*For classroom purposes, avoid discussion of any other options.*)

Research any of the following:

> • Current statistics on abstinence for teens

> • Current statistics on teen pregnancy

> • Laws regarding paternity rights and responsibilities

> • Child support payments

> • Adoption issues

The Birth of an Adult

The ultimate measure of a man is not where he stands in moments of comfort and convenience, but where he stands at times of challenge and controversy.

Martin Luther King Jr.

The doctors started to rush into the room. The delivery was going smoothly, but to me it felt like hysteria. The walls were a chalky gray like the wall of a jail cell. It wasn't the best setting for Jamie's labor, but it would have to do. Jamie was only a seventeen-year-old junior in high school. And now she was giving birth. She lay back in pain. Her only movements consisted of shaking her head from side to side, in an effort to escape the pain.

I took Jamie's hand, comforting her and trying to soothe her agony. Her eyes opened, and she looked at me. Our eyes met, and suddenly I felt every emotion I have ever known. I always knew Jamie would challenge me to better myself; however, I didn't think it would entail being her sidekick during her pregnancy.

All this began on the afternoon of New Year's Eve, 1997. I sat in Jamie's basement awaiting the urgent news she had to tell me. She collapsed onto the couch and told me how she had broken up with her boyfriend, Eric, who had left the country to study abroad. This came as something of a relief, although I did my best not to show it. I didn't think Eric, or any other guy she had dated, was good enough for her. Okay, I'll admit it, I was—how should I put it—a little jealous. But I'd convinced myself we were better off as friends, anyway. And now she needed one.

Then the real news came: She was six weeks pregnant. Tears rolled down her face as she told me. I sat in shock and disbelief. The words were not registering in my head. She reached out and gave me a hug, which must have lasted only a few seconds but seemed like hours. My arms were still at my sides. We talked for a little while, and then I left her house and drove around in my car. I was in shock. I was upset about her lack of birth control because this whole ordeal could have been prevented. I was too young to deal with her pregnancy. Being a seventeen-year-old and a junior in high school was confusing enough without dealing with my own real-life after-school special.

That evening I arrived at a party to drink my worries away. The air was filled with smoke and the partygoers reeked of alcohol. I could not take the atmosphere for long, so I left. I went to Jamie's house and stood on her front porch staring at the front door. What should I do? I asked myself. My foot started to turn from the door, but my hand reached out and pushed the doorbell. I wanted to run and go back to the party. I wanted to have fun this New Year's Eve. Suddenly, the door opened and Jamie stood in the doorway with her head down. "You can't spend New Year's Eve by yourself," I blurted out. She smiled, and we hugged in the doorway. This symbolized the beginning of the new journey that lay ahead for us. That night, we sat and laughed like usual while watching Dick Clark ring in the New Year. After that night, my life would change. I wouldn't be a crazy teenager anymore. I would become a young adult.

Weeks passed, and Jamie told her parents about the pregnancy. She and her parents made the decision to go through with the pregnancy, but to give the baby up for adoption. My parents talked with her parents and offered their support, almost like they were discussing our marriage; Jamie and I were growing and maturing together.

During her first trimester, I found myself at Jamie's house every day after school, giving her foot massages while she relaxed and watched her soap opera. She wasn't able to walk very much. I made snacks for her and enough food runs to Taco Bell to last us both a lifetime. My friends were not considerate about what I was going through. While I was busy helping a friend, they were busy making fun of me. They would call Jamie's house wondering what I was doing. They already knew, but they just wanted to poke fun. At school, the jokes surfaced like, "Gonna be a good daddy?" and "What are you doing this weekend . . . Lamaze class?" I shrugged them off and ignored them. I went on with my daily chores and focused on Jamie. I tried to make her life as easy as possible.

Later, one Saturday afternoon as I was catching up on sleep, Jamie called.

"Did you want to do something today?" she asked.

"What did you have in mind?" I replied.

"I want you to help me choose the baby's family," she said.

My ears turned hot, and I felt uneasy. But I told her I would pick her up. As I drove to her house, I thought about how much I had changed. I was more responsible, but I still considered myself a child. I felt I had no business choosing a path for an unborn baby. I groaned and doubted myself. I arrived at her house and helped her into the car. As we were driving to the adoption agency, Jamie pointed out to me, "You're not speeding."

It occurred to me that I was no longer a crazy driver, thinking about how quickly I could get from one place to the other. I was now responsible for making sure we got there safely.

"I'm driving for three people now," I told her.

We arrived at the agency and were seated in a conference room. Fifty manila folders lay on the table, each containing a couple. One of these folders would be the lucky one. One of these couples would be the parents of Jamie's baby. The counselor and Jamie and I went through each folder discussing their spiritual, psychological, financial, genealogical, and emotional backgrounds. I began browsing through one folder, which read "Jennifer and Ben." The folder was more like a booklet chronicling their life with pictures of where they'd been, who they are, and who they wanted to become. Their explanation of why they wanted a baby caught my attention. This couple intrigued me. We kept narrowing down the couples, until we were down to two couples: Jennifer and Ben, and Jamie's pick. We discussed both couples, finally agreeing on Jennifer and Ben.

As we were getting ready to leave, I took a picture of Jennifer and Ben out of the folder and slipped it into my jacket pocket without Jamie noticing. I wanted to have a record of them before their life was to be changed forever. I put on my jacket, and we left the agency.

It was a miserably cold spring day. After helping Jamie into the car, I walked around the car and a warm breeze struck me. I stood by the trunk of my car feeling the summer draft. I couldn't understand it. It was a cold day, but the wind was warmer than an August breeze. It felt like a sign, an anonymous thank you. We drove away and I thought about the decision we made. I thought about the families we didn't pick. How much longer would it take for them to receive the gift of a child?

A few weeks later we met Jennifer and Ben for the first time. They impressed me. They were a close couple, and I knew they would apply the love they had for each other to their child. Jamie told them that I urged her to pick them, which made this meeting even more overwhelming for me. I tried not to show it, though, as we bonded almost immediately. They urged Jamie to take a childbirth class so she would be ready for all of the upcoming events. She needed a partner for the class, so I agreed. She signed up for a class, and every Tuesday night Jamie and I attended together.

The first class was awkward. I had never felt so out of place in my entire life. Jamie and I sat down together, trying to ignore the seven married couples staring at us. We were too young and too ignorant to be going through a pregnancy and a birthing class. Nevertheless, Jamie had to do it, and I would not let her be alone. After time, we all began to bond and develop a tremendous amount of respect for each other. Everyone realized what a struggle it was for us to get this far.

During the "Mom Time," the dads and I sat outside talking about the babies' futures. The dads talked about peewee football, mutual funds, and insurance. I talked about Shakespeare and geometry. I was out of place, for sure, but I realized there is more to giving birth than nine months and a doctor. So much freedom was sacrificed, replaced with a huge amount of responsibility. The dads respected me and praised me for my humanity towards a friend, not to mention my maturity. I still just couldn't believe I was sitting around talking about babies. I wanted to be innocent again. I wanted to drive my car fast and go to parties, but more important responsibilities called me. I was maturing.

I was getting ready for school one morning when Jamie called me from the hospital. "Um, do you want to get over here?" she asked.

"It's only another sonogram. Besides, I can't miss class," I said.

"Well, I think you might want to get over here, 'cause I'm having the baby!" she shouted.

I ran out of the house and darted to the hospital. At the hospital, the nurse handed me scrubs and I entered her room. She lay there as I sat next to her.

"Well, this is it," she said. "Nine months, and it's finally here." She grimaced with pain and moved her head back and forth. Doctors were in and out of her room every two seconds with medication. She was about to give birth. After a few hours of getting Jamie settled, she was fully dilated.

"Okay, here we go. When I say 'push,' you push," the doctor said.

She acknowledged him while grabbing my hands and nodding her head quickly several times. Jamie gave three pushes of strength and, with one final push, she breathed life into a new baby. The doctors cut the umbilical cord and cleaned the baby off. I sat in awe. Every possible human emotion struck me like a freight train.

"It's a boy," they exclaimed.

I smiled, and tears of joy ran down my cheek. No more fear, no more chores, just pure happiness. The baby was handed to Jamie, and she spent the first moments of the baby's life holding him in her arms. She looked up at me, and I looked at her.

"You did it, kiddo," I whispered in her ear.

The doctors left with the baby to run tests and weigh him. Jennifer and Ben came in with the birth certificate. "What's his name?" Ben asked. Jamie motioned for him to come closer, and she whispered in his ear. Ben smiled and went into a different room. I walked outside to get a drink. I came back in a few minutes and saw the completed birth certificate. It read "Blake Jonathan."

I smiled and cried. The doctors brought Blake back in. They passed Blake to me, and I held new life in my hands. I thought about the dads in birth class. Then I thought about Blake's future. His first steps, peewee football games, the first day of school, and his first broken heart. All the dads' talk finally caught up with me. Jennifer and Ben looked at me and smiled. Tears rolled down their cheeks. I gave Blake to Ben and received a gracious hug from Jennifer. They were his parents now. They were his keepers. Jamie still lay there, crying but filled with delight. I went over to her and gave her a big hug.

"Everything okay?" she asked.

"Fine. Absolutely fine," I whispered, and kissed her softly on her forehead. I would never be the same.

Jonathan Krasnoff

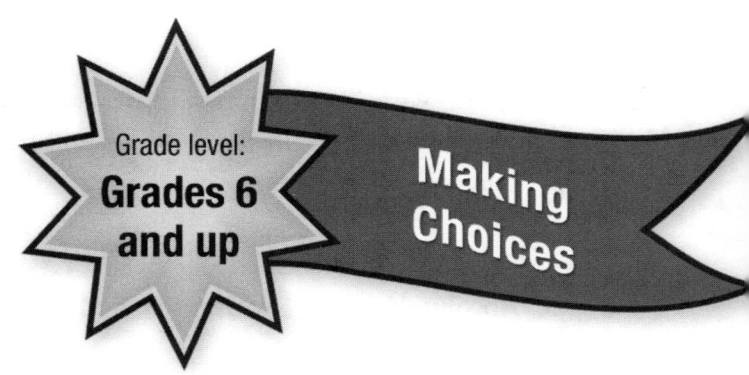

TITLE: **TO HAVE A BOYFRIEND—OR NOT?**

BOOK: **Chicken Soup for the Girl's Soul**

PAGE: **217**

TIME TO READ: **8 minutes**

TOPICS: **Making Choices**
Tough stuff—peer pressure
Living and learning
Acceptance and belonging

AGE LEVEL: **Grades 6 and up**

SYNOPSIS: **Initially, Patty is thrilled to have Ty come into her life, but quickly finds that having a boyfriend doesn't mean that you have to be "owned" by him, nor "Velcro-ed" together in all that you do.**

NOTES TO TEACHER:

This story is introduced at the middle school level, when dating relationships first begin. We have included it here because it is equally suitable for any high school class, particularly if you include information on dating abuse. (*We recommend that you invite a speaker on the subject from a local shelter-house or agency for the prevention of abuse.*)

For a wonderfully humorous story of a first kiss, read, "My First Kiss, and Then Some," included in the Just for Fun chapter of this book.

Or, for a nicer "first kiss" outcome, read "First Kiss," found on page 277 of *Chicken Soup for the Soul on Love and Friendship.*

For a story relating to a totally different kind of pressure—that of riding with someone who has been drinking—read "Just One Drink," found on page 216 of *Chicken Soup for the Teenage Soul.*

Chicken Soup for the Girl's Soul,
To Have a Boyfriend—or Not?

HIGH SCHOOL:

PRE-QUESTIONS:

Have you ever felt left out of something, seeming as though everyone but you participated? If so, what was the occasion?

How much peer pressure do you think comes from within (*e.g., wanting to be accepted*) versus pressure that comes from others (*e.g., someone pushing you to do something*)?

(*Dares and taunts to do something happen more often with younger kids. The desire to do things in order to be accepted is a pressure that comes from within, and it occurs more frequently with older teens.*)

Read Story

POST-QUESTIONS:

Do you think that Patty really was the "... only one without a member of the opposite sex in her life"? Explain your answer.

Was Ty's possessiveness a sign of affection, or control? Is this normal in a relationship?

Initially, Patty liked the idea of "belonging" to Ty. What happened at the party that made Patty want to end things with Ty?

STUDENT ACTIVITIES:

Make a list of relationship behaviors that are normal and healthy, and another list of unhealthy actions or words between couples.

Write a story or song about a healthy first love.

Role-play various scenarios that involve peer pressure (*e.g., drinking, smoking, skipping school, having sex, shoplifting, cheating, etc.*).

Use the **Saying No** handout (Appendix, page 341) to practice some of these situations.

Write an "inner script" of conversations that you have with yourself when you are under pressure to do something that you don't want to do. Discuss ways that you resolve these inner conflicts.

Have a poster contest within your class with the theme of "healthy relationships do not include ownership." Post the winners throughout the school.

Invite a speaker from a shelter house to talk about the progression of abuse (*e.g., often an early warning sign of abuse is extreme possessiveness*).

To Have a Boyfriend—or Not?

The best protection any woman can have . . . is courage.

Elizabeth Cady Stanton

All of a sudden it seemed like all my friends were starting to have boyfriends. Last year in eighth grade, when we talked on the phone, we had talked about all kinds of stuff; like horses, our 'rents, homework, and boys—but it wasn't all about boys. Now every conversation was all, "My boyfriend this, my boyfriend that," and I had nothing to contribute. The last straw was when one of my best friends told me about her upcoming birthday party.

"Since my birthday is so close to Valentine's Day, my mom said I can have a couples-only party, Patty. Isn't that cool?"

Huh? Cool? Definitely NOT, I thought. I am the only one without a member of the opposite sex in my life, and I sure won't have one by next weekend. "Yeah, that's cool, Heather," I managed to stammer out, and I hung up the phone. Great. Just great.

The very next day that all changed when I ran into Tyrone Raymond—literally. I was late to one of my classes (as usual), and as I was barreling around the corner of the building, I ran right into Ty, scattering my books and homework everywhere. He bent down to help me pick up my papers, and as he stacked up what he could reach, he looked up at me and grinned. Not bad, I realized with a shock. Not too bad at all. In fact, kinda cute.

Ty Raymond was in our class, but he was a year younger than the rest of us because he had skipped a year of school somewhere along the way to ninth grade. We all figured he must be really smart to have done that. I had heard that his parents had gotten a divorce over the summer and that it had been really hard on Ty and his three little brothers. Other than that, I didn't know much about him; except that now, looking at him, I realized that he was much better looking than I had remembered. His deep brown eyes were dark and sparkling under long eyelashes as he gazed up at me, and his black hair wasn't just a careless buzz cut anymore—it had actually grown into kind of a neat style.

"Patty . . ."

I snapped back into reality as I realized he was trying to hand me my papers.

"Huh?"

"I've got to get to class. Here's your stuff . . ."

"Oh . . . thanks. Ummm . . . hey, Ty, would you like to go to a party with me on Friday?" Ohmigod. I can't believe I just said that.

"Ahhhh . . . sure," he answered.

What?????? I was astounded.

He continued, "Give me your number, and I'll call you after school. Sounds like fun." I scribbled my phone number on one of the pieces of paper and gave it to him. Then he turned and walked away, leaving me with my jaw hanging open. That was the beginning.

Ty did call me that night. And every night after that. And he called me in the morning before school every morning to tell me where we would meet so that we could walk to school together. As we walked together, Ty would do one of three things to show the rest of the world that I was HIS: He would have his arm around my back with his hand in the back pocket of my jeans, or wrap his arm around my waist, or grab the back of my neck with his hand as we tried to maneuver though the busy school halls like some cojoined, weird set of Siamese twins.

That first couple of days, I was in heaven. Ty obviously liked me a lot. No boy had ever shown me this kind of attention before, and I felt proud of his possessive attitude and that he was always by my side.

On Friday night, my dad drove me over to Ty's house to pick him up for the party. His mom seemed like a nice person but kind of frazzled. It looked like she depended on Ty to help her take care of his three wild little brothers, and she asked us more than once what time the party would be over and when he would be coming back home. Before we left, she asked if I could come over for a family dinner on Sunday, and when I looked to my dad for the answer, he nodded yes, so I accepted. More than ever, I was convinced that this was my first real relationship.

When we got to Heather's house, I was excited. Her family room was dimly lit, and love songs were coming from the sound system. It was the first time I had gone to a party with a guy, and it felt so romantic . . . at first.

After about two hours of slow dancing with our faces stuck together from nervous sweat and Ty's hands roaming around my back as he held me tightly against him, I was ready to go home. I realized, too late, that I hated kissing Ty. He mashed his mouth so hard against mine that it HURT. I turned my face away so that he couldn't kiss me anymore and managed to mumble something about my braces hurting my lips, so he stopped for a while—but then he started right up again. When I went to the bathroom, he followed me and waited outside of the door until I was done. If I wanted food or something to drink, we visited the table together. I started to feel dizzy and sick from the sweating, the groping, the music, the lack of air in the room, and Ty trying to kiss me. I felt trapped and suffocated.

Finally, FINALLY . . . my dad came to get us. As we dropped Ty off at his house, Ty turned to me, smiled, and said, "I'll see you on Sunday, Patty."

"Uhhh . . . okay . . . see ya." When he closed the door of the car and went into his house, I heaved a sigh of relief. I couldn't wait to get home and hide beneath the covers of my bed. My bed in my room. Away from him.

All day Saturday, I thought about Ty and how I was feeling. Every time the phone rang, I let my mom or dad answer it. When he did call, I was conveniently too busy to answer. *If this is how a relationship is supposed to be,* I thought, *I don't want any part of it.* I felt like I couldn't breathe. I didn't know how to tell him that I just couldn't do this anymore, so I did the logical thing—I chickened out. On Sunday, I pleaded with my mom to call Ty's mom to let her know I wasn't feeling well enough to go to dinner at their house. It actually was the truth—just the thought of seeing Ty right then made my stomach turn.

As I expected, Ty called me the first thing on Monday morning.

"What happened to you yesterday, Patty? My mom was looking forward to having you for dinner, and she missed seeing you. And what about all day Saturday? I called and called, but I never got you."

My mind was spinning like an animal in a cage. What was I going to say to get out of this?

"Never mind," Ty said. "You can tell me all about it on the way to school. I'll meet you at the usual corner."

"Uh, Ty, I'm not going to walk to school with you," I blurted.

"WHAT!!?" He shouted.

"I don't want to date you anymore. I want to break up," I ventured timidly.

"What are you talking about? Is there someone else? That's it—you have been seeing someone else behind my back. Who is it? I'm going to beat the snot out of him! I'm going to . . ."

"Ty!" I interrupted. "I'm not seeing anyone at all. It isn't that! I think I'm just not ready for a boyfriend. I don't want to date anyone yet." I was barely able to breathe from the pressure of trying to understand my own feelings and to explain myself. "I don't want to belong to someone. I . . . I just don't want to . . ."

"All right, you baby. Whatever!" And he slammed the phone down.

I barely made it to school at all that day. My mom had to give me a tardy excuse because it took me so long to stop crying and do something about my red swollen eyes. But the reality is I did make it to school. And I made it the next day and the next—and I walked down the halls alone or with my girlfriends. I didn't need Ty to be glued to my side to be okay. He moved shortly after that, and luckily I didn't have to worry about running into him in the halls anymore.

It took me a while to realize that Ty's possessive behavior wasn't normal and that wasn't how a healthy relationship should be. You should never feel pressured into doing something you are not ready to do, like you are trapped or owned, or be made to feel guilty if you want to hang out with your friends or like you can't do anything on your own without making your boyfriend mad at you. It's just way better to be a boyfriend have-not!

Patty Hansen

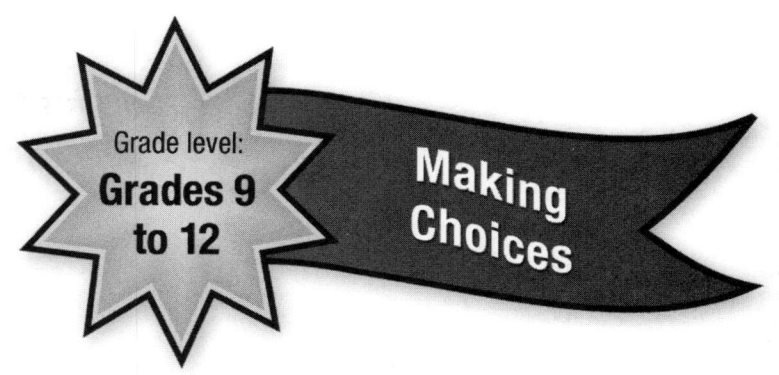

Title: THE TWO ROADS

Book: Chicken Soup for the Teenage Soul III

Page: 300

Time to read: 4 minutes

Topics: **Making Choices**
Following your dreams
Acceptance and belonging
Tough stuff—pain and regret

Age level: Grades 9 to12

Synopsis: This is a poem about following your heart rather than following the crowd.

NOTES TO TEACHER:

We have chosen to take a creative approach with the activities in this plan. You could, however, use this story to discuss the more analytical aspects, such as different decision-making styles, the basic steps to decision-making, etc, (Appendix, pages 342–347).

Chicken Soup for the Teenage Soul III,
The Two Roads

PRE-QUESTIONS:

On a daily basis, we are all faced with choices.

- What procedure do you use to make your decisions (*e.g., ask a friend, flip a coin, ask a parent, research options, etc.*)?

Do you ever "trust your gut" when making a decision?

- If so, how does that work for you?

(The Appendix, pages 342–347, provides additional tools for ***decision-making***).

Read Story

POST-QUESTIONS:

While it may seem that we are stuck with our choices in life, most people have other options they aren't aware of when they examine the situation more carefully.

- List, then discuss, the kinds of decisions that are irreversible.

Write about a time when you either did, or didn't, trust your heart or your intuition.

- What was the outcome?

STUDENT ACTIVITIES:

Paraphrase this piece of poetry by rewriting its key concepts in your own words.

Use art, music, and/or dance to reflect the key concepts of this poem.

The Two Roads

There was a path
Deep in the woods.
Once it forked—
The bad, the good.

I chose to take
The left-hand path,
I did not know
I had no map.

Now this road that I travel
Is dirty and battered.
It's littered with dreams
That are broken and tattered.

Paved with wrongdoings
And dotted with hearts,
That were taken from people
And just torn apart.

Pain and regret
Are common here.
wherever you turn,
They're always near.

I want to cross
To the other path,
And leave behind
This painful wrath.

I thought I was forever
doomed to walk.
And all the gates
were tightly locked.

But as I continued,
A footbridge I could see.
A Bridge of Hope
called out to me.

Slowly I crossed
to the path of good.
Finally I was on the path
Of which I thought I should.

Now hidden deep
Within the woods.
The one that forked;
Paths bad and good.

I once was wrong,
But now I'm right.
And before me
Glows a guiding light.

Altered by
A little step.
So close to falling
In darkened depths.

But I was finally
Pulled to hope.
I found that footbridge,
And learned to cope.

My simple mistake
Following the crowd.
Ignoring the heart
That speaks so loud.

The choices you make
Can change your life.
One will bring happiness,
The other brings strife.

Following the crowd,
Won't lead you to right.
If you follow your heart,
You'll be guided by light.

There was a path,
Deep in the woods.
Once it forked—
The bad, the good.

Heed my warning,
Because I know.
Follow your heart—
You know where to go.

Whitney Welch

TITLE: **LIFE IS SHORT**

BOOK: **Chicken Soup for the Preteen Soul**

PAGE: **150**

TIME TO READ: **6 minutes**

TOPICS: **Making a Difference**
Tough stuff—death
World issues—organ donations
Friendship and community

AGE LEVEL: **Grades 6 and up**

SYNOPSIS: A sixteen-year-old dies in a snowboard accident, but lives on in almost fifty other people who received parts of him as organ donations.

NOTES TO TEACHER:

l   Consider classroom values before emphasizing organ donations with this story.

Chicken Soup for the Preteen Soul,
Life Is Short

PRE-QUESTIONS:

Are you familiar with the concept of organ donations?

- Who does it?

- When, how, and why is it done? (*A person can delegate that at the time of their death, if various organs are functional, that they be donated for others to use. Eyes, heart, liver, and almost any organ can be "matched" and used to improve, or save, the life of others. Family members may also make this decision for a deceased loved one.*)

Have you had a close friend who has died?

- Do you want to share your experience?

Do worksheet on grief (see Appendix, page 356).

Read Story

POST-QUESTIONS:

What happened to Gabe?

What did Scott, the author, learn from this experience?

- What does he do differently as a result of Gabe's death?

Do you wear a helmet when doing risky sporting events (*e.g., biking, skateboarding, snowboarding, roller blading, etc.*)?

Will you wear one now, after hearing this story?

- Why, or why not?

Why is it important to live life with passion *now*?

STUDENT ACTIVITIES:

Complete a **Timeline** of your life (see Appendix, page 374). Be sure to include things you have accomplished already in life, as well as things you wish to do before you die.

Do **Unfinished Business** assignment (Appendix, page 357).

Go to the website at the end of the story, or search online to find out information about organ donations.

- If this concept captures your heart, communicate your wishes to your family members.

Life Is Short

For you and me, today is all we have; tomorrow is a mirage that may never become a reality.

Louis L'Amour

"Hey, man, I'm hungry," I said. "I'm going to go get something to eat."

My friend Gabe smiled and warmly responded, "Alright, but you're crazy. I can't stop. The weather's too good! Look for me here at the bottom of this lift when you're done. I'm gonna go take some more runs."

I released my bindings and began to walk in the direction of the smell of hot pizza. I shouted over my shoulder, "I'll catch up to you later."

I didn't think twice about those few little words at the time. My friend, Gabe Moura, and I had been snowboarding all morning. I was too hungry to take another run, so I decided to eat something at the lodge.

I remember the weather that day. It was one of those flawlessly sunny, crisp winter Sundays where it was just brisk enough to get your blood rushing but warm enough to wear a T-shirt. I had been riding in a T-shirt all day, and despite the occasional patch of ice, the snow was great.

Earlier that morning, we had been tearing up the mountain. Huge aerials, blazing speed, and unfading smiles were common for us. After a quick slice of pizza in the lodge, I would soon be back on the mountain with my friend. But taking a break from this snow-capped playground was just not something Gabe would do. He continued back to the crowded lift line with a sparkle in his eyes. I remember thinking, *That guy is never going to stop riding, not on a day like this at least.*

I finished my lunch and headed back out. The lifts were open and I didn't see Gabe anywhere, so I went on up. I figured he was having fun up there somewhere, and I was determined not to miss out just to wait around down at the bottom for him.

On the lift, I remember seeing a big crowd at a fork in the runs. I assumed it was just another minor collision and that somebody was just complaining about their back again. I rode for a few more hours with an intoxicating combination of adrenaline and excitement flowing through my veins. I recall seeing a crowd at the fork several more times and wondering what Gabe was up to.

The day flew by, and soon it was time to go back to the hotel. As I waited for my mom at the lodge, I saw the other kids Gabe and I had been riding with that day. Mona, one of Gabe's friends, was standing by the parking lot, and she looked beat. I naturally figured it was from the insane day of riding we had all had.

As she was standing there with her shoulders drooped, I walked over to her. As I got closer, I saw that she had tears in her eyes. She told me that Gabe had been in an accident and was being flown by air-evac to Tucson. He was in a coma.

WHAT!?! My mind screamed, but my voice quivered. She explained that he had collided with a skier at full speed and the back of his head had landed on a patch of ice. The skier had gotten up, said a few words, then disappeared, leaving Gabe on the ground.

The car ride home to Tucson was undoubtedly one of the longest I recall. My mind played cruel games on me while my nerves wreaked havoc on my body. I remember crying uncontrollably and vomiting. That night I called the hospital, but there had been no change. Gabe was still unconscious and the doctors had no prognosis.

The next day, my friends and I bought some get-well cards and headed for the hospital. Once there, we were herded into a large conference room with probably two hundred or so people. A chaplain took the podium and informed us that Gabe was brain-dead. They were taking him off life-support, and he would be officially dead within ten minutes.

My comical get-well card seemed so trivial now. My friend, who just yesterday had shared life with me on a beautiful mountaintop, was gone forever.

The ensuing weeks were filled with a funeral, candlelight vigils, and mostly struggling to comprehend why. Why did someone so completely innocent, so full of life, die? How could this happen?

It's been about eight months since Gabe died, and I still don't know the answers to these questions. I know I never will. I do, however, know—more intimately now—that all those clichéd sports commercials are so true. Life is short. There is no method or reason to life if you just wander through day to day. You must find your passion and live it, but be safe. There is no reason to take chances with your life. If Gabe had been wearing a helmet he would probably be alive today. Life is fragile enough as it is. It comes and goes as fleetingly as a falling star.

I strive to make my life exceptional and extraordinary, but it is difficult. You can eat well and exercise daily for an hour at the gym, but unless you truly experience life, it is all for nothing. It is so much easier to become apathetic or lazy. I see people letting their lives revolve around the TV. I see people overcome by greed and the almighty dollar, working horrendous hours at jobs they despise.

But I know I must be different. I must strive to make a difference. Gabe is my inspiration. He made a difference, in life and now in death. While he was here, Gabe brightened people's days and made the world a richer, more loving place for his family and friends. His passion for life was something he spread to everyone, but an extraordinary person like Gabe couldn't stop there.

Just a few months prior to his accident, he told a family member, "If anything ever happens to me, I would want all of my organs to be donated."

The heart that so many girls fought for is now beating strongly inside of a sixty-two-year-old man, who is engaged to be married soon. Gabe's liver went to a thirty-three-year-old husband and father. One kidney went to a woman and the other to a man. Two people who could not see before now do, thanks to Gabe's eyes. Between thirty-five and fifty people received tissue from Gabe's body.

Gabe not only still lives in the memories of his family and friends, he lives on in the hearts and lives of fifty other people, who are now alive and healthy because of him. Gabe set an example for all of us. You never know how much time you are going to have to live your life, so pursue your passions and make the right choice now. Make your life matter.

Scott Klinger, age sixteen

TITLE: **MY TOUGHEST DECISION**

BOOK: **Chicken Soup for the Teenage Soul II**

PAGE: **139**

TIME TO READ: **2 minutes**

TOPICS: **On Love**
Tough stuff—teen pregnancy
Tough stuff—adoption
Living and learning
Making choices

AGE LEVEL: **Grades 9 to12**

SYNOPSIS: **A "good kid" gets pregnant and makes the tough decision to release her daughter for adoption.**

NOTES TO TEACHER:

It is suggested that you do the ***Valued Treasure Activity*** on page 212, and then read the story to your students.

If you wish to focus on the decision-making aspect of this story, refer to the Appendix, pages 342–347, for information and practice sheets.

HIGH SCHOOL:

PRE-QUESTIONS:

What is the one thing in your life you value the most?

What is the biggest mistake you've made in your life?

What is your most important dream or goal for your future?

Read Story

POST-QUESTIONS:

Discuss your feelings after hearing this story.

What percentage of teens release their unplanned children for adoption?

• Why is this number so low?

What percentage of teen fathers are involved in the life of the child they helped to create?

What rights and responsibilities does the father have?

How often is a fifteen-year-old capable of quality parenting?

What does a teen have to give up in order to parent a child (*e.g., prom, homecoming, class ring, dating, new car, etc.*)?

Discuss the issue of the child's best interest and lifestyle.

STUDENT ACTIVITIES:

Do the **Valued Treasure Activity** that follows on page 212.

Discuss your feelings about the **Valued Treasure Activity**.

• Does it give you a better understanding of the adoption process?

• Explain your answer.

Have a speaker from an adoption agency discuss adoption issues, including open adoptions.

VALUED TREASURE ACTIVITY

For this "Valued Treasure" activity, have students search through their purses, pockets, fingers, necks, or wrists, for the most *valuable* thing in their possession at the moment. Collect these items in a box, and if possible, remove them from the room or place them in a closet—any *out-of-sight* place that is safe and secure.

Go on with the story and the discussion questions. Come back to their *feelings* of parting with this "possession," and how they might *feel* if they released a child for adoption. The longer you can keep their "possessions" out of sight, the more powerful this activity will be.

My Toughest Decision

Mistakes, mistakes, mistakes. Everyone makes them. No one saw mine coming.

Overall, I was a really good kid. At fifteen, I was a sophomore at a Catholic high school and a member of the National Honor Society. I played softball and ran cross-country. I had, and still have, aspirations of becoming a doctor. If someone would have told me that at the age of fifteen I would become pregnant, I would have said they were crazy. Why would anyone do something so foolish? It's still hard for me to believe, but it happened.

October 11, 1997, was the day my daughter was born. I took one look at her, and it was love at first sight. It was so overwhelming—a flood of emotions that I have never experienced. I loved her in a way that could only be described as unconditional. I looked at her, and in my heart I knew that I could not give her all the things that she needed and deserved to have, no matter how badly I wanted to. Physically, emotionally, and in every other way, I was not capable of being a mother. I knew what had to be done. Putting all my emotions aside and doing what I felt was best for my daughter, I decided to give her up for adoption.

Placing my baby in the arms of her mother was the hardest thing I've ever had to do. My very soul ached. Even though I still get to see my daughter because I am blessed with having an open adoption, the pain is still there. I can feel it burning inside me every day, whenever I think about Katelyn. I only hope that when she gets older, she realizes how much I love her. I love her more than anything in the world.

Today is my daughter's first Christmas. I won't be there to share with her the joy of this season, or to play Santa and open her presents for her (she's only two months old). In fact, I won't be there to see her first step or hear her first word. I won't be there to take pictures on her first day of kindergarten. When she cries for her mommy, it won't be me that she wants. I know in my heart that I made the right choice. I just wish with all my heart that it was a choice I never had to make.

Kristina Dulcey

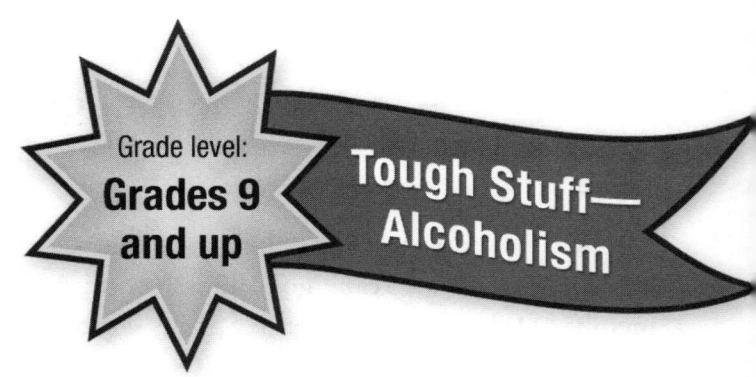

TITLE: FRIENDS OF BILL W., PLEASE COME TO THE GATE . . .

BOOK: Chicken Soup for the Recovering Soul

PAGE: 48

TIME TO READ: 3 minutes

TOPICS: **Tough Stuff—Alcoholism**
Overcoming obstacles
Asking for help

AGE LEVEL: Grades 9 and up

SYNOPSIS: Having a weak moment in recovery, Grace uses an airport paging system to send an Alcoholics Anonymous message to seek help from anyone, and everyone, in the Los Angeles International Airport.

NOTES TO TEACHER:

In assigning any projects regarding AA (Alcoholics Anonymous) or Al-Anon (for families of alcoholics), it is important to remind students of the anonymity and confidentiality of the program.

For an ancillary story on alcoholism, read "For You, Dad," the story of a young teenage girl who uses the death of her alcoholic father to speak to schools and encourage young people not to drink. This story is found on page 268 of *Chicken Soup for the Teenage Soul II*.

"Ask, Ask, Ask," (on page 119) and "Suzannah's Story," (on page 171) also deal with the topic of asking for help. You might wish to read these stories to your students, then have them compare and contrast the main characters in all three stories.

For detailed background information on asking, see pages 302–304 in the Appendix, taken with permission from *The Success Principles: How to Get from Where You Are to Where You Want to Be.*

Chicken Soup for the Recovering Soul,
Friends of Bill W., Please Come to the Gate . . .

PRE-QUESTIONS:

When was the last time that you asked anyone for help with anything?
- Who did you ask?
- What did you ask for?
- Was your request met?
- Why, or why not?

What is the difference between AA and Al-Anon? (*AA is for the alcoholic, Al-Anon is for their families.*)

Name other programs for addictions (*e.g., narcotics, overeaters, gamblers, etc.*).

Read Story

POST-QUESTIONS:

Who is Bill W.?

Why did some people miss their plane in order to help?

Is there an age requirement to join AA?

What are the rules or requirements for AA membership?

What are the rules or requirements for Al-Anon membership?

STUDENT ACTIVITIES:

Read "Ask, Ask, Ask" (page 119) and "Suzannah's Story" (page 171).
- Create a Venn diagram comparing the three main characters.

Research and report on AA or other recovery groups.

Many adults in our society can't even imagine a party without alcohol. Find out what occurs at a typical AA party.

Plan a nonalcohol party for adults or young adults.

Research other recovery programs besides twelve-step programs.
- Compare, contrast, and note varying success rates.

Invite speakers from AA to explain or demonstrate what happens at a typical AA meeting, as well as to explain how the program works.

Write a sequel story or poem to Grace's AA experience at the airport.

Write a sequel with Grace not having paged the friends of Bill W.

Friends of Bill W.,
Please Come to the Gate...

Once you learn to walk, crawling is out of the question.

James D. Davis

Sometime in the early 1990s I was treating a woman in an intensive outpatient chemical dependency group. Let's call her "Grace." Grace was a flight attendant and had been suspended from her job with a major airline due to her untreated alcoholism. She had been stealing the little miniature liquor bottles, drinking in airport bars in uniform, and so on. Her employer, realizing she needed treatment, sent her to us.

After the eight-week program, I suggested to her it might be a good idea to solidify her foundation in recovery before returning to work as she would be working in a high-risk environment (serving alcohol, being out of town alone, etc.). Grace did, however, return to work shortly after completing outpatient treatment. One day while she was departing from a plane at the end of a long day, a major craving for alcohol overpowered her. There she was, in the Los Angeles International Airport, pulling her roller-bag behind her when this massive craving to drink came over her. She tried to just "think through it," or "just forget about it," but it was way too powerful. It was so powerful, in fact, that she was resigned to the fact that she would just go drink. Grace thought, *Oh, the heck with it, I'll get another job . . . or maybe no one will find out anyway.* But deep down inside Grace did not want to drink. She truly had wanted to stay sober, but she was in trouble.

On her way to the bar in the airport, Grace had a moment of sanity. She stopped, picked up the airport paging phone and said, "Will you please page friends of Bill W.," she paused, quickly looking around for an empty gate, "to come to Gate Twelve?"

Within minutes, over the paging system in the L.A. International Airport came, "Will friends of Bill W. please come to Gate Twelve. Will friends of Bill W. please come to Gate Twelve." Most people in recovery know that asking if you are a friend of Bill W. is an anonymous way to identify yourself as a member of AA.

In less than five minutes there were about fifteen people at that gate from all over the world. That brought tears of amazement, relief, and joy to Grace. They had a little meeting there in that empty gate, total strangers prior to that moment. Grace discovered that two of those people had gotten out of their boarding lines and missed their flights to answer that call for help. They had remembered what they had seen on many walls of meeting rooms: "When anyone, anywhere reaches out their hand for help, I want the hand of AA to be there, and for that I am responsible."

Grace did not drink that day. I would venture to guess that none of the people who came to Gate Twelve drank that day either. Instead, Grace had a moment of sanity, realized she could not do it on her own, took the action of asking for help, and received it immediately. This help is available to all of us if we want it and sincerely ask for it. It never fails.

Jim C. Jr.

Grade level:
**Grades 9
to 12**

**Tough Stuff—
Cutting**

TITLE: **COOKIE CUTTER HANDS**

BOOK: **Chicken Soup for the Teenage Soul on Tough Stuff**

PAGE: **254**

TIME TO READ: **5 minutes**

TOPICS: **Tough Stuff—Cutting**
Asking for help
Living and learning
Making choices

AGE LEVEL: **Grades 9 to12**

SYNOPSIS: **The loss of her mother, then her boyfriend, causes a freshman girl to suppress her emotional pain by turning to cutting as a release.**

NOTES TO TEACHER:

Use caution if you choose to read this story to younger or more immature students. Focus on asking for help, as well as the importance of developing healthy coping skills to deal with pain that we all face during our lives.

For detailed background information on learning to ask, turn to the Appendix, page 302.

Chicken Soup for the Teenage Soul on Tough Stuff,
Cookie Cutter Hands

PRE-QUESTIONS:

In writing, list the coping devices you use when dealing with emotional pain.

- Put a + next to ones that would be considered healthy.
- Put a – next to those considered to be harmful.
- What does your list tell you about yourself?

Read Story

POST-QUESTIONS:

Brainstorm healthy ways to deal with emotional pain.

Make a combined classroom list of ways to cope with and heal one's pain.

STUDENT ACTIVITIES:

Using the class list from above, choose activities that fit for you.

- From that list, make an artistic deck of cards, entitled, "Healthy Things To Do When I'm Down."
- Whenever you are in an emotional slump, randomly select a card and then do the positive activity suggested.

Cookie Cutter Hands

It started a few years ago—the cutting. My boyfriend had just broken up with me, and my mother disappeared. She left a note—that was it—and then was gone.

On the outside I was your typical high-school freshman. I was in the popular group. Older boys liked me, and I earned straight A's. I was told to be grateful, to rejoice that I didn't have to keep a job after school, and that I could attend a private college back east after graduation. I was told that everything was going to be okay. I was told to smile and not to think about Mom or stress out over school. I was told not to care. Except, the problem was that I did care. I cared about Mom leaving and my boyfriend dumping me—and not being able to talk to anyone. I cared that my dad was always working and that I was always alone. I cared about everything—and I felt so alone.

On the inside I was tormented by feelings of angst, loneliness, and self-loathing. My mother's leaving confused me. I was ashamed and humiliated over my breakup with my boyfriend. In a sense, I felt dead. It was as if I went to school mummified. No one knew that my insides were rotting away, slowly.

I never talked about these feelings with my friends. Why would I? What would they say? How would they react? I was happy and fun to hang out with at school, and nothing was ever wrong. I grew up in a neighborhood where the grass was always cut and sixteen candles on the cake justified a shiny new car.

Somehow, even though I was suffering, I couldn't feel it. I wanted to feel the pain that I could not understand. I wanted to reshape the crooked emotions into a neat little line that stretched across my right arm, a line that curved around my ankle, a line that liberated the caged ghosts screaming inside me. The razor was like a tool, a wrench used to tighten the screws on my innards and keep them in place so that I didn't have to cry in public or talk about my pain or feel alone.

With every red beaded line, I would sigh in calm relief. I didn't cry when I was hurt or upset. Instead, I cut. The complex emotions leaked from my flesh in the form of blood, rather than from my eyes in the form of tears. Anytime I felt empty or stressed or confused, anytime I looked in the mirror—hating myself and my cursed reflection—I would cut. I would cut just to bleed, to know that I was still breathing, to feel my heart race and my nerves stir.

My secret kept me safe. I became addicted to a pain that didn't hurt, but instead felt nice. I sought refuge in the shower with my cookie-cutter-like razor, making imprints on my soft flesh: circles and lines, hearts and stars. I was steady with my razor. The whole world seemed to blur and slow down, and the cuts left me calm as I watched the crimson tears drip onto the white shower tiles.

I hid my scars under designer blouses with long sleeves. Sometimes I let them show.

"Darn cat," I would say if anyone asked. "Darn friggin' cat."

My addiction to self-mutilation lasted all through high school. No one knew there was a war going on inside of me. I was really good at hiding it. Sometimes I flirted with the idea of pressing the razor harder into my wrist to make the whole world stop. I never did, though, thank God. Instead I got caught.

After four years of hiding my cookie-cutter hands and neatly sliced arms, my father finally noticed my self-inflicted wounds. I couldn't use the same excuse with him. He knew we didn't have a cat.

I felt naked showing my father my scars. I didn't want to share them with him. I was angry with him for being so unaware, for letting my mother leave, and for abandoning me with my pain. He scrutinized the red marks under my sleeves and the scabbed lines beneath my socks. And then he cried. My father had never cried before. I cried, too, and at that moment, I snapped. I suddenly realized how unhappy I was. I wasn't happy at school, and I wasn't happy after cutting myself. Cutting had been a release, an ephemeral exhale, a brief hope that I could make it hurt enough to release the pain so that I could smile again, and that my smile would be for real. I wanted to make myself bleed and then watch myself heal. I wanted to be in control of the wounds inflicted in order to see the pain I felt inside, and, yet, I realized at that moment that I wasn't in control of anything.

I started seeing a doctor and learning how to express my emotions and make my pain tangible. I wrote in my diary and played the guitar. I talked to my father and my friends at school. I talked to my new boyfriend. I tried to get out of the house as much as possible, exploring nature and the other side of the window. I took in the air and relaxed. Slowly, it became easier. Slowly, my addiction lessened, and I was okay. It was hard, but I grew stronger each time I faced my pain. I realized that for the past four years, I had been walking through shadows without taking the time to look up at the purple jacaranda trees that cast them.

Kelly Peters
As told to Rebecca Woolf

TITLE: **THE GRADUATION SPEECH**

BOOK: Chicken Soup for the Teenage Soul on Tough Stuff

PAGE: 212

TIME TO READ: **7 minutes**

TOPICS: **Tough Stuff—Suicide**
Tough stuff—taunting
Acceptance and belonging
Living and learning

AGE LEVEL: Grades 10-12

SYNOPSIS: In rhyming verse, Jesse, the senior president, speaks of the death of a class-mate—the valedictorian, who was endlessly taunted and teased. Now his dreams will never be attained, and the silence of his would-be speech is convincingly loud.

NOTES TO TEACHER:

It is recommended that you practice this one aloud, to get the proper rhythm to carry it through to its powerful and surprising ending.

HIGH SCHOOL:

PRE-QUESTIONS:

Have you ever taunted or teased someone?

• About what?

• How did you feel doing it?

Have you been on the receiving end of such teasing?

• How did that feel?

Have you ever witnessed taunting or teasing, and not done anything to stop it?

• How did that feel?

Taunting or teasing seems like such an elementary-school kind of thing—is it?

• Discuss this concept, and cite examples without using any names.

Read Story

POST-QUESTIONS:

Imagine being a senior at graduation and hearing Jesse's speech, followed by Charlie's "silence."

• Write your thoughts, feelings, and impressions as if you were there.

• Discuss these in dyads or **Circle Talk groups** (Appendix, page 311).

To capture some of your feelings about suicide, do the worksheet found in the Appendix, on page 358.

STUDENT ACTIVITIES:

Write a poem or short story as seen through Charlie's eyes.

Write Charlie's valedictory speech, as if he had been alive to present it.

Research the mass murders at Columbine or Virginia Tech where teasing and/or isolation seemed to play a role in the minds of the murderers.

• Design a "prevention program" that could be implemented at your school.

The Graduation Speech

Jesse was well liked by everyone, so everybody anticipated what he had to say
As he walked up to the microphone, on graduation day.
For a moment he remained silent, as he peered at the faces from his senior class,
And then Jesse leaned into the microphone, and finally spoke at last:

"As your class president, I'm here to speak to you today.
I was up most of the night, considering what words that I should say.
I reminisced on school days, and all the many things I've done,
So many memories came to mind, but my thoughts kept me focusing on one."

And then Jesse held up a photo, and he moved it all around,
As everyone leaned to view it, and silence was the only sound.
You could have heard a pin drop, as Jesse placed the picture in full view,
And began talking of a classmate, that no one really knew.

"Charlie's life seemed meaningless, compared to yours and mine,
Because none of us understood him, we never took the time.
We saw only what we wanted to, that Charlie was not cool,
He was far from being popular, the butt of all our jokes in school.

"That's what we knew of Charlie, that much we decided on our own,
He simply wasn't worth our time, he was an outsider who deserved to be alone.
But you see Charlie had a passion, deep within he had a dream,
It was his one desire, to play for our soccer team.

"And of course that was ludicrous, it was totally absurd,
Charlie was no athlete, he was the senior nerd.
In gym class he was never captain, he was always chosen last,
He was the poster child for unpopular, he preferred history, science, and math.

"And so some of us took it upon ourselves to keep Charlie from wanting to play,
For weeks we taunted him with insults, day after day after day.
We made sure that he wasn't welcomed, by anyone else on the team,
For whatever foolish reasons, we were set on destroying his dream.

"And I'm here now to tell you, as your class president, I was wrong
I'm here to speak for Charlie, who couldn't be here, because you see he's gone."
Jesse paused just for a moment, to give time for his words to sink in,
As he looked about at the faces, of parents, teachers and friends.

"I'm not sure if all of you know it, I'm not sure if anyone cares,
But the reason Charlie isn't with us is a reason I feel I must share.
Cruel words, they are definitely weapons, they destroyed Charlie's body and soul,
For all of the taunting and teasing left Charlie feeling out of control.

"And Charlie alone in a battle, gathered his weapons to fight.
He purchased some drugs from a dealer, his mother found his body last night.
Maybe it was only an accident, maybe Charlie wanted to die,
But no matter how it happened, we as his classmates know why.

"For who in their lives hasn't been teased, or made to feel unbearable shame,
I'm certain that everyone in this room has endured some heartache and pain.
And maybe boys will be boys and girls will be girls, and we each have our battles to fight,
But no matter our justification, hurting Charlie was never right."

And then Jesse took Charlie's picture and held it firm in his hand,
And spoke to the photo before him, words unrehearsed and unplanned.
"If only I'd helped somehow, given you guidance to conquer your dream,
If only a teacher, a classmate, if someone would have just intervened.

"But I know I can never go back, I can never undo what has been,
For you will never receive your diploma, or ever play soccer again.
But deep in my heart I wonder, I can't help asking what if . . .
I would have reached out to you Charlie,
Would your school years have ended like this?"

Jesse stood lost in his thoughts of a life that was ended too soon,
Until muffled coughs caught his attention, and nervous whispers began filling the room.
And then Jesse turned with a smile, before retreating back to his chair,
Teaching a valuable lesson, with his final words filling the air:

"I would like to introduce our valedictorian, he will be speaking today,
Please give him your full attention, please hear all that he has to say."
And then Jesse set Charlie's picture down, on the podium facing the crowd,
As the silence told Charlie's story, a message quite convincingly loud.

Cheryl Costello-Forshey

PART THREE

Additional Stories
That Inspire
and Motivate

Short Shorts

Sometimes, the most powerful lessons follow the period at the end of the final sentence of the story.

In the silence of the ending,
    thoughts form . . .
    the mind ponders . . .
    no questions are necessary . . .
    no activities to clutter the process . . .

It is with this concept in mind that we have included some of our favorite "short shorts."

These stories have no lesson plans, merely the space for thoughts to form. Most of them require only a couple of minutes to read, but their powerful impact leaves students with much to consider.

We recommend that these stories be read in the final minutes of class, as you send your students out the door with their private wonderings.

A Simple Hello

I have always felt sympathy and compassion for the kids I see at school walking all alone, for the ones who sit in the back of the room while everyone snickers and makes fun of them. But I never did anything about it. I guess I figured that someone else would. I did not take the time to really think about the depth of their pain. Then one day I thought, *What if I did take a moment out of my busy schedule to simply say hello to someone without a friend or stop and chat with someone eating by herself?* And I did. It felt good to brighten up someone else's life. How did I know I did? Because I remembered the day a simple kind hello changed my life forever.

Katie E. Houston

Night Watch

Not he who has much is rich, but he who gives much.

Erich Fromm

"Your son is here," the nurse said to the old man. She had to repeat the words several times before the man's eyes opened. He was heavily sedated and only partially conscious after a massive heart attack he had suffered the night before. He could see the dim outline of a young man in a U.S. Marine Corps uniform, standing alongside his bed.

The old man reached out his hand. The marine wrapped his toughened fingers around the old man's limp hand and squeezed gently. The nurse brought a chair, and the tired serviceman sat down at the bedside.

All through the night, the young marine sat in the poorly lighted ward, holding the old man's hand and offering words of encouragement. The dying man said nothing, but kept a feeble grip on the young man's hand. Oblivious to the noise of the oxygen tank, the moans of the other patients, and the bustle of the night staff coming in and out of the ward, the marine remained at the old man's side.

Every now and then, when she stopped by to check on her patients, the nurse heard the young marine whisper a few comforting words to the old man. Several times in the course of that long night, she returned and suggested that the marine leave to rest for a while. But every time, the young man refused.

Near dawn the old man died. The marine placed the old man's lifeless hand on the bed and left to find the nurse. While the nurse took the old man away and attended to the necessary duties, the young man waited. When the nurse returned, she began to offer words of sympathy, but the marine interrupted her.

"Who was that man?" he asked.

Startled, the nurse replied, "He was your father."

"No, he wasn't," the young man said. "I've never seen him before in my life."

"Then why didn't you say something when I took you to him?"

"I knew there had been a mistake by the people who sent me home on an emergency furlough. What happened was, there were two of us with the same name, from the same town, and we had similar serial numbers. They sent me by mistake," the young man explained. "But I also knew he needed his son, and his son wasn't there. I could tell he was too sick to know whether I was his son or not. When I realized how much he needed to have someone there, I just decided to stay."

Roy Popkin

Winning Isn't Everything

Great competitors are bred, and great sportsmen are born. I came to that conclusion at a Little League T-ball game in Davis, California, for which my son, Matt, was umpiring. This conclusion was cemented solidly just last week when a friend of mine related a horror story from her son's Little League game.

"One of the coaches just ripped off a kid's head for making a mistake," she noted. "What does that teach him?"

In both of our books, nothing.

We have become a nation addicted to winning. "We're number one" puts smiles on sports fans' faces. Running a good race doesn't always.

This premise relates to every facet of life, whether at home, at church, at school, at work, or at play. Numbers are crunched; awards are pursued; emotions are stifled in favor of one-upmanship. Even the Joneses have a hard time keeping up.

Life too often becomes a tough game with more losers than winners. When claiming the prize eliminates the good in playing, no one wins. Real rewards come from teamwork and playing the game unselfishly for the good of the whole.

On a hot, sunny afternoon, a small boy stepped up to bat. The crowd watched like hawks for his move, waiting for the sought-after home run that most likely wasn't to be. After all, these kids were five and six years old, much too little to stroke a ball past the pitcher, if at all.

The little guy's determination showed in his stance: gritted teeth, slightly bulging eyes, hat-clad head bobbing slightly, feet apart, hands with a death grip on the bat. In front of him was a small softball, sitting perched like a parrot on a lone tee, awaiting the six swings that the batter was allowed.

Strike one.

"Come on, you can do it!" came a solitary voice out of the bleachers.

Strike two.

"Go for it, son!" the proud father yelled encouragingly.

Strike three.

"Go, go, go . . ." the crowd joined in.

Strike four.

"You can do it!" just the father and a couple of viewers crooned, others losing interest and turning to bleacher conversations.

"YOU CAN DO IT!" And suddenly bat hit ball, amazing the crowd and the little boy, who stood rock still, watching it travel slowly past the pitcher on its way to second base.

"Run!"

The stands rumbled with stomping feet.

"Run, run!"

The little boy's head jerked ever so slightly and he took off toward third base.

"No!" the crowd yelled. "The other way!"

With a slight cast of his head toward the bleachers, the boy turned back toward home.

"NO!" My son, the umpire, waved him toward first base.

The kids on both teams pointed the way. The crowd continued to cheer him on. Confused, he ran back to third. Then following the third baseman's frantic directions, he finally ran toward first base, but stopped triumphantly on the pitcher's mound. The pitcher moved back, not sure what to do next. The crowd stood, shaking the bleachers with the momentum. All arms waved toward first base. And with no thought for his position, the first baseman dropped his ball and ran toward the pitcher.

"Come on," he yelled, grabbing the hand of the errant batter and tugging him toward first base while the crowd screamed its approval. The ball lay forgotten as a triumphant twosome hugged each other on the piece of square plastic that marked the spot where lives are forever shaped.

Two little boys, running hand in hand, toward a goal that only one should have reached. Both came out winners. In fact, there wasn't a loser in the stands or on the field that summer day, and that's a lesson none of us should ever forget.

Winning is more than being number one. Winning is helping another when the chips are down. It's remembering to love one another, as biblically directed, despite the flaws that sometimes appear in the fabric of daily life.

No one will ever remember the score of that summer afternoon encounter. Competition, usually fettered by jeering remands, lost to sportsmanship, an innate formula for winning.

When you get to first base with opposing teammates, families, friends, and grandstanders behind you, a home run is never that far down the road.

Mary Owen

I'll Get Another One

At his father's funeral, American Carl Lewis placed his one-hundred-meter gold medal from the 1984 Olympics in his father's hands. "Don't worry," he told his surprised mother. "I'll get another one."

A year later, in the one-hundred-meter final at the 1988 games, Lewis was competing against Canadian world-record-holder Ben Johnson. Halfway through the race, Johnson was five feet in front. Lewis was convinced he could catch him. But at eighty meters, he was still five feet behind. *It's over, Dad,* Lewis thought. As Johnson crossed the finish, he stared back at Lewis and thrust his right arm in the air, index finger extended.

Lewis was exasperated. He had noticed Johnson's bulging muscles and yellow-tinged eyes, both indications of steroid use. "I didn't have the medal, but I could still give to my father by acting with class and dignity," Lewis said later. He shook Johnson's hand and left the track.

But then came the announcement that Johnson had tested positive for anabolic steroids. He was stripped of his medal. The gold went to Lewis, a replacement for the medal he had given his father.

David Wallechinsky

A Brother's Love

She pulled back on the ropes, making the homemade swing fly higher and closer to the leafy branches of the tall sycamore tree. The breeze swished cool against her cheeks. She was five years old, and, at that moment, stomping mad at her eleven-year-old brother, David.

How could he have been so mean? she asked herself, remembering how he had made a face and called her a "big baby" at the breakfast table. *He hates me,* she thought, *just because I took the last muffin out from under his nose. He hates me!*

The swing carried her up so high that she could see for miles. It was fun looking down at the farmyard below. Her red sweater flashed brightly in the morning sunlight. She stopped thinking about being mad at her brother and started to sing a swinging song.

On a distant hill behind the swing, a huge bull with long, sharp horns watched the red sweater flashing in the sunlight. The bull had broken out of his pasture. He was cranky and ready to charge at anything that moved. He snorted and scraped the ground with his hoof. Then he lowered his massive head and began lumbering across the field toward the red sweater he saw swinging back and forth beneath the sycamore tree.

Meanwhile, David was in the barnyard, feeding the chickens. He looked out and saw his little sister on the swing. *Sisters are a pain in the neck,* he thought. Then, suddenly, he saw the bull charging across the field, heading straight for his sister. Without a second thought, David screamed as loudly as he could, "Look out behind you! Get out of there! Run!"

His sister didn't hear him; she just kept singing and swinging. The bull was halfway across the field and closing in fast. David's heart pounded. It was now or never. He ran across the chicken yard, jumped the fence, and dashed toward his sister. He ran faster than he had ever run before.

Grabbing one of the ropes, David jerked the swing to a stop, tumbling his sister sideways to the ground only a second before the snorting bull charged at the place she had been. She let out a terrified yell. The bull spun around, scraping the ground again with his hoof. He lowered his head to charge again.

David yanked on one sleeve of the red sweater and then the other. Pulling it off of his sister, he flung the sweater as far away as he could. The bull followed it.

With horns and hooves, he ripped it into a hundred shreds of red yarn, while David half dragged, half carried his frightened sister to safety.

I was that little girl, and ever since that day, I just laugh when my brother calls me a "big baby." He can't fool me—I know he loves me. He doesn't have to face a charging bull to prove it. But I'll never forget the day he did.

Diana L. James

The Crumpled Blue Ribbon

Mrs. Green, a fourth-grade teacher, was grief-stricken as she watched the news on TV. She had been teaching for more than twenty-two years, but she had never been faced with such disaster as this one on September 11, 2001. She was overwhelmed with despair, until suddenly she recalled the "Who You Are Makes a Difference" story she had read in the first *Chicken Soup for the Soul* book, in which a fourteen-year-old boy's life was saved when his father honored him with a blue ribbon. "That's the answer," she shouted. We don't have to focus all our energies on the terrorists. She thought, *I can teach my students how to love one another and make the world a healthier and more peaceful place right now.* She immediately called to purchase "Who I Am Makes a Difference" blue ribbons.

As she held the blue ribbons in her hands, her eyes twinkled as she announced to her students that today they would not be learning reading, writing, and arithmetic. Instead, they were going to have a hands-on experience of love, life, and what it means to be truly a great human being. One by one, she approached each of them, telling them how very special and unique they were to her. Then she placed a "Who I Am Makes a Difference" blue ribbon just above their heart. The sadness and pain of the recent days faded.

Her students' faces glowed, chests swelled, and spirits soared. If only for those thirty minutes, the gloom and doom of the recent days had lifted, and she was convinced that something very special had occurred on this day.

As her students left her classroom, she handed out extra blue ribbons saying, "Go home and tell your parents, brothers, sisters—everybody—how much you love them. Tell them today! Place a blue ribbon above their heart." The bell rang, her students raced out with a new vigor. She sat at her desk, crying with happiness. She felt such a relief. Love was definitely what needed to be taught in this world right now. At least she had done her part.

Now she hoped that her students would be able to pass on this love to others. But she could not have imagined the difference this exercise would have made to one father.

Less than a week later, a parent stormed into her classroom unannounced.

"I'm Timmy's father," he declared. "Was this your idea to do this blue ribbon project?"

"Yes," Mrs. Green answered.

"Well," the father mumbled, pulling out a crumpled blue ribbon from his pocket, "my son came home the other day and told me how much he loved me and what a good father I am. I've come here to tell you that I'm not a good father. I'm an alcoholic. But something happened to me when my son told me how much he loved me. At that moment, I decided to go to AA for the first time. I even attended church this past Sunday. You see," he said as he turned toward the door, "the world might be hurting, but I don't need to add to the pain. In fact," he said, "from now on, I'm going to become the father my son thinks I am."

Mrs. Green gasped as she watched the father go out her classroom door, knowing that the healing had begun and the world was going to get better . . . because she taught at least one child to love.

Helice Bridges

The Giving Trees

For it is in giving that we receive.

Saint Francis of Assisi

I was a single parent of four small children, working at a minimum-wage job. Money was always tight, but we had a roof over our heads, food on the table, clothes on our backs and, if not a lot, always enough. My kids told me that in those days they didn't know we were poor. They just thought Mom was cheap. I've always been glad about that.

It was Christmastime, and although there wasn't money for a lot of gifts, we planned to celebrate with church and family, parties and friends, drives downtown to see the Christmas lights, special dinners, and by decorating our home.

But the big excitement for the kids was the fun of Christmas shopping at the mall. They talked and planned for weeks ahead of time, asking each other and their grandparents what they wanted for Christmas. I dreaded it. I had saved $120 for presents to be shared by all five of us.

The big day arrived, and we started out early. I gave each of the four kids a twenty dollar bill and reminded them to look for gifts about four dollars each. Then everyone scattered. We had two hours to shop; then we would meet back at the "Santa's workshop" display.

Back in the car driving home, everyone was in high Christmas spirits, laughing and teasing each other with hints and clues about what they had bought. My younger daughter, Ginger, who was about eight years old, was unusually quiet. I noted she had only one small, flat bag with her after her shopping spree. I could see enough through the plastic bag to tell that she had bought candy bars—fifty-cent candy bars! I was so angry. "What did you do with that twenty dollar bill I gave you?" I wanted to yell at her, but I didn't say anything until we got home. I called her into my bedroom and closed the door, ready to be angry again when I asked her what she had done with the money. This is what she told me:

"I was looking around, thinking of what to buy, and I stopped to read the little cards on one of the Salvation Army's 'Giving Trees.' One of the cards was for a little girl, four years old, and all she wanted for Christmas was a doll with clothes and a hairbrush. So I took the card off the tree and bought the doll and the hairbrush for her and took it to the Salvation Army booth.

"I only had enough money left to buy candy bars for us," Ginger continued. "But we have so much and she doesn't have anything."

I never felt so rich as I did that day.

Kathleen Dixon

The Eyes Have It

*It took me a long time not to judge myself
through someone else's eyes.*

Sally Field

The exhibit was entitled "Anne Frank in the World," a collection of photographs that depicted what life was like for Anne Frank and other persecuted Europeans during the Nazi regime.

Although I am fortunate enough not to have lost any relatives to the Holocaust, I was nonetheless reared in its specter. Even as a child I innately understood that, had my great-grandfather emigrated from Russia to western Europe instead of to America, my destiny may have been very different.

So it seemed natural to volunteer my services to Facing History and Ourselves, an educational organization committed to eradicating prejudice via classroom curricula. Their hope is that students will connect the lessons of the Holocaust and other examples of collective violence with the moral choices they face today.

My time was spent stuffing envelopes and answering phones in the office. Though the staff was grateful for my help, I had doubts about my contribution's significance. They also serve who sit and stuff, I reminded myself. Not all crusaders wield swords.

When the call came for docents to lead groups through a touring photographic exhibit, I signed up immediately. This was the interactive role I craved, a chance to do something really useful. During our brief training period, we learned there would be no memorized text to reiterate; tours would consist of applicable information in whatever manner the docent chose to present it. The idea of ad-libbing turned my hands clammy. What if someone asked a question, and I didn't have the answer? I took a deep breath and plunged in.

After the first few knee-knocking tours, I became more at ease. Several children did ask questions that I couldn't answer immediately, but I realized it wasn't crucial that I know the answer. It was more important that the question had been asked.

The majority of students touring the exhibit were adolescents whose attention spans are not lengthy at best. For many of the kids, this excursion was a holiday from the classroom, nothing more. I quickly realized that I needed drastic measures to capture their attention at the start and sustain it throughout. I remembered hearing about an exercise that was used in the 1960s to show students how harmful the myth of white superiority is, and what, as a result of this myth, it meant to be black in America. I tried it first on a group of seventh-grade girls from a local Catholic school.

The students gathered around and looked at me expectantly. I gave them a warm smile.

"Would everyone with blue eyes please raise her hand?" I instructed without preamble.

A number of hands went up. "Good," I acknowledged. "Please come to the front of the group. Those whose eyes are not blue, step to the back wall."

The girls complied, looking bewildered but intrigued.

"Okay, all you blue eyes, come with me. Everyone else, stay by the wall. You will not be taking the tour."

At this point, the group eyed me warily. Had this crazy lady gone off the deep end?

I turned to the pairs of brown and hazel eyes huddled in the back. "Tell me, what did you think of my announcement?"

"It's not fair," one girl proffered. "It doesn't make any sense."

"You're right," I replied. "But that's exactly the way the Nazis treated people they considered inferior: Gypsies, Jehovah's Witnesses, homosexuals . . . not only the Jews."

A blonde girl in the front group looked puzzled. "But how could they tell who was Jewish and who wasn't?"

Out of the mouths of babes . . . "They couldn't. That's why Jews were forced to wear identifying insignias on their clothing."

The girl pondered this, verbalizing her thoughts. "I've never met a Jew before."

"Well, now you can say you have," I smiled.

Understanding dawned, and the blue eyes widened in astonishment. Involuntarily, she backed a few steps away from me. "You're Jewish?"

"I'm Jewish. And you see? I'm no different from anyone else."

I was surprised at my own hurt feelings. Her reaction was completely devoid of malice, yet it spoke volumes. What had fostered this girl's impulse to physically distance herself from the unfamiliar?

In our progression through the exhibit, I noticed that the girl paid close attention to my commentary. She asked introspective questions and digested my replies with a thoroughness that drew giggles from her classmates. The final leg of the tour was a brief oral presentation by a Holocaust survivor. As I watched the plaid skirts and navy-blue blazers shuffle into the lecture hall, the blonde girl glanced back and gave me a shy smile.

During the ensuing weeks, I escorted hundreds of children through the exhibit, running the gamut from inner-city public schools to ultra-Orthodox Jewish day schools. Somewhere in between was a twelve-year-old Catholic girl who went home that evening and told her parents about her class trip to "Anne Frank in the World." Maybe she even told them about the Jewish tour guide who looked just like a regular person.

And if that girl was the only one I had reached with a life-changing message about tolerance and understanding, then I had done something worthwhile.

Cynthia Polansky Gallagher

[EDITORS' NOTE: *For information on Facing History and Ourselves, contact 16 Hurd Rd., Brookline, MA 02445; 617-232-1595; e-mail:* info@facing.org.]

Inspirations

Courage is the discovery that you may not win,
and trying when you know you can lose.

Honor is standing for what you believe—
not for what you know.

Life isn't about living without problems.
Life is about solving problems.

If you plow the field every day—
the only thing that grows is resentment.

Compassion is passion with a heart.
The only thing in the whole universe people need to control are their attitudes.

How a person wins and loses is much more important
than how much a person wins and loses.

If you only do what you know you can do—
you never do very much.

There are no failures—
just experiences and your reactions to them.

Getting what you want is not nearly as important
as giving what you have.

Going on a journey with a map requires following directions—
going on a journey without one requires following your heart.

Talent without humility is wasted.
If you don't want it bad enough to risk losing it—
you don't want it bad enough.

When life knocks you down you have two choices—
stay down or get up.

Tom Krause

Making Sarah Cry

He stood among his friends from school,
He joined their childhood games
Laughing as they played kickball
And when they called poor Sarah names.
Sarah was unlike the rest;
She was slow and not as smart,
And it would seem to all his friends
She was born without a heart.
And so he gladly joined their fun
Of making Sarah cry.
But somewhere deep within his heart,
He never knew just why.
For he could hear his mother's voice,
Her lessons of right and wrong
Playing over and over inside his head
Just like a favorite song.
"Treat others with respect, son,
The way you'd want them treating you.
And remember, when you hurt others,
Someday, someone might hurt you."
He knew his mother wouldn't understand
The purpose of their game
Of teasing Sarah, who made them laugh
As her own tears fell like rain.
The funny faces that she made
And the way she'd stomp her feet
Whenever they mocked the way she walked
Or the stutter when she'd speak.
To him she must deserve it
Because she never tried to hide.
And if she truly wanted to be left alone,
Then she should stay inside.
But every day she'd do the same:
She'd come outside to play,
And stand there, tears upon her face,
Too upset to run away.
The game would soon be over
As tears dropped from her eyes,
For the purpose of their fun
Was making Sarah cry.
It was nearly two whole months
He hadn't seen his friends.

He was certain they all must wonder
What happened and where he'd been
So he felt a little nervous
As he limped his way to class.
He hoped no one would notice,
He prayed no one would ask
About that awful day:
The day his bike met with a car,
Leaving him with a dreadful limp
And a jagged-looking scar.
So he held his breath a little
As he hobbled into the room,
Where inside he saw a "Welcome Back" banner
And lots of red balloons.
He felt a smile cross his face
As his friends all smiled, too
And he couldn't wait to play outside—
His favorite thing to do.
So the second that he stepped outdoors
And saw his friends all waiting there,
He expected a few pats on the back—
Instead, they all stood back and stared.
He felt his face grow hotter
As he limped to join their side
To play a game of kickball
And of making Sarah cry.
An awkward smile crossed his face
When he heard somebody laugh
And heard the words, "Hey freak,
Where'd you get the ugly mask?"
He turned, expecting Sarah,
But Sarah could not be seen.
It was the scar upon his own face
That caused such words so mean.
He joined in their growing laughter,
Trying hard to not give in
To the awful urge inside to cry
Or the quivering of his chin.
They are only teasing,
He made himself believe.
They are still my friends;
They'd never think of hurting me.
But the cruel remarks continued
About the scar and then his limp.
And he knew if he shed a single tear

They'd label him a wimp.
And so the hurtful words went on,
And in his heart he wondered why.
But he knew without a doubt
The game would never end, until they made him cry.
And just when a tear had formed,
He heard a voice speak out from behind.
"Leave him alone you bullies,
Because he's a friend of mine."
He turned to see poor Sarah,
Determination on her face,
Sticking up for one of her own tormentors
And willing to take his place.
And when his friends did just that,
Trying their best to make poor Sarah cry,
This time he didn't join in,
And at last understood exactly why.
"Treat others with respect, son,
The way you'd want them treating you.
And remember, when you hurt others,
Someday, someone might hurt you."
It took a lot of courage
But he knew he must be strong,
For at last he saw the difference
Between what's right and wrong.
And Sarah didn't seem so weird
Through his understanding eyes.
Now he knew he'd never play again
The game of making Sarah cry.
It took several days of teasing
And razzing from his friends,
But when they saw his strength,
They chose to be like him.
And now out on the playground,
A group of kids meets every day
For a game of kickball and laughter
And teaching their new friend, Sarah, how to play.

Cheryl L. Costello-Forshey

One Price

There is only one price:
You pay for this experience with your life.
You can paint on a canvas
one inch square.
You can paint on a canvas
one mile square—
Or any size or shape in between.
The price is the same:
One life, due and payable;
One payment, in full, at the end.
And, you die knowing the scope of your choice:
Timid or expansive,
Cramped or capacious.
Listen to me!
One price.
One price buys all the rides,
or none.
The price is one life:
Spectator or player,
In or out of the arena.
One life.
Time is the only unknown,
And time matters not.
The price of admission—
for one minute or for one eternity—
Remains one life.
Hoarding adds not one second.
Giving subtracts not one breath.
Living itself is the defining action,
The shaping force;
Brave, fierce living,
In the body,
Heart open,
Arms open,
Eyes open.
The act of being shapes and sizes the canvas.
Carpe diem?
Not nearly enough.
Seize life!

Wring from it the payment's worth.
Spread out.
Unfold.
Stretch wide.
Paint in broad strokes
with bright colors.
Man or mouse,
A line or a six-lane freeway,
Gray or a rainbow,
A point or a universe.
Dance on a pinhead or across the stars.
The price remains the same:
One life.

Roberta R. Deen

The Ultimate Sacrifice

Linda Birtish literally gave herself away. Linda was an outstanding teacher who felt that if she had the time, she would like to create great art and poetry. When she was twenty-eight, however, she began to get severe headaches. Her doctors discovered that she had an enormous brain tumor. They told her that her chances of surviving an operation were about 2 percent. Therefore, rather than operate immediately, they chose to wait for six months.

She knew she had great artistry in her. So during those six months she wrote and drew feverishly. All of her poetry, except one piece, was published in magazines. All of her art, except one piece, was shown and sold at some of the leading galleries.

At the end of six months, she had the operation. The night before the operation, she decided to literally give herself away. In case of her death, she wrote a "will," in which she donated all of her body parts to those who needed them more than she would.

Unfortunately, Linda's operation was fatal. Subsequently, her eyes went to an eye bank in Bethesda, Maryland, and from there to a recipient in South Carolina. A young man, age twenty-eight, went from darkness to sight. That young man was so profoundly grateful that he wrote to the eye bank thanking them for existing. It was only the second "thank you" that the eye bank had received after giving out in excess of thirty thousand eyes!

Furthermore, he said he wanted to thank the parents of the donor. They must indeed be magnificent folks to have a child who would give away her eyes. He was given the name of the Birtish family and he decided to fly in to see them on Staten Island. He arrived unannounced and rang the doorbell. After hearing his introduction, Mrs. Birtish reached out and embraced him. She said, "Young man, if you've got nowhere to go, my husband and I would love for you to spend your weekend with us."

He stayed, and as he was looking around Linda's room, he saw that she'd read Plato. He'd read Plato in Braille. She'd read Hegel. He'd read Hegel in Braille.

The next morning Mrs. Birtish was looking at him and said, "You know, I'm sure I've seen you somewhere before, but I don't know where." All of a sudden she remembered. She ran upstairs and pulled out the last picture Linda had ever drawn. It was a portrait of her ideal man.

The picture was virtually identical to this young man who had received Linda's eyes.

Then her mother read the last poem Linda had written on her deathbed. It read:

Two hearts passing in the night
falling in love
never able to gain each other's sight.

Jack Canfield & Mark Victor Hansen

Abraham Lincoln Didn't Quit

The sense of obligation to continue is present in all of us. A duty to strive is the duty of us all. I felt a call to that duty.

Abraham Lincoln

Probably the greatest example of persistence is Abraham Lincoln. If you want to learn about somebody who didn't quit, look no further.

Born into poverty, Lincoln was faced with defeat throughout his life. He lost eight elections, twice failed in business, and suffered a nervous breakdown.

He could have quit many times—but he didn't, and because he didn't quit, he became one of the greatest presidents in the history of our country.

Lincoln was a champion, and he never gave up. Here is a sketch of Lincoln's road to the White House:

1816: His family was forced out of their home. He had to work to support them.

1818: His mother died.

1831: Failed in business.

1832: Ran for state legislature—lost.

1832: Also lost his job—wanted to go to law school, but couldn't get in.

1833: Borrowed some money from a friend to begin a business and by the end of the year he was bankrupt. He spent the next seventeen years of his life paying off this debt.

1834: Ran for state legislature again—won.

1835: Was engaged to be married, sweetheart died, and his heart was broken.

1836: Had a total nervous breakdown and was in bed for six months.

1838: Sought to become speaker of the state legislature—defeated.

1840: Sought to become elector—defeated.

1843: Ran for Congress—lost.

1846: Ran for Congress again—this time he won—went to Washington and did a good job.

1848: Ran for re-election to Congress—lost.

1849: Sought the job of land officer in his home state—rejected.

1854: Ran for Senate of the United States—lost.

1856: Sought the vice-presidential nomination at his party's national convention—got less than one hundred votes.

1858: Ran for U.S. Senate again—again he lost.

1860: Elected president of the United States.

The path was worn and slippery. My foot slipped from under me, knocking the other out of the way, but I recovered and said to myself, "It's a slip and not a fall."

Abraham Lincoln
Quoted after losing a senate race.

Jack Canfield & Mark Victor Hansen

My Moment of Truth

Hi, my name is Candice, and I'm fat. No, you did not just walk into an Overeaters Anonymous meeting. I just wanted to get that out, right away. Some people might think it's not politically correct to use such a vulgar term. They'd prefer I call myself some nice euphemism like "cherubic," "voluptuous," or for those lovers of Xena Warrior Princess, "Amazonian." However, when you are thirteen years old, stand five feet tall on tippy-toes, and weigh in at 150 pounds, most kids your age don't express your condition in such tender terms. I have been called such names as "Lardo," "Wide Load," and even "Candy, the Candy Terminator, No Candy Is Safe with Her Around."

Ironic, isn't it, that my parents named me after my own Achilles' heel—food? But an ice-cream sundae is no substitute for a social life. Not even when they give you extra sprinkles. There is simply not enough ice cream in the world that could make me impenetrable to the hurtful things kids say about me.

I have always enjoyed the movies. It is a way of buying a ticket to the ultimate escape. Movies are a common thread running through most of my memories. Like the summer my parents sent me to a camp for overweight kids in upstate New York. I hated it. Being raised in New York City, I preferred sterile concrete to tick-infested woods. The only nights I ever looked forward to were movie nights in the old casino house. The spray of light from the old projector mesmerized mosquitoes from across the Catskills. There was always that one rebel mosquito that was strangely attracted to the images on the old, worn-out movie screen. It would dance across the scenes; sometimes it was a mustache, sometimes a beard, sometimes it appeared as a kind of weird growth on an actor's nose. I felt like that lone insect in my own life. I was in the picture, and yet no one in the scene seemed to notice me.

That is what I remember most about my time at Camp Stanley. That, and the way we sat around at night discussing things like Chips Ahoy, Entenmann's, and Frito-Lay, as if they were friends back home we longed to see. And, for some, these were indeed their only friends.

I was a chubby toddler and progressed through life expanding ever larger. My size did not go unnoticed by my peers. You would think I would have grown tougher from the years of name-calling. You would be wrong. I enacted the classically wrong reaction every time: I cried. And I cried easily.

My mother would try to console me after school each day. She would lecture me, like a pathetic old football coach trying to boost the morale of his losing team. "They are just jealous of you, honey," she'd recite regularly. "Just ignore them!"

But I knew that she was lying to me. I knew that the whole entire school, including the janitorial staff, could not be jealous of me. Yes, even the school janitor had commented about my size.

My free-flowing tears only loaded my enemies' guns with powerful ammunition. Each of their shots hit the mark. Their constant taunts made me less than excited to go to school with each passing day. I was never going to be acceptable to them, and as a result, my self-esteem was becoming nonexistent.

One day, I was watching Oprah. She had a show called "Fighting Back." There was a middle-aged guy on the panel. He was obviously losing his hair. He had a black fringe of hair around the back of his head. Then, way, way up on top, only a few lonely hairs remained. They were like the lone survivors on a desert island. The man, in an effort to conceal his baldness, let his last few precious hairs grow quite long. With his comb, he could swirl them around his head like a cinnamon bun. He reminded me of a friend of my dad's. He swam at our community pool. Whenever he stepped out of the water, his long top hairs would flop over to the side of his head. The wet strands of hair congealed together and appeared as some sort of love-struck sea urchin, nibbling amorously at the poor man's sunburned ear. His bald head gleamed in the white-hot sun like an SOS. It was quickly noticed by all the neighborhood kids, who would laugh at his expense. But the bald man never seemed to care. He'd just carefully smooth the hairs back into place, suck in his gut, and step out of the troubled waters. Maybe he didn't notice those kids and their cruelty. Maybe he didn't care. Maybe he was in denial. Denial must be like a kind of Disneyland for the adult mind. However, I digress. The man on Oprah did not deal as well with the criticism he received from his coworkers. He admitted that he had never fought back. He grew those few, sad hairs longer, as if he could hide beneath them.

Oprah told him that he had to come out from hiding behind his hairs, that he was a smart man with a lot to offer the world. He should not let these bullies stand in his way. He must confront them. They did not dictate who he was in life.

"You," she told him, "are the only one who is in control of your destiny!"

The whole audience cheered for Oprah. They cheered for the balding man. But most of all, they cheered for the free foot-massager and bunion remover they would receive after the show.

Was I like the balding man? Was I eating my way into hiding? My weight, like his hair, was something I could never hide behind. It was that day that I decided to fight back.

The next day in class my science teacher, Mr. Roster, was leading the class in a lab. Of course, Jill and Haley, the popular girls, were chatting up a storm. Mr. Roster looked up quite suddenly. He was annoyed at their disturbance.

"Would you girls like to share what you are chatting about with the class?" asked Mr. Roster.

The whole class turned to watch what would happen next. They were like rubber-neckers around a three-car pileup. I also turned to look. Bad move on my part. Haley's eyes hit mine like a dart hitting its target.

"What are you looking at, Chubbo? Time for another feeding at the zoo?"

Now the whole class turned its eyes to me. As I turned and looked back at the smirking faces, something finally hit me. Maybe it was Oprah and the bald man. Maybe it was all those years of abuse, which had struck a final chord inside my very soul. Or maybe it was just the heartburn I felt from the tuna tortillas they had served for lunch that day in the cafeteria. It doesn't matter. Whatever it was, it was my moment of truth. I would not look away. I would not cry. I was in control of my destiny. I would confront my fears. With fire in my eyes and total conviction on my side, I looked Haley and all the others who had ever hurt me in my life straight in the eyes and said, "Maybe your little friends aren't afraid of you . . . but I am!"

Of course, right away I knew I had said the wrong thing. What I meant to say was, "Maybe your little friends are afraid of you . . . but I'm not!"

Well, it seems it didn't matter what I said that day. The point is, I stuck up for myself. I didn't run away. Haley and her friends never bothered me again. Maybe it was because they saw the fire in my eyes, or maybe it was because they thought I was totally insane. It just doesn't matter. The important thing is that I confronted my fears, and I was still standing. That was the day I felt like I was no longer watching the world from the outside looking in. I was no longer that dull mosquito thrashing wildly against the movie screen. I was in this movie now, and I liked the ending.

As told to C. S. Dweck

Nothing but Problems

On Christmas Eve 1993, Norman Vincent Peale, the author of the all-time bestseller *The Power of Positive Thinking*, died at age 95. He was at home surrounded by love, peace, and tender care. Norman Vincent Peale deserved nothing less. His positive-thinking ministry had brought peace and renewed confidence to generations of people who realized from his sermons, speeches, radio shows, and books that we are responsible for the condition we're in. Since he felt God did not make junk, Norman reminded us that we have two choices every morning when we wake up: we can choose to feel good about ourselves or choose to feel lousy. I can still hear Norman clearly shouting out, "Why would you choose the latter?"

I first met Norman in July 1986. Larry Hughes, who was president of my publishing company, William Morrow & Co., had suggested we think about writing a book together on ethics. We decided to do that, and the next two years working with Norman on *The Power of Ethical Management* was one of the greatest delights I have ever had in my life.

Ever since that first meeting, Norman had a great impact on my life. He always contended that positive thinkers get positive results because they are not afraid of problems. In fact, rather than thinking of a problem as something that is negative and ought to be removed as quickly as possible, Norman felt problems were a sign of life. To illustrate that point, here is one of his favorite stories, one I have used frequently in my presentations:

> *One day I was walking down the street, when I saw my friend George approaching. It was evident from his downtrodden look that he wasn't overflowing with the ecstasy and exuberance of human existence, which is a high-class way of saying George was dragging bottom.*
>
> *Naturally I asked him, "How are you, George?" While that was meant to be a routine inquiry, George took me very seriously and for 15 minutes he enlightened me on how bad he felt. And the more he talked, the worse I felt.*
>
> *Finally I said to him, "Well, George, I'm sorry to see you in such a depressed state. How did you get this way?" That really set him off.*
>
> *"It's my problems," he said. "Problems—nothing but problems. I'm fed up with problems. If you could get rid of all my problems, I would contribute $5,000 to your favorite charity."*
>
> *Well now, I am never one to turn a deaf ear to such an offer, and so I meditated, ruminated and cogitated on the proposition and came up with an answer that I thought was pretty good.*
>
> *I said, "Yesterday I went to a place where thousands of people reside. As far as I could determine, not one of them has any problems. Would you like to go there?"*
>
> *"When can we leave? That sounds like my kind of place," answered George.*
>
> *"If that's the case, George," I said, "I'll be happy to take you tomorrow to Woodlawn Cemetery because the only people I know who don't have any problems are dead."*

I love that story. It really puts life in perspective. I heard Norman say many times, "If you have no problems at all—I warn you—you're in grave jeopardy—you're on the way out and you don't know it! If you don't believe you have any problems, I suggest that you immediately race from wherever you are, jump into your car, and drive home as fast but as safely as possible, run into your house, and go straight to your bedroom, and slam the door. Then get on your knees and pray, 'What's the matter, Lord? Don't you trust me anymore? Give me some problems.'"

Ken Blanchard

It's Never Your Fault

Yesterday I dared to struggle, today I dare to win.

Bernadette Devlin

I sat there with my body trembling from head to toe, wondering what was happening to me and what would happen next. I knew that what was occurring was not right, but I didn't know how to stop it. I wanted with all my might to push his dark soul away from me, but being about three feet tall and only weighing around forty-five pounds, I didn't have the physical capability.

I was four, and my parents were busy with work and social lives, so they began looking for baby-sitters near our house who could watch my sister and me at night. They found two guys who lived down the street who were more than willing to be our baby-sitters. Although they looked a little scary when I first saw them, my parents assured me that everything would be okay and that I should be on my best behavior. I still had a feeling of insecurity running through my veins. I didn't know why, but I thought the men weren't good people.

After they were there for a couple of hours, I needed to go to the bathroom, so I went upstairs and shut the door. Shortly after, the door opened and in came the older of the two. I thought at first that maybe he just thought I needed some help since I was so young, but then he just stayed there and watched me. As I was getting up to leave, he started feeling me in places that aren't meant to be seen by other people. I didn't do anything to stop it. I was so small, and he was so big. Eventually he stopped, probably so my sister wouldn't become suspicious. He told me not to tell anyone what had happened and that it was to be kept a secret.

Having an older sister, I knew what secrets were and I knew that they were meant to be kept, so I never said a word to anyone. Each time he came over to baby-sit, the same pattern would occur, and I began to feel really uncomfortable and violated; but he was starting to get more threatening, and I was beginning to fear losing my life if I told, so I remained quiet.

In elementary school, visitors from child abuse organizations would come and talk to us. That's when I learned that what was happening to me was called sexual molestation and that it's never the victim's fault. Up to that point, I had been blaming it on myself. They also said that it is very important to tell someone as soon as it happens to you and that telling is the most important thing to do. I really wanted to say something after hearing this, but I still didn't have the courage. I feared that he might come after me if the cops came after him.

The summer before sixth grade, I was walking back to my house after swim team practice. Normally, I walked back with my best friend, but she was staying at the pool all day, so I walked back on my own. As I headed up the long hill, a car started passing by very slowly, and the guys in the car were watching me. I could only make out one person—my former baby-sitter—and I started to run. I ran in between houses and went through backyards. I did everything possible to avoid getting into that car. After a half hour of that car chasing me, I made it into my house. I told my sister what had happened, and she called my mom at work, but she said that we should just lock the doors and watch for the car. I never saw that car ever again.

My junior year, I was on my high school's dance team. We had just finished performing our half-time routine and were in the process of heading back to the bleachers, where we had our bags, when someone who looked kind of familiar spit at me from over the fence and cursed at me. I wasn't sure at the time where I knew the face from, but I got extremely scared. A senior member on the team overheard what had happened and took me to the coaches. She explained to them what had happened, and my coach was about ready to jump over the fence and punch the guy's lights out, but I knew that wouldn't solve anything. That would only make me seem weak and would show that I let his hostility get to me. I wanted to be stronger than that and not give in, so I asked my coach if we could just forget about what happened and just enjoy the rest of the game.

Although I wanted to forget what had happened, I couldn't. I started having panic attacks and nightmares with flashbacks from that football game. I lost my appetite and became really depressed. After a couple months of not being able to eat much at all, my family and friends became very worried and wanted to help in any way that they could. However, I wasn't ready to admit the fact that I had a problem.

One night, after a dance practice, I got these intense pains in my side, and my mom rushed me to the hospital. I was given many tests, but they couldn't figure out what was wrong with me. I wasn't too sure myself. Finally, they took me back for a question-and-answer session, and a psychologist started asking me a ton of questions and had me respond to them. He asked me if I had ever had sexual contact. I wasn't quite sure how to answer that because I never had any willingly, but it did happen, so I told him the whole story. He was shocked to hear me say it so quickly and was glad that I did—and so was I. He asked why it had taken me so many years to tell, and I answered that I had been worried that I would be hunted down if I ever told. He found that quite understandable and contacted some social workers and legal offices to see if anything could be done about the sexual molester. Since I had waited so long and didn't have a witness, there really wasn't anything that could be done except that I should start seeing a psychologist regularly and that would help all the physical pain my body had been enduring.

I'm telling this story not to get sympathy, but because it was an important lesson that I learned. If something happens to you that you suspect isn't right, tell someone right away. It will only help. Your life will become more tranquil. I used to have nightmares any time my eyes would shut, but after telling someone, I can now sleep peacefully. My only regret is not having told earlier.

Hattie Frost, 18

[EDITORS' NOTE: *To get help with child abuse issues of any kind, call Childhelp USA at 800-4-A-CHILD.*]

The Purple Belt

A few years ago, I organized the Kick Drugs Out of America Foundation. It is an organization designed to work with high-risk, inner-city children. The idea is to teach the kids martial arts, to help raise their self-esteem, and instill discipline and respect for themselves and others. Many of the kids, boys as well as girls, come from broken homes and are having trouble in school and in their lives in general. I'm pleased to say that the program has been working phenomenally well. Most young people quickly adapt to the philosophy of the martial arts.

After more than thirty-five years in the martial arts, competing and training thousands of young people, there is one story that is engraved in my memory. It was told to me by Alice McCleary, one of my Kick Drugs Out of America black belt instructors.

One of her young students showed up for karate training without his purple belt. Alice reminded him that part of his responsibility as a student was to have his karate uniform and belt with him at all times.

"Where is your belt?" she asked.

The boy looked at the floor and said he didn't have it.

"Where is it?" Alice repeated. After pressing the boy to answer, he quietly lifted his head and looked at her and replied, "My baby sister died and I put it in her coffin to take to heaven with her."

Alice had tears in her eyes as she told me the story. "That belt was probably his most important possession," she said.

The boy had learned to give his best, unselfishly.

Chuck Norris

Just for Fun

These stories are simply . . . just for fun . . . and may well be the most important chapter of this book to inspire students to read.

In order to create *joyful reading* for your students, we believe it is important to share your favorite fun stories, *without* attaching homework to every story. So we have chosen several favorites for you to simply enjoy with your students. These stories are all play and no work, and many of them take less than a minute to read. We think you will find the time well-spent as you share the playfulness of a fun story. Additionally, we found that this sharing of laughter helps to build a sense of community within the classroom.

We hope you will find the pure *joy of story* evidenced in each of these selections.

A Child's Gift

About a year ago, as I prepared to leave the house, the telephone rang. For a fleeting moment I toyed with the idea of not answering it, but I ran back to the kitchen anyway.

My husband called and said, "Sorry, honey, but I have to work overtime. Guess you'll have to pick up Taylor at school today. I'll be home as soon as I can."

Each week I set aside several hours to bring a little joy into the lives of the women at a nearby home. On this particular day, I was bringing freshly cut red and yellow snapdragons and mammoth zinnias.

Accompanied by my unexpected companion, we started our rounds with bundles of blossoms in my arms and Taylor at my side. After we visited the third or fourth room, I noticed that, just as we were ready to leave each room, my son would hug each woman and then whisper something into her ear. Because I wanted to make sure that we had enough time to visit all of the residents, I didn't ask him what he was whispering, but he elicited a smile from every lady.

Later that evening, during dinner, my husband asked how my volunteer job worked out with our son in tow.

"It was actually lots of fun," I said. "We were quite a pair. Whatever Taylor said to the ladies, it definitely made them happy." Puzzled, I stopped and glanced across the table at our son. "What was it that you whispered?"

Looking at both his dad and me with an angelic face, he responded, "All I said was 'I love you, Grandma. You look soooo beautiful today.' I wanted to make them feel good."

Pamela Strome-Merewether

Surprise Santa

A few days before Christmas, a devout Christian couple held the hands of their young son and walked briskly to their nearby church. But the boy pulled back a bit, slowed, and came to an abrupt halt.

"Santa," he whispered. "Santa!"

The four-year-old broke free of his parents' grasp and ran toward an elderly gentleman with a long, flowing white beard.

Tugging on the stranger's coattail, the youngster begged, "Santa, will you bring me a teddy bear for Christmas?"

Embarrassed, the couple started to apologize, but the man merely waved them aside. Instead, he patted their son on the head, nodded once, winked wryly at the youngster and—without a word—went on his way.

On Christmas morning, a knock interrupted the family's festivities. In the doorway stood the old man holding out a large bear with a plaid bow around its neck.

"I didn't want the little fellow to be disappointed on his holiday," he explained with an awkward grimace and turned to leave.

Uncomfortable and stunned, the parents could only stutter a weak, "Uh, th-thanks. And M-merry Christmas to you . . . Rabbi."

Henry Boye

Discouraged?

As I was driving home from work one day, I stopped to watch a local Little League baseball game that was being played in a park near my home. As I sat down behind the bench on the first baseline, I asked one of the boys what the score was.

"We're behind fourteen to nothing," he answered with a smile.

"Really," I said. "I have to say you don't look very discouraged."

"Discouraged?" the boy asked with a puzzled look on his face. "Why should we be discouraged? We haven't been up to bat yet."

Jack Canfield

Just Do What You Can

It was a chilly fall day when the farmer spied the little sparrow lying on its back in the middle of his field. The farmer stopped his plowing, looked down at the frail, feathered creature, and inquired, "Why are you lying upside down like that?"

"I heard the sky is going to fall today," replied the bird.

The old farmer chuckled. "And I suppose your spindly little legs can hold up the sky?"

"One does what one can," replied the plucky sparrow.

D'ette Corona

Mosquitoes

While on a campout at Cumberland Falls State Resort Park several years ago, my son Tim and I spent the night sleeping in the back of our van.

In the middle of the night, Tim awoke scratching one of many mosquito bites and whispered, "Daddy, why did God put mosquitoes on Earth?"

I didn't have an answer, so I countered with a question, "Why do you think he did, Tim?"

He didn't respond and quickly fell back asleep.

The next morning, as we headed home, Tim suddenly exclaimed, "Daddy, I know why God put mosquitoes on Earth!"

I looked over and couldn't wait for the answer from his proud face.

"Because he didn't want them in heaven, that's why!"

Guy Lustig

The Power of Motivation

People are always asking me: "Tommy, when did you first realize that you could motivate people."

I think I have always had the ability to motivate, but I remember one time in particular, early on in my minor-league coaching career for the Los Angeles Dodgers, when I had a situation that really tested my motivational skills.

I was coaching in the Pacific Coast League for Spokane. It was the bottom of the eighth inning and we were leading 3–2. Bobby O'Brien was pitching, and I knew that if we could just get this next batter out we could go on to win this game.

So I went out to the mound and I asked O'Brien a question.

"Bobby," I asked, "if the heavens came apart right now, and that great Dodger in the sky came down to get you, would you rather go as having gotten this final batter out, or would you rather face the Lord after having given up a hit to this guy?"

Bobby hardly hesitated. "I would rather get him out," he said.

"Okay then," I told him, "then that's how I want you to pitch—as if you were going to die getting this guy out."

I felt good having shared such an inspiring visual message with Bobby and I left the mound and started back toward the dugout. But before I even got there, O'Brien threw the next pitch, and gave up a hit. The other team scored two runs and we went on to lose the game 4–3.

After the game I called Bobby aside.

"What happened?" I asked him. "You said you wanted to get this guy out if it was the last thing you ever did."

"Skipper," he said, "you had me so afraid of dying, I couldn't concentrate on pitching."

Tommy Lasorda
As told to Ernie Witham

Green Salami

That is the best—to laugh with someone
because you both think the same things are funny.

Gloria Vanderbilt

Sometime during the seventh grade two things happened to me. The first was that I got hooked on salami. Salami sandwiches, salami and cheese, salami on crackers—I couldn't get enough of the salty, spicy sausage. The other thing was that my mom and I weren't getting along really well. We weren't fighting really badly or anything, but it just seemed as if all she wanted to do was argue with me and tell me what to do. We also didn't laugh together much anymore. Things were changing, and my mom and I were the first to feel it.

As far as the salami went, my mom wouldn't buy any because she said it was too expensive and not that good for me. To prove my emerging independence, I decided to go ahead and eat what I wanted anyway. So one day I used my allowance to buy a full sausage of dry salami.

Now a problem had to be solved: Where would I put the salami? I didn't want my mom to see it. So I hid it in the only place that I knew was totally safe—under my bed. There was a special corner under the bed that the upright Hoover couldn't reach and that my mom rarely had the ambition to clean. Under the bed went the salami, back in the corner—in the dark and the dust.

A couple of weeks later, I remembered the delicious treat that was waiting for me. I peered beneath the bed and saw . . . not the salami that I had hidden, but some green and hairy object that didn't look like anything I had ever seen before. The salami had grown about an inch of hair, and the hair was standing straight up, as if the salami had been surprised by the sudden appearance of my face next to its hiding place. Being the picky eater I was, I was not interested in consuming any of this object. The best thing I could think of to do was . . . absolutely nothing.

Sometime later, my mom became obsessed with spring cleaning, which in her case meant she would clean places that had never seen the light of day. Of course, that meant under my bed. I knew in my heart that the moment would soon come when she would find the object in its hiding place. During the first two days of her frenzy, I watched carefully to judge the time when I thought she would find the salami. She washed, she scrubbed, she dusted . . . she screamed! She screamed and screamed and screamed. "Ahhhhhh . . . ahhhhhh . . . ahhhhhh!" The screams were coming from my room. Alarms went off in my head. She had found the salami!

"What is it, Mom?" I yelled as I ran into my room.

"There is something under your bed!"

"What's under my bed?" I opened my eyes very wide to show my complete innocence.

"Something . . . something . . . I don't know what it is!" She finally stopped screaming. Then she whispered, "Maybe it's alive."

I got down to look under my bed.

"Watch out!" she shouted. "I don't know what it is!" she said again. She pushed me to one side. I was proud of the bravery she was demonstrating to save me from the "something" in spite of her distress.

I was amazed at what I saw. The last time I had looked at the salami, the hair on it was about an inch long and fuzzy all over. Now, the hair had grown another three inches, was a gray-green color and had actually started to grow on the surrounding area as well. You could no longer tell the actual shape of what the hair was covering. I looked at my mom. Except for the color, her hair closely resembled the hair on the salami: It was standing straight up, too! Abruptly she got up and left the room, only to return five seconds later with the broom.

Using the handle of the broom, she poked the salami. It didn't move. She poked it harder. It still didn't move. At that point, I wanted to tell her what it was, but I couldn't seem to make my mouth work. My chest was squeezing with an effort to repress the laughter that, unbidden, was threatening to explode. At the same time, I was terrified of her rage when she finally discovered what it was. I was also afraid she was going to have a heart attack because she looked so scared.

Finally, my mom got up her nerve and pushed the salami really hard. At that same exact moment, the laughter I had been trying to hold back exploded from my mouth. She dropped the broom and looked at me.

"What's so funny?" my mom asked. Up close, two inches from my face, she looked furious. Maybe it was just the position of having her head lower than her bottom that made her face so red, but I was sure she was about to poke me with the broom handle. I sure didn't want that to happen because it still had some gray-green hair sticking to it. I felt kind of sick, but then another one of my huge laughs erupted. It was as if I had no control over my body. One followed another, and pretty soon I was rolling on the floor. My mom sat down—hard.

"What is so funny?!"

"Salami," I managed to get out despite the gales of laughter that I had no control over. "Salami! Salami!" I rolled on the floor. "It's a salami!"

My mother gazed at me with disbelief. What did salami have to do with anything? The object under the bed did not look like any salami she had ever seen. In fact, it did not look like anything she (or I) had ever seen.

I gasped for breath. "Mom, it's a salami—you know, one of those big salami sausages!"

She asked what any sane mother would ask in this situation. "What is a salami doing under your bed?"

"I bought it with my allowance." My laughter was subsiding, and fear was beginning to take its place. I looked at her. She had the strangest expression on her face that I had ever seen: a combination of disgust, confusion, exhaustion, fear—and anger! Her hair was standing on end, perspiration beaded on her flushed face, and her eyes looked as if they were going to jump out of her head. I couldn't help it. I started to laugh again.

And then the miracle of miracles happened. My mom started to laugh, too. First just a nervous release, a titter really, but then it turned into the full-on belly laugh that only my mom's side of the family is capable of. The two of us laughed until tears rolled down our cheeks and I thought I would pee my pants.

When we finally were able to stop laughing, my mom shoved the broom into my hands.

"Okay, Patty Jean Shaw, clean it up, no matter what it is!"

I had no idea how to clean up something and not look at it or touch it. So, of course, I got my little sister to help me. I could get her to help with anything, as long as I bribed or threatened her.

Because she didn't know what the object was supposed to look like to begin with, she didn't have much fear attached to helping. Between the two of us, we managed to roll it onto the evening newspaper (my dad never knew what happened to it). I carefully, carefully carried it outside and put it into the trash. Then I had my sister remove the remaining fuzz from the carpet. I had convinced her that I was too large to get into the small corner where it had grown. I ended up owing her my allowance for two weeks.

My mom never got mad at me for buying the salami. I guess she thought I had already paid a price. The salami provided a memory of shared, unrestrained laughter. For years to come, all I had to do was threaten to buy salami to make my mom laugh.

Patty Hansen

Be Yourself

President Calvin Coolidge once invited friends from his hometown to dine at the White House. Worried about their table manners, the guests decided to do everything that Coolidge did. This strategy succeeded, until coffee was served. The president poured his coffee into the saucer. The guests did the same. Coolidge added sugar and cream. His guests did, too. Then Coolidge bent over and put his saucer on the floor for the cat.

Erik Oleson

My First Kiss, and Then Some

I was a very shy teenager, and so was my first boyfriend. We were high school sophomores in a small town. We had been dating for about six months. There was a lot of sweaty hand-holding, actually watching movies, and talking about nothing in particular. We often came close to kissing—we both knew that we wanted to be kissed—but neither of us had the courage to make the first move.

Finally, while sitting on my living room couch, he decided to go for it. We talked about the weather (really), then he leaned forward. I put a pillow up to my face to block him! He kissed the pillow.

I wanted to be kissed sooooo badly, but I was too nervous to let him get close. So I moved away, down the couch. He moved closer. We talked about the movie (who cared!), he leaned forward again. I blocked him again.

I moved to the end of the couch. He followed, we talked. He leaned . . . I stood up! (I must have had a spasm in my legs.) I walked over near the front door and stood there, leaning against the wall with my arms crossed, and said impatiently, "Well, are you going to kiss me or not?"

"Yes," he said. So I stood tall, closed my eyes tight, puckered my lips and faced upwards. I waited . . . and waited. (Why wasn't he kissing me?) I opened my eyes; he was coming right at me. I smiled. HE KISSED MY TEETH!

I could have died.

He left.

I wondered if he had told anyone about my clumsy behavior. Since I was so extremely and painfully shy, I practically hid for the next two years, causing me to never have another date all through high school. As a matter of fact, when I walked down the hallway at school, if I saw him or any other great guy walking toward me, I quickly stepped into the nearest room until he passed. And these were boys I had known since kindergarten.

The first year at college, I was determined not to be shy any longer. I wanted to learn how to kiss with confidence and grace. I did.

In the spring, I went home. I walked into the latest hangout, and who do you suppose I see sitting at the bar, but my old kissing partner. I walked over to his bar stool and tapped him on the shoulder. Without hesitation, I took him in my arms, dipped him back over his stool, and kissed him with my most assertive kiss. I sat him up, looked at him victoriously, and said, "So there!"

He pointed to the lady next to him and said to me, "Mary Jane, I'd like you to meet my wife."

Mary Jane West-Delgado

Practical Application

He's teaching her arithmetic,
He said it was his mission,
He kissed her once, he kissed her twice and said,
"Now that's addition."

And as he added smack by smack
In silent satisfaction,
She sweetly gave the kisses back and said,
"Now that's subtraction."

Then he kissed her, she kissed him,
Without an explanation,
And both together smiled and said,
"That's multiplication."

Then Dad appeared upon the scene and
Made a quick decision.
He kicked that kid three blocks away
And said, "That's long division!"

Dan Clark

Consider This . . .

Consider This . . . consists of several lists of famous people who *"failed"* or met with extreme adversity in their rise to the top.

There are no lesson plans with this chapter. The intent is simply to motivate and inspire students.

We recommend reading or posting one example each day for students to ponder, helping them to realize that failures and setbacks are merely "stepping stones to success."

Anna Unkovich found it useful to post one of these success stories, or a famous quote, on the board each day. Students were instructed to write about the story or quote for five minutes in their personal journals, reflecting on what it meant to them. This settled the students into a quiet, classroom mode, while allowing her to take attendance, deal with previously absent students, or complete any other necessary teacher duties. It also was a daily writing assignment, and a safe way for students to deal with feelings about failure or adversity. In many cases, it became a written dialogue between teacher and student that created a sense of caring and security in the classroom.

Overcoming Obstacles

Consider This . . . .*Jack Canfield & Mark Victor Hansen*
Consider This . . . .*Jack Canfield & Mark Victor Hansen*

For other wonderful examples of overcoming obstacles to rise to success, look for "Consider This . . ." in the following books:

A 2nd Helping of Chicken Soup for the Soul, page 251

A 3rd Serving of Chicken Soup for the Soul, page 283

A 4th Course of Chicken Soul for the Soul, page 261

A 5th Portion of Chicken Soup for the Soul, page 301

A 6th Bowl of Chicken Soup for the Soul, page 263

Chicken Soup for the Soul: Living Your Dreams, page 320

Consider This . . .

Consider this:

- After Fred Astaire's first screen test, the memo from the testing director of MGM, dated 1933, said, "Can't act! Slightly bald! Can dance a little!" Astaire kept that memo over the fireplace in his Beverly Hills home.

- An expert said of Vince Lombardi: "He possesses minimal football knowledge. Lacks motivation."

- Socrates was called "An immoral corrupter of youth."

- When Peter J. Daniels was in the fourth grade, his teacher, Miss Phillips, constantly said, "Peter J. Daniels, you're no good, you're a bad apple, and you're never going to amount to anything." Peter was totally illiterate until he was twenty-six. A friend stayed up with him all night and read him a copy of *Think and Grow Rich.* Now he owns the street corners he used to fight on and published a book: *Miss Phillips, You Were Wrong!*

- Louisa May Alcott, the author of *Little Women,* was encouraged to find work as a servant or seamstress by her family.

- Beethoven handled the violin awkwardly and preferred playing his own compositions instead of improving his technique. His teacher called him hopeless as a composer.

- The parents of the famous opera singer Enrico Caruso wanted him to be an engineer. His teacher said he had no voice at all and could not sing.

- Charles Darwin, father of the theory of evolution, gave up a medical career and was told by his father, "You care for nothing but shooting, dogs, and rat catching." In his autobiography, Darwin wrote, "I was considered by all my masters and by my father, a very ordinary boy, rather below the common standard in intellect."

- Walt Disney was fired by a newspaper editor for lack of ideas. Walt Disney also went bankrupt several times before he built Disneyland.

- Thomas Edison's teachers said he was too stupid to learn anything.

- Albert Einstein did not speak until he was four years old and didn't read until he was seven. His teacher described him as "mentally slow, unsociable, and adrift forever in his foolish dreams." He was expelled and was refused admittance to the Zurich Polytechnic School.

- Louis Pasteur was only a mediocre pupil in undergraduate studies and ranked fifteenth out of twenty-two in chemistry.

- Isaac Newton did very poorly in grade school.

- The sculptor Rodin's father said, "I have an idiot for a son." Described as the worst pupil in the school, Rodin failed three times to secure admittance to the school of art. His uncle called him uneducable.

- Leo Tolstoy, author of *War and Peace,* flunked out of college. He was described as "both unable and unwilling to learn."

- Playwright Tennessee Williams was enraged when his play *Me, Vasha* was not chosen in a class competition at Washington University, where he was enrolled in English XVI. The teacher recalled that Williams denounced the judges' choices and their intelligence.

- F. W. Woolworth's employers at the dry goods store said he had not enough sense to wait upon customers.
- Henry Ford failed and went broke five times before he finally succeeded.
- Babe Ruth, considered by sports historians to be the greatest athlete of all time and famous for setting a long-standing home run record, also holds the record for strikeouts.
- Winston Churchill failed sixth grade. He did not become prime minister of England until he was sixty-two, and then only after a lifetime of defeats and setbacks. His greatest contributions came when he was a "senior citizen."
- Eighteen publishers turned down Richard Bach's ten-thousand-word story about a "soaring" seagull, *Jonathan Livingston Seagull,* before Macmillan finally published it in 1970. By 1975 it had sold more than 7 million copies in the United States alone.
- Richard Hooker worked for seven years on his humorous war novel, *M*A*S*H,* only to have it rejected by twenty-one publishers before Morrow decided to publish it. It became a runaway bestseller, spawning a blockbuster movie and a highly successful television series.

Jack Canfield & Mark Victor Hansen

Consider This . . .

My mother taught me very early to believe
I could achieve any accomplishment I wanted to.
The first was to walk without braces.

Wilma Rudolph, three-time Olympic gold medalist in track

Consider this . . .

- Basketball superstar Michael Jordan was cut from his high school basketball team.
- Rafer Johnson, the decathlon champion, was born with a clubfoot.
- Early in her career, Whoopi Goldberg worked in a funeral parlor and as a bricklayer while taking small parts on Broadway.
- Sidney Poitier was told at his first acting audition that he should stick with dishwashing.
- Beyoncé Knowles says she was the really shy, quiet kid in school.
- Eddie Murphy was once paid one dollar per minute as a stand-up comedian.
- Wesley Snipes installed telephones before getting his first movie role.
- It was not until he reached his fifties that Morgan Freeman become a movie star.
- Alex Haley received a rejection letter once a week for four years as a budding writer. Later in his career, he was ready to give up on the book *Roots: The Saga of an American Family.* After nine years on the project, he felt inadequate to the task and was ready to throw himself off a freighter in the middle of the Pacific Ocean. As he was standing at the back of the freighter, looking at the wake, he heard the voices of his ancestors saying, "You go do what you got to do because they are all up there watching. Don't give up. You can do it. We're counting on you!" In subsequent weeks, the final draft of *Roots* poured out of him.
- Wilma Rudolph was the twentieth of twenty-two children. She was born prematurely and wasn't expected to survive. When she was four years old, Wilma contracted double pneumonia and scarlet fever, which left her with a paralyzed left leg. At age nine, she removed the metal leg brace and began to walk without it. By thirteen, she had developed a rhythmic walk, which doctors claimed as a miracle. That same year, she decided to become a runner. She entered a race and came in last. For the next few years, every race she entered, she came in last. Everyone told her to quit, but Wilma kept on running. One day, she actually won. From then on she won many of the races she entered. Eventually this little girl, who was told she would never walk normally, went on to win three Olympic gold medals.
- In 1962, four young women started a professional singing career. They began performing in their church and doing small concerts. Then they cut a record. It was a flop. Later, another record was recorded. The sales were a fiasco. The third, fourth, fifth, and on through their ninth recordings were all failures. Early in 1964, they were booked for Dick Clark's show, *American Bandstand.* He barely paid enough to meet expenses, and no great contracts resulted from their national exposure. Later that summer, they recorded "Where Did Our Love Go?" This song

raced to the top of the charts, and Diana Ross and the Supremes gained national recognition and prominence as a musical sensation.

- Scottie Pippen, who won six NBA championship rings and two Olympic gold medals, received no athletic scholarship from any university and originally made his small college basketball team only as the equipment manager.
- Renowned photographer Howard Bingham flunked his college photography class and was fired from his first job as staff photographer at a Los Angeles newspaper. He went on to become one of the top photographers in the world, working with such notables as Bill Cosby and Dr. Martin Luther King Jr., and circling the globe with Muhammad Ali.
- One of the most beautiful speaking voices on stage and screen belongs to James Earl Jones. Did you know that Jones has long battled a severe stuttering problem? From age nine until his mid-teens, he had to communicate with teachers and classmates by handwritten notes. A high school English teacher gave him the help he needed, but he still struggles. Yet there is no finer speaking voice than his.

Jack Canfield & Mark Victor Hansen

Teacher Motivation

Most teachers are not in education for the pay, the prestige, nor the respect given to the profession. To sum up the reason for teaching in one word, it's passion.

However, even passion runs a little thin at times. So, this chapter, "Teacher Motivation," is to recall the reason for this career choice.

These old favorites, along with new, previously unpublished stories, are designed to remind teachers of their purpose. They may also be read to students to show them a little of their teachers' love of their work.

Some of these stories are fun, while others are more serious. All of them are heartwarming episodes of the passion we feel for our students. We hope you will enjoy these inspiring selections for teachers of all kinds.

Manners

The tired ex-teacher edged closer to the counter at Kmart. Her left leg hurt and she hoped she had taken all of her pills for the day: the ones for her high blood pressure, dizziness, and a host of other ills. *Thank goodness I retired years ago,* she thought to herself. *I don't have the energy to teach these days.*

Just before the line to the counter formed, she spotted a young man with four children and a pregnant wife or girlfriend in tow. The teacher couldn't miss the tattoo on his neck. *He's been to prison,* she thought. She continued checking him out. His white T-shirt, shaved hair, and baggy pants led her to surmise, *He's a gang member.*

The teacher tried to let the man go ahead of her.

"You can go first," she offered.

"No, you go first," he insisted.

"No, you have more people with you," said the teacher.

"We should respect our elders," parried the man. And with that, he gestured with a sweeping motion indicating the way for the woman.

A brief smile flickered on her lips as she hobbled in front of him. The teacher in her decided she couldn't let the moment go and she turned back to him and asked, "Who taught you your good manners?"

"You did Mrs. Simpson, in third grade."

Paul Karrer

The Fragile Eight

Hold a true friend with both hands.

African Proverb

"Please," appealed the principal. "Nobody can handle him. Please take him."

It was the fall of 1987, in Albuquerque, New Mexico. She stood in the spacious hall with Brad Earlewine, the new D-Level special education teacher, discussing eight-year-old Roscoe Williams. This child's aggressive behavior seemed devoid of sensitivity and reason, yet he was so likable. The veteran principal couldn't understand the boy.

Roscoe was a hyperactive, severely learning-disabled child with a communication disorder. He couldn't walk down a hall without causing trouble. He was a whirl of motion, a tiny, black-bespectacled tempest in a teapot. A spindly legged catastrophe dressed in a Superman cape. There was talk about a behavior disorder to add to the baggage he was already carrying.

After batteries of tests, Roscoe was placed in Earlewine's class. The minute the pair looked at each other, there was a certain magic, like two elements combining, both stimulating and challenging each other. Single, caring, and gentle, Earlewine held a degree in special education and had even trained for the priesthood.

A maverick to tradition, he looked for ways to get inside his kids' heads, trying to find a key. His eight "Fragile Ds," as he soon called them, provided his first experience at this level. The bunch had it all. Some were orphans, some sexually abused. Some were full of rage, some immeasurable sorrow. Some possessed every kind of handicap, even genius imprisoned by mixed-up neurology. Like human pincushions stuck with dozens of fluttering labels, they were often the butt of cruel jokes.

"We just don't stand being called names!" he instructed his kids hotly. "Face up to them! Be brave. Don't take it!"

But they took it.

He taught the three Rs, placing each child on an individualized program of studies, but after weeks he couldn't find the spark. One day he thought of his beloved, crusty old uncle who'd taught him chess.

Unorthodox? he mused. Yeah. Why not! It's worth a shot.

He brought a children's chess book to class and began reading the fairytale-like myths that explained the basics. Within a week, the Fragiles, especially Roscoe, gobbled up everything. Earlewine purchased boards for school and sent one home with each kid. While they all showed real promise with the game, Roscoe was the bold, tactical player.

A few weeks later, Earlewine, an adept player, realized that the boy was thinking five to seven moves ahead after only the barest of instruction. Roscoe started studying his teacher's moves and beat him five times in a row.

Something else began to happen in that portable classroom as well. The Fragiles were changing. As they grasped more and more chess, a newfound courage began to emerge. They were absorbed, more confident, purposeful, and even proud.

Earlewine began a before-school chess club. Dozens of kids flocked in, to be taught and played by the Fragiles. It was only a matter of time before the little team began beating junior- and senior-high chess clubs. Boldly, Earlewine entered the whole team in the chess nationals to be held in Albuquerque, where eight hundred top U.S. kids would assemble for the challenge.

Tiny Roscoe Williams became America's newest junior chess champion. Sitting atop four telephone books, he beat a large junior-high boy who never knew what happened until the checkmate. Newspaper reporters stared incredulously when Earlewine explained that his Fragiles, dressed in hand-decorated school Ts instead of classy wool blazers with team crests, were D-level special education students.

Saturday, February 11, 1989, dawned sunny after many days of snow and rain. Roscoe, full of starch and vinegar, hopped onto his bike to deliver candy for the chess club's recent fund-raiser. Laughing at a friend, he looked back over his shoulder, and sailed right through the stop sign. There was a screech of brakes and a horrible thud.

Roscoe hit the side of the automobile, rolled over the hood, flew thirty feet through the air, and struck the median with the right side of his head.

A week later Earlewine was finally allowed to see his young student. Roscoe's face was unrecognizable. His body was there, but it was a hollow shell more dead than alive. Earlewine joined the ancient practice of the laying-on of hands by adding his white hands to a dozen black ones, all members of the Pilgrim's Rest Church, who touched the bandaged, broken lump under the covers. Voices sang old spirituals that rose and floated softly into the beautiful Southwest's burgeoning spring evenings.

Roscoe was transferred to the Carrie Tingley Hospital for Crippled Children, unable to move or talk. He was tube-fed because of mouth sutures and fractured teeth. It looked as if he was going to keep his eyes, but mental functioning was almost zero.

At school, Earlewine set up a tape recording station where the Fragiles could make daily personal messages to their friend.

"Please come back, we miss you," they'd record. "Do you remember me?"

The teacher asked that the videotapes of past chess matches be played twenty-four hours a day. He sneaked kids to the bedside. One day, Earlewine brought a chessboard and set it up in front of the zombie that was Roscoe. By now, Roscoe's eyes were open, but no recognition, no spark, no life was living within.

"Okay, Buddy," the teacher began, "when I hold my hand over a piece, and you see a move you want to make, blink your eyes."

Earlewine touched pieces one at a time, pointing to all the possible moves, looking up and waiting. On the last choice, he detected the barest twitch.

"He's awake!" the teacher ran hollering down the hall.

Nobody believed him, but Earlewine didn't give up.

Finally released home, one day Roscoe said, "Uh-huh," his old stock phrase. But he made little progress past that. When authorities wanted to put him in a training school for the mentally handicapped, Earlewine demanded his student back.

"I can do this! My kids can do this," he beseeched. "Give us two weeks. Please."

The Fragiles cut Roscoe's food. They fed him, toileted him. They never left his side, nor did they stop talking to him or wrapping him in their arms. Earlewine told the kids they had to believe Roscoe was in there, that he would return. Every one of them surrounded their friend with such patient compassion and such unending tenderness that one day there was a spark in his eyes—just the barest flash of memory.

"You remember!" they cheered.

"Uh-huh," he chuckled.

And the remembering continued. Things flooded back in torrents. Through the days, their old Roscoe came back for longer and longer periods, and so did the sparkle and even the two-step. The kids supplied missing pieces anytime he needed them. The little group of barrio kids and their very special teacher never broke the circle of kind and gentle caring, praise, and celebrations. They simply willed him, loved him, back to life.

In the spring of 1990, the Fragiles, including Roscoe, went to the Kansas City Nationals, a chess tournament that attracted one thousand players. The boy who was loved back to health won a gold medal and placed tenth in the nation.

Isabel Bearman Bucher

[AUTHOR'S NOTE: *Roscoe Williams and Brad Earlewine are still close. Every couple of months, they meet and set up the board. Roscoe volunteers his time, teaching chess to kids in after school programs, and Brad still dazzles his students with the game of Kings.*]

I Like Myself Now

Once you see a child's self-image begin to improve, you will see significant gains in achievement areas, but even more important, you will see a child who is beginning to enjoy life more.

Wayne Dyer

I had a great feeling of relief when I began to understand that a youngster needs more than just subject matter. I know mathematics well, and I teach it well. I used to think that was all I needed to do. Now I teach children, not math. I accept the fact that I can only succeed partially with some of them. When I don't have to know all the answers, I seem to have more answers than when I tried to be the expert. The youngster who really made me understand this was Eddie. I asked him one day why he thought he was doing so much better than last year. He gave meaning to my whole new orientation. "It's because I like myself now when I'm with you," he said.

A teacher quoted by
Everett Shostrom in Man, The Manipulator

One Child

*Live to shed joys to others. Thus best shall
your own happiness be secured.*

Henry Ward Beecher

Sorting through my mail while standing in the school office, I was surprised to see a letter from my previous principal. I skipped through the rest of the mail and quickly opened that letter, curious to see why she was contacting me. Inside the envelope, I found a submission for a Teacher of the Year award. A Post-it note stuck on top bore my principal's handwriting: "How wonderful to have touched someone's life in this way." As I looked down to see which student had written the essay, I saw "Lisa Nicholson"* written in another familiar hand. My eyes immediately filled with tears. It was late June, the very end of the school year, and I was in the process of packing up my room, but not just for summer vacation. My husband and I were relocating to another state, and I didn't even know if I would be teaching the following year. I was very emotional as it was and could not handle this, so I stuck the essay at the bottom of the mail pile and returned to my classroom.

As I sat at my desk in my quiet classroom, long after my students had gone home, I began to think about Lisa. I was surprised she had written anything about me, and although I knew how hard I had worked to help her, I didn't think she realized all I had done. I remembered how bitter and angry she was when she first entered my fourth-grade classroom three years before. She was very volatile, oscillating between being withdrawn and sharp; sometimes, she was even warm. I knew something was going on with her, and I tried several times to talk to her to see what was wrong. At first, she resisted, but then, one day, while she chose to have lunch with me in the classroom instead of in the cafeteria with her friends, she burst into tears and told me how her teenage brother had been murdered the year before. I had never encountered such a tragedy, and I didn't even know how to respond. I listened to her, and my eyes filled with tears. Soon, she regained her composure and the rest of the students returned from lunch, but I felt sick all day. I wanted so desperately to help her, to take away her pain, but I didn't know how. I knew that coddling her would turn her away.

For the rest of the year, I did what I could without making it obvious that my heart was breaking for her. I started an after-school club and always had a snack for any of the kids who stayed so that she (along with several other students who were dealing with personal demons) would stick around a little while longer for extra personal attention and academic help. I attended a workshop on helping children deal with grieving and death. I tried to establish a relationship with her mother to work together to help her, but I don't think she was ready for it. I wanted to do more, but I didn't know how. Before I knew it, the school year was coming to an end. As the year progressed, I took every opportunity to spend one-on-one time with Lisa. Sometimes, our time together would leave me feeling optimistic, but mostly I would be an emotional wreck for a week after listening to her pain.

One day in spring, Lisa asked me if she could sing "God Bless America" after the Pledge of Allegiance. I quickly agreed, although I was surprised at such an odd request. After hearing her sing,

---

Not her real name.

I was awestruck. I couldn't believe a nine-year-old could have such a voice. She had the vocal power of a gospel singer combined with the sweet tone of an angel. The entire class cheered for her as she quietly took her seat. That same day, I went to the music teacher, who was preparing for the summer concert, and I asked her if Lisa could do a solo in the show. She told me that she normally didn't consider fourth-graders for solos, but when I told her about Lisa's voice and about the hard time she'd been having, she agreed to let Lisa audition.

I will always remember how proud Lisa was when she announced that she would be the only fourth-grade student singing a solo at the concert; I will also always remember how proud I was of her when I heard her sing her heart out in front of a huge audience of strangers. I had thought that was the one contribution I had made to her life. I didn't think she would remember anything else about me. Then I read her essay.

I couldn't believe the words that I was reading. Lisa, in very straightforward and simple words, described how she was terribly depressed at the time I taught her, which I already knew, but went on to say that there were many times during that period that she thought of killing herself but resisted because of me. My eyes welled up as I continued to read her account of the way I had impacted her life and prevented her from taking her life by being there for her at such a difficult time. I sobbed for some time after reading her nomination. So many emotions rushed through me at once. I was shocked to realize how desperate she really was, but simultaneously grateful that she didn't act on that desperation. Then I was proud of myself for being such a significant instrument in someone else's life. Mostly, I was humbled at the miracle of our everyday simple efforts. I did work extremely hard to help Lisa, but never did I realize just how high the stakes had been.

If Lisa hadn't heard of the Teacher of the Year award, and if the newspaper sponsoring it didn't forward her nomination to the principal of the school, and if the principal hadn't then forwarded it to me, I never would have fathomed the impact I had on such a precious little girl. I wondered how many other teachers helped students in similar ways, without ever having the opportunity to realize the impact they had. I wondered how many other human beings, who do good every day for the people around them, go unacknowledged, never knowing of the power of their simple acts of kindness and caring.

When I finally pulled myself together enough to gather my things to go home for the night, I looked around my classroom and thought about each of the little lives I had been so blessed to spend the past ten months with. I loved each and every one of them. While I realized I might never see any of them again, I felt such peacefulness knowing that I had given them my best every day we were together.

Regina Hellinger

Hulk Heaven

You cannot shake hands with a clenched fist.

Indira Gandhi

I was a young teacher, the new kid in the department, and so I got to teach the third-period sopho-more English C class. Every day, I walked to that classroom with chest tightened, hands clenched, and the sternest look I could muster. Period Three meant facing a class of twenty-five insolent hulks, with a few girls mixed in. Everyone knew that C was a euphemism for bored, intransigent, lazy—or any combination thereof.

At 10:23 every morning, I sat terrified and sweating as the hulks lumbered into my class. Walt, short and stocky, had a police record. John had been kicked off the football team and now sat with his long legs raising and lowering the desk so that it made intermittent clunks that echoed on the wood floor. Nick sat near the outside wall, twisting the window-blind cord into knots. And Vin kept dropping his books during some of the rare moments of silence.

They talked to each other, called out answers at random and banged knuckles on the desks. When I asked them to write, they dropped pencils, crumpled their notes, and sent paper airplanes flying. I set down rules. I pronounced consequences. I gave ultimatums. I told them in no uncertain terms that they had to change their behavior. The daily quizzes I gave to keep them quiet resulted in daily piles of papers for me to correct, but brought no noticeable improvement to their behavior.

One day, the police came to the door to question Walt about something, and that inspired John to clunk the desk even louder. Out of sheer desperation, I ordered John to the principal's office. He looked at me in disbelief, saying, "Why me?" then proceeded to take a full five minutes to unwind his lanky frame from his desk and clomp to the front of the room. When he reached the door, he turned to face the class and bowed while they all clapped.

I left school that day—and every day—frustrated and exhausted. By the time I finished grading all my disciplinary quizzes, I barely had the time and energy to walk my dog. Clearly, I was spending my personal resources and the taxpayers' money on enforcing discipline, not on teaching English. What a waste! I finally got it: the only behavior I could change was my own. What if, instead of act-ing from fear, I acted from love? What if, instead of standing over them in all my imposing sixty-one inches, I worked side by side with them as a fellow learner? Clearly, the clenched fist wasn't working. Why not open my hands and my heart?

The next morning, I convinced the principal's secretary to give me enough small, soft-covered notebooks for my Period Three class. At 10:23, after giving one notebook to each of my students and one to myself, I announced that we were going to write as fast as we could for three minutes without stopping, and without any regard for spelling, punctuation, or grammar. During a moment of stunned silence, I saw a number of sideways glances, raised eyebrows, and shrugged shoulders. I said, "Look. I'm working on my writing, too, and I'm going to write along with you. No questions asked. If you don't know what to say, then just write 'I don't know what to write' for three minutes without stopping." Nick punched John in the back while John's eyes rolled in disbelief. "Let's go," I said. My heart was pounding as I began to write. After three minutes, I cautiously looked up and saw twenty-five hulks bent over small soft-covered notebooks, scribbling away.

We continued this drill every day at the beginning of the class period for the rest of the year. The change occurred slowly. The little notebooks became sources of information and instruction. We started by sharing words that jumped out at us from someone's writing. Then it grew. It became cool to talk about writing, to expand vocabulary, and even to spell correctly. We went to the notebooks to use our own sentences for revision, and we learned how to work in pairs and groups. When they wrote, I wrote. I didn't diminish my subject-matter expertise, but I did let them know that I found writing hard work, too. And that was the truth. I read some of my work to them and told them where I was stuck. They offered suggestions and asked helpful questions. When Walt said, "You mean you don't know all the answers?" I realized that this time they were laughing with me instead of at me.

Books stopped dropping on the floor, knuckles no longer banged on the desks, and John's desk stayed miraculously in place. On a memorable Tuesday, I heard Walt call out to Vin, "Hey, what do you think of this description of how the inside of a police car smells? Pungent."

Vin said, "Great word. I've never been inside a police car. What else did you smell and see in there?"

Gradually, Vin started to turn his love of sudden and unexpected sound and rhythm into poetry. Nick disengaged himself from the window cords and became the class vocabulary expert, keeping a thesaurus on his desk for general consultation. On the day John got applause for the piece he wrote on motorcycles instead of his walk to the principal's office, I wanted to dance in the streets.

The notebooks became inspirations for longer pieces. After about six weeks of small, daily steps that built on the three-minute writing, I got to class early one day to find Walt writing busily in his notebook. Head down, he said, "Last night I thought of more stuff that I wanted to say about that day in the police car." When he looked up at me for an instant, I saw tears in his eyes. I touched his shoulder gently and said, "Let me know if you want to share any of this with me." He looked up once again, this time with a tearful smile, and we began to share our stories.

From that point on, we all unclenched our fists—and our hearts. The threats and ultimatums were gone. I went home energized instead of depleted, and the taxpayers were finally getting what they paid for. Caring and mutual respect, mixed with a bit of humor, worked every time. It was so simple once I got it. The hulks were really angels at heart.

Dee Montalbano

When I Was . . .

When I was five,
I wanted to be a gardener.

When I was ten,
I wanted to be a nurse.

When I was fifteen,
I wanted to be a dancer.

When I was twenty,
I wanted to be a mother.

When I was twenty-five,
I wanted to be an actor.

When I was thirty,
I wanted to be an artist.

When I was thirty-five,
I wanted to be a librarian.

When I was forty,
I wanted to be a counselor.

Now that I am forty-five, I have—
Planted
Cared
Inspired
Nourished
Entertained
Enlightened
Discovered
Guided

I AM A TEACHER

I am living my DREAMS!!!

Filomena Solis Saenz

"Who's on First?"

Do you remember that hilarious "Who's on first?" sketch made famous by Abbott and Costello? Remember how confused and flustered the poor little guy was? As unbelievable as it sounds, I can now identify with him.

The whole thing started when I informed my speech students that their only homework was to come to class the following day with a subject for their next speech. I threatened them with all sorts of unimaginable punishment if they returned unprepared. The next day I traveled up and down the aisles, personally quizzing each student.

"What's your subject?"

"Playing basketball."

"What's your subject?"

"What I did last summer." And so on.

And everything was fine until I came to one very quiet, very timid little girl who sat in the front of the middle row.

"What's the subject you're speaking on?" I asked.

"I don't know," she timidly responded.

"What do you mean, you don't know? You were supposed to have your subject when you came to class. Why don't you have it?"

"I do have it."

"Okay then, what is it?"

"I don't know."

"You said you knew it."

"I do."

"Then what is it?"

"I don't know."

It was beginning to get bizarre. "Look, do you know your subject?" She nodded. "Then tell me what it is."

Close to tears, she barely breathed, "I don't know."

In spite of what you might think, I am not an ogre and the child was obviously in danger of coming unglued. So, quite concerned, I asked, "Did you do the assignment?" She nodded. "Good. And do you know your subject?" Another nod. "Okay, very good. Now what is your subject?"

"I don't know," she whispered.

I was beginning to feel as if I was caught in the Twilight Zone. Meanwhile, the rest of the class was having a field day.

"Just tell me your subject." I begged.

"I don't know," she responded.

Then, from somewhere in the dim recesses of my mind, I realized what she was saying.

"Are you trying to tell me that your subject is 'Things you don't understand or know about'"?

"Yes. *Things I don't know,*" she nodded gratefully.

I do know exactly how Lou Costello felt.

Ron Schnitzuis

Geography Lesson

They came into my classroom carrying bags of clothing. No, it was not clothes-swapping day, nor were we collecting clothes for orphans or the homeless. It was *homework* for my four- and five-year olds—*geography homework,* to be precise.

It all started with Brendan. He forgot to bring an item to show for Share Day. I liked the shirt he was wearing. It was dark blue with an interesting Hawaiian-type print. "Let's read the label and see where your shirt came from." I read, "Bangladesh," pointing to that country on the map. "Bangladesh, Bangladesh" repeated the children. They seemed to love the melodic flow of that word.

Soon, I was reading the labels of all the T-shirts, dresses, sweaters, and jackets walking into the classroom, then finding the countries on the map. It became a daily ritual.

"Let's see where your clothes came from today. Let's see if we can find a new country." It was truly exciting. That year we found more than sixty different countries that made our clothing.

The labels became our magic carpets that took us to fascinating places all over the world. We traveled down the biggest rivers, climbed the tallest mountains, viewed Paris from the Eiffel Tower, and made the Tower of Pisa lean even more. All clocks became Big Ben, we played the Stradivarius in Italy, hopped with the kangaroos in Australia, and chewed on bamboo with the pandas in China.

That was just the beginning. In the process, we understood why the Panama and Suez Canals were built, and by whom. We discussed why many countries speak English, while others speak Spanish. Other questions arose: Why do so many different countries make our clothes for us? Why do Kenyans run so well? Why do Austrians ski?

We began to read food labels, discovering apples from New Zealand, butter from France, jam from Switzerland. The list was endless.

We read postage stamps, finding the countries on the map. Some of the poorest countries had the largest stamps. And we realized that some of the countries had different names on the stamps, not the names we found on our map.

Since everything we talked about in class originated *"somewhere"*—whether it was a current event, classical music, literature, art, an invention, idea, food, animal, clothing, toy, or anything else—we always found that *"somewhere"* on the map.

If we are to love our worldly neighbors, we have to know something about them. For my students, the world became a smaller place, and a more friendly and familiar one. We sympathized with countries going through tough times, and we rejoiced in the blessings of others.

"What's the longest, skinniest country in the world?" I asked. "I know, it's a pepper," said Amy with a laugh. "Okay class, what is it?" "Chile," they giggled, pointing at the map.

Irene Husaruk-Leon
Kindergarten Ranch School
Covina, California

Writing About Favorite Things

Oh, no! Here he comes again, I thought. Juan** was my most challenging student—*ever!* The scenario was unfolding in my mind. He will flop under the table and begin his chant again, "You can't teach me. You can't *make* me read."

Not only was Juan annoying, but he was making me look incompetent! We were trying an innovative concept called Inclusion. Instead of taking my students with learning disabilities to a separate room, I would help them learn to read within their own classroom setting. Now he was ruining our chances. His third grade classroom teacher, Mrs. Realdo,** wasn't excited about inclusion, nor did she think co-teaching would be successful. I knew it could work, but she still wasn't convinced.

Now, on our second day, this boy might end it all. I had been praying about him on my drive into school. Now I sent up another quick prayer for guidance, "Please, God, help! *Now!!!*"

One of the boys at the table spoke above the chanting and said, "Mrs. Wiepking. Juan's a really good artist. You should see his dinosaur pictures." Quickly I grabbed a clipboard and snapped on a piece of paper. I slid it with some crayons under the table and told Juan to draw his favorite dinosaur.

The chanting stopped, and I was able to finish the reading lesson with my other students. Juan tapped me on my foot as he slid the clipboard back to me. When I bent over, I was amazed at his drawing and the details that he had included.

"Juan, tell me what you know about this dinosaur."

"His name is T-Rex. He was a meat eater. He was huge!" I wrote Juan's words down under his picture *exactly* as he had said them to me. Then I had him trace over the words with a thin yellow marker. I explained that writing with the yellow marker would make these words belong to him. In addition, it would show him how the letters were made.

After tracing the letters, I asked him to read his story to me. From past experience, I knew that children could always read their own words if they were written down *exactly* as they were said. The trick was to make sure to write precisely what the student said, even if the grammar wasn't correct. Grammar could be learned later.

One of my former students once told me, "I can read my own words. I just can't read your stupid books!" It turned out that Juan was no exception. He read his descriptions of T-Rex verbatim.

The next day I was prepared with the clipboard and crayons waiting for him. He crawled under the table and drew a different dinosaur, and we filled in his words after my regular lesson was finished. Mrs. Realdo asked me how long I intended to keep this up. I assured her it would only be a few more days.

On the following day, Juan joined us at the table while he drew a third dinosaur. By the end of that week, we had five pictures with his words written beneath them. Juan then made a cover where we listed his name as the author and the illustrator. After school, I laminated all of the pages, and put them in a plastic spiral binding, making it his official "book."

On Monday, when I gave Juan the book, he grabbed it, hugged it tightly to his chest, and ran around the room laughing with pleasure. Then he disappeared out the door. Now what? I chased after him and caught up with him just as he was telling the principal that he *had* to show it to her. Then

---

**Names were changed.

Juan proceeded to read his dinosaur book to her. He was beaming and so were we, amidst a few joyful tears.

When we returned, Mrs. Realdo asked Juan to read his book to the entire class.

Personal storybooks became the best teaching tools of my career. From then on, every time I got a new student, the first thing we did was make a book about his or her favorite things.

Once the student saw that his or her words were important and that they were worthy enough to be made into an easy-to-read book, *then* the student was willing to give other books a try. They seemed to understand that other people's words must be important to them, too, and therefore were worth reading.

With this attachment to our own words, there is a bonus concept that relates to writing assignments. If students need to know how to spell a word, they can often find it in their personal books where they have used it before. It opens up the entire reading and writing process, because the stories are about things that the students are interested in and can relate to.

Furthermore, this idea can be adapted to any age group, or learning situation regarding the development of reading skills—special education, ESL, or virtually any person or group that struggles with the written word.

It is a fairly universal phenomenon, that people enjoy seeing their own words in print.

Elaine Wiepking

Mystery Reader

Teaching first graders to read can be a challenging undertaking. In order for the children to find a true love of reading, I add excitement to these story periods by incorporating a Mystery Reader.

Parents volunteer to bring their favorite book to read to the students, and to add to the thrill, they are disguised. They cover up their heads and bodies, and sit with their backs facing the class. The students then ask questions, and the mystery person shakes his or her head to answer, or raises fingers to indicate numbers.

On this particular day, MacKenzie's mom was our Mystery Reader. Our first grade classroom was made up of all Caucasian children except for MacKenzie, who was African American.

When MacKenzie's mom arrived, she was draped in a blanket but she didn't have her hands covered. I knew that if the children asked her how many kids she had, or a similar question, she would have to put her fingers up, and the students would then guess who she was by the color of her hands.

We quickly solved the problem by having her wear a pair of gloves. She sat down with her back facing the group of very excited children. They asked their normal questions such as "Do you have a child in this classroom?" "How many children do you have?" et cetera.

The questions continued until the students finally guessed that it was MacKenzie's mom. She read the story to the class and everyone had a great time. We thanked her and she left.

Shortly after her departure, I was telling MacKenzie how I gave her mom the gloves so we wouldn't be able to see her skin.

MacKenzie laughed at me and said, "Mr. Zielinski, it wouldn't have mattered. All moms have skin."

Wouldn't it be great if we could all see the world the way MacKenzie does?

Mark Zielinski

Parent Inspiration

Many parents are searching for a little extra guidance in dealing with their children. In some cases, it is the *parents* who need the guidance.

In either situation, this Parent Inspiration chapter offers stories of help and humor.

We found these stories, especially the humorous ones, to be great introductory ice breakers at any type of parent meeting. The fun stories particularly help to "lighten" situations with groups of parents.

The more serious stories help to set the tone for what may be expected of parents in this important joint venture of educating their child.

Typical of almost all Chicken Soup for the Soul stories, they are heartwarming while providing guidance or lessons in living. We found that our students enjoyed hearing these messages, as well as their parents.

Living and Learning

Be Careful What You Teach Them

Don't worry that your children don't listen to you.
Worry that they are watching everything you do.

Weatherly

Katie was in trouble, and I mean BIG trouble. She was such a sweet and caring kid; I just couldn't imagine what she had done to make her mom so angry. A third-grade teacher always dreams of having a classroom filled with Katies. She worked hard, loved learning, did her homework, had concerned and active parents, and was attentive and a risk taker. And she was never, ever a discipline problem.

So when I received a phone call one evening, I was surprised. Katie's mom was not the type to overreact to situations, and she said she needed my help. It seemed that Katie had been running up sizable charges in the lunchroom. Her mother and father explained that she did not have permission to be buying snacks at school. She brought a great homemade lunch each day, and there was no reason for her to be charging extra items. They assumed a sit-down with Katie would solve the problem. It always had in the past. But when they got another bill from the school cafeteria the following month, her mom and dad became very concerned. It was so unlike Katie to purposefully misbehave, and it was totally out of character for her to ignore her parents.

It was at this point that her parents asked me if I could help them get to the bottom of this situation. I told them that I would try to find out what was going on and would be in contact with them by the end of the week. When I went to the cafeteria to inquire about Katie's charges, the lady told me that Katie charged a lunch every day and took the tray to her table and ate it. This made no sense at all. I had seen the lunches Katie brought and had thought to myself that I wouldn't mind if her mom packed me a lunch once in a while. There was no way Katie would prefer to eat the school lunch. Hey, nothing against school lunches, but really!

I asked Katie to stay in for recess the next day, hoping to solve the mystery. I had a few theories of what might be happening, but I planned on letting her tell me the story in her own time.

She was a rock.

She wouldn't crack.

I couldn't believe it!

There was no way Katie could ignore the stern manner I took with her . . . but she did. I have a pretty good "disappointed teacher" look, but it had no effect on her.

"Why are you charging lunches, Katie?" I asked.

"Because I need to eat lunch," she responded.

"What happens to the lunch your mother makes for you every morning?" I countered, sure that I had her with this one.

"I lose it," she responded, matter-of-factly.

"You lose it?" I asked incredulously.

"Yup, I lose it."

"Every day?" I asked.

"Every day."

I leaned back in my chair, fixed her with my sternest gaze and said, "I don't believe you, Katie." She didn't care. . . .

Well, as upset as it made me to be ignored, there was something about all this, something that just didn't fit.

So I took a new tack.

In my most understanding and concerned voice I asked, "Is someone stealing your lunch, Katie? Is that what is happening?"

"Nope," she said in a tight-lipped sort of way.

"Katie, if someone is bullying you and stealing your lunch, I can help." I really thought I was on the right track with this theory.

"No one is stealing my lunch, Mr. D. I just lose it."

Well, she had me. There was nothing else I could do.

Schools have a law that a student with no lunch must be provided with a lunch. The family is to be billed for the lunch unless they qualify for a free or reduced lunch. There was no way Katie's family qualified for free lunch, so they would have to pay the charges as long as Katie asked for a lunch.

I called her parents on Friday night. We talked about the whole situation, bouncing different theories off one another, but nothing made sense.

The problem was still unresolved the next week when I noticed a boy who was new to the school sitting alone at a lunch table. Other kids had not warmed up to him very quickly, and he always looked sad. I thought I would go and sit with him for a few minutes. As I walked toward him, I noticed the lunch bag on the table in front of him. The name on the bag said "Katie."

He was munching away on a big, delicious, homemade sandwich.

Now I understood.

I talked to Katie that afternoon.

It seemed the new boy never brought a lunch, and he wouldn't go to the lunch line for a free lunch. He had confided in Katie and asked her not to tell anyone that his parents would never take a "handout" from the school. And if he did charge a lunch, he got in a lot of trouble at home. Katie asked me not to tell her parents.

But I did. I told on her.

In fact, I drove to Katie's house that evening after I was sure that she was in bed. I have never seen parents so proud of their child. Katie didn't care that her parents had grounded her. She didn't care that I was disappointed in her. She didn't care about any of these things as much as she cared about a little boy who was hungry and scared and keeping his embarrassment a secret.

Katie still buys lunch every day at school. And every day, as she heads out the door, her mom hands her a delicious homemade lunch.

David Diamond

He Is Just a Little Boy

He stands at the plate
with his heart pounding fast.
The bases are loaded,
the die has been cast.
Mom and Dad cannot help him,
he stands all alone.
A hit at this moment
would send the team home.
The ball meets the plate,
he swings and he misses.
There's a groan from the crowd,
with some boos and some hisses.
A thoughtless voice cries,
"Strike out the bum."
Tears fill his eyes,
the game's no longer fun.
So open your heart and give him a break,
for it's moments like this
a man you can make.
Please keep this in mind
when you hear someone forget.
He is just a little boy, and not a man yet.

Chaplain Bob Fox

If I Had My Child to Raise Over Again

If I had my child to raise all over again,
I'd finger-paint more and point the finger less.
I'd do less correcting and more connecting.
I'd take my eyes off my watch, and watch with my eyes.
I would care to know less and know to care more.
I'd take more hikes and fly more kites.
I'd stop playing serious, and seriously play.
I'd run through more fields and gaze at more stars.
I'd do more hugging and less tugging.
I would be firm less often, and affirm much more.
I'd build self-esteem first, and the house later.
I'd teach less about the love of power,
and more about the power of love.

Diane Loomans

From the book, Full Esteem Ahead, 100 Ways to Build Self-Esteem in Children & Adults. ©1994 Diane Loomans.

Pay Attention

Jason came from a good family with two loving parents, two brothers, and a sister. They were all successful academically and socially. They lived in a posh neighborhood. Jason had everything a boy could desire. But he was always into some kind of mischief. He wasn't a bad kid who caused trouble, but he always wound up in the thick of things.

In first grade, Jason was labeled Special Ed. They tried to keep him out of the regular classes. In middle school, he was the "misfit troublemaker." In high school, although never officially tested, Jason was tagged with having attention deficit disorder (ADD). More often than not, his teachers kicked him out of class. His first report card had one C and the rest Ds.

One Sunday the family was enjoying brunch at the country club when a teacher stopped and said, "Jason is doing so well these days. We're pleased and delighted."

"You must be mixing us up with another family," said the father. "Our Jason is worthless. He is always in trouble. We are so embarrassed and just can't figure out why."

As the teacher walked away, the mother remarked, "You know, honey, come to think of it, Jason hasn't been in trouble for a month. He's even been going to school early and staying late. I wonder what's up?"

The second nine-week grading period was finally up. As usual, Jason's mom and dad expected low grades and unsatisfactory marks in behavior. Instead, he achieved four As and three Bs and honors in citizenship. His parents were baffled.

"Who did you sit by to get these grades?" the dad asked sarcastically.

"I did it all myself," Jason humbly answered.

Perplexed and still not satisfied, the parents took Jason back to school to meet with the principal. He assured them that Jason was doing very well.

"We have a new guidance counselor and she seems to have touched your son in a special way," he said. "His self-esteem is much better, and he's doing great this term. I think you should meet her."

When the trio approached, the woman had her head down. It took a moment for her to notice she had visitors. When she did, she leaped to her feet and began gesturing with her hands.

"What's this?" asked Jason's father indignantly. "Sign language? Why, she can't even hear."

"That's why she's so great," said Jason, jumping in between them. "She does more than hear, Dad. She listens!"

Dan Clark

Remember, We're Raising Children, Not Flowers!

David, my next-door neighbor, has two young kids ages five and seven. One day he was teaching his seven-year-old son Kelly how to push the gas-powered lawn mower around the yard. As he was teaching him how to turn the mower around at the end of the lawn, his wife, Jan, called to him to ask a question. As David turned to answer the question, Kelly pushed the lawn mower right through the flower bed at the edge of the lawn—leaving a two-foot wide path leveled to the ground!

When David turned back around and saw what had happened, he began to lose control. David had put a lot of time and effort into making those flower beds the envy of the neighborhood. As he began to raise his voice to his son, Jan walked quickly over to him, put her hand on his shoulder and said, "David, please remember . . . we're raising children, not flowers!"

Jan reminded me how important it is as a parent to remember our priorities. Kids and their self-esteem are more important than any physical object they might break or destroy. The window pane shattered by a baseball, a lamp knocked over by a careless child, or a plate dropped in the kitchen are already broken. The flowers are already dead. I must remember not to add to the destruction by breaking a child's spirit and deadening his sense of liveliness.

* * *

I was buying a sport coat a few weeks ago and Mark Michaels, the owner of the store, and I were discussing parenting. He told me that while he and his wife and seven-year-old daughter were out for dinner, his daughter knocked over her water glass. After the water was cleaned up without any recriminating remarks from her parents, she looked up and said, "You know, I really want to thank you guys for not being like other parents. Most of my friends' parents would have yelled at them and given them a lecture about paying more attention. Thanks for not doing that!"

Once, when I was having dinner with some friends, a similar incident happened. Their five-year-old son knocked over a glass of milk at the dinner table. When they immediately started in on him, I intentionally knocked my glass over, too. When I started to explain how I still knock things over even at the age of 48, the boy started to beam and the parents seemingly got the message and backed off. How easy it is to forget that we are all still learning.

* * *

I recently heard a story from Stephen Glenn about a famous research scientist who had made several very important medical breakthroughs. He was being interviewed by a newspaper reporter who asked him why he thought he was able to be so much more creative than the average person. What set him so far apart from others?

He responded that, in his opinion, it all came from an experience with his mother that occurred when he was about two years old. He had been trying to remove a bottle of milk from the refrigerator when he lost his grip on the slippery bottle and it fell, spilling its contents all over the kitchen floor—a veritable sea of milk!

When his mother came into the kitchen, instead of yelling at him, giving him a lecture or punishing him, she said, "Robert, what a great and wonderful mess you have made! I have rarely seen such a huge puddle of milk. Well, the damage has already been done. Would you like to get down and play in the milk for a few minutes before we clean it up?"

Indeed, he did. After a few minutes, his mother said, "You know, Robert, whenever you make a mess like this, eventually you have to clean it up and restore everything to its proper order. So, how would you like to do that? We could use a sponge, a towel, or a mop. Which do you prefer?" He chose the sponge and together they cleaned up the spilled milk.

His mother then said, "You know, what we have here is a failed experiment in how to effectively carry a big milk bottle with two tiny hands. Let's go out in the back yard and fill the bottle with water and see if you can discover a way to carry it without dropping it." The little boy learned that if he grasped the bottle at the top near the lip with both hands, he could carry it without dropping it. What a wonderful lesson!

This renowned scientist then remarked that it was at that moment that he knew he didn't need to be afraid to make mistakes. Instead, he learned that mistakes were just opportunities for learning something new, which is, after all, what scientific experiments are all about. Even if the experiment "doesn't work," we usually learn something valuable from it.

Wouldn't it be great if all parents would respond the way Robert's mother responded to him?

* * *

One last story that illustrates the application of this attitude in an adult context was told by Paul Harvey on the radio several years back. A young woman was driving home from work when she snagged her fender on the bumper of another car. She was in tears as she explained that it was a new car, only a few days from the showroom. How was she ever going to explain the damaged car to her husband?

The driver of the other car was sympathetic, but explained that they must note each other's license numbers and registration numbers. As the young woman reached into a large brown envelope to retrieve the documents, a piece of paper fell out. In a heavy masculine scrawl were these words: "In case of accident . . . remember, honey, it's you I love, not the car!"

* * *

Let's remember that our children's spirits are more important than any material things. When we do, self-esteem and love blossom and grow more beautifully than any bed of flowers ever could.

Jack Canfield

Final Thoughts

Some final thoughts for you to ponder . . .

In these final moments of this book, we want to send you out the door with some thoughts on success, and a short reminder of how important it is to *teach to the heart*!

Our blessings to you on your journey.

Anna, Jack, and Mark

The Successful You

If your ship doesn't come in, swim out to meet it.

Jonathan Winters

You probably know me best as that Chicken Soup guy who, along with that other Chicken Soup guy (a.k.a. Mark Victor Hansen), founded the Chicken Soup for the Soul series in the early 1990s. Well, yes, you're right, and I'm extremely fortunate to have this extraordinary series be a part of my life over the last decade.

But before I became that "Chicken Soup guy," I was, and continue to be, one of America's leading experts in motivating, training, and coaching entrepreneurs, corporate leaders, managers, sales professionals, employees, and educators. For the last thirty years, I have helped hundreds of thousands of individuals the world over achieve their dreams. I love what I do—and I do what I love—and I wish the same for you. Thus, I'm excited to share some of my wisdom with you, to inspire you into action. Are you game?

* * *

One of the most pervasive myths in American culture today is that we are entitled to a great life— that somehow, somewhere, someone is responsible for filling our lives with continual happiness, exciting career options, nurturing family time, and blissful personal relationships—simply because we exist.

But the real truth is that there is only one person responsible for the quality of the life you live. That person is you.

If you want to be successful, you have to take 100 percent responsibility for everything that you experience in your life. This includes the level of your achievements, the results you produce, the quality of your relationships, the state of your health and physical fitness, your income, your debts, your feelings—everything!

And this is not easy, especially when you're either contemplating starting your own business or you currently own a business. But I can help you get from where you are to where you want to be.

In my 2005 book—*The Success Principles: How to Get from Where You Are to Where You Want to Be,* penned with Janet Switzer (HarperCollins)—I write about sixty-four principles and strategies that will give you the courage and the heart to start living successfully today. For the purposes of entrepreneurship, I have selected ten principles from my book to share with you:

1. **Decide what you want.** If you are going to get what you really want out of life, you will have to stop saying, "I don't know; I don't care; it doesn't matter to me," or my current favorite of teenagers, "Whatever!" When you are confronted with a choice, no matter how small or insignificant, act as if you have a preference. Ask yourself, *If I did know, what would it be? If I did care, which would I prefer? If it did matter, what would I rather do?*

2. **Unleash the power of goal-setting.** Experts on the science of success know the brain is a goal-seeking organism. Whatever goal you give to your subconscious mind, it will work night and day to achieve. Much of this can be obtained through visualization (Principle #3, below), but it is up to you

to figure out what you want and desire. When you create your goals, be sure to write down some big ones that will stretch you. It pays to have goals that will require you to grow to achieve them. Why? Because the ultimate goal, in addition to achieving your material goals, is to become a master at life. And to do this, you will need to learn new skills, expand your vision of what's possible, build new relationships, and learn to overcome your fears, your intellectual considerations, and any external roadblocks you encounter.

3. **See what you want, get what you see.** Visualization—or the act of creating compelling and vivid pictures in your mind of what it is that you want—may be the most underutilized success tool you possess because it greatly accelerates the achievement of any success in many ways. When you consistently visualize your goal as already achieved, your brain will do three things: (1) generate creative solutions for achieving your dreams, (2) perceive more resources that can help you, and (3) increase your motivation to act. Sports psychologists and peak-performance experts have been popularizing the power of visualization since the 1980s, and almost all Olympic and professional athletes now employ the power of visualization. Remember, to get what you want, you need to first visualize it in your mind.

4. **Take action.** The world doesn't pay you for what you know; it pays you for what you do. There's an enduring axiom of success that says "The universe rewards action." It is as simple and as true as this principle; it's surprising how many people get bogged down in analyzing, planning, and organizing, when all they really need to do is take action. Many people fail to do so because they're afraid to fail. Successful people, on the other hand, realize that failure is an important part of the learning process. They know that failure is just the way we learn by trial and error. Simply get started, make mistakes, pay attention to feedback, correct, and keep moving forward toward the goal. Every experience will yield more useful information that you can apply the next time.

5. **Use feedback to your advantage.** Once you begin to take action, you'll start getting feedback about whether you're doing the right thing or not. You'll get data, advice, help, suggestions, direction, and even criticism that will continually enhance your knowledge, abilities, attitudes, and relationships. But what you do with that feedback is critical. Be it good or bad, favorable or unfavorable, it is up to you to absorb the information and use it in a positive manner that will help you constantly adjust and move forward.

To ensure you get valuable feedback, ask for it. For example, the most valuable question you can ever ask as an entrepreneur is the following: "On a scale of one to ten, how would you rate our product/service/relationship/etc.?" Anything less than a ten gets a follow-up question: "What would it take to make it a ten?" Ask this question of your clients, employees, and suppliers. Ask it often, and then put new policies and procedures in place to constantly get closer to a ten.

6. **Commit to constant and never-ending improvement.** In Japan, the word for constant and never-ending improvement is *kaizen*. Not only is this an operating philosophy for modern Japanese businesses, it is also the age-old philosophy of warriors—and it's become the personal mantra of millions of successful people. Whenever you set out to improve your skills, change your behavior, or better your family life or business, start with small, achievable goals that can be easily mastered. By consistently taking little steps, your belief that you can easily improve in that area will be greatly reinforced.

7. **Exceed expectations.** Are you someone who consistently goes the extra mile and routinely over delivers on your promises? A rarity these days, this is the hallmark of high achievers who know that

exceeding expectations will help them stand out above the crowd. Almost by habit, successful people simply do more. As a result, they experience not only greater financial rewards for their extra efforts, but also a personal transformation; they become more self-confident, more self-reliant, and more influential with those around them. Always ask yourself, How can I give my customers and clients more? How can I surprise them?

8. **Stay motivated with the masters.** The title of this principle sounds a lot like the title of an exercise video, and it is—but for your brain. So many of us are trained (or brainwashed) by the media, parents, schools, and culture to have limiting beliefs. It's not possible. I don't deserve it. Well, you do deserve it, and only you can make it possible, by reading inspiring books and listening to motivational and educational CDs. Did you know that the average person commutes a total of one hour each day? In five years, that's 1,250 hours in the car, enough time to give yourself the equivalent of a college education! Use that commute as a time for maintaining high levels of motivation, learning a language, honing your management skills, or creating sales and marketing strategies. Use this time to learn virtually anything you want or need to know to succeed at a higher level. A comprehensive list of books and audio programs can be found on pages 441 to 451 of *The Success Principles.*

9. **Hire a personal coach.** Of all the things successful people do to accelerate their trip down the path to success, participating in some kind of coaching program is at the top of their list. A coach will help you clarify your vision and goals, support you through your fears, keep you focused, confront your unconscious behaviors and old patterns, expect you to do your best, help you live by your values, show you how to earn more while working less, and keep you focused on your core genius.

10. **Mastermind your way to success.** We all know that two heads are better than one when it comes to solving a problem or creating a result. So imagine having a permanent group of five to six people who meet every week for the purpose of problem solving, brainstorming, networking, encouraging, and motivating each other. This process, called masterminding, is one of the most powerful tools for success presented in my book. I don't know anybody who has become super-successful who has not employed the principle of masterminding. If you are not already in a mastermind group, join or start one now.

* * *

I simply leave you with one of my favorite ancient Chinese proverbs—"A journey of one thousand miles must begin with one step." Godspeed.

Jack Canfield

[EDITORS' NOTE: *To learn more about* The Success Principles *and Jack's mentorship, coaching, audio, and speaking programs, please visit www.successprinciples.com or call toll-free 800-237-8336.*]

I Taught Them All

I have taught in high school for ten years. During that time I have given assignments, among others, to a murderer, a pugilist, a thief, and an imbecile. The murderer was a quiet little boy who sat on the front seat and regarded me with pale blue eyes; the pugilist lounged by the window and let loose at intervals in a raucous laugh that startled even the geraniums; the thief was a gay-hearted Lothario with a song on his lips; and the imbecile, a shifty-eyed little animal seeking the shadows.

The murderer awaits death in the state penitentiary; the pugilist lost an eye in a brawl in Hong Kong; the thief, by standing on tip-toe, can see the window of my room from the county jail; and the once gentle-eyed little moron beats his head against a padded wall in the state asylum.

All these pupils once sat in my room, sat and looked at me gravely across worn, brown desks. I must have been a great help to those pupils. . . . I taught them the rhyming scheme of the Elizabethan sonnet and how to diagram a complex sentence.

Naomi White
Progressive Education
November, 1943

Appendix

This final section will provide you with a variety of supplemental materials for your use.

Some of the information found here is the foundation for this entire curriculum and can be used to support any plan or any teaching situation. Issues of self-esteem, learning how to ask for help, writing goals and affirmations, or making commitments can be used anywhere in classrooms, or in life.

In other cases you will find activities with extensive directions or several options, too lengthy to attach directly to the story lesson plans. Demonstrations of the power of thought, examining attitude, or creative ways to form student groupings are examples of this. Or, in some instances, you will simply find a worksheet that is appropriate for use with two or three stories.

Additionally, there are several miscellaneous student worksheets that are not specifically tied to a story, but can be adapted for use with several stories or several age levels, or with a classroom activity totally unrelated to this curriculum. These materials were found to be very successful with our teacher test groups, so we have included them for your benefit. We hope you will enjoy using them in addition to the other activities and lesson plans found in this document.

Appendix Contents

Jack Canfield

The Success Principles

100 Ways to Enhance Self-Concept in the Classroom

Self-Esteem in the Classroom: A Curriculum Guide

Breakthrough to Success-Training Materials

101 Ways to Develop Student Self-Esteem and Responsibility

Joel Goodman and Matt Weinstein

Playfair

Anna Unkovich

Communication

Decisions

Games and Projects

Goals

Issues of Loss

Self-Esteem

Miscellaneous Worksheets

Ask, Ask, Ask: Creating Win/Win Relationships

In the Bible, Matthew 7:7 says, "Ask and it will be given to you; knock and the door will be opened to you." History is filled with examples of incredible riches and astounding benefits people have received simply by asking for them. Yet asking—perhaps the most powerful Success Principle of all—is *still* the challenge that holds people back.

Why People Are Afraid to Ask

Why are people so afraid to ask? They are afraid of several things: looking needy, foolish, or stupid. But mostly they're afraid of experiencing rejection. They are afraid of hearing the word "no." The sad thing is that they're actually rejecting themselves in advance. They're saying "no" to themselves before anyone else even has a chance to say "no."

You've Got Nothing to Lose by Asking

As executive coach Marcia Martin likes to say, "If you apply to Harvard and you don't get in, you weren't in Harvard before you applied and you're not in Harvard after you applied. Your life didn't get worse. And think about it. You've spent your whole life not going to Harvard and you know how to handle that."

This is so true!

Jack teaches a phrase in his seminars: "Oh, what the heck . . . go for it anyway."

How to Ask for What You Want

There's a specific science to asking for and getting what you want or need in life. And while we recommend you learn more by reading *The Aladdin Factor* (Jack Canfield and Mark Victor Hansen), here are some quick tips to get you started:

1. Ask as if you expect to get it. Ask with a positive expectation. Ask from the place that you have already been given it. It is a done deal. Ask as if you expect to get a "yes."

2. Assume you can. Don't start with the assumption that you can't get it. If you are going to assume, assume you can get an upgrade. Assume you can get a table by the window. Assume that you can return it without a sales slip. Assume that you can get a scholarship, that you can get a raise. Don't ever assume *against* yourself.

3. Ask someone who can give it to you. Qualify the person. Who would I have to speak to, in order to get . . .? Who is authorized to make a decision about . . .? What would have to happen for me to get . . .?

4. Be clear and specific. In his seminars, Jack often asks, "Who wants more money in their life?" He picks someone who raised their hand and he gives them a quarter, asking, "Is that enough for you?" Then, "No? Well, how would I know how much you want? How would anybody know?" You need to ask for a specific number. Too many people are walking around wanting more money, but not being specific. Do you want enough to buy an iPod? Enough to buy a new bike? Enough to go to camp this summer? Enough to go to Stanford University? Well, how much is that? If you're not sure, do the research and find out.

Take a look at these examples:

Don't say. "I want a later curfew."

Do say, "I want to be able to stay out until midnight on weekends."

Don't say, "I want to spend some time with you this weekend."

Do say, "I would like to go out for dinner and a movie with you on Saturday night. Would that work for you?"

5. **Ask repeatedly.** One of the most important Success Principles is the commitment to not give up. Whenever we're asking others to participate in the fulfillment of our goals, some people are going to say "no." They may have other priorities, commitments, and reasons not to participate. It's no reflection on you.

Just get used to the idea there's going to be a lot of rejection along the way to success. The key is to not give up. When someone says "No," you say "NEXT!"

Why? Because when you keep on asking, even the same person again and again, they might say "yes" . . .

. . . on a different day

. . . when they are in a better mood

. . . after you've proven your commitment to them

. . . when circumstances have changed

. . . when you've asked in a different way

. . . when you've established better rapport

. . . when they trust you more . . . and so on.

Kids know this Success Principle better than anyone. They will ask the same person over and over again without any hesitation.

Ask someone else. The other option is to ask someone else. Remember, there are more than six billion people on the planet! Someone will say "yes." Don't get stuck in your fear. Move on to the next person, and the next person, and the next!

It is a numbers game. Someone out there is waiting to say "yes." When a nineteen-year-old Rick Little wanted to start a program in the high schools that would teach kids how to deal with their feelings, handle conflict, clarify their life goals, learn communication skills, and determine values that would help them live more effective and fulfilling lives, he wrote a proposal and sent it to more than 143 foundations. During that two-year period, he slept in the back of his car, and most of the time he ate peanut butter on crackers. But he never gave up on his dream.

Eventually, the Kellogg Foundation gave Rick $140,000. Since that time, Rick and his team have implemented the Quest Program in more than one thousand high schools and junior high schools, and his International Youth Foundation has raised tens of millions of dollars for programs that benefit children around the world.

What if Rick had given up after the hundredth rejection and said to himself, "Well, I guess this just isn't supposed to happen." What a great loss that would have been to the world and to Rick's higher purpose for being.

How the NEXT Principle Built an Empire

Jack tells this story about how *Chicken Soup for the Soul* came to be—simply by asking repeatedly: "When Mark Victor Hansen and I went to find a publisher for the original Chicken Soup for the Soul, our agent took us to New York, where we were turned down by more than thirty-three publishers. He tried another twenty-two publishers on his own, who also rejected it. Then he returned the book to us and said no one was ever going to publish it.

"What did we do? We said, 'NEXT!'

"We took the book to the 1992 American Booksellers Association convention in Anaheim, California. We walked from booth to booth for two days, talking to every publisher that would listen. There were more than four thousand booths at that convention. Again and again, we were turned down. Again and again, we said, 'NEXT!'

"Finally, toward the end of the second day, a little publisher from Florida—Health Communications—said they would look at the manuscript. They called us back a week later and said, 'We love it! We want to publish it.'

"The hundreds of NEXTs paid off! There are more than eight million copies of that first book, and more than one hundred million books in print (in more than thirty-nine languages!) from the more than one hundred titles in the Chicken Soup for the Soul series that sprung from that first effort.

"What if Mark and I had given up after all the New York publishing houses had said 'No?' What would have happened if we had quit after our agent had given us back the book? What would have happened if we had stopped trying after the first days of continual rejections at the ABA convention? Nothing! That's what would have happened. Absolutely nothing.

"Fortunately, Mark and I walked our talk of consistent and perseverant action in the face of obstacles to our goals. We lived the NEXT principle."

SW ... SW ... SW ... SW

Some will, some won't, so what . . . someone's waiting. This powerful phrase helps us remember that, ultimately, someone is in the market for what you have to offer. Keep asking. Say, "Next."*

---

* *Used with permission:* The Success Principles: Your 30-Day Journey From Where You Are to Where You Want to Be, *by Jack Canfield and Janet Switzer. (Santa Barbara, CA: The Canfield Group, 2003)*

99 Percent Is Tough; 100 Percent Is Easy

There is a difference between interest and commitment. When you're interested in doing something, you do it only when it's convenient. When you're committed to something, you accept no excuses, only results.

Ken Blanchard, Chief Spiritual Officer of the Ken Blanchard Companies and
coauthor of more than thirty books, including the classic bestseller *The One Minute Manager*

In life, the spoils of victory go to those who make a 100 percent commitment to the outcome, to those who have a "no matter what it takes" attitude. They give it their all; they put everything they have into getting their desired result—whether it be an Olympic gold medal, being at the top of their class, a perfect birthday party, an A in biology, or their dream car.

What a simple concept this is—yet you'd be surprised how many people wake up every day and fight with themselves over whether or not to keep their commitments, stick to their disciplines, or carry out their action plans.

The "No Exceptions Rule"

Successful people adhere to the "no exceptions rule" when it comes to their daily disciplines. Once you make a 100 percent commitment to something, there are no exceptions. It's a done deal. Non-negotiable. Case closed! Over and out. If I make a 100 percent commitment to avoiding drinking sodas, that is it. I never have to think about it again. There are no exceptions, no matter what the circumstances. It ends the discussion, closes the door, permits no other possibility. I don't have to wrestle with that decision every day. It's already been made. The die has been cast. All the bridges are burned. It makes life easier and simpler and keeps me on focus. It frees up tons of energy that would otherwise be spent internally debating the topic over and over and over, because all the energy I expend on internal conflict is unavailable to use for creating outer achievement.

If you make the 100 percent commitment to exercise every day for thirty minutes, no matter what, then it is settled. You simply just do it. It doesn't matter if you are traveling, if you have a 7 AM class, if it's raining outside, if you went to bed late last night, if your schedule is full, or if you simply don't feel like it. You just do it anyway. It's like brushing your teeth before you go to bed. You always do it, no matter what. If you find yourself in bed and you have forgotten, you get out of bed and brush them. It doesn't matter how tired you are or how late it is. You just do it.

Dr. Wayne Dyer, internationally renowned motivational speaker and host of the PBS show *The Power of Intention,* has made a similar commitment to his health and fitness. For twenty-two years, Wayne ran every day for a minimum of eight miles—every day without fail! Wayne has been known to run up and down hotel stairwells and hallways during freezing weather in New York—and even up and down airplane aisles during international flights. Whether your discipline is to read for an hour, practice the piano five days a week, do your homework daily before 5 PM, learn a new language, practice typing, do fifty sit-ups, run six miles, meditate, pray, read the Bible, spend sixty quality minutes with your family—or whatever else you need to do to achieve your goals—commit 100 percent to those daily disciplines that will get you there.

One Final Reason That 100 Percent Is So Important

This powerful 100 percent commitment also figures critically in other important areas—for instance, the workplace. Consider how a commitment to just 99.9 percent quality would mean in the following work situations.

It would mean:

One hour of unsafe drinking water every month
Two unsafe landings at O'Hare International Airport each day
16,000 lost pieces of mail per hour
20,000 incorrectly filled drug prescriptions every year
500 incorrect surgical operations performed each week
50 newborn babies dropped at birth by doctors every day
22,000 checks deducted from the wrong account each hour
Your heart failing to beat 32,000 times each year!

Can you see why 100 percent is such an important percentage? Just think how much better your life, and the whole world would be, if everyone were committed to 100 percent excellence in everything they do. *

---

* Adapted with permission, The Success Principles *by Jack Canfield and Janet Switzer (New York, NY: HarperCollins, 2005).*

THE MIRROR EXERCISE

The Mirror Exercise gives your subconscious mind the positive strokes it needs to pursue further achievements, and it helps change any negative beliefs you have toward praise and accomplishment, which puts you in an achieving frame of mind. Do this exercise for a minimum of three months. After that, you can decide whether you want to continue. Some very successful people have been doing this for years.

Just before going to bed, stand in front of a mirror and appreciate yourself for all that you have accomplished during the day. Start with a few seconds of looking directly into the eyes of the person in the mirror—your mirror image looking back at you. Then address yourself by name and begin appreciating yourself *out loud* for the following things:

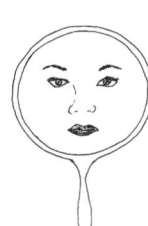

* Any achievements: school, work, personal, physical, spiritual, or emotional
* Any personal disciplines you kept: dietary, exercise, reading, meditation, prayer
* Any temptations that you did not give in to: eating dessert, lying, watching too much TV, staying up too late

Maintain eye contact with yourself throughout the exercise. When you're finished appreciating yourself, complete the exercise by continuing to look deep into your own eyes and saying, "I love you." Then stand there for another few seconds to really feel the impact of the experience—as if you were the one in the mirror who had just listened to all of this appreciation. The trick during this last part is to not just turn away from the mirror feeling embarrassed or thinking of yourself or the exercise as stupid or silly.

Here is an example of what your exercise might sound like:

Jack, I want to appreciate you for the following things today: First, I want to appreciate you for going to bed on time last night without staying up too late watching TV so that you got up bright and early this morning and you had a really good conversation with Mom. You helped with getting your sisters' lunches together, and you ate a healthy breakfast. You got to school on time and turned in all of your homework. In math class, you asked a question when you didn't understand. You focused on having a more positive attitude in English class . . . and it did help the hour to be more fun. At basketball practice, you didn't whine when the team had to run extra laps. Instead, you led the group and finished first. Before you left school, you double-checked your planner to make sure you had all of your materials to get your homework done. And when you got home, you spent quality time playing with your sisters and then you read them a book. That was really special. Then you did your homework before you got too tired. And now you're going to bed at a good time again and not staying up all night surfing the Internet. You were great today. And one more thing, Jack—I love you!

At this point, don't forget to maintain eye contact with yourself for an additional ten to fifteen seconds. It's not unusual to have a number of reactions the first few times you do this. You might feel silly, embarrassed, like crying (or actually begin crying), or just generally uncomfortable. Occasionally, people have even reported breaking out in hives, feeling hot and sweaty, or feeling a little light-headed. These are natural and normal reactions, as this is a very unfamiliar thing to be doing. We are not trained to acknowledge ourselves. In fact, we are mostly trained to do the opposite: "Don't toot your own horn. Don't get a swelled head. Don't get a stuffed shirt. Pride is a sin." As you begin to act more positive and nurturing toward yourself, it is natural to have physical and emotional reactions as you release the old negative wounds, unrealistic expectations, and self-judgments. If you experience any of these things—and not all people do—don't let these things stop you. They are only temporary and will pass after a few days of doing the exercise.

The first time Jack did this exercise, after just forty days he noticed that all of his negative internal self-talk had totally vanished, crowded out by the daily positive focus of the Mirror Exercise. He used to berate himself for things like misplacing his car keys or his glasses. That critical voice just simply disappeared. The same kind of thing can happen for you, but only if you take the time to actually do the exercise.

One note to remember: If you find yourself lying in bed realizing you haven't done the Mirror Exercise yet, get out of bed and do it. Looking at yourself in the mirror is a critical part of the exercise. And one last bit of advice: Be sure to let your family know in advance that you will be doing this exercise each evening for the next three months or more. You don't want them to walk in on you and think you've lost your mind!**

** *Adapted from* The Success Principles *by Jack Canfield and Janet Switzer (New York, NY: HarperCollins, 2005).*

Worried Himself to Death

*N*ick *Sitzman was a strong, healthy, and ambitious young railroad yardman. He had a reputation as a diligent, hard worker, and he had a loving wife and two children and many friends.*

One midsummer day, the train crews were informed that they could quit an hour early in honor of the foreman's birthday. While performing one last check on some of the railroad cars, Nick was accidentally locked in a refrigerator boxcar. When he realized that the rest of the workmen had left the site, Nick began to panic.

He banged and shouted until his fists were bloody and his voice was hoarse, but no one heard him. With his knowledge of "the numbers and the facts," he predicted the temperature to be zero degrees. Nick's thought was "If I can't get out, I'll freeze to death in here." Wanting to let his wife and family know exactly what had happened to him, Nick found a knife and began to etch words on the wooden floor. He wrote, "It's so cold, my body is getting numb. If I could just go to sleep. These may be my last words."

The next morning, the crew slid open the heavy doors of the boxcar and found Nick dead. An autopsy revealed that every physical sign of his body indicated he had frozen to death. And yet the refrigeration unit of the car was inoperative, and the temperature inside indicated 55 degrees Fahrenheit. Nick had killed himself by the power of his own thoughts.*

You, too, if you're not careful, can kill yourself with your limiting thoughts—not all at once like Nick Sitzman, but little by little, day after day, until you have slowly deadened your natural ability to achieve your dreams.

---

*From The Speaker's Sourcebook, by Glen Van Ekeren (Englewood-Cliffs, N.J.: Prentice-Hall, 1988.)

POKER CHIP THEORY OF LEARNING

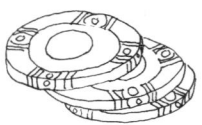

All learning is the result of a risk-taking situation somewhat like a poker game. In any potential learning situation, you are asked to take a risk: to write a paper that will be evaluated, to make a recitation that may be laughed at, to do board work that may be wrong, to create an object of art that might be judged, etc. In each situation you are risking error, judgment, disapproval, censure, rejection, and, in extreme cases, even punishment. At a deeper level you are risking your self-concept.

Imagine that your self-concept is a stack of poker chips. Some of you will start the learning game with a lot of poker chips; others will start with very few. If you have the higher number of chips, you have a great advantage. To continue the poker analogy, if you have one hundred chips, you can sustain twenty losses of five chips each. If you have only fifteen chips, you can only sustain three losses of five chips each. If you are the latter student, you will be much more cautions and reticent about stepping into the arena and may manifest a variety of behaviors indicating your reluctance to risk learning. They range from "This is stupid, I don't want to do it" (translation: "I am stupid; I'm afraid I can't do it") and withdrawn silence on one extreme to mischievous acting out on the other.

If you are a student who has had a good deal of success in the past, you will be likely to risk success again; if you should fail, your self-concept can "afford" it. If you are a student with a history predominantly filled with failures, you will be reluctant to risk failure again. Your depleted self-concept cannot afford it. Similar to someone living on a limited income, you will shop cautiously and look for bargains.*

*Adapted with permission from 100 Ways to Enhance Self-Concept in the Classroom by Jack Canfield and Harold Wells (Needham Heights, MA: Allyn and Bacon, 1976).

SPECIAL NOTES TO THE TEACHER REGARDING THE "POKER CHIP THEORY":

You may delete these special notes to use the top portion of this page as a student handout.

One obvious recommendation in this situation is to make each learning step small enough so the student is asked to only risk one chip at a time, instead of five. But even more obvious, in our eyes, is the need to build up the student's supply of poker chips so he or she can begin to have a surplus of chips to risk.

If a student starts out, metaphorically speaking, with twenty chips and gains fifteen more through the exercises contained in this book, then, even if the student loses ten in a reading class, he or she is still five ahead of the game. But if the student loses ten from a starting position of twenty he or she is now down to ten and in a very precarious psychological position. Viewed in this way, self-concept building can be seen as making sure that every student has enough chips to stay in the game.*

* Adapted with permission from 100 Ways to Enhance Self-Concept in the Classroom by Jack Canfield and Harold Wells (Needham Heights, MA: Allyn and Bacon, 1976).

CIRCLE TALKS

One of the cornerstones of a comprehensive approach to building and maintaining high self-esteem is the use of Circle Talks. Circle Talks are conducted in small groups, usually four to six students in size. In a Circle Talk, students share their thoughts and feelings about a particular topic, usually chosen by the teacher (see page 314 for sample topics).

Purpose and Benefits

Circle Talks give students an opportunity to express their thoughts and feelings in a safe and nurturing setting. The positive benefits of Circle Talks are:

★ Students learn how to share their feelings, rather than to repress them. This is an important preventative to teen suicide and drug abuse.

★ Students learn valuable listening skills that can be applied to all relationships.

★ Shyer, more reticent students are provided a safe structure for communication, which assures them an opportunity to express themselves and be heard. (One of the greatest problems in American education is that many students suffer from a deficit of positive attention.)

★ Students learn about additional coping behaviors and life attitudes from other students, which they can apply to their own life situations.

★ Students discover they are not alone in their feelings and that there are, indeed, universal situations and challenges that everyone faces. As a result, students build deeper friendships with their peers, and unnecessary feelings of loneliness and isolation are overcome. This builds self-esteem and inner emotional strength to resist depression, drug abuse, teen suicide, and unwanted teen pregnancy.

Many students live in an isolated world, suffering from what Dr. Harry Stack Sullivan, a Harvard psychologist, called a "delusion of uniqueness"—a false belief that they alone suffer certain emotional stresses and life crises (such as divorced parents, alcoholic homes, sibling rivalry, fear of failure, loneliness, stress at school, disappointments in athletic and academic achievement, teasing, lack of money, fears of rejection, fears of participating in certain activities, hopes and dreams that are not supported, etc.). When a student discovers that others also have these same longings, fears, conflicts and doubts, they no longer feel alone. Instead, they feel bolstered by the realization that these things are shared with others. This, in turn, helps them to accept and feel comfortable with their own emotions. Students no longer think of themselves and their feelings as strange, weird, or unacceptable. Self-acceptance, self-expression, and self-confidence are nurtured and expanded.

Another benefit is that teachers who regularly conduct Circle Talks in their classrooms begin to know their students at a much deeper level. They begin to better understand the causes of their students' behavior, their hidden motivations, their fears, and their desires. Teachers find they have more information to use in individualizing their instruction and in helping a student overcome what may appear to be learning blocks.

The Process

Gather students into groups of four to six each. These may be ongoing groups or newly formed groups.

Each group is given a "focus object," which is used to indicate whose turn it is to speak. Objects that have been used successfully are hearts (filled with seeds), teddy bears, stuffed animals, tennis balls, Native American peace pipes, baseballs, or rocks. The object serves the purpose of denoting whose turn it is to talk and it gives the speaker something to hold on to.

While one student is holding the object, everyone else remains silent. The object acts as a visual reminder that no one may interrupt the speaker. Students learn to await their turn by waiting for the object to reach them. Students also report that the holding of the focus object makes it easier to speak. It gives their hands something to do and it is comforting.

Introduce the guidelines to the students:

1. Only the person holding the object may talk. Everyone else is to remain silent and give the speaker their complete attention and support.
2. Pass the object gently to the left. The object is never to be thrown from one person to another.
3. You have the right to "pass." There is no requirement or pressure to share. . . . Just say, "I pass," and hand the object to the person on your left.
4. Talk only about what you think and feel. Do not talk about what other people have said. Focus on your *feelings* about a topic.
5. No put-downs. Listen to the speaker without judgment or criticism.
6. Confidentiality—do not share what is said outside of the Circle Talk.
7. Talk as long as you need to, but be aware that other people also want a turn.
8. Do not leave the group during the Circle Talk.

In grades five to twelve, we suggest that you post a list of the Circle Talk guidelines in your classroom so students can refer to them as needed.

Ask the students if they have any questions about the guidelines. Tell them that they may find it difficult to listen without interrupting at first, but there is great value in learning how to give others their total attention. If you have the time, you may also wish to lead a brief discussion using the following questions as discussion starters:

★ Has anyone here ever experienced somebody not paying attention to them when they are talking? (Perhaps they are distracted by TV or by someone else?) How do you feel when someone looks away when you are talking to them? Does it make you feel less important? Does it make you feel angry?

★ Have you ever been talking about something that is really important to you and had someone interrupt you and start talking about what they wanted to say? Has anyone ever taken the focus away from you in a group discussion? Did you like that? How did you feel? What did you want instead?

The fact is that we all yearn to be listened to, understood, and accepted by others. We all need to be the center of attention on a regular basis. In order to receive attention, we must also learn to give it to others. True listening is one of the greatest gifts we can give another person.

After you have introduced the guidelines, make sure that everyone understands them and is willing to play by the rules. If there are students who do not agree to the guidelines, ask them to sit outside of the circle or group and provide them with quiet desk work to do. Emphasize to the whole class that their decision not to participate is acceptable.

How Long Should a Circle Talk Last?

The length of a Circle Talk depends on several things—the age and maturity level of the students, the interest level and intensity of the topic under discussion, and the time available for the activity. In general, a Circle Talk lasts eight to fourteen minutes. We recommend that the students continue to pass the focus object around the circle, with students taking repeated turns until the time has elapsed, thus assuring that all groups end at the same time. It is usually a good idea to tell the class when half the time has elapsed, giving the students an opportunity to speed things up if less than half the group has shared.

If your time frame is open-ended, you can continue the Circle Talk until everyone says, "I pass," indicating that there is no more to be said on the subject, or you can limit the passing of the focus object to one round.

If there is time after a Circle Talk it can be valuable to share "I learned . . ." statements from the class.

When Circle Talks Are Recommended

There are two important times that we suggest using Circle Talks in your classroom. The first is whenever there is any kind of emotional upset. These occasions can include:

* ★ The death of a classmate
* ★ The loss of a major athletic event
* ★ After a fight or a bout of teasing
* ★ When a major privilege has been taken away
* ★ When a lot of students have failed a test
* ★ When an interracial incident has occurred
* ★ After the loss of a pet or class mascot
* ★ After cancellation of a field trip due to bad weather
* ★ After viewing an emotionally stimulating film such as *The Holocaust*
* ★ After reading a particularly emotional passage in English
* ★ After the announcement of the election of class officers
* ★ The dissection of an animal in biology class
* ★ Following a heated political debate in a social sciences class
* ★ The day before SAT tests or final exams

Perhaps even more significant is the use of Circle Talks in a developmental way. We suggest conducting Circle Talks one to three times a week depending on the class and the time available. We believe once a week is the absolute minimum for effectively building high self-esteem.

Topics for Circle Talks

When first beginning to use Circle Talks, you may choose to begin with simple, positively focused topics. Some examples are:

1. A success you recently had (during the summer, last year, etc.)
2. What you would do if you won the state lottery (inherited $1 million, etc.)?
3. Where you would like to live if you could live anywhere in the world?
4. Something you would like to achieve in the next three years
5. Your favorite movie, TV show, song (favorite anything)
6. Something you like about yourself
7. How you feel about doing a Circle Talk
8. Something you wish you could do better
9. Your favorite thing to do
10. A fun thing that happened this week
11. Something you are good at doing
12. Something you have always wanted to do
13. Something you think about a lot
14. If you had three wishes they would be . . .
15. Something you wished for that came true

Here are several more topics:

16. Something about my body that makes me feel OK
17. Something about my body that makes me feel not OK
18. Something I don't like about myself
19. Something I sometimes wonder about
20. An especially good dream I had
21. An especially bad dream I had
22. Something I sometimes worry about
23. Something I feel afraid of
24. A way I get over being afraid
25. A time that I was scared and it was fun
26. A time that I was scared and it wasn't fun
27. A good result of something I do
28. A bad result of something I do
29. Something that makes me angry with myself
30. What I do when I'm very angry
31. What I do when I'm very afraid
32. Something I feel sad about
33. What I do when I am sad
34. A time that I acted like a leader
35. A time that I enjoyed being a follower
36. A time that I had to struggle with someone for power and I won
37. A time that I had to struggle with someone for power and I lost

38. A time that I shared power with someone
39. The worst trouble I ever got into
40. A time when I couldn't get what I needed
41. A time when I knew the truth and lied anyway . . . and what happened
42. A time I told the truth even though it was difficult
43. A way I have of getting attention from others
44. A decision I made that was very hard to make
45. A decision I had to make where either way it seemed like I would lose
46. A decision I had to make between things I wanted very much
47. A time I said "no" to peer pressure
48. A time I had to resist others to do what I wanted
49. A time I helped change a rule or a policy
50. Something I did that helped someone else feel good
51. Something that someone did for me that helped me feel good
52. The things I do to keep a friend
53. A time I found a way to meet someone I wanted to know
54. A time I got someone else to change their mind about something
55. A time I did something that someone else did not like
56. A time I wanted attention and did not get it
57. A time I gave someone attention because they needed it
58. A time I didn't know how to get attention
59. A time I was new and didn't know how to break in
60. A time someone did something that helped me feel included
61. A time I did something that helped someone feel included
62. A time someone did something that kept me out
63. A time I did something that excluded someone
64. A time I made a promise and did not keep it
65. A time someone made a promise to me and did not keep it
66. A time I kept my word
67. How someone hurt my feelings
68. A time I did not know how to ask for a favor
69. A time I told someone something but did not mean it
70. A time I disappointed someone
71. A time someone disappointed me
72. Something I have to do that I don't like to do
73. A time I went along with the crowd, even though I didn't like it
74. Something I can't stand in people
75. Something I do that bugs other people
76. Something that I appreciate about my parents
77. A time I resisted authority
78. Something it's hard to "go against the crowd" about
79. Something I did that someone else criticized
80. How I get people to do what I want them to do

81. A secret fear I have

82. A secret wish I have

83. How I feel about . . . war . . . the homeless . . . the environment . . . teacher/student relationships . . . parent/student relationships . . . boy/girl relationships . . . cliques . . . gangs . . . drugs . . . dress codes . . . homework . . . global warming . . . this school . . . the list is as endless as your imagination!

NOTE: When dealing with issue-related Circle Talks it is important to remember that the purpose is not to obtain agreements of any sort. This is not a rap session or a discussion. Each person merely states his or her *feelings* about the issue. The emphasis is on listening to one another's feelings and, through that experience, discovering more about one's own feelings. Remember, this is a *feeling exercise* so thoughts and opinions, while acknowledged, are not the primary focus. Circle Talks are not meant to clarify thoughts and opinions (although they often do), but rather to introduce and provide practice in how to talk about and listen to each others' feelings.

———

*Used with permission from Self-Esteem in the Classroom: A Curriculum Guide by Jack Canfield, et al (Culver City, CA: Self-Esteem Seminars, 1986).

GOOD BOY/BAD BOY KINESIOLOGY DEMONSTRATIONS

Purpose

★ To demonstrate to students the power of their minds over their feelings and their bodies
★ To show experientially that by changing what students think or imagine about themselves and others, they can alter their internal and psychological experience
★ To stress the importance of positive thinking

Background

Kinesiology is a form of muscle testing that chiropractors and other health professionals employ for diagnostic purposes. The technique is also useful in exploring the relationship of thoughts to physiological strength. When we think negative thoughts about ourselves or talk to ourselves in negative ways, we weaken the body's physiology. Negative thinking does, indeed, have a negative effect upon how we feel and our ability to perform. Similarly, negative images of the past or the future also produce a negative effect. The following exercise dramatically demonstrates just how powerful these negative thoughts can be.

Anecdotal Material

Research shows that people who are peak performers in all walks of life, people whom we normally consider "winners," such as Olympic athletes, bank presidents, and successful business people, tend to focus on their past successes. People we'd call "losers" tend to focus only on their past failures.

One of the key points we will continually reinforce is the importance of acknowledging and focusing on our successes rather than our failures.

The former president of the Levi Strauss Company, Peter Thigpen, kept a "victory log" on his desk. Every time he had a small or large victory, he wrote it down in this notebook. When he was about to do something that might be scary, he read through his log of past accomplishments. This brought forward images of past successes rather than failures, and empowered him to take more risks while feeling good about himself. Peter Thigpen is a very successful person. You've heard of Levi jeans, haven't you?

Procedure

Demonstration with Volunteer

Ask for a volunteer to come up to the front of the room. Tell the student the following:

"We are going to be working with something called 'muscle testing' to see how strong you are and to see how certain thoughts and words affect our strength. Before we begin, do you have any problems with your shoulders or arms, such as tennis elbow or any recent injuries? No? Great. Now what I'd like you to do is extend your right arm straight out in front of you at shoulder level, parallel to the floor."

"Make a fist, and now rotate your fist so that your thumb is pointing down. We're going to test the muscles in your back to see how strong you are at this point."

Place two fingers on the small bone which protrudes upward on the outside of his wrist.

"What I'm going to do is to take my first two fingers and press down on your wrist bone. You resist my downward motion. Ready? Resist."

Push slowly, increasing the pressure until his or her arm begins to move.

"Good. You're strong! This is called his 'base strength.' We'll be using this base strength measurement to compare all other tests. Okay, (volunteer), what I'd like you to do is to lower your arm, close your eyes, and say out loud with great force and conviction, 'I'm a bad boy/girl' about eight times. The reason you are saying this will become clear shortly."

After he has said "I am a bad boy/girl" about eight or ten times:

"Raise your arm again, make a fist, point your thumb down and continue saying 'I am a bad boy/girl' while I push down on your wrist. Ready? Resist."

Ninety-nine percent of the time, the arm will be dramatically weaker than during the base strength test, and the student will feel unable to resist your downward pressure.

At this point, ask the volunteer to share with the class what his experience was the second time. The usual response is, "I was much weaker and couldn't resist."

"Don't sit down yet, because there's a second step to this exercise. Once again, close your eyes. This time say out loud with great force and conviction, 'I am a good boy/girl.' Keep saying this over and over, about eight to ten times, keeping your eyes closed. When I think you're ready, I'll ask you to raise your arm and we'll test you again."

Once again, with two fingers on the small wrist bone, apply increasing pressure. Again, in 99 percent of the cases, the volunteer will be at least as strong as he or she was at the beginning of the test, if not stronger. Ask the student to share his or her impressions with the class. Most report a significant increase in feelings of strength and/or sense of well-being.

Now turn to the class and say the following:

"What we have demonstrated here is the power of our thoughts over our bodies. When we say negative things to ourselves or to others about ourselves, we tend to weaken our bodies. When we think or say positive thoughts to ourselves, we tend to feel stronger. No one knows why this is true—just that it is. It makes sense, then, to notice our internal dialogue and begin to say only positive things to ourselves about ourselves."

"I'd like to take this a step further and demonstrate how this works in terms of the pictures we imagine in our minds."

Say the following to the volunteer:

"Close your eyes and think of a time in the past when you had a 'failure experience,' a time when you set a goal or tried to do something that didn't work out—a time when you felt you failed to achieve your chosen goal. You will not be sharing this with the class aloud, so be as honest with yourself as possible. As soon as you have such an event vividly imagined in your head so you can feel, hear, and see what it was like, nod once."

Pause until she or he nods.

"Now raise your arm to shoulder level and make a fist with your thumb pointing down."

Reach out and push down with your two fingers on the wrist bone. Once again you will find that the arm is weak.

"Lower your arm and, with your eyes still closed, remember a time when you had a 'success experience,' a time when you achieved something that was important to you, a time when you set a goal and accomplished it, perhaps even felt proud. Let me know when you are there by nodding your head again."

Pause.

"Keeping this positive experience clearly in your imagination, raise your arm to shoulder level and again make a fist with your thumb pointing down. I'm going to press down. Resist."

Press down on the wrist. In almost all cases the arm will be strong again, perhaps even stronger than the first time. Ask the student to lower his or her arm, and when he or she is ready, describe her experience. Turn to the class again and say:

"It's not only the thoughts we think but the images and the memories that we choose to focus on in our mind, which either weaken or strengthen us."

"Finally, (volunteer), what is your least favorite subject in school? Okay, what I want you to say out loud eight or ten times is, 'I hate (subject)! I hate (subject)!' Then I'm going to test your arm again."

The students' arm will once again be weak.

"Now, I know this isn't true, but what I want you to say for the sake of the experiment is, 'I love (subject)! I love (subject)!' eight to ten times. Then I'm going to test your arm again."

In almost every case when the student says, "I love (subject)" the arm is much stronger, and when they say, "I hate (subject)" the arm weakens again. Now turn to the class and say:

"You see, whenever you are in a state where you hate something, you weaken yourself. If you are feeling and saying to yourself, 'I love _____,' you strengthen yourself. So when you are doing your math homework and you are thinking, 'I hate math,' you are really weakening your ability to be effective in math. If you say, 'I love math,' even though it might not feel true at the time, you are not only strengthening your ability to do math, but also drawing from your subconscious mind the resources necessary to be more effective. When you say you hate another person, you also weaken yourself. When you say, 'I love or I like _____,' you strengthen yourself."

"You see, the essence of who you are is love. When you deny that essence—even a little—you tend to weaken your body, which will affect your thinking, too. So, for the rest of this class we are going to monitor ourselves and focus on speaking only those things that are positive—not that we will deny that we have angry feelings or dislikes, but we will consciously *choose* to focus on the positive in ourselves and in each other. In this way we not only strengthen ourselves, but create a more harmonious and loving environment in which to grow."

Answer any questions the class may have. Then ask the class to acknowledge the volunteer by giving him or her a warm round of applause. Thank the student for being courageous enough to come to the front of the room to participate. Acknowledge his or her contribution to the whole class.

NOTE: *When the student is receiving applause, monitor to make sure he or she is letting it in. See that they are making eye contact with the class and breathing deeply, rather than looking shyly at the floor.*

Class Participation

Ask everyone in the class to find a partner of approximately the same height and size they are, and to spread out throughout the room. Have them decide who will be the Experimenter and who will be the Volunteer for the first round of testing. Tell them that they will be switching roles after the Volunteer goes through the entire set of tests.

Direct them to conduct the same experiment with each other that you just demonstrated in front of the room. Give the volunteers and experimenters the following reminders and instructions:

Instructions to Volunteers

1. Place your arm straight out to your side at shoulder height, parallel to the floor.
2. Make a fist and rotate it so that your thumb is pointing down.
3. Do not raise your shoulder while the Experimenter presses down, as this will defeat the test.
4. Keep your eyes closed during the experience and say the lines with as much conviction as is possible.

Instructions to Experimenters

1. Place your hand on the outside wrist bone of the Volunteer.
2. Push gently at first, and then increase the pressure slowly until you achieve some kind of movement in the Volunteer's arm.
3. Don't jerk his/her arm down quickly in an attempt to overpower the other person. This will not work and runs the risk of straining muscles.

Sequence of Directions for Testing

1A. "I am a good girl/boy."
1B. "I am a bad girl/boy."
2A. Failure experience
2B. Success experience
3A. "I hate (subject)."
3B. "I love (subject)."

Following the testing, ask how many participants found that they did, in fact, get weaker when they said negative things about themselves and others. With those who seemingly had no reaction, check to see if you can detect a change in their strength.

There is a minority of people who will not experience much change. If this arises, just acknowledge it. If someone asks what this means, explain that while the experiment might not have the same effect on all people, focusing on saying and imagining positive thoughts about yourself will make you feel better, and it will empower you to take healthy risks and to grow.

Additional Activities

1. Ask students to make a list at the end of each day of all the academic, social/interpersonal, athletic, and domestic successes they enjoyed. Have them list these successes in their journals and circle the ones that they feel are the most enjoyable or significant.

2. Ask students to make their own Victory Log out of a pocket spiral notebook, and have them keep it with them so they may write down their successes as they occur. Ask them to commit to keeping the log for at least two weeks. Challenge them to maintain the log for the entire quarter or semester.*

---

* Used with permission, Self-Esteem in the Classroom: A Curriculum Guide *by Jack Canfield, et al (Culver City, CA: Self-Esteem Seminars, 1986.)*

FINGERS COME TOGETHER

Purpose

★ To demonstrate the power of the mind over the body
★ To reinforce the principles in the Good Boy/Bad Boy Kinesiology Demonstration

Procedure

Ask the students to lace their fingers. Have them separate their forefingers while keeping their other fingers laced. Their forefingers should be straight in front of them so they are approximately one inch apart. Pause, and ask if everyone is able to do this. When everyone assents, continue.

Tell them to look at their fingers. Without trying to make anything happen, and without trying to resist anything happening, have them say out loud, over and over, "Fingers come together . . . fingers come together . . ." for approximately one minute.

In most cases the forefingers will begin to move toward each other until they are actually touching.

This simple little exercise takes less than two minutes and reinforces the principle that the thoughts we think affect our bodies.*

---

* *Used with permission,* Self-Esteem in the Classroom—A Curriculum Guide *by Jack Canfield, et al (Culver City, CA: Self-Esteem Seminars, 1986).*

INNER SMILE VISUALIZATION

Before doing this exercise, you may want to review a diagram of the major internal body organs with your students.

Give the students the following instructions:

1. "Sit up straight in your chairs. Your legs should be a hip's width apart, and your feet should be flat on the floor. Put your hands comfortably on your lap. Close your eyes and breathe normally.

2. "Begin to relax all the muscles in your face. Imagine being in a very relaxing place—perhaps the place where you have felt the most relaxed in your whole life.

3. "Now imagine seeing your own smiling face out in front of you. Feel that smiling energy, like sunshine, being drawn into your eyes. Feel it relaxing all the skin on your face. . . . Feel it going deep inside your facial muscles and relaxing and warming your whole face.

4. "Let the smile flow into your mouth, gently lifting its outer corners. And as you continue to smile, bring that swirling energy into your jaw, and feel the jaw release any tension that is held there.

5. "Smile down into your neck and throat and feel the energy melting any tension there.

6. "Let the smiling energy flow down into your heart in the left side of your chest. Smile to your heart and thank it for its constant and essential work in pumping blood throughout your whole body. Feel your heart relax as it works more easily. Let the energy of your smile fill your heart with love and joy.

7. "Now smile into your lungs, thanking them for their wonderful work in supplying oxygen to the body. As you breathe into your lungs, feel them fill with goodness and courage.

8. "Smile now into your liver and kidneys, thanking them for helping you to keep your blood clean. You can feel yourself letting go of any anger or fear that may be there.

9. "Send your smiling energy to your stomach now, and thank it for the work it does digesting the food you eat. Then smile into your intestines and thank them for absorbing the nutrients from your food into your body.

10. "Continue to send your smiling energy down into your hips and upper legs. Feel the warm energy of your smile relaxing all the muscles there.

11. "And, finally, feel your inner smile extending down into your lower legs and feet.

12. "Feel your whole body now feeling loved and appreciated.

13. "Very good. Whenever you are ready, just slowly open your eyes and give me your attention up here . . . (pause) . . . Great! You may want to stretch your arms and legs for a moment before we continue."

After teaching this exercise to your students, you may wish to encourage them to practice it at home when they first wake up in the morning and any other time they just want to relax or increase their sense of self-appreciation.

GUIDELINES FOR AFFIRMATIONS

Affirmations will help you take action toward your goals.

Remember an affirmation is a statement with a thought picture that says you already have your goal.

There are eight rules for making an affirmation that will work:

1. Affirmations start with the words "I AM . . ."

2. Affirmations are positive. Never use the word "not" in an affirmation.

    WRONG: I am not afraid of job interviews.
    RIGHT: I am calmly answering every question in my job interviews.

3. Affirmations are stated in the present tense. Say it as if it is happening now.

4. Affirmations are short.

5. Affirmations are specific.

    WRONG: I am driving a new car.
    RIGHT: I am driving a new red 2008 Pontiac Firebird.

6. Affirmations need words that end in "ing" (an action verb).
    I am driv**ing** a new red 2008 Pontiac Firebird.
    I am teach**ing** kindergarten.

7. Affirmations have a feeling word in them (happily, proudly, thrilled, excited, exhilarated, peacefully, calmly, gratefully, or an action verb that express feelings such as enjoying, adoring, or feeling great).
    I am **happily** driving my new red Pontiac Firebird.
    I am **enjoying** teaching kindergarten.

8. Affirmations are about yourself.
    All of your affirmations should be to change your own behavior, not the behavior of someone else.

    WRONG: Johnny's keeping his room clean.
    RIGHT: I am calmly and effectively communicating with (or teaching) Johnny about keeping his room clean.

HOW TO USE AFFIRMATIONS AND VISUALIZATIONS

1. Repeat your affirmations three times per day. The best times are first thing in the morning, in the middle of the day for course correction, and around bedtime.
2 It is better to work in depth with a few affirmations than to occasionally repeat a lot of them.
3. If you are in a private place, read each affirmation out loud. If not, read it silently to yourself.
4. Close your eyes and visualize yourself as the affirmation describes. See the scene as you would see it if you were to look at it through your eyes, as if it were happening around you.
5. Hear any sounds/images you might hear when you successfully achieve what your affirmation describes. Include other important people in your life congratulating you and telling you how pleased they are with your success.
6. Feel the feelings that you will have when you achieve this success. The stronger the feelings, the more powerful the process becomes. (If you have difficulty creating the feelings, you can affirm, "I am enjoying creating powerful feelings in my effective work with affirmations.")
7. Say your affirmation again, and then repeat this process with the next affirmation.

Other Ways to Use Affirmations and Visualization

1. Post three-by-five cards with your affirmations on them around your house.
2. Post pictures of the things you want around your house or room. You can put a picture of yourself in the picture.
3. Repeat your affirmations during "wasted time," such as waiting in line, exercising, and driving. You can repeat them silently or out loud.
4. Record your affirmations and listen to them while you work, drive, or fall asleep. You can use endless loop tapes for this. See your audio supply dealers for endless loop tapes.

MY AFFIRMATIONS

1. _____
   _____

2. _____

   _____

3. _____

   _____

4. _____

   _____

5. _____

   _____

Guideline Recap
1. Positive
2. Starts with I am . . .
3. Present tense
4. Specific
5. "ing" verb
6. Feeling word
7. Brief
8. Personal

6. _____

   _____

7. _____

   _____

8. _____

   _____

9. _____

   _____

10. _____

    _____

11. _____

    _____

12. _____

    _____

13. _____

    _____

14. _____

    _____

15. _____

    _____

Chicken Soup for the Soul in the Classroom

E + R = O (EVENT + RESPONSE = OUTCOME)

Background

In order to achieve complete and full self-esteem, we have to take full responsibility for our lives, including both our internal and external experiences. Often we fall into the trap of blaming other people for how we feel and for what happens to us; this provides the distraction of looking for solutions to problems by focusing on supposed outside causes. It is much more profitable, however, to look inside ourselves: regardless of who is to blame, we are at least in charge of how we feel. Taking the point of view that we are responsible for our responses to the world gives us more power.

E + R = O

E stands for all the "events" of our lives.
R stands for our "response" to those events.
O stands for the "outcomes" we experience.

What most people complain about in their lives are the "outcomes" of this equation. For instance, people complain about having constant headaches, being depressed, feeling sad, feeling guilty, feeling angry, being yelled at by their parents, or getting a D or an F in school. They complain about how their boyfriend or girlfriend treats them.

These are all Os that have been created as the result of how they have responded to the events—the Es—in their lives.

For instance, would it be possible to come into this classroom where there are many, many people and feel lonely? (Yes.) Would it be possible to come into this same classroom and create connection, warmth, and friendship? (Yes.) It's the same classroom. The E is the same: there are the same people, with the same gender, it's the same number, same day, same temperature, same circumstances. Yet two people can enter the same room and produce a very different outcome for themselves. Why is this possible?

Because the R, the response, of the different individuals is different. For example, one person might enter, look around the room, and decide that everyone is too uptight, too judgmental, too much older, too much more sophisticated, too weird, too strange—and then sit back and observe everyone. At the end of the day that person leaves saying, "What an unfriendly classroom. I didn't have any fun. I felt very lonely."

Another person might come into the same room, same time, same circumstances, and go up to someone and say, "Hi, my name is Sheila, and I just moved here from Cleveland." That person had a different response to the same set of circumstances and events, the same E. As a result, she produced a different outcome in her life.

Often, what we do in life is to hope, pray, or demand that the E, the outside event, changes. We often hear this in the form of "If only's": "If only my teacher were more understanding" "If only my father were more loving" "If only my boyfriend understood how I feel" "If only . . ."

The fact is that Es, those environmental influences and other people, rarely change in the way we want them to. It's not impossible, but it doesn't often happen. In order to produce a different outcome, we have to change our behavior and our response.

"If I want a different outcome in the classroom, I'm going to have to do something different: reach out, participate more, raise my hand, do my homework. If I want a different response to my mother, I'm going to have to do something different in order to get her to respond differently to me."

2 + 2 = 4

$2 + 2 = 4$ and will always equal 4 from now until the end of time. If you don't like the outcome, 4, you will have to change either the first 2 or the second 2. We've already seen that other people and outside events are not likely to change very quickly. But we do have the power to change our response. We can change our 2 to a 3 or 4 or 5 or 6, producing a different result or outcome.

Sometimes the events in our lives have already happened. Our girlfriend has already decided to leave; the baseball has already crashed through the neighbor's living room window. At that point we again have a choice—we can choose to depress ourselves by telling ourselves that no one will ever love us again the way Sally did. We can tell ourselves that we're going to die and feel depressed. A different response would be to say: "There are many people in the world that I can have a loving relationship with. I'll start to look around and find them."

This response produces a totally different outcome. If I hit a baseball through a neighbor's window and start to imagine negative events, I'm likely to feel nervous inside—that is the outcome I have produced. The baseball going through the window didn't produce that. Another choice is to realize that I've made a mistake. I'll own up to it, talk to the neighbor, and replace the window. Then I have a good feeling inside.

If I have a boss who is negative or critical and judgmental, I have a choice, too. I can go inside and agree with the boss that I'm a bad person, or I can choose to tell myself that their point of view is their point of view and that I'm still a good person. This leaves me feeling okay. If they are the kind of boss who is constantly putting down people who make funny remarks, I can continue to be the office clown and get in trouble, or I can adjust my behavior—acknowledging that they might be the one who's uptight—but change my behavior so I no longer get reprimanded. This is the choice I always have.

$E + R = O$ means that if we want changes in our lives, we need to stop blaming the events, circumstances, and other people, and start focusing on our feelings and actions—our response. That's where the power is to produce the kinds of outcomes we truly want.

Biggest Idiot

"Suppose I approach John and say, 'John, of all the people I've ever met in my ten years of teaching, you have to be the biggest idiot I have ever had in one of my classes.' How many of you think that that would raise John's self-esteem? [No participants raise their hands.] How many of you think that that statement would lower John's self-esteem? [Most participants raise their hands.]

"How many of you think it doesn't matter what I say to John, but rather what John says to himself after I stop talking that affects his self-esteem? [Participants who have been paying attention will raise their hands.]

"It's important that you understand fully that it's not what I say to John, but what John says to John after I stop talking that affects how he feels about himself. If John goes inside after I stop talking and says, 'My God, how did he find out so soon?' that will affect his self-esteem in a negative way. If he goes inside and says to himself, 'Well, the trainer just picked on me because he knows that I have a strong self-concept and can take this kind of teasing,' John will feel good about himself.

"Remember, when someone says something to you that hurts, look inside and see what it is you are telling yourself about yourself."

To complete the discussion, answer participant's questions. Then challenge them to hold the attitude—at least in this class—that nobody else makes them feel anything and that they don't make other people feel certain ways.

Green Hair

This interactive demonstration helps make the explanation above more real for the participants. Say the following:

"The E + R = O formula works well in terms of seeing how we let other people 'make us feel bad.' For example, suppose I go up to Mary and tell her, 'Mary, you have green hair.' Would that make you feel bad? [Mary would answer 'No.'] 'Why not?' 'Because I know I don't have green hair.' So it's not what I say to Mary that affects how she feels. What Mary believes to be true about her hair before or after I say what I say is what conditions her response to me.

"What if I said to you, 'Mary, you are a mean, selfish, cruel person'? Would that hurt you? [Most participants will answer 'Yes.'] I believe that my statement would only hurt Mary if she has any doubts about whether or not she is mean, selfish, or cruel. If she is totally clear that she is a loving, warm, and generous person, then she wouldn't be hurt by that statement because she would know the truth of who she is.

"Anytime someone says something to you and you feel hurt, it's because at some level you have a doubt about yourself in that area. If I say 'You have green hair!' and you know you don't, there is no problem. The same is true with anything else in your life."

At this point conduct a discussion about hurtful things people have said. Ask students to look inside to see if they have doubts about those particular issues in their lives.

The Law of Attraction

Your feelings energize your thoughts and propel them from your inner being to your outer reality. The stronger or more emotional your feelings are, the more accelerated the process of attraction becomes.

When you go into a restaurant and the waiter comes to take your order, do you say, "I don't want lasagna" or, "I don't want tomato soup" or, "I don't want roast beef"? Of course not! You place your order for steak (medium rare), broccoli, rice, and a mixed greens salad (with the dressing on the side). You order from the menu with the *clarity* of what you want and the *absolute confidence* that you will get exactly what you ordered.

What You Resist Persists

When you focus on what you don't want by complaining about the way things are at home, at school, or with friends, or how hard your life is, you will attract more of the very things you say you don't want. By being *against* something, you are continually recreating it, as this becomes your focus. The war against drugs and the war against poverty were doomed from the beginning. If you focus on drugs, you get more drugs. If you focus on drug-free people, you get more of that. The war on terrorism has created more terrorism. The antiwar movement created more war within the country. The peace movement has a much greater chance of succeeding because it focuses on peace. There has never been a war to end all wars. Wars just keep perpetuating more wars. Focus on what you *want,* not on what you don't want.

Don't you find it interesting that we have five military academies, and not one peace academy in the United States? I am all for protecting ourselves against those who would harm us. But I am also aware that until we focus on creating peace, rather than defending against aggression, we will always have someone we must defend ourselves against.

What should you do when your find yourself complaining? Just acknowledge it and realize this is contrast playing itself out. You are getting clear about what you don't want. That's okay. But don't get stuck there. Ask yourself, "What is it that I *do* want?" Describe it in great detail. Write about it. Put it down on paper as a request, a purchase order, or a desire statement. Then affirm that you already have it. Close our eyes and visualize already possessing it or experiencing it, and create the emotions of what it would feel like if you already had it in your life. Do this for at least seventeen seconds of uninterrupted time—sixty-eight seconds is better.

Finally, saturate yourself with inspiring people, books, events, movies, videos, DVDs, seminars, workshops, lectures, and musical experiences, and your energy will soar to new levels of enthusiasm and exuberance. *

---

* Used with permission from Jack Canfield's Breakthrough to Success *training materials, 2006*

REPEATING QUESTION TECHNIQUE

This technique is designed to go deeply into that inner core place where all of our answers reside.

Initial answers to questions tend to represent surface thoughts and ideas. Repeatedly answering the same question takes us to a deeper level to find the answer.

Procedure

★ Find a partner.

★ Sit or stand comfortably facing that person.

★ Decide who will be Partner **A**, and who will be Partner **B**.

★ Partner **B** begins by asking Partner **A** the question:

What are you grateful for?

What do you want in life?

What do you like about school?

What brings you happiness?

Any question may be asked for which you desire a deep-level answer.

★ Partner **A** responds to the question.

★ Partner **B** asks the *same question.*

★ Partner **A** responds.

★ Partner **B** asks the *same question.*

★ **A** responds . . .

★ Continue until the time is up (two to five minutes).

Switch roles and begin again.

Share with your partner, or write about your feelings, after both partners have had a chance to repeatedly answer the question.

The partner asking the question only asks the question. Do not judge, agree, nod your head, or give any kind of feedback. Simply, and repeatedly, ask the question.

THE COMPLETION PROCESS PROCEDURE

The original intent of this assignment for you, as a teacher, is to help you to let go of past resentments or unfulfilled expectations that may interfere with your satisfaction in your career.

We recommend that you use the questions and prompts as joyful reminders of the journey you are undertaking with thousands of students, and how your attitude will set the tone for the journey.

Procedure

1. Find a time and place where you can be alone with your thoughts and feelings for awhile.
2. Read each question of the Completion Process, and either write down your answers or just spend time thinking about them. Let yourself get in touch with any feelings that arise, then work toward releasing them. (You can also do this exercise as a partner process, with your partner asking you each question, and you answering honestly.)
3. Reflect on the idea that "This is it," or that in terms of your experience all there is exists *now*.
   * When the past happened, it was in that moment of *now*.
   * All that is available to you now about the past are the thoughts that you carry about the past, and these thoughts exist *now* in your mind.
   * The past, as an event, is over. What happened has already happened. You cannot change that; you can only change your thoughts about it.
   * What is available to you is *now*; you have the opportunity to interact with what is happening in this moment. Don't waste it by worrying about the past.
   * *This is it!*
4. When you feel you understand this fully, contemplate the implications of this insight for your future.

The Completion Process Questions

1. Recall the moment you decided to become a teacher.
   * What was your inspiration?
   * What did you hope to accomplish?
   * Are you more enthusiastic about teaching now, or less?
   * What happened to make the difference?
2. Recall the earliest significant failure you experienced in teaching.
   * What happened?
   * How did you feel?
   * What interpretation did you place on this?
3. What do you consider the biggest mistake you've made as a teacher?
   * What happened?
   * To what did you attribute this?
   * What did you learn from it?
4. What was your most embarrassing moment as a teacher?
   * What happened?
   * What did you learn from this?
5. Recall a more recent disappointment you've experienced as a teacher.
   * What happened?
   * How did you feel?
   * What interpretation did you place on this?
6. What resentments have you had about being in education?
7. What regrets relating to being a teacher have you had?
8. What has been your biggest fear as a teacher?
   * What would be the worst thing about this happening?
9. Have you ever considered quitting the profession?
   * What prompted this thought?
10. If you were to do it over again, what about your career as an educator would you do differently?
11. What would need to happen in order for you to feel at peace with the past and be ready to move forward, open to new and exciting possibilities?
    * Whom would you need to forgive?
    * For what would you need to forgive yourself?
    * What is present that would need to be eliminated?
    * What is missing that would need to be created?
    * How could you shift focus from the "rear view mirror" to looking ahead through the windshield, fully in the driver's seat? *

---

* Adapted from 101 Ways to Develop Student Self-Esteem and Responsibility *by Jack Canfield and Frank Siccone (Needham Heights, MA: Allyn and Bacon, 1993).*

FORMING GROUPS

Were you ever the last one chosen to join a team, or the last person selected when asked to find a partner in the classroom? If so, it might cause you to break out in a cold sweat, even fifty years later. The following pages provide suggestions to take the angst out of forming groups. Indeed, many of these ideas are so much fun that students look forward to group work in a new way.

Some General Procedures for Grouping

Pick and choose the group size based on the lesson's objectives, the time constraints, and the properties of each group size.

Each group size has different advantages. In a group of two, each person is guaranteed an opportunity to talk. In a group of three, there is a larger range of experience and opinion, but there is the possibility of two people dominating the conversation or ganging up on the third member. One way to avoid this is to have one person at a time observe the other two and then give them feedback before rotating roles.

A group of four has inherent flexibility, because it can be formed by joining together two pairs, or dyads. One option is to use dyads for an exercise or two, and then create quartets for the closing set of exercises. In this way, each person in the quartet feels close to at least one other person before interacting in the larger group.

Groups of five or six provide a cross-section of experiences and a greater potential for creativity and problem-solving. Exercises that elicit feelings sometimes feel safer when in groups of five or six.

For time constraints, the rule of thumb is that if there are just a few minutes at the end of class, use partners or triads. If there is more time, start with smaller groups and then build to larger ones.

Possible Methods of Subgrouping

There are many ways to form pairs and groups. Some are traditional, others more fun. Here are some examples of directions you might give:

★ "I'd like you to look around the room and find a partner, someone you'd be willing to work with for the next ten minutes."

★ "I'd like you to look around the room and choose a partner of the opposite sex with whom you'd be willing to work for the next five minutes."

★ "I'd like you to pick a partner, someone with whom you haven't been partners yet."

★ "I'd like you to find a partner. Good. Now, I'd like the two of you to join another pair and form a group of four. When you have a group of four, please sit down so people who are still looking for partners will be able to see who is still available."

★ "I'd like you to count off by threes (or sixes) . . . 1, 2, 3 . . . 1, 2, 3 . . . 1, 2, 3 . . . Good. Now, ones over here, twos in the middle, and threes over there."

★ "I'd like you to find a partner who is approximately as tall as you."

★ "I'd like you to find two other people and form groups of three."

Here are some of the more creative and fun ways to get people into pairs or groups:
★ "I'd like you to find a partner (or get into groups of three, four, five, or six) who
—is the same height as you are, or the closest to it."
—has the same color clothing you do."
—was born in the same month you were."
—has the same birth order in their family as you (that is, first born, middle child, youngest, and so on)."
—is someone you would not normally pick."
—has the same size thumb you do, or the closest to it."

Adapted with permission from 101 Ways to Develop Student Self-Esteem and Responsibility, *Jack Canfield and Frank Siccone (Needham Heights, MA: Allyn and Bacon, 1993).*

CREATIVE WAYS TO GET INTO GROUPS

We have borrowed, with permission, some wonderfully creative ideas from Matt Weinstein and Joel Goodman, in their book entitled *Playfair* (see full citation noted at the conclusion). Have fun seeing how many different ways you can group your students, while lessening their anxiety.

A Note on Choosing Partners and Forming Groups

A seemingly innocuous suggestion like "Everybody pick a partner!" can strike terror into the hearts of many players. All sorts of questions race through people's heads:

* "Should I pick somebody or wait to be picked?"
* "What if nobody picks me?"
* "What if I pick somebody and she doesn't want to play with me?"
* "How can I pick her without making her think I'm coming on to her?"
* "If I pick him, is he going to follow me around all day after this?"
* "Does he really want to play with me or is he just being polite?"

And on and on . . .

In order to create a safe and supportive play environment, it is important to invent ways to get the players into pairs and groups without anyone being left out, and without putting the players into anxiety-provoking positions. "Pick a partner" is interpreted by many people to mean "Get together with the person you are the most attracted to," and that is an embarrassing thing for many people to do openly. There are many random ways to get people into groups. The more specific you can be about your instructions, the more comfortable the players will be. We've suggested a number of ideas for you here:

* Put either your left thumb or your right pinky in the air, and get together with one other person who's doing the same thing you are. Or, find three other people who are doing the same thing you are and sit down with them, forming a group of four.
* Put from zero to five fingers in the air, and find one other partner so that when you add your fingers to that person's fingers you get an even number.
* Put one or two fingers out and keep them out. Now find four people with the same number of fingers out and form a group of five and sit down in a circle.
* Check to see whether you're wearing a belt or not. Find one other partner who, like you, is or is not wearing a belt.
* Find a partner who is or is not wearing a ring, as you are.
* Count up the number of letters in your first name, and see if you have an odd or even number of letters. Now find a partner who, like you, has an even or odd number of letters in his or her name.
* Start hopping around on either your right foot or your left foot and find a partner who is hopping with the same foot as you are.
* Find a partner who has a different number of brothers and sisters than you do.

* Find a partner who is wearing one item of clothing the same color as you are.
* Close your eyes, and in your mind flip a coin. If it comes up heads, find a partner who is taller than you. If it comes up tails, find a partner who is shorter than you.

There are lots of elements at play here:

People looking carefully at each other, calling out things, moving around, raising their hands into the air—and you can decide which of those works best for your particular group and environment.

You could go on and on inventing ways to get the players into pairs. In fact, that's a good idea! Get a group of people together and play the Partner Game. One person calls out a way to get people into partners, and everybody finds a partner through that method. Then somebody else calls out another way to get into partners, and everyone reshuffles into new pairs. There's no need to verbally criticize anybody's suggestions, because it will be evident as you move from one to the other which ones work and which don't.

In a few minutes, a group can brainstorm dozens of usable pair-ups from this game. There are lots of interesting things you'll find out as the game goes on. For example, "Turn to your right and pick that person for your partner" sounds like a reasonable idea; however, as everybody turns to their right at once . . .

"Put either your left hand or your right hand into the air, and pair up with someone who's doing the opposite" also sounds like a good suggestion. But suppose that only one person has her left hand in the air, and everyone else has their right hands in the air. You'll soon find out that if you give people two choices, they'll have to pair up with someone who has chosen the *same thing* as they have for it to work out in even pairs.

Forming the players into groups and teams is also something about which to be very careful. Many people have childhood memories of "choosing up teams," desperately hoping not to be chosen last. Those feelings are still latent, even in the most confident of adults. Giving all the players a "forced choice" and letting them select their teams simultaneously is an anxiety-free way of getting groups formed. For example, "Imagine that you could go on a vacation to the tropics as soon as you wanted to. If you'd rather go to Hawaii, go over there; if you want to go to Puerto Rico, over there; and if you want to go to Mozambique, over there." Voila: three groups! For many "team" games, it doesn't matter if the teams are of unequal size.

If you want to release somewhat more energy during the formation of the groups, you can let them sort themselves out without giving them specific meeting points. For example, "Decide if you would like to eat a banana, a peach, or a bunch of grapes right now. Get together in one large group with everyone else who wants to eat the same thing you do!"

** This is excerpted with permission from Playfair: Everybody's Guide to Non-Competitive Play, by Matt Weinstien and Joel Goodman. Matt is the founder and emperor of Playfair, Inc., an international consulting firm based in Berkeley, California. His latest book is Gently Down the Stream. Contact Matt at Playfair, Inc., 2207 Oregon St., Berkeley, CA, 94705 (website http://www.Playfair.com). Joel is the founder of The HUMOR Project, Inc., the first organization in the world to focus full-time on the positive power of humor. For more info on The HUMOR Project's international conference, HUMOResources mail-order bookstore, and Speakers Bureau, contact Joel at The HUMOR Project, 10 Madison Avenue, Saratoga Springs, NY 12866 (www.HumorProject.com).

ASSERTIVE COMMUNICATION

Assertive communication is clear and direct communication in which the sender takes responsibility for the message.

The key word is "I," rather than "you," which is aggressive and makes the recipient feel attacked.

"I am not feeling appreciated right now," rather than, *"You don't appreciate me."*
"I want to do this work by myself," rather than, *"You never let me do things on my own."*

The Message Is Clear

★ Tone of voice, body language, and the words all send the same message. Less than one third of our total communication is the wording that we use. All messages need to be congruent.
★ Be clear about your desires and feelings and tell the other person what they are. Do not assume that someone can read your mind, or that they know what you are feeling.
★ Don't add tag-questions to your statements.

"We need to be done with this project by Friday," rather than
"We need this done by Friday, okay?"

The Communication Is Current and Supportive

Express your message in a positive and immediate fashion. Don't stockpile your feelings for a big dumping session later. And focus on the problem without name-calling, sarcasm, or other negative behaviors.

Avoid the Passive or Passive-aggressive Styles

While aggressive, you-based communication is not recommended, the passive style can actually be dangerous to your health. When one is being passive, feelings are not expressed; they are suppressed. Stuffed feelings can lead to physical maladies such as ulcers, high blood pressure, and migraines, or they may tie into socially unacceptable behaviors. Vandalism is often passive-aggressive and is exhibited by stuffed feelings now, followed by aggression later.

Assertive communication is clearer and more likely to get you the results you desire.

HOW TO SAY "NO"

We all know that when we're under pressure, saying "No" is not all that easy. In our hearts, we believe that saying "no" . . .

to drugs
to alcohol
to smoking
to unprotected sex
to cheating
to stealing
to lying
to fighting, and . . .
to many other things is probably the best idea.

But how? What happens when you want to say "no," but all of your friends are saying, "Aw, come on!" And what happens when you really don't want to say "no," but you feel that you should?

The steps to saying "no" really are pretty simple . . . but they are not easy.

1. First, you must be committed to your answer. Know how you feel about the choice.

2. It's best to decide this before the situation and not in the middle of it, whenever possible.

    You're going to a party. There may be alcohol there. Decide before the party whether or not you'll drink if alcohol is presented to you.

3. Next, try to find a friend who shares your belief. It's much easier to stick to it if there's more than one of you who feels the same way.

    Jim and John are twins. They hate drinking because their father was killed by a drunken driver. They vow never to drink, and they get Tom and Sam to join them in their plan. Saying "no" to alcohol at the party suddenly became easy.

Now, follow these three steps when saying "No":

1. **A simple yet firm "No!" is best.** You need not give an explanation . . . someone else will always have a reason why you should do what you are declining to do. Make certain that your body language and tone of voice matches your words.

   "Would you like a beer?"
   "No!"

2. **Express how you feel about being pressured.**
   "Come on, it's only a beer."

   "Eric, I'm really feeling uncomfortable about you pressuring me. If you're really my friend, lay off! The answer is no!"

3. **If the pressure gets too great, remove yourself from the situation.**

   "This stuff is really great. You don't know what you're missing."
   "I've already said 'No!' Now I'm going for a walk. Want to join me?"

It's as simple as one, two, three. But it won't become easy unless you practice it. And the more you practice it, the better you will be at this skill of saying "no" when you want to say "no."

A final reminder: your body language and tone of voice help to communicate the "no" much more loudly than merely your words. Use them to your advantage. The more you do it, the easier it gets.

Focus on the "Yes" in Your Life

While it's important to know how to say "no" in some circumstances, it is far more powerful to focus on the things that are "yes" in your life—the positive things that make your heart sing, that bring you inner peace and joy. What you focus on, you attract. So, turn your attitude and your attention to the things, people, and experiences that you want to experience even more.

SAYING "NO!"

Three Simple, But Not Easy, Steps:

1. Simply, and **repeatedly, say "no."**
   Do not give a reason, nor get drawn into a debate.

2. **Turn the tables.**
   "Why are you pressuring me into doing this?"
   "Why do you feel it is necessary for me to do this with you?"
   "What part of 'no' don't you understand?"

3. If pressure continues or escalates, **leave the scene.**
   "You obviously don't understand my feelings on this . . .
        I think it's time for me to go."
   "I'm leaving!"
   Or, simply leave without saying anything.

Role-play saying "No"
Practice it at least three different times in the following ways:
   ★ saying "no" when you are the only one doing so
   ★ saying "no" with one other friend at your side
   ★ saying "no" with several friends who have the same convictions

Note: *It is usually easier to say "no" when you have friends who are there to help you. Do not put yourself in situations where you are the ONLY one who feels a certain way. Make sure when communicating that your body language and tone of voice match your message.*

Practice Makes Perfect

Saying "no" (or saying "yes") gets easier and easier each time you say it. The first time is always the most difficult. The choice is yours to make. If you say "yes" to that first beer, beers number two, three, and four get successively easier. If you say "yes" to shoplifting just once (perhaps on a dare), the next time will get easier. The third time is easier yet. The longer you break the law, the greater your chances are of getting caught.

The same is true of saying "no." With each time you say it, you get the strength of your convictions and more ease with every "no" that you give. Learning to say "no" when it is in our best interest is an important skill to develop.

Know Your Values

Spend time thinking about your beliefs and what is important to you. Clearly *KNOW* what you will do before you are in the middle of a sticky situation. It's very difficult to make a clear choice in the middle of a passionate kiss in the back seat of a car!

EXAMPLE OF MODEL A FOR DECISION-MAKING

1. State your concern. What are you trying to decide? Write out the problem clearly in the space below.

    How should I spend my free time after school?

2. List all possible solutions you can think of (good, bad, silly, practical) for the problem stated above.

    watch TV

    take a nap

    clean bedroom **

    ~~eat a pint of ice cream~~

    do math for tomorrow **

    write an English report for next week **

    ~~sneak some of dad's beer~~

    take little brother/sister to the park **

    hang out at the mall

    join a sport or club at school**

Cross out the ideas you know are not good choices. Star (**) the good choices.

3. List your best solution.

    Do math assignment for tomorrow.

What is the worst possible thing that will happen if you use this solution?

    Do the assignment all wrong and fail the class.

What is the best possible thing that will happen if you use this solution?

    Get an A+ on math homework and ace the class.

What is the *most likely* thing to happen with this solution?

    Do the homework correctly and do well in the class.

4. Are you satisfied with the most likely results to your decision (part three)?

    Yes.

If not, go back to one of your other solutions and repeat step three on the back of this page. You can repeat step three as often as necessary until you are satisfied with the most likely results of your solution.

MAKING DECISIONS—PRACTICE MODEL A

Mark has been a pretty good student in social studies. He pays attention in class and takes good notes. All of his assignments have been turned in, and he has an A- average so far. But Mark has fallen far behind on his reading assignments. Now the teacher has told him that the big six-week test tomorrow will cover the reading material, not the class work. He has tickets to watch his friends play in the state finals basketball game tonight. What should Mark do? Use this Model A for Decision Making to decide for Mark.

1. State your concern. What are you trying to decide? Write out the problem clearly in the space below.

2. List all possible solutions you can think of (good, bad, silly, practical) for problem stated above. List all possible solutions below.

1.

2.

3.

4.

5.

6.

Cross out the ideas that you know are not good choices. Star (**) the good choices.

3. List your best solution.

What is the worst possible thing that will happen if you use this solution?

What is the best possible thing that will happen if you use this solution?

What is the most likely thing to happen with this solution?

4. Are you satisfied with the most likely results to your decision (part three)?

If not, go back to one of your other solutions and repeat step three on the back of this page. You can repeat step three as often as necessary until you are satisfied with the most likely results of your solution.

EXAMPLE OF MODEL B FOR DECISION-MAKING

The example below shows a typical student decision, followed by several options and the consequences, both good and bad, of each option. Add to the lists of choices and prices with things that you might do with your leisure time.

DECISIONS	CHOICES (options)	PRICES (the good and bad result of your choice)
How to spend leisure time?	*1) Reading*	*1. a) + building reading skills*
		b) - too much can give you a headache
	2) Homework	*2. a) + better grades*
	3) Biking	*3. a) + get in shape for basketball*
		b) – sore muscles
	4) "Party" with friends	*4. a) + helps social life*
		b) + a chance to meet people
		c) – possible illegal activities
		d) – lack of sleep
		e) – get in trouble with parents

MAKING DECISIONS—PRACTICE MODEL B

*S*arah and Jane, ages fourteen and fifteen, went to a party with Sarah's older brother, Scott. They didn't know there would be drinking at the party, but it was no big deal. Neither Sarah nor Jane was tempted by the alcohol offered to them.

The problem occurred when it was time to go home. To the surprise of both girls, Scott was drunk. It was miles from home and very late. Both girls knew the risks of riding with someone who had been drinking. Neither was old enough to have a legal driver's license.

What should they do? Using Decision-Making Model B, make the decision for Sarah and Jane below:

DECISIONS	CHOICES (options)	PRICES (list all prices, + and –)
How should Sarah and Jane get home?	1.	1. a)
		b)
		c)
		d)
	2.	2. a)
		b)
		c)
		d)
	3.	3. a)
		b)
		c)
		d)

MAKING DECISIONS

This step-by-step process can be used for any decision you need to make:

1. What is the problem? What are you trying to decide?

2. What are your options or choices?
   (Think of it like looking at a roadmap and considering all possible ways to get to your destination.)

3. Focus on your outcome. What do you want as an end result?
   (Where are you trying to go?)

4. Consider the results of each choice. What are the consequences, or what might happen to you with each choice?
   (Will the road be a dead end? Could you end up in the ocean?)

5. Make a selection or make a choice.
   (Choose a road or a highway. Do you want to take the Interstate and get there quickly? Or do you want to take small side-roads to enjoy the journey?)

6. Carry out your solution.
   (Get in your vehicle and drive down that road.)

7. Look back and evaluate your decision. Was it the best decision for you right now?
   (Perhaps the road you chose was only a minor detour. Maybe you need to take a slightly different route to get to your destination.)

Note: *There are roads taken that could permanently jeopardize your health or your life. Oftentimes, these fall into the category of thoughtless actions rather than conscious decisions. With most decisions, where consequences are considered, you can change your mind and take another course or another route.*

Another caution is the tendency to make a decision by avoiding the decision. Some people will put it off and put it off, until the opportunity has passed, and the decision is made by default. Fear of taking responsibility for the decision is really a way of giving up personal control of one's life, and this only leads to unhappiness and frustration.

Make your decisions as conscious choices to get what you want in life.

"TELEPHONE" DIRECTIONS

1. Have students sit in a circle.

2. The teacher begins by quickly whispering a sentence to one of the students.

3. This student, in turn, quickly repeats the sentence to the next student, who repeats it to the next, etc.

4. It continues around the circle until it gets back to the teacher, who repeats it aloud. The original message is usually very distorted by the time it gets to the end of the circle. Relate this game of "telephone" to see how gossip becomes distorted over time. Spend time discussing how hurtful these distorted or untrue messages can be.

SPREADING ACTS OF KINDNESS: A SCHOOL-WIDE CAMPAIGN

Whenever there is an act of kindness, the giver, the receiver, and the witness of that act all have increased serotonin levels in their brains and an enhanced immune system (paraphrased from a talk by Dr. Wayne W. Dyer on "The Power of Intention").

The focus of this project is to introduce or reinforce the intrinsic reward of doing nice things (*e.g., the inner joy that one feels*).

Step 1 . . .

• Introduce the concept with a story:

> "A Simple Hello"
> "Night Watch"
> "Winning Isn't Everything"
> "Kindness Is Contagious"
> "Innocent Homeless"
> "Surprise Santa"

These are a few of the stories in this book that focus on kindness.

Step 2 . . .

• Spend some time brainstorming acts of kindness with students:

> ★ picking up an item that someone has dropped
> ★ holding a door open for someone
> ★ making breakfast for Mom on Saturday morning
> ★ writing a letter of gratitude to a teacher from your past
> ★ visiting someone in a nursing home and having them tell you their life story
> ★ picking up litter in the school hallways or on the school grounds
> ★ buying a sandwich for a homeless person
> ★ anonymously sending something to someone in need (*flowers, a hand-made gift, etc.*)

Opportunities are as varied as the imaginations of your students.

Step 3 . . .

• Have each student make a poster promoting kind acts (*at home, in school, out in the community, on world travels, etc.*).

> The feel-good aspects can be stressed.
> Examples can be given.

Step 4 . . .

• Instruct students to complete three kind acts in a week (*at home, school, or in the community*).

An auxiliary assignment would be to have students write about how it felt to give in such a way.

Step 5 . . .

- Anyone receiving an act of kindness would be instructed to pass it on to at least three other people in the following week.

An auxiliary assignment would be for students to write about how it felt to receive an act of kindness.

Optional Community Involvement

Doing this portion of the activity shifts the energy away from intrinsic (*e.g., inner joy*) to extrinsic (*e.g., external reward*). Bringing community awareness to the project, however, can be worth the shift.

If you choose to do this portion of the activity, it is suggested that you remind students of the real value of doing a kind deed, of the intrinsic good feeling of doing nice things for others.

Step 6 . . .

- Contact local businesses to solicit a cash award to be donated to a local charity selected by the winning class.

Step 7 . . .

- Contact local media to cover the story, and to thereby give free advertising to the supporting media.

Step 8 . . .

- Instruct each classroom to keep records of who delivered acts of kindness, as well as what was done (*the "what" provides a good possibility list for the following year*).

Step 9 . . .

- Ask for further media coverage when the charity money is delivered.

Step 10 . . .

- Possibly follow up with an essay contest on "How It Feels to Be Kind."
  Submit the winning entry to the media as closure for the project.

TRUTH AND LIES (A.K.A. TWO TRUTHS AND A LIE)

This is a good introductory game or a good bonding activity that works well for any age group.

Preparation

1. Students are asked to think of two things their classmates do not know about them.

   I was born in New York in a blizzard
   I had heart surgery at age two
   My mother was in the astronaut program
   I weighed eleven pounds at birth
   I have twelve adopted siblings
   I won an art contest at age five
   I can speak fluent French
   I love to sing
   I spent my summer vacation helping to rebuild houses following a hurricane

2. Additionally, students are asked to create one lie of a similar content.

Procedure

Each student tells their two truths and one lie in a random order. Classmates attempt to guess which statement is the lie, while also learning two truths about each person in the class.

Variations

- The game may be played in smaller groups.
- The teacher can collect all entries, type them, and have students enter their guesses on paper, sharing aloud over a period of several days or weeks.
- I Have a Secret is a version done on paper, with only one entry per student. For example, classmates try to guess which student is the one who weighed eleven pounds at birth.

WARM FUZZY DIRECTIONS

1. These are written, **anonymous** compliments to everyone else in the room. To receive full credit, you should use a different word to describe each person.

2. Focus on **inner qualities** such as humor, friendship, honesty, trust, kindness, etc. Use a Thesaurus for different versions of a similar thought.

3. You may only use three statements about their physical attributes or their abilities like cute, good soccer player, etc. "You like to play soccer" is not a compliment. It is merely a statement about what they like to do. **Make sure that your warm fuzzies are all compliments.**

4. Spend time getting to know your classmates so you can determine their inner strengths. **Do not ask them to describe an inner quality for you.** You must find that inner quality as you interact with them.

5. Make your fuzzies at least as large as a credit card.

6. **Do not sign each fuzzy.** They are to remain anonymous.

7. **Be HONEST!** A false compliment is no compliment at all.

8. These must be **positive.**

9. Your teacher will give you an alphabetical listing of your classmates. Follow that list to make sure that you include everyone. Then place the list on top. It should indicate all of the compliments that you gave to each person on top of your stack of fuzzies.

10. These may be two-dimensional like a deck of cards, or 3-D like a small booklet, a furry creature, a balloon with the message inside, or a decorated candy bar for each classmate. While it is wonderful to see how creative you can get, remember that it is the message that is the intent of this assignment.

Warm fuzzies are due _____. Your grade will be lowered one full grade for each day it is late.

WRITING GOALS IN SMART FORMAT

S = **S**pecific. State exactly what you want.

(I want to get three As and two Bs on my next report card. Not, I want to get better grades.)

M = **M**easurable. Tell how you will know you have achieved it. How much? How far? Can you see it? How will you know when you are there?

(On my next report card, I expect to see three As and two Bs.)

A = **A**ction. What can you do in the next twenty-four hours to start your goal? What can you do next week? Next month? In six months?

(Starting today, I'm going to do thirty minutes of homework right after school. This week, I will purchase a day-planner in order to organize my study time. By next month, I will cut an hour of television out of each week so that I might devote that time to homework.)

R = **R**ealistic. Is this real for you? How does it fit into your lifestyle? Your values? Is it your goal, or someone else's?

(Getting good grades is important to me, and I am capable of achieving three As and 2 Bs with only slight adjustments in my day.)

T = **T**ime-limited. When will it be done? A week? A month? A year? By the time you are age thirty?

(It is only two months until the end of the semester grading period . . . I will accomplish my goal by that time.)

GOAL BOOK/GOAL POSTER

Choose three of your most important goals.

Write each goal in SMART format.
  S = **S**pecific. State exactly what you want.
  M = **M**easurable. Tell how you will know you have achieved it (How much? How far? Can you see it?)
  A = **A**ction (What can you do in the next twenty-four hours to start your goal? In a week? In a month?)
  R = **R**ealistic (Is this real for you? How does it fit into your lifestyle? Your values?)
  T = **T**ime-limited (When will it be done? A week? A month? A year? By the time you are age thirty?)

Show at least one picture representing each goal.

Label each goal as ST (short-term = less than a year),
                        MT (medium-term = one to three years), or
                        LT (long-term = more than three years).

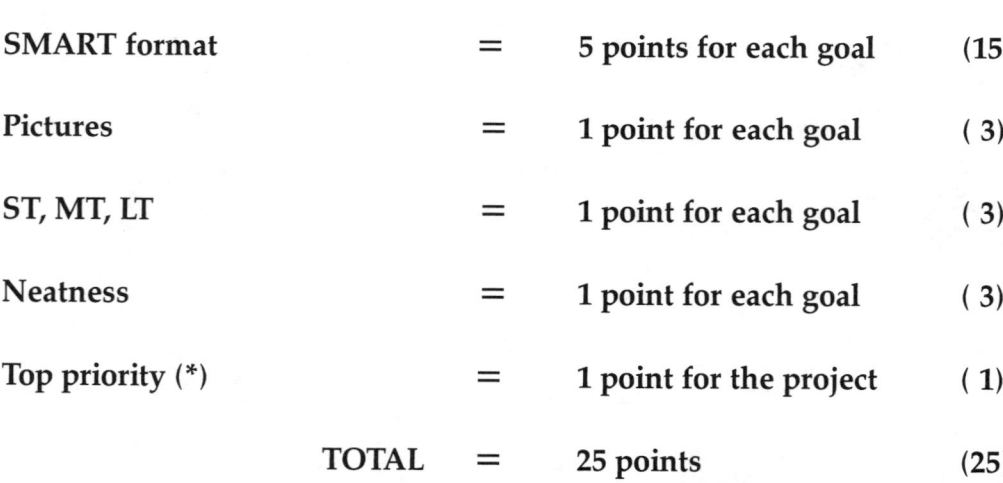

Place a * next to the goal that is your TOP priority.

Make sure that your project is NEAT.

GRADING SCALE FOR THE PROJECT:

SMART format	=	5 points for each goal	(15)
Pictures	=	1 point for each goal	(3)
ST, MT, LT	=	1 point for each goal	(3)
Neatness	=	1 point for each goal	(3)
Top priority (*)	=	1 point for the project	(1)
TOTAL	=	25 points	(25)

YOUR NAME_____ POINTS_____

Chicken Soup for the Soul in the Classroom

DIVORCE AND BLENDED FAMILY ISSUES

Divorce is a fact of life in our society today. Everyone knows of someone who has been divorced. In fact, you or many of your friends may be part of a blended family that has to deal with daily issues involving step-families. Respond to the following questions or statements regarding this topic.

1. Why do you think people get divorced?

2. List some emotions commonly associated with divorce.

3. What are some of the problems of divorce? Consider before, during, and after the divorce.

4. What do you think would happen if it were impossible to get a divorce? List as many things as possible. Even silly answers count on this one.

5. List some pros and cons of living within blended families.

6. If I didn't get along with my stepparent, I would . . .

7. The ideal stepparent is . . .

8. Having a stepbrother or stepsister . . .

GRIEF

Whenever you experience the loss of something significant, you also experience grief. Your teacher may choose to explain some of the stages of grief to you.

Imagine that your very best friend has just moved to another state. Describe below how you are feeling and what you are thinking.

Imagine that your closest friend came to school in tears this morning and would not explain why but simply told you to "get lost." What would you do?

During lunch, you find out that her dog was killed by a car last night. Now what do you do? How do you think she is feeling?

List as many ways as possible to describe death without saying "dead" (e.g., "passed away").

UNFINISHED BUSINESS

The purpose of this assignment is to complete, in a positive way, anything that might be emotionally left undone with someone, so if that person were to die tomorrow, you would feel completion, or at peace with the issue.

The guidelines are:

1. It must be *positive*. This is not a time for purging your anger or getting even.

2. It can be as big or as small as you feel comfortable with.

3. It can be verbal, in writing, or an action.

4. The outcome is not important. You cannot control how the other person will respond. What is important is you having done it.

5. To get credit for this assignment, you must write a follow-up paragraph explaining:

   ★ what you said or did
   ★ the response from the recipient
   ★ how you *felt* doing it

Some examples are:

   ★ give a gratitude hug to someone
   ★ apologize to a friend
   ★ write a letter to a sibling telling them how much you love them
   ★ thank someone for being such a good friend to you
   ★ write a letter of thanks to a favorite teacher, past or present
   ★ tell your parents you love them (if you haven't done this in a while)

The deadline for this assignment is _____ .
        (Procrastination only makes this task more difficult.)

A related assignment is to write a letter of completion for someone who is already deceased.

YOUR THOUGHTS ON SUICIDE

Suicide is a leading cause of death among young people. Why do you think this is so?

It is said that suicide is the most selfish of acts. Do you agree or disagree? Defend your position.

If your best friend talked to you about wanting to commit suicide, and asked you to maintain confidentiality, what would you do?

What do you think is the best way to prevent adolescent suicide?

Suicide is said to be "a permanent solution to a temporary problem." What does this mean to you?

List one or two trusted adults that you would seek out in the event you might feel suicidal, or if you had a friend who reported suicidal thoughts.

Chicken Soup for the Soul in the Classroom

FINDING AND KEEPING SELF-ESTEEM

Even if you enter your teenage years with a good self-image or good self-esteem, you are likely to run into some rough spots. Hormones are changing your body physically and emotionally. One moment you might feel confident, and the next moment you may feel frightened. One day, a look in the mirror reveals a pleasant reflection, and the next day all you see are new pimples and hair that just won't stay in place. It is perfectly normal to have these kinds of ups and downs throughout life.

However, some people choose to spend their lives blaming their parents for their lack of self-esteem. You can choose to do this, but it may mean a long and unhappy life and we don't recommend it. You have choices. It's a matter of focus and of putting your energy, and your time, with the people who support you in a positive way. Use the following lists to help start you on this journey:

Five People Who Like Me As I Am

List five people in your life who like you just as you are.

1.

2.

3.

4.

5.

Make it a point to start spending more time with these people.

Five Things I Like About Me

List five positive things about yourself. Are you a good cook? A good friend? A good student? You are what you think about, so think positively and you will be more positive.

1.

2.

3.

4.

5.

Five Things I Like to Do

List five things you like to do.

1.

2.

3.

4.

5.

Five Things I'd Like to Try

List five things you'd like to try, or groups you'd like to join.

1.

2.

3.

4.

5.

Don't feel you have to be perfect. No one is, so why should you feel like you should be? Remember that failure is a part of success. And no one does things perfectly the first time around.

No Vultures Allowed

Finally, get rid of the "vultures" who thrive on negative energy. Stay away from those who put you down all the time. And, just as importantly, don't put yourself down. What you say to yourself can be the most important tool toward reaching a positive self-image. Learn to change your negative thoughts to positive ones.

For example: A friend compliments you on a gorgeous sweater. You say, "Oh, it's just an old hand-me-down." You could say, "Thank-you. It's one of my favorites" and simply smile inside at the positive energy being generated from the encounter.

HOW DO YOU FEEL?

Look at the list of emotion words below. Circle those that you frequently feel

Happy	Fun	Honest
Intelligent	Likeable	Brave
Handsome	Knowledgeable	Considerate
Vivacious	Responsible	Tolerant
Clean	Fair	Sharing
Curious	Positive	Dependable
Humorous	Calm	Warm
Communicative	Sympathetic	Reliable
Accomplished	Graceful	Friendly
Real	Healthy	Social
Cheerful	Considerate	Out-going
Optimistic	Entertaining	Honest
Confident	Antagonistic	Brave
Sad	Selfish	Mature
Argumentative	Silly	Considerate
Cruel	Untruthful	Tolerant
Dull	Crude	Sharing
Stubborn	Gullible	Competent
Dishonest	Careless	Unfriendly
Clumsy	Uninvolved	Moody
Lazy	Unhealthy	Rude
Immature	Dreary	Unclean
Impulsive	Submissive	Afraid
Messy	Nervous	
Temperamental	Prejudiced	
Edgy	Gloomy	
Unhappy	Hostile	
Hurt	Uptight	
Negative	Bossy	
Pessimistic	Opinionated	
Angry	Annoying	
Phony	Jealous	
Defiant	Suspicious	

Chicken Soup for the Soul in the Classroom

LISTENING FOR FEELINGS

While it is important to learn how to listen for facts or information, especially in school, the focus of this activity is to learn how to listen when *feelings* or *emotions* are involved.

Here are some steps to help you with this skill:

1. Don't think about what you are going to say when the other person stops talking. Really listen to what *they* are saying.

2. Don't take what the other person is saying *personally.* Stop listening to how it affects you, and start *hearing* how it affects *them*.

3. Focus on the problem, the idea, the feeling, and not on the person.

4. Look for body language. It is expressing as much as two-thirds of the real communication.

5. Use feedback. With this technique, you repeat their message in your own words to be sure that you understand their message.

6. Speak for yourself. Learn to use "*I*" statements, rather than *"You are . . . "*

7. Be honest. Giving cheery advice just to make someone feel better is dishonest, and it will not help them to truly deal with the issue.

8. Don't give advice. What worked for you may not be appropriate for the other person. Just be there to *listen* and to *support*.

9. Avoid judging them, or what they are saying. Merely listen without adding your personal assessment or evaluation. Give your estimate of the situation *only* if it is requested.

PRACTICE LISTENING FOR FEELINGS

Your teacher will tell you the procedure to be used to select a partner for this activity.

Share with your partner your feelings about one
of the following topics:

★ The time I was most happy was . . .

★ The saddest I ever felt was when . . .

★ An embarrassing thing that happened to me
   was . . .

★ A time I felt really lonely was . . .

★ One time when I was very angry, I . . .

★ The thing that frustrates me the most is . . .

★ Something that really hurt my feelings was . . .

★ The most terrifying thing that happened to
   me was . . .

★ The thing that causes me the most regret in my life is . . .

★ A time that I felt discrimination was . . .

Switch partners, and share either the same situation or a different one from the list above.
What factors contribute to the ease or the difficulty of sharing your feelings?

Chicken Soup for the Soul in the Classroom

RANKING YOUR FEARS

The following is a list of common fears or phobias that people have.

Rank your reaction to each of these in the manner described.

0 = no fear at all
1 = a very small amount of fear, almost nonexistent
2 = a small amount of fear
3 = a moderate amount of fear
4 = slightly above average fear for you
5 = something that causes you a great amount of fear
6 = something that causes you terror!

1.____insects

2.____darkness

3.____heights

4.____pain

5.____open spaces

6.____needles

7.____cats

8.____God

9.____choking

10.____floods

11.____bees

12.____spiders

13.____thunder/lightning

14.____failure

15.____being alone

16.____disease

17.____cemeteries

18.____dogs

19.____flying

20.____crowds

21.____dentists

22.____accidents

23.____doctors

24.____crawly things

25.____Hell

26.____mice/rats

27.____blood

28.____firearms

29.____being robbed

30.____public speaking

31.____death/dying

32.____making decisions

33.____hospitals

34.____gaining weight

35.____being ridiculed

36.____snakes

37.____dreams/nightmares

38.____Heaven

39.____fire

40.____operations

41.____terrorists

42.____war

SELF-AWARENESS ACTIVITY SHEET

Directions: choose one activity from each set that follows.

Activities from Set A will be due on _____.

Activities from Set B will be due on _____.

Set A Activities

1. If you had a son or daughter, would you rather have him or her be athletically talented or academically gifted in school? Minimum length is one page.

2. Someone gives you $1 million. Make a list, in order, of what you would do with the money. Write the reasons for every decision you make.

3. What do you worry about the most? What can be done to solve or eliminate this worry? Write at least three paragraphs.

4. Your name appears in Saturday's headline. What is the headline? Write the full article that appears in the paper.

5. Write two paragraphs on what you would hate most to lose and why.

6. Write a poem, story, or play about yourself and your family.

7. If you could trade places with anyone for one day, who would it be and why? Write at least one page.

Set B Activities

1. Design your own flag or banner that represents you. On it, put the things you believe in.

2. Make an advertisement to sell yourself. You should include a written paragraph that lists your worthwhile qualities.

3. Write a last will and testament. What would you leave and to whom? Make it look very legal and official, with a place for witnesses, signatures, etc.

4. Design a bumper sticker that represents your personal view of what you would like people to know about how you feel about life, the world, etc.

5. Make a vision board of your life at ten and twenty years from now. Include pictures that represent what you will be doing, where you will be living, and if anyone else will be sharing this dream with you.

WHAT DO YOU THINK?

An important part of who you are is how you think about things. Respond to ten of the following twelve questions. Remember that there are no right or wrong answers. This is merely a way for you to figure out what is important to you. It is a credit/no credit assignment. It is not optional, however.

1. Tell about a time you laughed until it hurt.

2. Tell about a time you stood up for a strong belief.

3. Tell about a time you over-reacted to something.

4. Tell about something that you would like to stop doing, or would like to change about yourself.

5. Who is one person you know who seems to have it "more together" than you? What can you "borrow" from his/her life? What qualities would you like to have?

6. What is one thing you would change in our world? Our country? Our school?

7. What is something in the news that really disturbed you lately?

8. What is something you really want to learn how to do before you die?

9. Tell about a time you said something when it would have been easier to remain silent.

10. Tell how you feel about an issue that might be considered controversial, such as gun control, global warming, war, etc. . . .

11. Tell about the most exciting thing that ever happened in your life.

12. Tell about a time you believed something to be one way, but found out it was something entirely different.

WHO AM I?

List as many words to describe yourself as you can. Describe yourself physically (*e.g., tall, short, etc.*), by your personality (*e.g., funny, messy, etc.*), by your relationships (*e.g., friend, sister, etc.*), and even by the things you do (*e.g., basketball player, musician, etc.*).

You must have thirty qualities. Begin all sentences with the words "I am". . .

1. I am	16.
2.	17.
3.	18.
4.	19.
5.	20.
6.	21.
7.	22.
8.	23.
9.	24.
10.	25.
11.	26.
12.	27.
13.	28.
14.	29.
15.	30.

Put an asterisk (*) next to the five things that you think are the most important things about you. Put a plus (+) next to the positive things about you and a minus (−) next to those things that might be considered negative.

DO YOU KNOW ANYONE WHO GETS "PICKED ON" BECAUSE OF HOW THEY LOOK? WHAT COULD YOU SAY OR DO SO THAT THIS DOES NOT HAPPEN?

_____

_____

_____

_____

_____

_____

_____

_____

_____

_____

_____

IN LOVING MEMORY OF

_____

(WHO IS REMEMBERED FOR ALL THESE GOOD THINGS:

_____

_____

_____

_____

_____

_____

_____

_____

" WHEN YOUR LIFE IS OVER, "
HOW DO YOU WANT
TO BE REMEMBERED?

SAMPLE TIMELINE

Age	Event
0	birth
1	learned to walk
5	learned to read
6	learned arithmetic
7	learned how to ride a bike
12	NOW
14	pass Spanish class
16	get a driver's license
17	graduate high school
18	go to college
20	pass college physics
21	graduate college
22	become a teacher
24	coach a track team
27	get married
28	publish a children's book
29	have a child
31	have a second child
40	fly in a hot air balloon
45	buy a Harley-Davidson motorcycle and ride it to Alaska
46	publish another book that receives national awards
52	retire from teaching
53	buy a sailboat and take it on a long journey
63	start a reading program for young children in my community
83	ride a camel in Egypt
87	ride an elephant in Thailand
97	start a foundation to support literacy and empowerment for young people
106	die feeling happy and fulfilled

Chicken Soup for the Soul in the Classroom

SIMPLE STEPS TO VISUALIZATION

1. Close your eyes and take a few deep breaths to quiet your body and your mind.

2. Focus on the outcome you desire.

3. See this outcome as if you were there and already experiencing it. Do not see yourself as if on a movie screen. Rather, see it as if you were doing it, from the viewpoint from your eyes looking outward.

4. Use all of your senses in this experience
   ★ what do you *see*?
   ★ what do you *smell*?
   ★ what do you *taste*?
   ★ what do you physically *feel* in or on your body?
   ★ what do you *hear*?

5. Most importantly, what do you feel emotionally as you experience this goal in your mind? Hold onto this feeling for a few moments.

This can be done in a five-minute sitting, and ideally should be done three times a day. It is most powerful to visualize when first awakening and when drifting off to sleep.

Visualize on any specific outcome for thirty consecutive days, and you will see results.

Example: If I wanted to run a five-minute mile, I would see the track, see the crowds in the stands, see the lane lines, see the backs of my hand and arms and tops of my feet and front of my legs, see the uniform on my body, see other runners (out of the corner of my eye—behind me!), see the official at the starting line, smell the newly mowed grass on the infield, smell the sunscreen lotion, smell my sweat, taste my saliva, taste the dryness in my mouth on the final lap, feel the wind on my face, feel the sun on my back, feel the effortless movement of my body, feel the sun now on my face as I round the curve, hear the official's commands, hear the starting gun, hear the roar of the crowd, feel my feet connecting on the track with every stride, see the finish line, emotionally feel the exhilaration of running, feel the rush of adrenalin, feel the joy in my heart, see the stopwatch at 5:00.00 minutes as I finish, feel the pride of accomplishing my goal, see and feel my friends and family sharing in my success and excitement!

Resources

Some of the worksheets and activities presented here have been taken from and/or adapted from the following primary list of sources:

Self-Esteem in the Classroom: A Curriculum Guide by Jack Canfield, Marie Reese Banuelos, Sandra Lynn Limina, Ron Rowland, Ellen Fleischmann, Michael Hesse, Ann Meril, Georgia Noble, and Chris Hummel. Culver City, CA: Self-Esteem Seminars, 1986. Available from Self-Esteem Seminars. Phone: 800-237-8336 or 805-563-2935. Website: www.jackcanfield.com

The Success Principles: How to Get from Where You Are to Where You Want to Be by Jack Canfield and Janet Switzer. New York, NY: HarperCollins Publishing Inc., 2005.

The Success Principles: Your 30-Day Journey from Where You Are to Where You Want to Be by Jack Canfield and Janet Switzer. 2003. Audio set available from The Canfield Training Group, P.O. Box 30880, Santa Barbara, CA, 93130. Website: www.jackcanfield.com

Several other strategies suggested in this book are taken from Jack's seven-day summer training, which is now called Breakthrough to Success. For more information, visit www.jackcanfield.com or call 800-2ES-TEEM (800-237-8336).

The following list includes the primary sources of research used in this document:

"Can All Your Kids Read?" cover story, *NEA Today* (National Education Association), February, 2005.

"Children's Television Viewing and Cognitive Outcomes," Robert J. Hancox, et al, *Archives of Pediatrics and Adolescent Medicine,* July, 2005.

"Early Television Exposure and Subsequent Attentional Problems in Children," Christakis, Zimmerman, DiGiuseppe, and McCarty, *Pediatrics,* April, 2004.

"Education: The Shame of the Nation," speech by Jonathan Kozol, Portland, Oregon, September 30, 2005.

"How To Tune Up Your Brain," *Time* Magazine Special Report, January 16, 2006.

I Hear America Reading: Why We Read—What We Read, by Jim Burke. Portsmouth, NH: Heinemann, 1999.

"Race and Class in Public Education," speech by Jonathan Kozol, State University of New York at Albany, October 17, 1997.

The Read-Aloud Handbook, by Jim Trelease. New York, NY: Penguin Books, 2001.

Reading Reminders, by Jim Burke, Portsmouth, NH: Heinemann-Boynton/Cook, 2000.

"Reflections on the Problem Novel," by Barbara Feinberg, *American Educator* (American Federation of Teachers), Winter 2004/2005.

The following lists additional materials, or other information used for this project:

100 Ways to Enhance Self-Concept in the Classroom: A Handbook for Teachers and Parents, by Jack Canfield and Harold C. Wells. Needham Heights, MA: Allyn & Bacon, 1976.

101 Ways to Develop Self-Esteem and Responsibility, by Jack Canfield and Frank Siccone. Needham Heights, MA: Allyn & Bacon, 1993.

The Aladdin Factor, by Jack Canfield and Mark Victor Hansen. New York, NY: Berkley Publishing Group, 1995.

Dare To Win, by Jack Canfield and Mark Victor Hansen. New York, NY: Berkley Publishing Group, 1994.

Playfair, by Matt Weinstein and Joel Goodman. San Luis Obispo, CA: Impact Publishers, 1993.

The Power Of Focus, by Jack Canfield, Mark Victor Hansen and Les Hewitt. Deerfield Beach, FL: Health Communications, 2000.

The Secret is a documentary-drama DVD that teaches you how to manifest what you want in life. It is available for purchase at www.thesecret.tv.com. Book by Rhonda Byrne, New York, NY: ATRIA Books, 2006.

You've Got To Read This Book! by Jack Canfield and Gay Hendricks. New York, NY: HarperCollins, 2006.

Additionally, we referred to *Bloom's Taxonomy* to be certain that we were addressing all levels and domains of learning skills, and to Thomas Armstrong's and Howard Gardner's work with *Multiple Intelligences.*

Over the years we have identified other great story resources that are so powerful in content that they have a life-changing impact on students. This short list of supplemental books and videos are referenced within the plans, and are documented here for your use:

A Class Divided—a part of the PBS Frontline series, this documentary is based on a study in which a third grade teacher made eye color a deliberate criteria for discrimination. Check out http://www.PBS.org to purchase VHS or DVD.

Alexander and the Terrible, Horrible, No Good, Very Bad Day, by Judith Viorst. A children's book for all ages about overcoming a bad day. New York, NY: Aladdin Paperbacks, 1972.

Armed With Hope—the behind-the-scenes story of John Foppe, who was born without arms and learned to do everything with his feet. Check out John's website at http://www.johnfoppe.com to obtain books, audiotapes, VHS, or DVD.

The Children, by David Halberstam is the story of the young people who marched in the Civil Rights movement in the 1960s. New York, NY: Ballantine Publishing Group, 1998.

Ironweed, by William Kennedy. A Pulitzer Prize-winning story of the homeless, for use with grades 8-12. New York, NY: Penguin Group, 1983.

Messages from Water, by Dr. Masaru Emoto consists of two volumes based on his research that changed the molecular structure of water by using positive thinking. Tokyo: HADO Publishing, Vol; I, 1999, Vol. II; 2002. For more information on his research, go to one of his websites: http://thank-water.net or http://www.hado.com.

Night, by Elie Wiesel is the story of a young Jewish boy in a concentration camp. New York, NY: Bantam Books, 1982.

No Excuses: The True Story of a Congenital Amputee Who Became a Champion in Wrestling and in Life, by Kyle Maynard. With no self-pity allowed, Kyle first learns to survive, then to thrive and become a state champion athlete. Washington, DC: Regenery Publishing, Inc., 2006.

Pay It Forward, by Catherine Ryan Hyde is the story of twelve-year-old Trevor, who takes on an extra credit assignment. His action is to do a good deed for three people, and in exchange, to ask each of them to "pay it forward" to three others. New York, NY: Pocket Books, 1999. DVD available with Kevin Spacey and Helen Hunt, 2000.

Random Acts of Kindness, by the editors of Conari Press, includes several vignettes of simple acts of kindness that change the world. Berkley, CA: Conari Press, 1993. For many wonderful classroom ideas on this topic, see the Random Acts of Kindness Foundation at their website: www.actsofkindness.org/classroom.

Schindler's List is the story of a member of the Nazi party and prominent German businessman who helped to save Jewish lives. The movie *Schindler's List* appeared in 1993. The story of Schindler was also told in the book *Schindler's Ark,* by Thomas Keneally, published in 1982. The book was later retitled *Schindler's List.*

The Sneetches and Other Stories, by Dr. Suess, is a story for all ages about changing oneself in order to become popular. New York, NY: Random House, 1961.

Think Big (1992), *Gifted Hands* (1990), and *The Big Picture* (1999), all by Dr. Ben Carson, M.D., are the stories of his life journey from the slums of Detroit to becoming a famous surgeon. Grand Rapids, MI: Zondervan.

Tuesdays with Morrie, by Mitch Albom, is a bestselling nonfiction book about "living" until you die, for use with grades seven through twelve. New York, NY: Doubleday Publishing, 1997. A related video is *Nightline—Ted Koppel's Interview with Morrie Schwartz.* Go to http://www.ABCNewsStore.com to purchase this, and/or Morrie's *Lessons on Living.*

Finally, here are a couple of sources relating to world change:

An Inconvenient Truth: The Planetary Emergency of Global Warming and What We Can Do About It, book and DVD by Al Gore. Check out www.climatecrisis.net.

If I Can Change, So Can the World: Forty Positive Steps to Global Togetherness, by Paula Pluck. London: Ploair Publishing, 2005.

The focus of this project is on the messages of the Chicken Soup for the Soul stories, and on their life-changing impact. The questions posed, and the tasks suggested relate to each story, but nothing is set in concrete. Virtually everything in this document can be modified to fit another audience or another story. The resources that have been suggested here have been successfully used to enhance the Chicken Soup for the Soul stories within the classroom.

We recommend that you ask your librarian or media specialist to stock up on a variety of Chicken Soup for the Soul books. According to our sources, these books are the most highly checked-out books in school libraries. In addition, we suggest that you personally obtain other Chicken Soup for the Soul books whose titles appeal to you. As you begin to see your students' attitudes and behaviors changing, you may get hooked on using these stories to teach, and you will want more than the stories presented here.

Permissions

Kindness Is Contagious. Reprinted by permission of Kristin Seuntjens. ©1998 Kristin Seuntjens.

Glenna's Goal Book. Reprinted by permission of Glenna Salsbury. ©1994 Glenna Salsbury.

A Silent Voice. Reprinted by permission of David R. Collins. ©1980 David R. Collins.

To Be Enormously Gorgeous. Reprinted by permission of Carla O'Brien. ©1998 Carla O'Brien.

Lost and Found. Reprinted by permission of Antonio Angulo Jr. and Marisol Muqoz-Kiehne. ©2000 Antonio Angulo Jr. and Marisol Muqoz-Kiehne.

The Power to Shine. Reprinted by permission of Deborah Rosado Shaw 2000 Deborah Rosado Shaw.

A Good Reason to Look Up. Reprinted by permission of Shaquille O'Neal. ©1998 Shaquille O'Neal.

School—Moving Up. Reprined by permission of Dr. Ben Carson. ©1998 Dr. Ben Carson.

The Greatest Baseball Story Ever. From *How to Make a Habit of Succeeding* by Mack R. Douglas. ©1994, 1996 used by permission of the publisher, Pelican Publishing Company, Inc.

Innocent Homeless. Reprinted by permission of Lori. S. Mohr. ©1997 Lori S. Mohr.

On Courage. Reprinted by permission of Dan Millman. ©1991. "As appeared in *Source Book: Sacred Journey of the Peaceful Warrior* HJ Kramer/New World Library."

Just Ben. Just Ben. Reprinted by permission of Adrian Wagner. ©1998 Adrian Wagner.

The Power of Determination. Reprinted by permission of Burt Dubin. ©1992 Burt Dubin.

Their Bullet, My Life. Reprinted by permission of Ernelda Carrasco for Cruz Carrasco. ©2005 Ernelda Carrasco for Cruz Carrasco.

Did the Earth Move for You? Reprinted by permission of Dr. Hanoch McCarty. ©2000 Hanoch McCarty and Associates.

Just Me. Reprinted by permission of Tom Krause. ©1996 Tom Krause.

Nobody Knows the Difference. Reprinted by permission of Deborah J. Rasmussen. ©1998 Deborah J. Rasmussen.

The Power of an Attitude. Reprinted by permission of Melea A. Wendell. ©2007 Melea A. Wendell.

Rest in Peace: The "I Can't Funeral". Reprinted by permission of Chick Moorman. ©1992 Chick Moorman.

River Recipe. From *River of Words: The Natural World as Viewed by Young People*, edited by Robert Hass, ©2000 River of Words.

Troubled. Reprinted by permission of Gregory S. Woodburn ©2003 Gregory S. Woodburn.

The Anonymous Donor. Reprinted by permission of Deb Wilson. ©2002 Deb Wilson.

She Didn't Pray for a Miracle. Reprinted by permission of Cynthia Mercati. ©1999 Cynthia Mercati.

A Friend. . . . Reprinted by permission of Danielle Fishel and Jennifer Fishel. ©1998 Danielle Fishel.

What a Difference a Walk Makes. Reprinted by permission of Bruce Thoreau Northam. ©1998 Bruce Thoreau Northam.

A True Hero. Reprinted by permission of Joseph Haakenson. ©2000 Joseph Haakenson.

Do It Now. Reprinted by permission of Dennis Mannering. From the book *Attitudes Are Contagious . . . Are Yours Worth Catching?* ©1986 by Dennis E. Mannering.

If You Could Change the World. Reprinted by permission of ©2000 Scarlett Kotlarczyk, Wilson Cook, Brandon Barger, Timothy Blevans, Stacy Bergman, Rachel Force, Sarah Hampton, Lisa Cline,

The Purple Belt. From *The Secret Power Within* by Chuck Norris. Reprinted by permission of Little, Brown and Company. ©1996 by Top Kick Productions.

A Child's Gift. Reprinted by permission of Pamela Strome-Merewether. © 1999 Pamela Strome-Merewether.

Surprise Santa. Reprinted by permission of Henry Boye 2005 Henry Boye.

Just Do What You Can. Reprinted by permission of D'ette Corona. ©1999 D'ette Corona.

Mosquitos. Reprinted by permission of Virgina Lustig. © 2007 Virginia Lusting.

The Power of Motivation. Reprinted by permission of Ernie Witham. © 2001 Ernie Witham.

Green Salami. Reprinted by permission of Patty Hansen. © 1998 Patty Hansen.

Be Yourself. Reprinted by permission of Erik Oleson. © 1993 Erik Oleson.

My First Kiss and Then Some. Reprinted by permission of Mary Jane West-Delgado. © 2007 Mary Jane West-Delgado.

Practical Application and *Pay Attention.* Reprinted by permission of Dan Clark. ©1998 Dan Clark.

Manners. Reprinted by permission of Paul Karrer. ©1999 Paul Karrer.

The Fragile Eight. Reprinted by permission of Isabel Bearman Bucher. ©2003 Isabel Bearman Bucher.

I Like Myself Now. From *Man, The Manipulator* by Everett L. Shostrom. Used by permission. © 1967 Abingdon Press.

One Child. Reprinted by permission of Regina Hellinger © 2001 Regina Hellinger.

Hulk Heaven. Reprinted by permission of Dolores M. Montalbano © 2004 Dolores M. Montalbano.

When I Was. Reprinted by permission of Filomena Solis Saenz. © 2006 Filomena Solis Saenz.

Who's on First. Reprinted by permission of Ronald H. Schnitzius. © 2004 Ronald H. Schnitzius.

Geography Lesson. Reprinted by permission of Irene Husaruk Leon. ©2002 Irene Husaruk Leon.

Writing About Favorite Things. Reprinted by permission of Elaine Susan Wiepking. ©2004 Elaine Susan Wiepking.

Mystery Reader. Reprinted by permission of Maria Zielinski. ©2001 Maria Zielinski.

Be Careful What You Teach Them. Reprinted by permission of David S. Diamond ©2003 David S. Diamond .

He's Just A Little Boy. Reprinted by permission of Bob Fox. ©1994 Bob Fox.

If I Had My Child To Raise. . . . From *Full Esteem Ahead* by Diane Loomans with Julia Loomans. Reprinted by permissionof H J Kramer c/o Global Learning, Box 1203, Solana Beach, CA 92075. All rights reserved.

Pay Attention. Reprinted by permission of Dan Clark. ©1998 Dan Clark.

Index